Robert L. Thompson
630 Stewart Ave. Q

THE THEORY OF
ECONOMIC GROWTH

THE THEORY OF
ECONOMIC GROWTH

by W. Arthur Lewis

Stanley Jevons Professor of Political Economy
in the University of Manchester

1955
RICHARD D. IRWIN, INC.
HOMEWOOD, ILLINOIS

PRINTED IN THE UNITED STATES OF AMERICA

PREFACE

The purpose of this book is not to present original ideas on its subject, but to try to provide an appropriate framework for studying economic development. The place for original ideas is articles in the technical journals, and my articles on this subject are listed in the bibliographical notes. A book of this kind seemed to be necessary because the theory of economic growth once more engages world-wide interest, and because no comprehensive treatise on the subject has been published for about a century. The last great book covering this wide range was John Stuart Mill's *Principles of Political Economy*, published in 1848. After this economists grew wiser; they were too sensible to try to cover such an enormous field in a single volume, and they even abandoned parts of the subject altogether, as being beyond their competence. It is partly irrepressible curiosity and partly the practical needs of contemporary policy-makers that have driven me to range over this enormous area; but I suppose it is also mainly an excess of courage that has permitted me to offer to a critical public a book whose subject matter is so vast that most of it must inevitably be treated superficially.

My title is misleading if it suggests that there can be a single theory of economic growth. The factors which determine growth are very numerous, and each has its own set of theories. There is not much in common between the theories which one uses in studying land tenure, or the diffusion of new ideas, or the trade cycle, the growth of population, or the government's budgets. 'Theories' of economic growth might have been a more appropriate title, but it would have been just as misleading in suggesting that the book set out to review the literature of economic growth. What I have done is to make not a theory, but a map. So many factors are relevant in studying economic growth that it is easy to be lost unless one has a general perspective of the subject. This also is my excuse for superficiality. Maps are published in many different scales, for many different purposes. The articles in the technical journal correspond to a scale of an inch to the mile. This book is on a scale more like an inch to a hundred miles; this too should have its uses.

The same combination of curiosity and of practical need which drove me to this subject has also determined the shape of the book. Curiosity demands a philosophical enquiry into the processes of human history, while practical need demands a handbook of things to do. Since I am equally interested in both, what I have written will suit neither those who care only for philosophy, nor those who want to know precisely what to do next. It seems inevitable that a book

should reflect the personality of its author, with its diversity of traits.

A book must also reflect its author's craft. Economists and sociologists deal in generalizations, where anthropologists and historians deal in particular cases. I would much have liked to strengthen the book by including in it two or three case studies of economic growth or economic stagnation. I set out with this intention, and have had much pleasure reading of Ancient Egypt and Greece and Rome and Islam, not to speak of China, and Japan and the end of the Middle Ages. But in truth I derived more pleasure than knowledge, especially of periods before 1500 A.D., partly because so little is known with certainty about early economic history. To write up a single case adequately, covering all the matters dealt with in this book, requires immense researches, and a separate treatise. I have collaborated very closely with Mrs. Gisela Eisner, who is writing up the economic development of Jamaica from 1830 to 1930, as a member of the research staff of the University of Manchester. In a sense that volume, when it is published in 1956, will be a case study corresponding to this.

I have had generous treatment from many friends and acquaintances. Those who have taken time off, in South East Asia, or Africa, or the Caribbean, to show me what they were doing, to exchange ideas, and to entertain me hospitably, are so numerous that I cannot even begin to recite their names. Then there is also the debt one owes to the academic fraternity for innumerable conversations in many countries, as well as the ceaseless flow of articles in journals. Mr. Peter Bauer, Professor Max Gluckman, Mr. J. M. Low, Dr. J. Mars, Dr. K. Martin, the Rev. R. H. Preston, Dr. P. Rosenstein-Rodan and Professor M. N. Srinivas have been kind enough to read the book in typescript, and to offer detailed criticisms. I have benefited immensely from their comments, whilst obstinately adhering, here and there, to formulations which they still consider false or misleading. An immense labour has fallen upon my secretary, Miss Dora Walkden, who has typed the manuscript with patience and with care, and whose forbearance I gratefully acknowledge.

My wife and children have paid a heavy price for the writing of this book, in absences and silences; but I cannot begin to speak of what I owe to their affection.

W.A.L.

Manchester
July, 1954

CONTENTS

CHAPTER I

INTRODUCTION

1. DEFINITIONS

THE subject matter of this book is the growth of output per head of population. What follows does not depend upon precise definitions of these terms; nevertheless some comment on their meaning may be helpful.

First it should be noted that our subject matter is growth, and not distribution. It is possible that output may be growing, and yet that the mass of the people may be becoming poorer. We shall have to consider the relationship between the growth and the distribution of output, but our primary interest is in analysing not distribution but growth.

Secondly, our concern is not primarily with consumption but with output. Output may be growing while consumption is declining, either because saving is increasing, or because the government is using up more output for its own purposes. We shall certainly have to consider the relationships between output, consumption, saving and government activity, but we shall be doing this from the angle of the growth of output, and not from the angle of the growth of consumption.

The definition of output we leave to the theorists of national income. There are difficult index number problems in comparing one year's output with another. There is the difficult problem of deciding what is to be treated as output, and what is to be treated as the cost of output; is increasing expenditure on retail distribution, or advertising, or transportation to be taken as an increase in output, or merely as a cost of increasing specialization? If work which was formerly done by the consumer for himself (e.g. making clothes) is now transferred to factories, is this an increase of output? We mention these problems so that pedantic reviewers shall not be able to say that we are not aware of them. We do not, however, have to solve them. For our concern is not with the measurement of output, but with its growth. For the purposes of this book any consistent definition of the output of goods and services will do.

The definition must, however, relate to goods and services—'economic' output, in the old fashioned meaning of 'economic'—and not to some such concept as welfare, satisfaction or happiness. It is possible that a person may become less happy in the process

of acquiring greater command over goods and services. This frequently happens to individuals, and it may also happen to groups. This book is not, however, an essay on whether people ought to have or to want more goods and services; its concern is merely with the processes by which more goods and services become available. The author believes that it is good to have more goods and services, but the analysis of the book does not in any way depend upon this belief. In order to emphasize the fact that the book is about the growth and not about the desirability of output, he has relegated what he has to say about desirability to an Appendix at the end of the book.

We have next to distinguish between output and output per head of population. The relation between population and total output is an obvious part of our subject matter. Output per head will not however be our sole concern, for we are also interested in output per hour of work done, which may differ from output per head if people work longer or shorter hours, or if a greater or smaller part of the population is at work. All these matters will come under review.

The unit of enquiry is the group. Most commonly this will be the nation-group, in the peculiar statistical sense of the group about whose activities separate statistics of foreign trade are published; or the group in respect of whom separate censuses are taken. This is a definition of convenience, which comes near enough to defining the group as the people under one government, without entering into the difficulty of distinguishing between colonial governments, federal governments, and other variations of 'one' government. Much of the analysis will, however, apply equally to other groups, for example, sometimes to minority groups, and sometimes to regional groupings.

Finally, it should be noted that we shall have frequently to resort to abbreviation. 'Growth of output per head of the population' is rather a long phrase to repeat over and over again in a book. Most often we shall refer only to 'growth' or to 'output', or even occasionally, for the sake of variety, to 'progress' or to 'development'. Whatever the short term used, 'per head of the population' should be understood, unless total output is clearly specified or clearly intended by the context.

2. METHODOLOGY

The growth of output per head depends on the one hand on the natural resources available, and on the other hand on human behaviour. This book is primarily interested in human behaviour, and concerns itself with natural resources only in so far as they affect

human behaviour. Thus it is obvious that poverty of natural resources sets sharp limits to the growth of output per head, and that a
considerable part of differences in wealth between different countries
has to be explained in terms of richness of resources. But it is also
clear that there are great differences in development between
countries which seem to have roughly equal resources, so it is
necessary to enquire into the differences in human behaviour which
influence economic growth.

The enquiry into human actions has to be conducted at different
levels, because there are proximate causes of growth, as well as causes
of these causes. The proximate causes are principally three. First
there is the effort to economize, either by reducing the cost of any
given product, or by increasing the yield from any given input
of effort or of other resources. This effort to economize shows
itself in various ways; in experimentation, or risk-taking; in mobility,
occupational or geographical; and in specialization, to mention
only its chief manifestations. If the effort is not made, either
because the desire to economize does not exist, or else because
either custom or institutions discourage its expression, then economic
growth will not occur. Secondly, there is the increase of knowledge
and its application. This process has occurred throughout human
history, but the more rapid growth of output in recent centuries is
associated obviously with the more rapid accumulation and application of knowledge in production. And thirdly, growth depends upon
increasing the amount of capital or other resources per head. These
three proximate causes, though clearly distinguishable conceptually,
are usually found together.

The second stage of the analysis takes us behind these proximate
causes to ask why it is that they are found strongly operating in some
societies but not in others, or at some stages of history but less so in
others. What environments are most favourable to the emergence
of these forces which promote growth? This stage of the enquiry
subdivides itself. First we must enquire which kinds of institutions
are favourable to growth, and which are inimical to effort, to
innovation or to investment. Then we must move into the realm of
beliefs and ask what causes a nation to create institutions which are
favourable, rather than those which are inimical to growth? Is a part
of the answer to be found in the different valuations which different
societies place upon goods and services relatively to their valuation
of such non-material satisfactions as leisure, security, equality, good
fellowship or religious salvation? It is necessary to establish how far
the spiritual and the material values conflict, if they do, and how far
the institutions reflect particular ideas of the right way to live. Still
further behind this lie questions relating to nature and environment.

What causes a people to have one set of beliefs, rather than another set of beliefs, more or less favourable to growth? Are the differences of beliefs and institutions due to differences of race, or of geography; or is it just historical accident?

These questions are all questions of consistency: they ask what institutions or beliefs or environments are consistent with economic growth. But there are also questions of evolution. How do beliefs and institutions change? Why do they change in ways favourable to or hostile to growth? How does growth itself react upon them? Is growth cumulative, in the sense that once it has begun, beliefs and institutions are inevitably fashioned in such a way as to facilitate further growth; or is it self-arresting, in the dialectical sense that new beliefs and institutions are inevitably created to resist growth, and to slow it down? Are there self-reversing swings over the centuries in human attitudes and institutions, which make the process of growth inevitably cyclical?

The field of analysis which we have thus set out is customarily said to be divided out between different branches of the social sciences, but if the division has ever been made it has never been effective. Thus, one might have expected economists to study the proximate causes, but they have done so only very selectively. Economists have studied specialization and capital. They have also stressed the importance of mobility, of invention and of risk-taking, and analysed with care and elegance the logical implications of the will to economize. Some economists have gone on to study institutions; nineteenth-century economists especially refer frequently to land tenure, or to primogeniture, or to joint stock company legislation. However, such interests ceased to be fashionable in the second quarter of the twentieth century, and were even authoritatively stated not to be the proper business of economists. All the rest of the field belongs to sociologists, to historians, to students of beliefs, to lawyers, to biologists or to geographers, but they have done little more than to look at it, and to put in a spade here and there. One suspects that the sociologists have left the study of economic institutions to the economists, while the economists have left the subject to the sociologists. Where the general attitude is to leave the field to someone else, perhaps there will be no jealousy at the boldness of this writer in attempting a general survey. Perhaps too the field will no longer seem so discouraging if there is provided at least a crude map of its resources and its potentialities.

The questions of consistency are much easier to tackle than the questions of evolution. This is because, like the theories of economics or of mathematics, questions of consistency lend themselves to the process of deduction from simple premises. For, in the light of one or

two simple generalizations, it is not difficult to see why some beliefs
or institutions promote growth more than others. Relevant generalizations are such as that men are more likely to invest if they value
extra goods highly than if they do not; or if they will reap the fruit
of the investment for themselves than if it becomes common property; or if there is freedom to buy or hire co-operating resources than
if there is not. Economists are applying the deductive method all the
time to those of their problems which are quantifiable, at least conceptually, and which can therefore be handled mathematically. The
consistency of beliefs and of institutions with growth is not a problem
in mathematics, and this is why we have in recent years fought shy of
tackling such matters. But the deductive method is nevertheless
applicable and fruitful.

Some of the most elegant work of economic theorists in recent
years has been concerned with the stability of economic growth.
Starting by assuming capitalist institutions and habits, economists
have built mathematical models which oscillate, or rise logistically
towards a limit, or ultimately swing round from growth to secular
decline. These results are achieved by assuming various coefficients,
and various relations between parameters—for such matters as the
propensity to save, or the birth rate, or the determinants of investment decisions. This work in turn has stimulated statistical enquiry
to discover what relationships and coefficients best fit recent experience in the United States and other advanced economies. This work
is essentially in the area of consistency rather than of evolution. It
seeks to discover what the relationships and propensities are, and
how far they are consistent with stable growth; it does not tell us
why the coefficients are what they are, or why they change over time.
The result is an indispensable tool for short-term analysis, to be used
when we are enquiring into the history of some particular group
during some short period of time, during which the basic institutions
and attitudes can be assumed to change very little. But if we are concerned with long-term studies of changes in propensities, or if we
wish to account for differences between groups or countries, we have
usually to look beyond the boundaries of contemporary economic
theory.

In applying the deductive method to the consistency of institutions
with growth, the danger we have to avoid is that of bias. There is a
natural tendency to assume that things which are associated in the
society we know must necessarily also be associated in all other
societies. An important example of this is in the association between
individualism and growth. In Western capitalistic societies men
recognize fewer social obligations than they do in most other
societies, and we naturally tend to assume that a man is more likely

to make economizing efforts if the fruit accrues to himself alone than he would if the fruit had also to be shared by more distant members of his family, or by a whole clan, or by religious or political leaders, or by others whose claims he would not automatically recognize in an individualistic society. This assumption may be false. Institutions which would hinder progress in Western Europe may be conducive to progress in a society whose tests of whether effort is worth while are quite different because of their different conception of what is worth having. There is no way of guarding against this bias except observation. From the studies made by anthropologists and by sociologists we have to try to decide what is universal, in the sense of what is common to human behaviour in different social contexts, and so to arrive at basic generalizations which stand up to comparisons between societies, and which can therefore in turn be used for assessing institutions.

It should of course be added that some institutions or beliefs may be consistent with growth but not with each other. For example, economic growth is consistent with the state investing twenty per cent of the national income in public capital formation, or with private enterprise investing twenty per cent of the national income in private capital formation. But it is doubtful whether it would be possible to have one and the same society in which the state invested twenty per cent and private enterprise invested another twenty per cent in capital formation. The consistency of institutions with each other is a problem of special interest in the analysis of social change, and it is mainly in this context that we shall have to keep it in mind.

The most difficult problem in consistency is to explain why people hold the beliefs they do. Economic growth depends on attitudes to work, to wealth, to thrift, to having children, to invention, to strangers, to adventure, and so on, and all these attitudes flow from deep springs in the human mind. There have been attempts to explain why these attitudes vary from one community to another. One can look to differences in religion, but this is merely to restate the problem, since it raises the question why the particular religion holds these particular tenets, and why it has been accepted in this particular place and not elsewhere. Or one can look to differences in natural environment, in climate, in race, or, failing all else, in the accidents of history. The experienced sociologist knows that these questions are unanswerable, certainly in our present state of knowledge, and probably for all time. He will not expect any more in this book than that they should be briefly explored. We can say a fair amount about consistency between institutions and economic growth, and a fair amount about the relationship between attitudes and institutions; but when we come to explore the attitudes themselves, how they

emerge, and why they change, we reach sooner or later to the limits of our understanding of human history.

Questions of social evolution are even more difficult to handle than questions of consistency because the deductive method helps much less towards answering them. To understand how or why something happens, we must look at the facts; that is to say, we must apply the inductive method to historical data.

Every economist goes through a phase where he is dissatisfied with the deductive basis of economic theory, and feels sure that a much better insight into economic processes could be obtained by studying the facts of history. The instinct is sound; yet the enthusiasms of this phase seldom survive any serious attempt to get to grips with the facts of history. This is because there are very few facts of history in the relevant senses. We mean by this, in the first instance, that it is only for very few countries and for very recent periods that any adequate quantity of historical records exists; and even when there are plenty of records we cannot always be certain exactly what happened. We mean also, more significantly, that the 'facts' which would interest the theorist are not what happened but why it happened; and while history may record what happened, it is seldom able to record why it happened. The records may show what some people who lived at the time thought to be the cause. But, for most of the events that interest economists (and especially for gradual changes in institutions or beliefs), very few contemporaries even knew that they were happening, and most of the recorded opinions as to why they were happening have to be treated with reserve.

History therefore consists not of facts but of historians' opinions of what happened, and of why it happened. Historians' opinions of what happened are usually pretty reliable—with, of course, striking exceptions—since historians are trained in sifting historical evidence. But their opinions of why it happened are usually not more than a reflection of their personal theories of social causation, which determine which facts they select as important. Most economic historians explain economic events in terms of the economic theories current at the time of writing (or worse still, current in their undergraduate days when they were learning their economic theory), and a new crop of economic theories is liable to be followed by a new crop of historical articles rewriting history in terms of the new theory. A good historian's opinion of what happened, and of whether the facts he finds are consistent with this hypothesis or with that is always worth having, and is indispensable. Yet it is obvious that when the social theorist appeals to facts, in the sense of appealing to history, he is appealing to facts in quite a different sense from that in which the chemist or the biologist appeals to facts.

But our difficulties do not end here. For even if what happened were clear beyond all doubt, it would still be difficult to construct social theories from these facts. Each historical event has a number of contributing causes. The event may repeat itself several times, but the constellation of causes is usually different, since history cannot repeat itself exactly—if only because each successive event has more history behind it. The problem is therefore to decide which causes are more important than others. If the events with which we are dealing are measurable we can sometimes do this by means of statistical techniques, which result in equations where each cause is assigned a specific weight (coefficient). If we are dealing with non-measurable events, however, we are back in the realm of personal judgment. This is made still more difficult by the limitations of the human mind. No one person can know enough history—of different periods and different countries—to know enough facts—even if the facts were perfectly knowable—to feel confident that his theory is based upon a comparison of a sufficient number of events to justify generalization, that he has got all the facts right each time, and that his generalization could not be disproved by adducing other similar events which he has not considered.

It follows that theories of social evolution can never be placed upon as secure a foundation as can the theories of chemistry or biology, whose appeal is to repeatable experiments. The difference may be one of degree only, in the sense that the more speculative theories in the natural sciences are often upset by the discovery of new facts. But the facts of history are so much less securely established than are the facts of repeatable experiments that this is one of those differences of degree which is virtually a difference in kind.

It does not follow that we should cease to try to understand social change; man being a curious animal, it is beyond our nature to cease to try to understand. What follows is that we should be modest in our claims, and recognize how tentative is any hypothesis which we claim to base upon the study of history.

The formulation of theories of evolution proceeds at two levels. At the lower level we try to discover how things change and why; at the upper level we predict what is going to happen. The former is the essential business of social theorists, but it is of course the latter which offers the greatest excitements and follies.

At the lower level the social theorist attempts to discover which are the important variables, what are their relative weights, and how they are interconnected simultaneously and in time. At the upper level he has to predict how all the variables will change, and it is this which makes prediction impossible.

Most predictions are no more than exercises in method. We say:

the result depends on the behaviour of variables a to z; if we assume that a to g stay constant, and that h to r change in certain specified ways, then we can predict that the result will be such and such. To be able to predict what will happen we have to be able to know how all the variables are going to behave; we must know whether there is going to be a war within the specified time, or an earthquake, or an outbreak of influenza, or the birth or death of some influential person at a critical time, or a thousand other matters which influence the course of events. Many of these things can never be foreknown; even if they could be foreknown no single brain could ever set up a system of equations which could embrace all the millions of variables which determine the future. We cannot therefore hope to achieve more than partial predictions of the 'if . . . then . . .' variety. Examples of these are the difference equations which we use in exercising some problems of economic dynamics; or the Ricardian theory of economic growth through population and diminishing returns towards stagnation; or the Schumpeterian prognosis of institutional developments in Western capitalism. These exercises in method are often presented as something more than this, because the authors either do not realize themselves or fail to make clear to others the assumptions upon which the exercise is based. They usually also fail to predict the future correctly, because the coefficients were wrong or have changed, or because the relations between the variables were wrong or have changed, or because new variables which had been neglected turn out to be important. The failure of these exercises is no cause for shame, since it is only by finding out why hypotheses are inadequate that we can hope to glean a less imperfect understanding of the how and why of social change.

In this book we write with fair confidence on how society changes, but with little or no confidence on the directions in which it is likely to change. There are a few well established generalizations on the process of change—on such matters as who are the most likely innovators, on the role of imitation, on the sources of resistance to change, on the logistic process of growth, and so on. These generalizations seem also to have universal application, in the sense that the process of social change is much the same today as it was 2,000 years ago, and is much the same in societies of varying stages of development. Hence in writing about such matters we can take all human history for our province, without seeking to find different laws for different stages of social organization. Here we are in much the same position as when we discuss problems of consistency; human attitudes to property or to reward, or to child bearing do differ, but different societies have enough in common for it to be possible to deduce some general rules of human behaviour. We can tell how

B

change will occur if it occurs; what we cannot foresee is what change is going to occur.

This introductory statement on methodology may help to explain why this book does not pursue lines of enquiry which may be found in other analyses of economic evolution. We do not believe that it is possible to say how any particular social system is going to develop, and we do not, therefore, like Ricardo or Marx or Toynbee or Hansen or Schumpeter set out a theory of the laws of evolution of society. We do not believe that there are stages of development through which every society must pass, from primitive stages through feudalism to exchange economies, and do not therefore follow in the footsteps of Comte or Marx or Herbert Spencer or Weber. All our prediction is on the much more pedestrian level of enquiring how far the changes which occurred in the wealthier countries as they developed may be expected to repeat themselves in the poorer countries if they develop. Sometimes we can answer fairly confidently; for example, to say that the proportion of the population engaged in agriculture will fall, or that status relationships will give place increasingly to contractual relationships. In other places we do not know the answer, such as in predicting whether the birth rate will fall as the standard of living rises, or whether war is an inevitable product of economic growth. Much of the book is concerned with noting the changes which have occurred in developing societies, and in enquiring whether those who come after may be expected to follow in the footsteps of those who went before. As for the leading countries themselves, we hold it to be impossible to predict where they will go next, since we do not believe that the future of the human race is governed by immutable laws of which we have or can have knowledge.

3. LAYOUT

The layout of a book on economic growth is largely a matter of personal choice. The matters to be studied are so closely inter-related that it does not matter where one begins. This book begins with the effort to economize, and the beliefs and institutions which determine how vigorous this effort is. Next it considers the role of knowledge in growth, and the processes which facilitate both the accumulation and the diffusion of knowledge. The study of resources per head opens with a chapter on capital, and then continues with a chapter on population. This in turn leads naturally to international trade, since this is the outcome of different distributions of resources relatively to population. The role of government in economic development is not a separate subject; it really belongs to each of these chapters;

but it is convenient to treat government in a separate final chapter because of its importance. In each chapter the approach is the same; from the angle of consistency with growth we are interested in economic relations, in institutions and in beliefs; and from the angle of evolution we are interested in why things change, in how they change, and in whether any trends can be perceived.

This division of our subject matter between the various factors in economic growth makes it necessary to stress from time to time the inter-relationship between the several factors, in the sense that advance on any one front will bring about advance on the others as well. If more capital becomes available, for example from abroad, it will as likely as not be associated with new technologies, and will probably affect the pattern of institutions and of human attitudes. If new knowledge is discovered, investment will be stimulated, and institutions will feel the impact. If institutions are liberalized, human effort will increase, and more knowledge and more capital will be applied in production. Social change is cumulative, with the effect that different factors reinforce each other.

Despite this inter-relationship, there are fashions in asserting that some one factor is more important than all the others. To Adam Smith, for example, and a long line of liberal economists, what was needed to promote economic growth was primarily the right institutional framework; given this framework there was not much need to bother about willingness to make effort, or about the accumulation of knowledge, or about capital accumulation, since all these were instinctive human reactions, inhibited only by faulty institutions. To Malthus, on the other hand, one of the major obstacles in underdeveloped countries was lack of demand, which we would translate in these days as 'a low valuation of income in relation to leisure', and this point of view has many adherents today. Another school fastens upon low technological skill as *the* bottleneck; President Truman's programme for under-developed countries, for example, which claimed that technical assistance is what the under-developed chiefly need from the developed countries. Or there is the school which fastens upon capital as the bottleneck, claiming that if only the capital were available new technologies could be made available too, and that in the process of economic growth all institutions hostile to economic growth would be altered or swept away. And finally there is the school which puts all the emphasis upon natural resources, claiming, in effect, that every country gets the capital and the institutions which its natural resources warrant. Corresponding to these different emphases, we get the different meanings of the word 'under-developed'. A country may be under-developed in the sense that its technology is backward, when compared with that of other

countries, or in the sense that its institutions are relatively un-favourable to investment, or in the sense that capital resources per head are low when compared say with Western Europe, or in the sense that output per head is low, or in the sense that it has valuable natural resources (minerals, water, soil) which it has not yet begun to use. A country may be more under-developed in one of these senses, and less so in others, but in practice there is such close relationship between these indices that it is odd to find men abusing each other for using the word 'under-developed' in one sense rather than in some other.

Of course, it is true that one obstacle to growth may stand out above all others, in some particular place at some particular time, either in the sense that the deficiency is greatest at this point, or else in the sense that it is easier to make a start there than at any other point. For example, it is possible to think of countries where the principal contemporary obstacle to growth is institutions (e.g. bad government, or bad tenancy laws) in the sense that more knowledge and capital would come forth if the institutions were changed, but not otherwise. It is equally possible to think of other places where current institutions are not an obstacle to economic growth, and where the principal shortage is capital. And there are still other places where a good start could be made by taking new technologies to the farmers, in the shape of fertilizers and better seeds. It is some-times desirable to concentrate one's attention on a single problem to the exclusion of most others. This, however, is only a temporary tactic, in the sense that if one succeeds in breaking one bottleneck, the result is usually that some other comes into prominence. If the farmers take to the seeds and fertilizers, new capital will be needed to handle the extra output; if capital becomes available, mortgage and other investment laws must be made appropriate; if institutions improve, some other obstacle to growth then comes into view. Hence though the reformer may begin by working upon one factor only, he has to bear in mind that if he is to have full success, much other change is involved beyond the factor with which he is im-mediately concerned.

In this book we separate the various causes of growth for analy-tical purposes only. Since the causes are inter-related, the book must be read as a whole if it is not to be misunderstood; each sentence, or paragraph or chapter takes for granted what is written elsewhere, and if torn from its context, may cease to be true. There are also certain topics, e.g. religion, which have to turn up in several chapters, each time in reference to some different aspect of economic growth. Some confusion is inevitable when one has to dissect a subject which cannot be dissected. We have tried to keep confusion to a minimum

by making frequent cross-references in the text, but the reader who wishes to get a complete view of any single topic must use the index for this purpose.

BIBLIOGRAPHICAL NOTE

At the end of each chapter there is a biliographical note giving references for some of the subjects discussed in that chapter. These notes are not intended to survey the whole of the literature; they list only a few references which the student may find particularly helpful. In this first note we deal with general works on economic development, with philosophies of history, and with country studies.

Eighteenth century economists were greatly concerned with economic growth, and almost any major treatise published in that century deals with virtually the whole subject matter of this book. The subject went out of fashion, however, in the second half of the nineteenth century. John Stuart Mill's *Principles of Political Economy*, London, 1848, is the culminating work of this tradition, and is still worth reading. Frederick List was a lesser writer, unorthodox in his approach to tariff problems, but also specially interesting for his influence on German and on American thought; see his *The National System of Political Economy*, London, 1909 (originally published in German in 1844). Karl Marx was also in the classical tradition; his output was enormous, but his economic writings are intelligible only to specialists. For a lucid account by a modern Marxist see P. M. Sweezy, *The Theory of Capitalist Development*, New York, 1942.

The only twentieth century economist who came anywhere near to a general survey of economic growth was J. A. Schumpeter, in his *Socialism, Capitalism, and Democracy*, New York, 1942. (His *The Theory of Economic Development*, Cambridge, 1934, originally published in German in 1912, is very much narrower in scope than its title implies.) B. S. Keirstead, *The Theory of Economic Change*, Montreal, 1948, also covers only a part of the subject. Students of Indian problems will find a very good statement in B. Datta, *The Economics of Industrialization*, Calcutta, 1952. W. W. Rostow's *The Process of Economic Growth*, Oxford, 1953, is interesting chiefly as a study in method. Half of S. H. Frankel's *The Economic Impact on Underdeveloped Countries*, Oxford, 1952, deals with the definition and measurement of national income, and the other half makes the point that capital formation by itself will not ensure economic growth. For a brief introductory survey see United Nations, *Measures for the Economic Development of Under-developed Countries*, New York, 1951.

Historians have given more attention to these matters than economists in the twentieth century. A. J. Toynbee's *A Study of History*, London, 1934-9, is beyond the general reader, but it has been finely summarized in a single volume by D. C. Somervell, *Toynbee's Study of History*, London, 1946, which is well worth reading, despite the general hostility of historians to Toynbee's work. Another interesting builder of historical theories is P. Sorokin, whose voluminous work is summarized by F. R. Cowell's *History, Civilization and Culture*, London, 1952. On the attitude of his-

torians to theory see R. G. Collingwood, *The Idea of History*, Oxford, 1946. Karl Popper also discusses theories of history and of prediction in *The Open Society and its Enemies*, London, 1945. See also M. Ginsberg, *The Idea of Progress*, London, 1953.

It is desirable to read as widely as possible in the field of economic history. There are many standard histories of the countries of Western Europe and of the United States of America. Something should be known of Soviet Russia; the most reliable statistics are in a book edited by A. Bergson, *Soviet Economic Growth*, Evanston, 1953. Good introductions to Japan are E. H. Norman, *Japan's Emergence as a Modern State*, New York, 1940; and G. C. Allen, *A Short Economic History of Japan*, London, 1946. All the problems dealt with in this book would be settled if we understood the rise and decline of Greece and Rome. Unfortunately, though there is a large literature on this subject, it is still highly speculative. The best treatment to date is in the appropriate volumes of the *Cambridge Ancient History*, London, various dates; see also M. Rostovtzeff, 'The Decay of the Ancient World and its Economic Explanations', *Economic History Review*, Vol. II, 1930.

Some acquaintance with the institutions of primitive peoples is also necessary. C. D. Forde, *Habitat, Economy and Society*, London, 1934; R. W. Firth, *Primitive Polynesian Economy*, London, 1939; M. J. Herskovits, *The Economic Life of Primitive Peoples*, New York, 1940; B. Malinowski, *Argonauts of the Western Pacific*, London, 1922.

CHAPTER II

THE WILL TO ECONOMIZE

THE three proximate causes of economic growth, as we have said, are economic activity, increasing knowledge, and increasing capital. In this and the succeeding chapter we pursue the first.

By economic activity we mean effort directed towards increasing the yield of a given effort or resource, or towards reducing the cost of a given yield. To say that economic activity is necessary to economic growth is to say no more than that men are not likely to get more unless they try to get more. Growth is the result of human effort. Nature is not particularly kind to man; left to herself she will overwhelm with weeds, with floods, with epidemics and with other disasters which man wards off by taking thought and action. It is by accepting the varied challenges presented by his environment that man is able, in innumerable ways, to wrest from nature more product for less effort.

To accept the challenge of nature is to be willing to experiment, to seek out opportunities, to respond to openings, and generally to manoeuvre. The greatest growth occurs in societies where men have an eye to the economic chance, and are willing to stir themselves to seize it.

Now societies differ widely from each other in the extent to which their members seek out and exploit economic opportunities. There is a difference between countries, between groups in the same country (e.g. regional, religious or racial groups), and between patterns of behaviour in the same country at different stages of its history. These differences may be traced to three distinct causes, namely to differences in the valuation of material goods relatively to the effort required to get them, to differences in available opportunities, and to differences in the extent to which institutions encourage effort, either by removing obstacles in its way, or by ensuring to the individual the fruit of his effort. Many of the observed differences in effort are due to institutional defects, and social reformers who wish to promote economic growth are mainly concerned with seeking to bring about appropriate changes in institutions, whether by propaganda or by law. There are, however, also real psychological differences in the willingness to make effort, and we must analyse these differences first. Needless to say the attitudes and the institutions are not independent of each other; we separate them here only for purposes of analysis.

1. THE DESIRE FOR GOODS

When we say that a particular group places a low valuation upon goods relatively to effort, the difference may lie either in a lesser appreciation of goods and services, or else in a higher psychological cost of the effort required to get them. Under the first heading, the lower valuation of goods may be due to asceticism, or to a higher valuation of other activities, or to limited horizons. Under the second heading we must remember that economic effort embraces all ways of seeking out and using opportunities, not only work, but also mobility and enterprise. We shall consider in turn attitudes to each of these matters.

(a) Asceticism

Ascetic codes recognize special merit in consuming less than the rest of one's fellows. Several paths lead to the conclusion that this is the superior way of life. In the first place, some codes stress the value of learning to control one's natural desires, for food, for sex, for comfort and for other satisfactions; they encourage forms of fasting and other discomforts as means of spiritual growth. In the second place, earning one's living consumes time which might be given to meditation or to religious exercises; not all religions take this view—in some God is glorified as much in work as in prayer, and work is a means of earning spiritual merit. In the third place, earning a living sometimes brings out aggressive tendencies towards one's fellows, and it is better to avoid this temptation by confining oneself to consuming as little as one can manage.

Most codes distinguish between what is expected of priests, or others professionally engaged in practising, safeguarding or disseminating the code, and what is expected of the laity. Priests are generally expected to be poor. This is not always so even in the theory of the matter; the priests of some religions, e.g. in Africa, are not expected to be more ascetic than their fellows. Also, the theory is not always put into practice, for, in many churches where asceticism is the ideal expected of priest, there is nevertheless much wining and dining and living in luxury. This distinction between theory and practice is facilitated where a distinction is drawn between the priests and the church. If the code does not prevent the church from growing rich—and hardly any religion opposes the accumulation of wealth by its church—it is hard to expect the individual priests, who administer the wealth of the church, to refrain from enjoying some of it for themselves.

The distinction between what the code expects of priests and what it expects of the laity cannot be watertight, if only because the laity are expected to model themselves to some extent upon the priests,

whose way of life is supposed to be the model of holiness. In the matter of asceticism, however, the code seldom demands of the layman more than that he should practise various forms of asceticism (especially fasting) from time to time, or on specified days, or for specified periods. And these periods of asceticism are usually matched by corresponding festivals or feast days, when the faithful are encouraged to give themselves over to indulgence in varying degrees. In origin, many of the fasts and the festivals are associated with the seasons of agriculture; one fasts in the hungry period before the harvest, and feasts in thanksgiving when the crop is garnered.

The only parts of the world in which the ascetic ideal is held before the laity with any emphasis are the parts where Hinduism and Buddhism hold sway, and even in those parts it is doubtful whether this ideal actually influences the conduct of many laymen. It may be that in these countries some people who might otherwise pursue a business career are attracted instead to the priestly life, but this happens everywhere. It may also be that the proportion so attracted is larger than it is elsewhere, and that there are 'too many priests' in the restricted economic sense that too much talent is withdrawn from economic pursuits, and also that resources which the laity could otherwise have used for capital formation have instead to be used for supporting a disproportionately large class of priests. But this, if it were so, would testify merely to the power of religion in those parts, and to the attractiveness of the priestly life. The power of a religion to attract large numbers into its professional service is not primarily a function of whether or not it stresses the merits of asceticism. Countries as widely separated as seventeenth century Spain and contemporary Tibet are alleged to have been drained economically by an excess of priests, but the allegation is more relevant to investigating the forces which determine how much resources are available for capital formation than it is to a discussion of the effect of asceticism upon the behaviour of the laity.

It is safe to assert that this effect is small. Nowhere in the world are laymen reluctant to seize opportunities of raising their standard of living simply because they believe that it would be bad for their souls to raise their current standard of living. They may not think it worth the effort, but that is a different proposition, which we shall discuss in a later section. If no effort were involved, very few laymen would refuse to enjoy a higher standard of consumption solely from fear that this might stand between them and salvation. Thus, if seeds of higher yield, or artificial fertilizers, were offered to the farmers of India or Burma, nothing in their religious outlook would stop them from applying these aids to their work, or from enjoying the superior fruit which would result. Religion may deter people

from seeking a living in certain ways—we shall come to this later—but it does not deter anyone from enjoying a higher standard of life which has been earned without sin.

(b) Wealth and Social Status

In most communities the attractions of asceticism are small when compared with the attractions of wealth, either as a means to power, or as a mark of superior social status.

The attractions of conspicuous consumption are a familiar theme. Goods may even be desired for this purpose even though they cannot be enjoyed. Many men acquire objects which they are not able to enjoy, solely to emphasize their status—the literature is full of pianos in houses where no one plays them, of private picture galleries owned by insensitive millionaires, of cattle kept to show tribal status instead of for meat or milk, of goods acquired for conspicuous waste or destruction, and of similar examples of goods desired for show rather than for personal enjoyment. These displays are practised particularly by persons who are moving from a lower to a higher social class, and who are anxious to be recognized in their superior status. In the industrial countries they are much indulged in by the *noveaux riches*. In the colonial countries, where the ruling classes differ in race from the ruled, it will also often be found that the middle and upper classes indulge excessively in conspicuous consumption. This is because one form which their nationalist self-assertiveness takes is to show that they are 'as good' as their rulers, at least in being able to build as big houses, or to drive in as big cars, or to throw as expensive parties. This excessive consumption often weakens the subject people, by throwing them into debt, and by reducing the amount which they might save and invest in accumulating wealth.

Wealth is also desired as a means to power—whether it be the power of bribery, political power, power over employees, or other forms of power.

Wealth is not, however, always the easiest road to power or prestige. In modern capitalist society anyone who becomes rich can move into the highest—or nearly the highest—social circles. In many other communities this is not so. As in Hindu society, it may be the priestly caste that all others respect; or as in old China, the learned man. Elsewhere, it is the soldier; or prestige goes to birth in noble families. In any country the most enterprising young men will try to distinguish themselves in the ways which win highest distinction; if the way lies in war, in hunting, in religion, in bureaucracy—wherever it may lie, thither they will go. They will turn their thoughts towards economic activity only if the successful organizers of economic

activity can achieve the highest honours. In the early days of the Soviet Union the organizers of economic activity were despised; there was glory for the party man, or for the trade unionist, or for the scientist, but the factory manager was held in low esteem. Today all is different. The successful manager is very highly paid; is accorded special privileges in housing, and in entertainment; is no longer subordinated to workers in his own factory; and moves in the highest social circles.

This is one sense in which it is true that wealth is desired more in some countries than in others, and that the amount of effort given to producing wealth is a function of the desire for wealth. This, however, is merely a matter of degree. In every country of the world wealth wins respect and prestige, even though in some there is a time lag, and wealth may not acquire its full prestige until the second generation. Making money, nevertheless, always competes with other ways of acquiring social status, and the proportion of intelligent and enterprising young men attracted to this way of life is partly a function of the relative status of money making and of other activities. Thus some believe that the relative status of money makers is higher in the U.S.A. than it is in England, and higher in England than it is in Burma, and that these differences of status partly account for the differences in the rate of economic growth with which they correspond. Similarly, most analyses of industrial revolutions, both of those which have come off and of those which have failed, enquire into the relative social status of the merchant class just before the revolution, as compared with the status of aristocrats, scholars and military classes. For example, differences in this respect between China and Japan are usually given as part of the explanation why their economic history has been so different in the last hundred years. Similarly, the low status of trade in Spain, compared with its status in Elizabethan England, is not irrelevant to explaining why Spain failed so signally to exploit her economic opportunities in the sixteenth and seventeenth centuries.

It was at one time the custom to associate the present high status of money making in Western capitalist countries with the changes in the Christian religion which occurred during the Reformation and the Counter-Reformation. It is true enough that mediaeval Christianity tended to condemn commercial activities as a way of life, and also regarded it as sinful for any man to want to become wealthy in order to raise his social status and that of his family. Nowadays, however, more importance is assigned to the growth of the opportunities for making money, which began to be evident from about the twelfth century, with the expansion of seaborne trade. As wealth accumulated it became more respectable, and long before the

Reformation the Christian theologians were engaged in adapting their precepts in order to show that trade and usury were not necessarily sinful activities. By the time the Reformation occurred in the fifteenth century, this adaptation was already advanced. This is an interesting illustration of the relationship between religious change and economic change, which we shall be discussing more fully in Chapter III (section 4(a)). Since religion reflects economic change, economic attitudes cannot be explained exclusively in religious terms. On the other hand, if only because of the time lag in religious change, the influence of religious beliefs upon economic behaviour is at any time of great significance.

In almost every society wealth, prestige and power are closely associated. Where societies differ fundamentally is in what the wealthy do with their wealth, and in the sources of wealth to which prestige attaches. In pre-capitalist societies rich men spend their wealth in unproductive ways, whereas in capitalist societies they invest it productively. There are not great differences in the degree of inequality of income, as between stagnating and expanding economies, but it makes a great difference to the rate of economic growth whether the rich spend their incomes on keeping retainers and on building monuments, or whether they invest it in irrigation works, or mines, or other productive activities. It is the habit of productive investment that distinguishes rich from poor nations, rather than differences in equality of income, or differences in the respect accorded to wealthy men. Again, in so far as there are differences in prestige attaching to wealth, what matters is the relative status of those whose wealth is made or represented by productive investment, as compared with those whose wealth springs from ownership or inheritance of land. In most societies the landowners constitute the aristocracy, and it is only in societies which have undergone considerable economic expansion that rich men whose wealth is founded upon commercial activities can move on equal terms with men whose wealth is founded upon land. The really significant turning point in the life of a society is not when it begins to respect wealth, as such, but when it places in the forefront productive investment and the wealth associated therewith.

Behind the differences in attitudes to productive investment lie many factors which we shall consider in more detail in Chapter V (section 2(b)). Not the least of these are differences of national aspiration. Countries which are anxious to be strong militarily, or to be independent, or to colonize or conquer other countries, usually also want to have economic strength, if only because this is necessary in war. In our own day we can see this nationalist aspiration at work in several countries. The colonial or formerly colonial countries are

busily enquiring into the causes of economic growth, and framing plans for economic expansion, partly because they want to raise the standard of living of their peoples, but also because they wish to raise their international status. The U.S.S.R. has forced through programmes of tremendous expansion at tremendous cost in human misery. Great Britain, anxious to retain her status as a first class power, is preaching the gospel of productivity, and so on. Differences between countries in their attitudes to wealth are rapidly diminishing because of the strong force of nationalist aspirations. And they will diminish all the more as the resulting study of the possibilities reveals opportunities for wealth hitherto unsuspected.

(c) Limited Horizons

We have argued so far that asceticism is not, in practice, a drag on economic effort, and also that most men desire wealth, whether for personal enjoyment, or for prestige and power, though it is also true that the prestige of wealth, relatively to the prestige of other forms of success, varies in different communities. We come now to what is probably the most important limitation on men's desire for goods, namely their limited horizons.

The point we wish to make here is that wants are limited because the goods one knows about and can use are limited. The degree of limitation varies widely from community to community, depending upon the accumulated physical capital, upon the accumulated cultural capital, upon habits and taboos, and upon sheer ignorance.

By physical capital we mean the physical environment which is necessary for the enjoyment of particular satisfactions. This may be a question of nature or of artifice. Thus people who have no access to water do not require boats. Ice cream is not popular at the Poles, nor furs at the Equator. There is not much demand for furniture among people whose houses are small and dark. Electrical equipment—gramophones, washing machines, toasters, vacuum-cleaners—cannot be used in places where no electric current is laid on. Motor cars cannot run where there are no roads, and so on. In most poor countries there is not the accumulated physical capital to support a high level of wants. The individual's house is small and there is no electricity, gas or water laid to it. And there is a similar lack of other capital. Thus the goods which the individual can buy and use are extremely restricted.

By cultural capital we mean the background of knowledge accumulated by the society. Thus, unless the individual can read he has no use for newspapers, books, and other consumer goods whose enjoyment depends on literacy. If the culture's musical appreciation is at a low level, there is little demand for musical instruments or for

musical entertainments. Similarly, the theatre, the cinema, the sports stadium, the dance hall, and similar purveyors of mass entertainment depend upon the nature of the people's culture.

Wants are limited, thirdly, by habits and taboos. At low levels of living, food and clothing account for two-thirds of income, or more. But these are just the fields of expenditure where social convention is important. Thus it is hard to get people to improve their diets, if this improvement means eating new sorts of food, or eating food prepared in new ways. And there is similarly a limited market for styles of dress which are not generally approved.

Finally, wants are limited by ignorance. In spite of the limitations of physical background, cultural background, and habit or taboo, there remain some goods which people would be willing to buy, and to make the effort to get, if they knew about them. But the process of spreading knowledge is slow.

These are among the reasons why in some primitive communities people work very little, and are not tempted by offers of employment even at what appear to be high wages. They are not tempted because they would not know what to do with the money; or more exactly because the things they could buy with the money yield low marginal satisfactions. It is also for these reasons that large increases of income are so often misspent, by western standards. The money cannot be spent as westerners would spend it. In particular, it has to be spent not so much in acquiring new goods, of a type not owned before, as in buying more of the same—more drink, or more wives, or more cloth.

If wants are limited, it is only natural that people will work fewer hours as the remuneration per hour increases. Conversely, if wants are expansible, it is theoretically possible that people will work more as remuneration per hour increases. In considering the elasticity of wants we have to distinguish between the short run and the long. In the short run a man has definite ideas of the standard of living which he has to try to maintain, this being the conventional standard of his class. If earnings increase his immediate reaction is to work less, and if earnings decrease his immediate reaction is to work more. In the longer run, however, his standards are adjustable. If life has become harder, he may lower his standard, and revert to shorter hours; if life has become easier he will raise his standard, and revert to longer hours. For, it is not only the standard of living that is conventional, but also the number of hours worked. The immediate effect of a change is to leave the standard more or less unchanged, while altering the hours substantially; whereas the ultimate effect is to alter the standard substantially while hours revert towards the previous convention.

In primitive societies extra income beyond the conventional level

cannot be enjoyed as much as in more advanced societies because of the limited range of possible uses. There will be a demand for goods if they can help to reduce further effort; bicycles reduce the need to walk; guns make it easier to kill wild beasts, for food or for protection; tanks conserve water. Extra income may also give greater power over one's fellows; by securing election to coveted positions; by bribery; by purchase of slaves; by moneylending. Or goods can be used for display; one can give big banquets; or have more wives; or buy more clothes or jewellery; build bigger tombs; or impress one's fellows by orgies of destruction, including destruction of some of one's equipment (e.g. fishing boats in Polynesia). There is also a temporary demand for useless novelties, both to satisfy curiosity, and also for display. All these motives, of course, are present in all societies, whatever their degree of development. What distinguishes the primitive from the advanced societies is firstly that in the advanced societies there can be more enjoyment of extra commodities for themselves, and not merely because of the opportunities they give for display or power or reduced effort; and secondly that the range of goods that can be enjoyed is so much wider.

The expansibility of wants increases as physical equipment increases, as the culture becomes more complex, as the hold of convention weakens, and as knowledge of new goods is spread. This last is naturally the key to the expansion of wants, since it is the knowledge of new goods which sets in motion the forces that destroy convention or change the physical environment. To understand how wants become more elastic we must therefore understand how knowledge of new goods is spread.

The process is one of imitation. New goods can be sold sometimes merely by persuasion. The domestic innovator, or the foreigner who brings the good from some other country, may try to sell it merely by persuading people to try it out, but the good is not likely to become popular until people see it in use by others. These others must usually be persons whose status in the community is somewhat superior, so that the rest of the people wish to imitate them. There are exceptions to this; television has everywhere spread more rapidly among the common people than it has among people of superior status. Nevertheless it is generally the rule that new goods are adopted first by the upper classes—if only because these can usually afford them first, and are freer from the restraints of convention—and are later taken up by the lower classes.

The speed of diffusion therefore depends, among other things, upon the relations between the upper and the lower classes. It depends on whether they live mixed up with each other, so that the poor can see what the rich consume; or whether the rich live in their own

separate part of the town or of the country, enjoy their leisure in exclusive clubs or other surroundings, and avoid social mixture with other classes. It depends, again, on whether the rich encourage the poor to imitate them, or whether there are laws or customs which deter the poor from consuming the sort of things which the rich consume. It depends also on the degree of social mobility, since if it is easy for members of the lower classes to rise, there will be some desire on the part of those who are rising to display their changing status by adopting the consumption habits of the rich. The more democratic the community, in terms of mixing together socially, the more elastic wants will be, in terms of effort.

Societies differ in the extent to which the spread of new goods is hindered by difficulties of diffusion, in comparison with other difficulties. In primitive societies it is more probably lack of equipment, and such cultural lags as illiteracy, that limit wants rather than ignorance of new goods. This was not so in the days when these countries were cut off from foreign contact. But in these days, with foreigners in their midst living at high and envied material standards, most of the people in these countries could think of ways of spending extra income, if it were not that their houses are small, and that electricity, gas and water are not available on tap. Much extra income flows into better housing and furniture. On the other hand, in a country like England, the limit to the desire of the lower classes for more goods is more probably lack of desire to imitate the better off, with telephones, or cars, or refrigerators or expensive clothes, and this is because the undemocratic social (as distinct from political) traditions of the country cause the lower classes to be more satisfied to accept their material station in life than are the corresponding classes in the United States.

2. THE COST OF EFFORT

So much for men's attitude to wealth. We turn next to men's attitude to the effort required to obtain wealth. For, given equal attitudes to wealth, men will nevertheless make unequal efforts to acquire it if their attitude to effort is different.

This is merely a way of saying that men value other things besides material wealth. They value leisure; they value their good relations with each other, which may be disturbed by a too aggressive search for wealth; they value the company of friends and relations whom they would have to leave behind if they migrated to better economic opportunities; and they have prejudices which prevent them from taking advantage of all the opportunities which they might otherwise exploit.

(a) The Attitude to Work

We begin with the attitude to work. Given an equal desire for goods men will work less if work seems more arduous to them than if it does not. This is partly an objective and partly a subjective matter.

Work is objectively more arduous if a given job exhausts one man more than it does another. This may be due to differences in his physical constitution, to differences in his state of health, or to differences in his environment. In addition work may seem subjectively more arduous if one is less well disposed to work as a way of life.

The physical constitution differs between races and between individuals of the same race. For example, when Indians were introduced to the West Indies after the emancipation of the Negro slaves, the planters preferred the Indians for the regularity with which they worked, but they preferred the Negroes for their superior physical strength. It is not certain how much of these differences in physique is due to differences in nutrition or in environment, and how much is due to biological inheritance. In any case, willingness to work and physical strength do not necessarily correlate well, as the example cited shows.

Malnutrition and chronic debilitating disease are probably the main reason why the inhabitants of most under-developed countries are easily exhausted. And this creates a chain which is hard to break, since malnutrition and disease cause low productivity, and low productivity in turn maintains conditions of malnutrition and disease. Modern capitalist firms, working in such environments, find that it pays them to take a close interest in the food and in the health of their employees. Some mining firms in Central Africa feed new recruits on improved diets for several days before sending the recruits into the mines. There are also many firms, not confined to mining, which issue free balanced rations, or provide a midday meal, or at least subsidize meals, in order to ensure that their employees are well fed. Similarly it pays to provide free medical treatment, and to ensure that the workers live in healthy surroundings. Even in advanced industrial countries, such as the U.S.A. and England, many firms think it pays them to provide cheap midday meals, especially if they have many women employees, since women especially are alleged to be willing to save on meals in the interest of their children, or of buying themselves clothes, or of other forms of expenditure.

The environment in which one works also determines how exhausting it is to work. Thus it is unpleasant to live in great cold or great heat; the body seems to function best at a temperature of between 60°F. and 75°F., with moderate humidity. This gives an

C

advantage to the temperate climates over the tropical climates. Similarly, students of modern factory practice emphasize the importance to productivity of correct lighting, heating and ventilation; of rest pauses; of correct seating; of the elimination of unnecessary motions; and generally of pleasant physical conditions. It is also exhausting and unpleasant to work if one's companions in work are not congenial, and this too has given the industrial psychologists food for thought. It is not easy to prescribe the conditions of congeniality. Some men like working with their relatives, while others do not; some like big groups, some small; some prefer strict discipline and regulation, while others prefer more scope for individual decision. It is hard to define the conditions for happiness in the working group, but there is no doubt of their importance.

Finally, some work is more exhausting than other work either because it requires more energy per unit of time, or because it is more unpleasant.

These factors may cancel each other out. Other things being equal, men may work longer in an exhausting job than in an easy job if the social atmosphere is more attractive in the former than in the latter. Or men in poor physical condition may work longer than men in better condition if they have also better conditions in which to work.

We turn next from differences in the strain imposed by the work itself to differences in the attitude to work.

Let us suppose that two men have the same wants, in the sense of their desire for material things; and that the jobs they do are objectively equally arduous and unattractive; but that one has a more remunerative job than the other. We cannot then conclude that the one with the more remunerative job will necessarily work shorter hours than the other. It depends on his attitude to work as such. Work is a means of acquiring goods and services, but it is also a way of life, and as such it is more attractive to some men than to others, and to some groups than to others. Everybody regards work partly as a nuisance, and partly as a virtue, but some groups emphasize more the nuisance aspect, while others hand down to their children the idea that work as such is a virtue.

These differences of attitude correspond often to differences of religion. Some religions teach that salvation, or spiritual fulfilment, is found mainly in meditation or in prayer. Others teach that it is found also or alternatively in work, both because work disciplines the soul, and also because we have a moral duty to make the best use of the talents and resources with which God has endowed us, and to serve our fellow-men thereby. There is, nevertheless, the usual difficulty in deciding how much importance to attribute to religion in economic matters. First, there is the distinction we drew before,

between what a religion expects of its priests, and what it expects of its laity. If as is so often the case, it expects its priests to pray but its laymen to work, it will diminish the community's economic effort only if it attracts excessive numbers into the priestly life. Even if the religion puts the emphasis upon meditation for the laity, and discourages economic preoccupations, there is the further difficulty of assessing how effective its precepts are, since so many men will seize opportunities for making wealth even if their religion disapproves. Behind all this lies the further question why a quietist religion is acceptable to the community. Religious precepts tend to accommodate themselves to the community's ways of making a living. Hence to say that people do not work hard because their religion does not encourage them to may not be to give a fundamental explanation; it may equally be that the religion does not at present stress work because the other circumstances of the community, environmental or social, do not bring hard work into the forefront of values.

We cannot be certain what these other circumstances are which produce differences in the attitude to work. Biological differences are alleged, as also the unpleasantness or productivity of the work, and also the social structure of the community. In analysing these factors it is important to remember that there is always a lag between an attitude and the conditions which have produced it. That is to say, if we want to know why a community believes what it believes, we must look not to its present biological composition, or social structure, or what you will, but to conditions decades or centuries earlier, when its traditions were being formed.

Let us take first the biological factor. Some individuals have more energy, or more disposition to work than others, because of a biological inheritance not related to their environment. There are millions of people who believe unshakeably that the proportion of these biologically industrious persons is greater in some races or countries than it is in other races or countries. There are also millions who believe that the distribution of the biologically industrious or lazy does not vary from race to race, and that the observed differences can all be explained in terms of physical environment and cultural tradition.

The great majority of the world's scientists deny that there is acceptable evidence linking human attitudes with racial biology. If we confine ourselves, however, to localities, while we are still devoid of evidence, we have at least some plausible theories. Thus, if a country is subject to repeated disasters or crises of a kind where the biologically energetic survive, while the rest perish, then it follows tautologically that the biological inheritance of this community will constantly improve in terms of energy. The difficulty of course is to

define the circumstances in which the difference between survival and death depends upon biologically inheritable energy: in most crises survival owes as much to upbringing, to cunning, and to luck. Again, we have the theory that a country peopled by immigrants will show more energy than one which has been settled for a longer period (all countries are peopled by immigrants) because immigrants tend to be more enterprising than those they leave behind, and because the hardships of migration and settlement tend to weed out the unfit. The difficulty here is to be certain that the biological factors are dominant in determining who becomes a successful immigrant. Immigrants certainly tend to be more energetic than those they leave behind, or than those they come to live amongst, but this may be merely because the stresses to which they are subject are greater, and so call forth greater performance.

Biological explanations of differences in group attitudes can neither be accepted nor be rejected. We can certainly reject the idea that one race is superior to another, in the sense that all members of one race are superior to all members of another in performance tests. But as to the distribution of superior, ordinary and inferior between different groups we can say nothing at present. Our explanations of group differences have therefore to be confined to differences in physical and cultural environment.

We come then secondly to the unpleasantness of the work. We have already seen that work may be particularly arduous in itself, or because of the physical condition of the worker, or because the physical or social environment in which it has to be done is uncongenial. We argued then that people might be expected to work less in these circumstances. The argument is reversed, however, if we are asking not how much work is done in pleasant compared with unpleasant circumstances, but rather what attitude to work grows up. For, if the work is unpleasant, people may have as it were to force themselves to do enough of it to keep themselves alive. And those who let themselves be put off by its unpleasantness may not survive. In these circumstances parents may begin to teach their children that work itself is a virtue, and is something to be done for its own sake, perhaps even because it is unpleasant. This tradition may be handed down, and may survive changed conditions, so that even when the work to be done ceases to be unpleasant men may continue to work with as much grim determination as before.

Exactly the same line of argument can be applied to work that is relatively unproductive. Thus one may reason as follows. In countries where it is easy to make a living, work is seldom regarded as a virtue, since men's habit is to make a virtue of necessity. At the other extreme, countries where it is exceptionally hard to make a living

may discourage effort. Intermediately, work is a virtue in countries which are hard, but not too hard. That is to say in countries where it is possible to attain a good standard by reasonable effort, but where without such effort men will perish. Hardness may be due to over-crowding, to soil of only moderate fertility, to recurrent drought or hurricane, or to other misfortune. In such countries children will be taught that work is a virtue, and will be shown the poverty of persons who failed to keep at their tasks; and they in turn will hand the tradition down to their children.

All explanations based on environment have, however, to face the fact that attitudes are not constant; the same country displays opposing tendencies at different times. Explanations of attitudes have therefore to be historical as well as environmental; that is to say, if they are relying upon environment they have to show when and why the environment changed to bring about the differences which they are explaining. This is particularly damaging to those explanations of attitudes which rely upon climate, since the same country shows quite different attitudes at different times in its history; this is why some of these explanations seek to show changes in climate, for example in accounting for the decline of the Roman Empire. Most of the environmental explanations of traditions of hard work involve some sort of historical shock to the community, which has challenged the people to display their best qualities of endurance—such as defeat in war, or the onset of famine, or the hardship of a great migration. However, it must take something more than a great historical hardship to stiffen the will of a people, or else it would seem to be a mere accident whether a community subjected to hardship becomes despondent and discouraged, or alternatively finds courage and inspiration therein.

A different kind of explanation connects the community's attitude to work with the behaviour of its upper classes. According to this explanation work is more highly regarded by the people in general in those communities where it is the tradition for everyone to work than it is in communities where the rich traditionally live in idleness. For men imitate their social betters, and if these find it degrading to work, others also will work as little as they can. For example, in the slave communities of the New World, the plantocracies were much given to going on picnics and to having a good time, and there was much absentee ownership. The middle and working classes of these communities to this day show a greater propensity to consume lavishly than they do to work, and this may plausibly be explained by saying that they have inherited the idea that work is fit only for slaves. The distinction we are making is not between equalitarian and inequalitarian societies, but between those where the rich work and those

where they live in idleness. Thus in the United States the rich usually work, if only from force of habit, whereas in England there is a long tradition, now almost dead, that the ideal life for the rich is one of hunting and shooting and fishing. It is not the case that the American workman works longer hours than the British workman—actually he works shorter hours—but there is some evidence that he works more intensively while he is working. Some people attribute this difference to different attitudes to work, and trace these differences back to different ideals as to how successful men should spend their time. The facts in this comparison are all disputable, but the comparison illustrates the line of argument.

Whatever the reasons may be why some people object to work, as such, more than others do, the fact remains that there are significant differences in this respect both between individuals and between groups. These differences show themselves not only in the number of hours work done at any time, but also in the reaction to increases in the productivity of work. In practice, the long run effect of raising the yield of work per hour is always to reduce the number of hours done (in theory either result is possible). We can see this whether we compare industrial countries, in which case we shall find in general that those with the highest productivity per man also work the shortest hours; or whether we compare hours in the same country as its standards of remuneration have increased. This is a natural reaction. Since leisure is one of the good things of life, men naturally use extra productivity to buy some extra leisure as well as some of other things. Besides, leisure and goods are complementary in enjoyment, since the more wealth one has, the more leisure one needs to enjoy it in. In the long run men work harder if wages are low than they do in more favourable conditions—provided that real earnings are still high enough to maintain good health and productivity. The extent of the difference between groups in this respect depends simply on the intensity of their desire for wealth, on the one hand, and on the intensity of their desire for leisure on the other hand.

When the entrepreneurs of Western countries first arrived in the more primitive countries they had great difficulty in getting labour. The native peoples were enjoying their conventional standards, and could not be tempted by offers of extra income. It was therefore thought necessary to resort to means of compulsion. Slaves were bought; or labour was brought from far countries on indenture. Natives were smoked out of their indolence by levying high taxes upon them, which had to be paid in money, which again could be had only by working for the foreigner; or by prohibiting them from growing commercial crops; or by taking their lands away; or by compelling chiefs to send young men to work in mines or on planta-

tions. These compulsions (except slavery) are still to be found in one or other of the African colonies of all the European powers, but they are not so necessary now as they were formerly thought to be. For imitation has done its work. The Africans have acquired new wants, and are willing to work to satisfy them without compulsion.

The ruling classes in any country are usually anxious that the people should be willing to work steadily and persistently, say for an average of forty hours a week or more. Capitalists and employers like the population to be hardworking, because it is easier to fulfil their industrial ambitions if labour is plentiful, and also because their profits increase as output increases. Governments, too, whether they be democratic or authoritarian, conservative or radical, like the people to work because the yield of taxation is greater with greater output; governments need large revenues whatever their purposes may be, whether they be the 'democratic' purpose of improving education, public health, communications and other public services, or the 'imperialistic' or 'anti-imperialistic' purpose of creating large military forces, or merely the 'corrupt' purpose of lining the politicians' pockets. (And so it happens that 'radical' governments, elected for their sympathy with the desire of the workers for shorter hours, usually revert, once they are firmly in the saddle, to appealing to the people for longer and steadier work.) Humanitarians, who have no personal interest in the matter, usually share the same sentiment that it is good for the people to be industrious, because humanitarians abhor poverty and its results, and prefer the people to have a reasonable standard of living.

A willingness to work long hours is not, however, a necessary condition of economic growth. It is obvious that the standard of living will be higher if people work more than if they work less—subject to their not working so hard as to reduce their productive powers—but it is not obvious that the standard of living will also *grow* faster. Our interest is not in the absolute level of output, but in its rate of growth. Apart from minor changes of hours, output usually grows not because people are working harder, but because they are working more productively, using more knowledge or more capital, and taking more favourable opportunities for specialization, for trade, and for investment.

Opportunities for greater productivity exist whatever level of work people may fix upon. It is true that some of these opportunities depend on willingness to make regular effort; factory routines, for example, require regular attendance and regular hours. Other opportunities also depend upon flexibility—on willingness to work at night, or on week-end shifts, or even at call. These opportunities, however, do not depend on the number of hours of work each person

is prepared to do in a year; both regularity and flexibility are consistent with each person stipulating beforehand upon a limited total number of hours. Some opportunities for greater production will also be missed, in the sense that some industries may not come into existence at all because people will not work in the way these industries require; but this is quite consistent with their working very productively in other industries whose working habits are more congenial.

Economic growth requires also that people should be willing to work conscientiously, but this is not the same thing as being willing to work long hours. A man should be willing to give his mind to what he is doing; to do it properly, to the best of his ability; and to be punctual in starting and in delivery. These qualities are sadly lacking in some communities where people seem to attach little importance to faithful fulfilment of their contracts. In primitive societies this is usually due to the strangeness of the new demands now made upon the individual. Where people are accustomed to working in the fields, at their own pace, without clocks, it is hardly a matter for surprise if they are unpunctual, or irregular in attendance at work. Similarly, where people are accustomed to relationships based upon kinship and upon status, it is difficult to get used to obligations which are exclusively pecuniary, and it may take two or three generations before the new contractual relationships acquire a new and generalized moral sanction. In more advanced societies, the community may be torn by internal dissensions: the 'employed class' may dislike the 'employing class', or the sellers may have a grievance against the buyers, so that there is no sense of moral obligation towards the other contracting parties. In a competitive society these things tend to sort themselves out with time. Those individuals who give the most conscientious service succeed (other things being equal) to a greater extent than the less conscientious, and their example is increasingly imitated, until the new moral tradition is firmly forged. But societies are not always competitive, and the forces moving in these directions may be weak.

Now it may be argued that willingness to use one's opportunities is positively correlated with willingness to work long hours, in the sense that people who cannot take the trouble to work long hours will also not take the trouble to seek out the most profitable opportunities, or to work regularly and conscientiously. The argument is not, however, very plausible. People may be very quick off the mark in seizing the most profitable opportunities, even though they are firm in their decision to work shorter hours than their fellows. It is, for example, hard to get the farmers in tropical countries to work as many hours as industrial workers in temperate countries, but this

does not prevent them from seizing opportunities to use better seeds, or fertilizers, or to plant more profitable crops. It has not prevented the Gold Coast farmer—who is said, no doubt erroneously, to be one of the laziest farmers in the world—from switching from subsistence production to creating the largest cocoa industry in the world, over a short space of time; or prevented the farmers of Uganda or of Indonesia from taking enthusiastically to cotton and to rubber respectively. It might even be suggested that the less one likes work the more likely one is to seek out opportunities for making one's work more profitable so that one may be free to work less. But this suggestion has no more plausibility than its converse. There is probably no correlation, positive or negative, between willingness to work long hours, and willingness to seek the most productive opportunities.

Again, we have already seen that as productivity increases people work shorter hours. If their demand for leisure is very high relatively to their demand for goods they will, in the extreme case, reduce their hours as fast as their productivity increases. Their standard of living will then fail to rise, despite increasing productivity. Growth will nevertheless be occurring. We have defined growth as taking place if output is increasing per hour of work done. This is the reasonable definition; it would be silly to deny that economic growth was taking place merely because people were preferring to use their increasing productivity to buy more leisure instead of to buy more goods.

If there is any correlation between industriousness and economic growth the link will be found in greater ability or willingness to make productive investment. Those who work hard have presumably greater income and less time for consuming it than do those who work less; they may therefore be in a better position to invest. It is not enough that they should be willing to save more. If peasants save by buying gold and jewellery, economic growth is not stimulated. Similarly if they save to buy more land, the effect is not to increase agricultural output, but merely to change the price and ownership of land. What matters to growth is the formation of productive capital, which is not necessarily associated either with willingness to work or with willingness to save. There is in fact no evidence that hard work and productive investment necessarily go together; the Chinese, for example, have for centuries had the reputation of being among the hardest working peoples of the world, but though the population of China has increased much less rapidly than that of Europe this hard work has not resulted in economic growth. When we are told of two different races living together that one is more industrious than the other, and that this is why it is more prosperous, we will usually find, on closer examination, that the real difference is that one is engaging

more extensively in productive capital formation than the other. Hard work and capital formation are an excellent formula for economic growth, but whereas capital formation without hard work will also produce substantial growth, hard work without capital formation makes little contribution to development.

Willingness to seek out and to seize opportunities, and to make productive investments is not a function of hours of work done, but it certainly relates to the intensity of thought which one gives to one's opportunities, and it may have high costs in nervous energy. Business men get stomach ulcers not so much because they work long hours as because they worry about their work; it takes a good deal of nervous energy to be always thinking of ways of saving another sixpence, or making another sixpence, as they are supposed to do. And it is, of course, an open question whether the game is worth the candle, that is to say whether it is better to think seriously about one's economic chances, and to progress materially, or whether it is better not to give much thought to such matters and to stay poor. In some societies economic growth is thought to be worth while for its own sake, and young men are encouraged to try to get on in life; whereas other societies prefer to give their minds to other things: to making war, to the arts, or just to the enjoyment of good talk or other pleasures.

While it is true that the individual is more likely to succeed in achieving greater productivity if he thinks the effort worth while, it is seldom the case that a large proportion of any community is keenly sensitive to its chances, and neither is it necessary for growth that the masses of the people should be so inclined. There must be a few people willing to pioneer; once they have pioneered successfully, the others will usually follow in their footsteps without giving much thought to the matter—provided they are not prevented from doing so by barriers of caste or race or religion. It is in this sense that growth depends on alert leadership. Of course, the larger this alert minority, and the more scope it is allowed for manoeuvring, the more rapidly the community will grow economically, and it is in the difference of proportions and of scope that the essential difference between societies is to be found.

(b) The Spirit of Adventure

We are leaving until the next chapter the analysis of the scope which society gives to those who wish to manoeuvre economically; in this chapter we continue to examine the individual's willingness to do so. This reveals itself in many ways, of which we shall now consider the most important. These are willingness to operate with a mind free from convention and taboo, willingness to take risks, and

willingness to move from one place to another, as the occasion demands.

Convention and taboo may restrict opportunity in various ways. For example, it may restrict the use of resources. A well known instance of this is the Hindu attitude to the sacred cow; beasts of inferior quality cannot be killed, or restrained from breeding; and the number of animals is so excessive that they are a drain on the farmers' resources. A similar instance is the prejudice which prevents most Western communities from using human excrement for manuring their fields, and which therefore means that valuable minerals extracted from the soil are annually poured into the sea. Every community has prejudices of this sort, which prevent it from using to the full resources which other countries would be glad to have, but some are much more ridden with taboos than others.

Probably the most important prejudices hampering economic development at the present time are the prejudices about livestock. Subject to what is said in the next chapter about the disincentive effects of faulty agrarian structure, it seems to be the case that peasant farmers are everywhere anxious to improve their material conditions, and responsive to innovations which have this effect. They gladly adopt new seeds, or fertilizers, or make use of water provided by new irrigation facilities, or turn over to more remunerative commercial crops. The suggestion that economic development is prevented by farmers not having worldly values is largely a myth, since farmers are almost everywhere an acquisitive class. It is not, however, at all mythical in relation to livestock. Both in Asia and in Africa there are some farming communities which take a noncommercial attitude to livestock, fail to exploit their cattle to best advantage in terms of work, meat and milk, carry excessive numbers of useless beasts, and ruin themselves in the process. This is a great nuisance to economic development because such development is tied up to a considerable extent with progress in agriculture, which in turn depends largely upon a better integration of animal and arable husbandry.

Next in importance are the taboos relating to family life, especially those relating to the sort of work which women may do (Chapter III, section 2(b)) and those relating to birth control (Chapter VI, section 1(a)). Fortunately, there is reason to think that these prejudices are dissipated by the process of economic development itself, but they can seriously keep down the standard of living in the early stages of economic growth. Prejudices in relation to livestock and in relation to the family are currently religion's most deadly contribution to the maintenance of poverty.

There may also be conventional ways of doing things, which have

to be followed on pain of social disapproval. Thus in some countries agricultural practices are controlled by priests, whose mysteries tell when and how and where to plant, and whose ritual ministrations are essential to success. As civilization progresses technology escapes from the control of religion, but there are always other dogmatists lying in wait for it. The regulation of techniques by the mediaeval guilds is not different in kind from the orthodoxies which hamper scientific progress, even in our own day. And the ambitions of the state to regulate techniques are exemplified equally by Colbert's seventeenth century edicts and by the Lysenko purge. It is impossible to have an absolutely open mind on how things should be done, and to be forever willing to experiment in all directions, but some societies are more successful than others in widening the freedom for individuals to experiment.

Then there are the prejudices relating to occupations. Early mediaeval theologians thought that the merchant's calling was virtually incompatible with the Christian life, and were even more certain of the sinfulness of moneylending. How effective these pronouncements were in practice is open to question; at any rate they were modified continuously as opportunities for profitable trading increased with the growth of towns. In the same class (though its origins were different) was the contempt for trade which was felt by the Spanish aristocracy, in the sixteenth century, and to which some historians attribute some part of Spain's failure to exploit successfully her ownership of and her easy access to the New World: certainly Queen Elizabeth and her nobles, if they felt any such prejudices, were not prevented thereby from sharing in trading adventures. In every community some occupations have lower status than others. Usually, however, there are plenty of people of low social status for these low status jobs. Sometimes, however, a change of conditions brings it about that these are just the jobs which now offer great opportunities for economic expansion, and the prejudice then becomes a brake on growth. Thus, it is unfortunate for England if, as is alleged, a social stigma attaches to coal mining, or if scientists who engage in technology have much lower status than scientists engaged in 'pure' research, or if a business career is ranked low in preference by good honours graduates from the universities. For, since the prejudices of one community are not the same as those of another, the chance which one community rejects is often taken instead by its rivals. Just so the predilection of Negro West Indians for the prestige of the liberal professions is one reason why, to their dismay, it is Indian and Chinese West Indians who are gaining increasing control of business.

Even within occupations there are prejudices against doing various

kinds of work. One of the most striking examples is the often reported refusal of engineers in under-developed countries to do work which would soil their hands, or of persons in administrative positions even to move a chair for themselves. The doctrine that manual work should be done only by people of low social status is well entrenched in all those communities where considerations of caste or social prestige bulk large. Often the fundamental explanation is over-population. In over-populated countries the tradition is established that there is a moral duty on the part of the better-off to provide as much employment as they can for the not-so-well-off, and hence, if people of higher status are seen doing manual work they lose respect —not only because they are lowering their caste, but also because their refusal to give the work to someone else shows either that they are mean and heartless, or else that they are not-so-well-off as they would like it to be thought. Such traditions are very appropriate to static over-populated communities; but they do not mix well with the philosophy of individualism and self-help with which more dynamic societies are associated.

Men differ also in their willingness to have economic relations with strangers, and in whom they consider to be strangers. Opportunities must be restricted if one can trade with, or employ, or lend money to one's relations only, or members of one's caste only, or only to people from one's own village, or country, or sex, or race, or religion, or political party, or whatever the restriction may be. Differences here are also related to differences in the impersonality of economic relations. In modern capitalist communities a contract is based primarily upon considerations of price and quality, leaving aside considerations of kinship, or of the personal merit, welfare, or good fortune of the party with whom one is doing business; but in most other communities a contract is to a greater extent a form of personal relationship, which originates in or creates personal ties not inherently connected with the transaction itself. Even in modern societies a personal element has to enter into many business relationships; some kinds of contract it is wise to make only with persons whom one can trust to execute them faithfully and without deceit; it may also be necessary to give special personal favours in order to get special personal favours in return (especially in imperfectly organized markets where supply and demand are not always in equilibrium); and it may sometimes be necessary to support one's own relations, or the members of one's race, or sex, or some other group to which one belongs if mutual protection is needed for economic self-defence. Apart from these cases where the personalization of business is an advantage to the person making the contract, on economic grounds, there is much personalization based only on sentiment or on preju-

dice. Whatever the case may be for it in its own terms—of kinship, or politics, or religion, or else—there is no doubt in these cases that impersonal economic relationships would offer wider opportunities for economic growth.

We are dealing with a phenomenon which causes much sadness to those who regret the passing of old ways. Most primitive societies rest upon status. Men have rights and expectations which depend upon their status in the community, and not upon their competitive performance in the market. When therefore services which they expect from others are sold instead to the highest bidder, or goods to which they have a traditional claim pass instead into the market, they cry out against the disintegration of old customs and institutions based upon personal relationships, and the substitution instead of what they call greed and lack of respect. The change from status to contract is revolutionary in any society. The old code of values goes, and the community may indeed disintegrate, even in the moral sense, until new traditions form and gain respect. It is not only the economic relations that are affected; the decline of status in economic affairs corrodes also the old ideas about status in political organization, and in the family, and simultaneously challenges the religious precepts which safeguarded the old rights of status, and thus religion itself. Reintegration does not therefore occur until the community has found new kinship and new political arrangements which accord with its new contractual outlook, and a new or reformed religion or moral code to sanction the new arrangements. This process took a long time to work itself out in Western Europe; it took some time to formulate a new political philosophy, based on the idea of the social contract; and to reconcile a contractual outlook with a religion based on revelation and authority. The process is not yet completed. Indeed, the twentieth century shows some tendency to return from contract to status, by way of legislation prescribing the rights and duties of various classes, and denying freedom to make contracts of employment or tenancy or hire purchase or sale except on terms stipulated by law. The less developed countries are only just entering upon this cycle. Some African societies already have political and marriage systems based on contractual ideas. But in most communities outside the Western world adaptation to impersonal economic relations cannot be done without resistance on the part of those whose status is thereby challenged, or without a general upheaval of ideas.

Another aspect of the adventurous spirit which causes sadness to some is the effect of competition in economic life. The competitive spirit runs through all human activity; men take pleasure in showing off their prowess in games, or hunting, or sexual attraction, or sing-

ing or what you will, and in some spheres, such as in the struggle for political power, or for leadership in religion or in social status, the struggle may be bitter, merciless, and unlimited. There is always, however, some sort of code within which competition is supposed to operate—such as the code which controls the struggle for political power—and there are always those who regard the competitive instinct as a danger to the soul, and who are anxious to curb it as much as possible. These sentiments apply as much to competition in economic life as to competition in any other sphere.

There is not much room for economic competition in a subsistence economy where there is little specialization or trade, but competition is found in every sphere of a market economy however hard monopolists may seek to eliminate it, since the buyer always has some freedom to decide to spend his money differently. Competition exists even though the sellers do not want it, so long as the buyers are free to choose between them—a choice which is narrowed if all the sellers in 'the same industry' collaborate, but which does not disappear since competition between 'different industries' (e.g. television and cinemas) may be just as important. If in addition some sellers are anxious to get a larger share of the market, whether by offering better quality, or by offering a lower price, by advertising, or merely by dishonesty, the competition will be even more acute.

Competition is almost certain to hurt somebody. Thus the factory worker who produces more than the norm may hurt the others, because he shows up their slackness, or because the employer is thereby encouraged to raise the norm, or because he leaves less work for the others to do; these results are not inevitable, but they are possible in some circumstances. Similarly in the industry the firm which tries to capture a larger share of the market puts a strain upon all the others, and may drive some bankrupt. One cannot make omelettes without breaking eggs.

In some societies the weakest goes to the wall, and few tears are shed over him. There is a certain ruthlessness towards established expectations in such countries (otherwise widely different) as the United States, the U.S.S.R. and Japan, which it is hard to dissociate altogether from the relatively high rates of economic growth which these countries have achieved in recent decades. In some other countries there is a greater desire to ensure that expectations are not rudely frustrated; it is 'bad form' to be too aggressive, or to work too hard, or otherwise to cause serious loss to one's rivals. We shall have to discuss this subject more fully in the succeeding chapter, when we come to institutional restraints upon effort; here we note merely how widely attitudes towards competition differ.

Another aspect of the adventurous spirit is the attitude towards

risk. Willingness to bear risk is partly a matter of temperament, partly a matter of what one can afford, and partly a matter of the tradition in which one has been raised. If we are comparing the attitudes of different groups we must ignore the question of temperament. It is possible that different groups of men inherit a biological propensity to risk in different proportions, but we know no more about this than we do about group differences in the biological inheritance of the propensity to be industrious.

The more secure one's economic foundation is, the more one can afford to risk. Thus a rich farmer can try out new seeds extensively, without knowing how well they stand up to conditions of drought or flood or other agricultural risks. But farmers who live near the level of subsistence are extremely reluctant to give up seeds which they know will give some yield in many varied conditions, however poor this yield may be on the average, since they simply cannot run the risk that the new seed, however bountiful on the average, may in one year fail, and reduce them to famine. On the other hand, the very poorest people, who have nothing to lose, may be more willing to try a chance than the more fortunate, who would lose if the chance failed. Thus, if there is a rumour of a gold strike a hundred miles away, the unemployed are more likely to be attracted than are people who have already a moderate source of income to which they could not return if they found no gold. More risk-taking is therefore to be expected in fairly rich or in very insecure communities than in those which have a modest competence.

The difference of traditions is probably more important. In the schools of twentieth century England many a Speech Day orator urges those who are graduating not to go for the secure jobs, but to cultivate a spirit of adventure; touching perhaps also on Drake and the Elizabethans and the splendid record of British enterprise. Similar speeches were not made in mediaeval England; and are not made in contemporary Morocco or Siam. As with work so with adventure; there are countries where the young are taught that it is a virtue, and countries where they are not so taught. It is equally difficult to account for the difference of traditions. Presumably countries which live by hazardous occupations learn to fear risk less than other countries. But all occupations are hazardous; the farmer's life in India, with uncertain rainfall, is as hazardous as is a life spent in fishing or in foreign trade. Whatever the origin, the tradition probably feeds on itself, in the sense that countries which have behind them a career of successful risk-taking develop a degree of confidence in the chances of success which other nations lack.

One aspect of risk-taking which is particularly important in a developing economy is willingness to change one's occupation. In

the extreme status-type economy the caste system seeks to compel a man to pursue only the trade into which he was born, and his father before him (except that all castes may farm); and even in societies which do not recognize caste, strong family feeling and filial sentiment may keep sons tied to an occupation for which they have no talents, or for which the demand is clearly shrinking. Family feeling apart, one may also have a special affection for a craft in which one has been trained, and may have a natural reluctance to leave it, even for some more profitable occupation. These again are matters where traditions vary between communities, some taking it for granted that a man will stick to one trade all his life, preferably his father's, while others encourage a more adventurous spirit.

Changing one's occupation is particularly hard when it involves leaving one's home and taking up residence somewhere else. Yet growth constantly demands movement of this kind: new resources are discovered in sparsely populated districts; or the resources of old districts are worked out; or some change in demand or in supply alters the assessment of known resources. In these days some governments are anxious to take work to people instead of people to work, and this may find economic justification if new industries would fit into the old location just as well as into any other. It is sometimes also supported on the basis that the old location has accumulated capital in houses, power supplies, schools and other public services, which it would be wasteful to replace elsewhere; but this argument, though it has some validity, is not as forceful as it might be since capital wears out and has to be replaced somewhere sometime. In any case, industries which depend upon such natural resources as the soil, minerals, or water have little choice but to go where these resources are to be found.

Willingness to move is partly a matter of sentiment, partly a matter of pressures, and partly a matter of the attractiveness of the place to which one might move.

The sentiment may lie in one's attachment to one's relations, or one's friends, to one's home, or to one's district, or to one's way of life. The biggest break is involved if the migration involves a new way of life; such as ceasing to be a farmer in a small community, in order to become a factory hand or a miner in a large community. Here also tradition helps. After a decade or so in which many have made the change, their successors become used to the idea. News travels home of what conditions are like in the other place, and knowledge may dispel fear, and may even kindle enthusiasm. There is not much more to be said about sentiment than that peoples who are used to moving move more than those who are not.

To start the habit in a big way usually requires some pressure. In

D

those agricultural countries where everybody has enough land to live on it is very difficult to get people to move even to much better opportunities, unless something happens to reduce their security at home. This may be the onset of famine, or of over-population, or of war or of some natural disaster. Or, as in Africa, governments may add the pressure of taxes, of taking away people's land, or of compulsion, to force Africans out of their reserves into wage-earning employment. The English classical economists often discussed the effect of primogeniture, and concluded that its effect was to force all but the heir to be more enterprising and more mobile. The strength of family connections is probably also important: if one can rely on a wide circle of relations for support one is less likely to make great efforts for oneself, and it is probably not without significance that extended family systems and rapid economic growth are seldom found together. In industrial communities people tend to move out of areas of heavy unemployment if there are other expanding areas into which to move; the existence of unemployment insurance may reduce their mobility somewhat, but most men prefer to be employed rather than unemployed, and in any case the difference between unemployment pay and wages is substantial for all but the lowest paid workers.

How important it is that the place where the migrants are wanted should be attractive is shown by the failure of many programmes. The migrant needs assurance of a friendly reception, of reasonable accommodation, of economic prospects, and of a chance to settle in to the new life. The great mining companies of Central and Southern Africa, who needed hundreds of thousands of Africans to move out of their reserves for work, offered at first hardly any of these attractions, so it is not surprising that pressures had to be exercised on their behalf. Good pay, good housing to which wives and children can be brought, prospects of promotion, and the establishment of the amenities of permanent town life now figure to a greater extent in their programmes, and have almost eliminated dependence on pressures in the reserves. We can see exactly the same attitudes at work in the suburban housing estates to which the great industrial towns of the Western world are trying to move populations out of congested slums in city centres. Often those who have been moved demand to go back. They say they miss their friends and the city streets and noises; in fact they dislike the much longer journeys to work, and the fact that there are not enough cinemas and public houses and other institutions round which to build a new community life. There is much less frustration when the new suburbs have their own factories, when groups of friends and relations are moved together, and when the new suburbs have all the facilities needed for creating a new community life. Still another example is the failure of

so many schemes for land settlement. Often settlers are given land without prior preparation of roads or water supplies; they are chosen haphazardly, without regard to agricultural experience, or to capital; and they are left to fend for themselves without advice, assistance or organization. Indonesian experience is particularly instructive. Prior to 1937 the government offered to transport Javanese to Sumatra, where it gave them land and financial assistance, but very few would go. Thereafter it was arranged that settlers should arrive just before the harvest, and should spend their first weeks working as labourers for previous settlers and lodging with them. This enabled them to earn some money, to get acclimatized to the new country in various senses, to get advice on the spot, and to make useful contacts. The system also ensured that the new settlers would in their turn be assisted with their harvests. The result was that the annual number of migrants nearly doubled between 1936 and 1940, and was increasing every year, in spite of the fact that the government also greatly reduced the amount of financial assistance it gave to the migrants.

While it is true that the individual is more likely to succeed if he is willing to be mobile, it is not necessary to economic growth that everyone should be mobile. Economic conditions change relatively slowly, and on the fringe, so that it is enough that some proportion of the people, usually a small percentage in any year, should be willing to move. Even this small percentage, however, will not be forthcoming unless there is a combination of the attractiveness of the new areas with either a tradition of mobility or strong pressures at home.

Much the same remark applies to all other aspects of 'adventure'. Economic growth requires not that all should be adventurous, but that there should be an adequate supply of innovators. This in turn is partly a matter of the rewards and prestige which can be gained by successful innovation. In every community there are some men whose natural bent is to experiment with new techniques, new products, or new economic forms, in defiance of established opinion or of vested interests. Some societies admire and encourage such people, while others regard them as buccaneers to be suppressed, but economic growth depends very largely on the extent to which the social atmosphere nourishes such people, and gives them scope. We shall be returning to this subject in later chapters.

3. RESOURCES AND RESPONSE

The most important natural resources are climate, fresh water, fertile soil, useful minerals, and a topography which facilitates trans-

portation. None of these features can be defined as rich or poor in any absolute sense, since what is considered valuable today in any one of these categories, may be considered useless tomorrow. The value of a resource depends upon its usefulness, and its usefulness is changing all the time through changes in taste, changes in technique, or new discovery. Coal was not a valued resource until men learnt to burn it; neither can anyone speak with confidence today as to its value in two hundred years' time. The Severn estuary was regarded chiefly as a barrier until the discovery of America made Bristol temporarily one of the greatest ports in the world. A hundred acres of fertile soil in Jamaica were once a fortune, but are not now so highly regarded since many other lands suitable for growing sugar have been opened up. Accordingly, when we say that a country is rich in resources the statement has meaning only in relation to contemporary knowledge and techniques. Similarly, a country which is considered to be poor in resources today may be considered very rich in resources at some later time, not merely because unknown resources are discovered, but equally because new uses are discovered for the known resources.

Bearing this temporal limitation in mind, it is interesting to enquire to what extent the rate of growth displayed by any particular country has resulted from the richness or poverty of its natural resources. There is an obvious sense in which the one depends upon the other. Other things being equal, men can make better use of rich resources than they can of poor resources, hence we expect those countries whose opportunities are greatest to show the greatest rates of development. Much of the world's economic history can be written very simply in these terms. In the earliest days when agriculture is the chief activity, the fertile river valleys show the greatest progress. At other times one can see how other places come into prominence through the discovery of minerals (e.g. Malaya's tin) or of new ways of using them (Middle East oil, Britain's coal); or through changes in trade routes (the ports of Western Europe after 1492); or through new means of transport (e.g. Bangkok's airport). The extent of a country's resources is quite obviously a limit on the amount and type of development which it can undergo. It is not the only limit, or even the primary limit. For most countries could make better use of their existing resources than they do. Given the country's resources, its rate of growth is determined by human behaviour and human institutions: by such things as energy of mind, the attitude towards material things, willingness to save and invest productively, or the freedom and flexibility of institutions. Natural resources determine the course of development, and constitute the challenge which may or may not be accepted by the human mind.

The more fundamental sense in which one probes into the relationship between resources and growth is therefore to enquire whether there is a connection between richness of resources and the quality of the human response. Given the effort which human beings make, the same effort will produce more rapid growth in rich than in barren countries. But is there also some law by which greater effort is induced in the richer than in the more barren countries, or is the reverse the case?

The question can be answered definitely only for one 'resource', namely accessibility, and very much less definitely, or not at all, for other resources. Accessibility is a resource in the sense that it stems from geographical features—the surface layout of the country, its rivers, its access to the sea, the quantity and quality of its harbours, and the presence or absence of impassable barriers such as high mountains, deserts or impenetrable jungle between the country and the rest of the civilized world. Accessibility plays a decisive part in stimulating economic growth. It stimulates trade, therefore widening the range of demand, encouraging effort, and furthering specialization. It also results in a mingling of peoples, with different customs and ideas; and this keeps the mind active, stimulates the growth of knowledge, and helps to keep institutions free and flexible. Degree of accessibility must play a large role in explaining the economic vigour of any people.

Next in degree of doubtfulness comes climate. It seems to be the case that the human body functions best in a temperature of 60° to 75°F., with moderate humidity, but the effects of climate on the human mind are not so clear. It is clear that extremes of temperature are unfavourable. Nevertheless, civilizations have flourished in the past in countries varying very widely in their climates, from the hot river valleys of the sub-tropics, to the high altitudes of Mexico and Peru, or the cold and dark winters of Northwestern Europe. Because economic growth is currently most rapid in the temperate zones it is fashionable to assert that economic growth requires a temperate climate, but the association between growth and temperate climates is a very recent phenomenon in human history.

As for other resources, such as a fertile soil, the argument turns on whether relative hardship stimulates people's wits, or exhausts their mental energies. There is, of course, an obvious relationship between resources and the growth of knowledge, namely that one learns to use only that which one has. Coal technology does not develop in a community which has no coal, nor architecture in a community without suitable stone. But, given some resources—or there would be no community—it seems very hard to establish any clear connection between the richness of the resources and the vigour of the com-

munity. It cannot be done by logical argument, since rich resources might equally well promote laziness or vigour; and it cannot be done by appealing to history, since countries with similar resources show dissimilar vigour, and since, also, the same country shows dissimilar vigour at different times in its history without any obvious change in its resources.

Some play has been made with an alleged relationship between character and occupation. Farmers and miners, it is said, are 'dull'; fishermen, merchants, and sailors are 'adventurous'; craftsmen and urban dwellers generally are 'ingenious'. On these characterizations one can build a relationship between growth and resources such that the countries showing most rapid growth will be those whose inhabitants take to making a living by the sea, or by manufacturing commodities which they export in exchange for food. This gives actually an inverse relationship between resources and growth, since the peoples who take to the sea or to exporting manufactures are usually those who have not enough fertile soil to feed themselves exclusively by home production. This kind of generalization fits a few cases—the Phoenicians or the Greeks at one stage of their history only—but it does not explain others—the Incas or the Egyptians. A 'law' which does not fit all the cases cannot be accepted as a law.

There is more to be said for the argument that resources influence the human response through the cumulative effects of economic growth. Suppose two countries to be newly settled by immigrants from the same old country, with the same attitudes and institutions. Suppose that one of the new countries turns out to be much richer in resources than the other. It will then show more rapid economic growth. The question is now: will this more rapid growth so transform the attitudes and institutions of the inhabitants as to add to the rate of growth, or to check it; will the human response in the rich country in due course rise above or fall below that in the poorer country? Some people argue that the response will become more favourable. More rapid growth will stimulate new consumption demands. Technological knowledge will grow more rapidly, and this is a cumulative process, increasing the willingness of the human mind to experiment and to adventure. There will be greater social mobility, and greater flexibility of institutions. Greater opportunity will call forth greater response. Other people argue the opposite case. Greater riches increase the demand for leisure, and reduce the willingness to work. Reduction of economic pressure reduces the need to adventure, and to make the best use of limited resources. Riches stimulate envy, democratic discontents, internal strife and civil war. Society, like men, grows 'fat and lazy'. This has long been the cry of prophets, religious revivalists, fascist dictators, militarists, schoolmasters and

all those other who regard comfort as one of the great destroyers of the human spirit.

If one cannot settle this argument by appealing to history, can it be settled by an appeal to anthropology? It is known that some primitive communities have richer natural resources at their disposal than have other primitive communities. Is there evidence that those with the richer resources work harder, or more intelligently than those whose resources are less favourable? Alas, one can get either answer by choosing one's favourite anthropologist, just as by choosing one's favourite historian. The truth appears to be that there is no direct correlation, positive or negative, between resources and human behaviour. Some peoples with superior resources make more effort than some with inferior resources; while some other people with inferior resources make more effort than some others with superior resources. If we set out to explain the vigorous response of a particular people we call to our aid all that we can find in biology, in geography, and in psychology, but in the end we are forced to admit that this is really still one of the unsolved mysteries of the universe. To this writer the most plausible of all the explanations is the accident of leadership. If a community is fortunate to have a good leader, born at a crucial time in its history, who catches the imagination of his people and guides them through a formative experience, he will create traditions and legends and standards which weave themselves into the thinking of his people, and govern their behaviour through many centuries. This is to some extent a biological accident. The alternative view, that men are made by the circumstances in which they find themselves, and that leaders are mere creatures of their times, is quite untenable. To hold it is like believing that in every country in every year there is born a potential Beethoven, a potential Buddha, and a potential Newton. The distribution of men with the highest creative power seems to be a rare statistical accident, in place as well as in time. The circumstances of place and time help to determine whether these qualities will be recognized and used, but they cannot create what is not already there, and the community is most fortunate if the leadership it needs is there when it needs it.

BIBLIOGRAPHICAL NOTE

There is a large literature on the relationship between religion and economic attitudes; the best introduction is R. H. Tawney's *Religion and the Rise of Capitalism*, 2nd Edn., London, 1937; see also the extended summary of Max Weber's study of Indian, Chinese, and Jewish religion in Talcott Parsons' *The Structure of Social Action*, New York, 1937; Weber's original, *Gesammelte Aufsaetze zur Religionssoziologie*, Vols. 2 and 3, Tübingen, 1920-1, has not yet appeared in an English translation; see also

H. H. Gerth and C. W. Mills, *From Max Weber*, London, 1947. On the spread of new wants see H. G. Barnett, *Innovation, the Basis of Cultural Change*, New York, 1953; E. Hoyt, 'Want Development in Under-developed Areas', *Journal of Political Economy*, June 1951; and T. Veblen, *The Theory of the Leisure Class*, New York, 1899. W. E. Moore's *Industrialization and Labour*, New York, 1951, is an excellent survey of the problems involved in recruiting labour for industrial employment in agricultural countries. O. Klineberg, *Race Differences*, New York, 1935, surveys the whole literature of this subject up to the time of its publication. E. Huntington's *The Mainsprings of Civilization*, New York, 1945, summarizes the voluminous writings of this learned and famous author, on the theme that mental attitudes depend in the last resort upon geographical factors. See also the references to A. J. Toynbee at the end of Chapter I. I have discussed the problems involved in settling people on the land in two articles, 'Issues in Land Settlement Policy', *Caribbean Economic Review*, October 1951; and 'Thoughts on Land Settlement', *Journal of Agricultural Economics*, June 1954.

CHAPTER III

ECONOMIC INSTITUTIONS

IN the preceding chapter we considered the willingness of people to make the effort required for economic growth; in this chapter we consider the scope which the community's institutions offer to such effort. The two are not unrelated; if the institutions are favourable, willingness to make effort is encouraged and grows; and if this willingness is strong, institutions will be remodelled to accommodate it. We separate the two only for convenience of analysis.

Institutions promote or restrict growth according to the protection they accord to effort, according to the opportunities they provide for specialization, and according to the freedom of manoeuvre they permit. We shall consider each of these matters in turn. Then, after a more detailed analysis of certain institutions, we shall turn from the consistency of institutions with growth to consider the evolution of institutions, and the processes of change.

1. THE RIGHT TO REWARD

Men will not make effort unless the fruit of that effort is assured to themselves or to those whose claims they recognize: this is the fundamental argument of this section. Much of the effort of social reformers is directed towards changing institutions so that they accord protection to effort. Nevertheless, the proposition is by no means simple; one may argue both about 'those whose claims they recognize', and also about the assignment of 'fruit' to 'effort'.

(a) Non-Material Rewards

Utopian philosophers have often challenged the idea that material reward needs to be in some sense proportional to effort if effort is to be stimulated. Some have suggested that man is, or can become, a creature who will work for the pleasure of creative effort alone, or for the pleasure of serving his fellows; while others, less boldly, have suggested that he is or can become content with social recognitions not involving material reward.

Now it is certainly not to be denied that men derive from work satisfactions other than the material reward. Some kinds of work, which permit creative self-expression, are done for little and sometimes even for no reward. But most work is not of this type. Not only is it true that most occupations are not of this type, but even in the

attractive occupations most of the work to be done is mere drudgery. After the surgeon has taken out his twenty-fifth appendix, the operation becomes a bore; and even the university teacher tires of repeating himself. If the community relied on people doing only what they found it attractive to do, most of its work would not be done.

Again, it is true that the sense of serving one's fellows adds pleasure to work. Most people are glad to work for little or no material reward on some occasion or other—for one's church, or one's village, or in face of sudden disaster. But it is also true that, in our relations with the other members of our group, we have also other inclinations besides the inclination to serve, which may conflict with it. Some have a highly developed propensity to shirk; and others have a strong sense of justice which makes them resent being expected to do more than their fair share. In a group where all the members have highly developed propensities to serve each other, men will work without comparing closely their shares in the group effort and in the group reward. But very few groups, other than the small family group itself, can rely exclusively or primarily on these ideals.

Where the utopians are right is in insisting that men are more likely to work without differential reward if their work benefits all alike than if someone else in particular is obviously reaping a fortune therefrom. In a community where everybody gets more or less the same remuneration people are not angered by the fact that other people are benefiting from their work. But they have also no incentive to make special effort, or even to avoid shirking their share of the work to be done. It is important to ensure that one man does not make a fortune out of some other man's work; but this is not enough. For unless we match differential effort with differential reward, men are unlikely to take the trouble to develop their talents and resources to the utmost of their capabilities.

To say that men put forth more effort if the fruit is to be enjoyed by themselves and by their intimate circle than if it has to be shared with a wider group is not to deny that it is desirable that men should also be able to find creative pleasure in their work, or that men take pleasure in serving their fellows, or that recognition by the conferment of distinctions adds sweetness to labour. Men will work all the more if their work is creative, if it serves social ends that they value, and if it is recognized; but they will also work the less if the material reward is withheld. Nowhere is this now better recognized than in Soviet Russia. When that state was created, its leaders believed that effort would not be reduced if earnings were equalized, and if orders and decorations were substituted for differences in pay. Experience belied their expectation, and when rapid economic growth became a major object of policy, the Soviet rulers returned to reliance upon

wide differences in earnings, and made it an offence to suggest that men should be paid equally, irrespective of the work they do.

The power of communalism is seen ideally in a modern dress in the progress in recent years of the movement for 'community development' in rural areas. In these schemes villagers are encouraged to give their labour freely for works of special benefit to the village, such as building roads, or schools, or wells, or community centres, or other public property. It takes some organization to get these schemes working; there must be government officials to plan them, and to work up enthusiasm for them; and public funds must also be provided to meet the cost of materials or of skills which the village cannot itself provide. Given such organization, experience shows that villagers will gladly turn out to work freely on local public works. The idea that they will do this seems strange to townsmen, especially in our individualistic societies; but, in a small village, where everybody knows everybody else, a sense of communal effort for communal purposes may be a very effective incentive to the betterment of social conditions. All the same, there are definite limits to what can be achieved in this way. In the first place, the works must be of local benefit: the villagers will build a minor road connecting their village to a main road, but they will not build a main road for all and sundry without payment; or they may dig drainage works for their village freely, but will not do so if the benefit is to be diffused widely outside their area. Secondly, the works must benefit the village as a whole, and must not be obviously of much greater advantage to some than to the rest.

These limitations of 'community development' illustrate very well the limitations of group loyalties as incentives. These loyalties function very well in stable economic situations, where routine action is all that is required, and not individual initiative; in such situations each individual grows up knowing what he is expected to give, and what he can expect to get, and the economic system may function merrily. The system may even adapt itself to change, if the change is of the kind that benefits nearly everybody to the same extent. Usually, however, economic growth does not benefit everybody to the same extent; some benefit more than others, and it is difficult to get people to do something more than or different from what they have been doing in the past if the benefit is to accrue mainly to others. Economic growth requires something more than that people should be willing to carry out established routines cheerfully, without counting effort and reward. Growth involves changes in the kinds and quantities of work done by different individuals; and even if innovation is introduced by order from above, growth involves also some willingness on the part of individual members of the clan to

adjust spontaneously to changing opportunities, and to seek and exploit new chances. Of course, some societies appear to have reached the limits of what they can achieve in the hard geographical conditions in which they live, and with the technology at their command. It is possible, for example, that the Eskimos are doing as well as they can; that greater individualism would not discover improved techniques of living; and that a loosening of ties of obedience and of obligation might on the contrary reduce the chance of survival. If growth is not possible, the absence of individual initiative is no handicap. Most communities, however, are capable of economic growth, if not by improving their techniques from within, then at least by absorbing new techniques from abroad, or by responding to new opportunities created by foreign trade. Then, once we move out of stable into changing conditions, it is doubtful whether a sense of one's communal obligations is adequate to bring forth the necessary adaptations, in the absence of a close relationship between individual effort and reward. It is equally doubtful whether this sense of obligations can survive opportunities for individual profit. Individualism seems to make great strides in all societies which are subjected to accelerated economic change, and this seems to be inevitable.

(b) The Management of Property

Capital formation is one of the conditions of economic growth, and the existence of a law of property is one of the conditions of capital formation. By property we mean the legal right to exclude other people from using a particular resource. This right may vest in a private person, or in a group, or in a public authority; the numbers enjoying the right may be large or small; but whoever may exercise the right, this right of exclusion is fundamental. This is emphasized because the term property is so often used to mean only private property. A battleship owned by the government is as much property as the farmer's acre; it is property because, despite the fact that the battleship in some theoretical sense belongs to 'all the people', in law and in practice individual members of the public are excluded from having anything to do with battleships except under strict authorization.

The legal concept of property is enshrined in all economies, capitalist, socialist, feudal or otherwise. For if a resource and its fruit could not be protected against the public at large, it would certainly be misused, and hardly any person would find it worth while to invest in its improvement. The legal protection of property is therefore extended to all resources as soon as they become scarce. Thus, in countries which are sparsely populated relatively to their resources, some resources may remain free for many centuries. Individuals may be allowed to cut forest trees at will; to fish freely in rivers; to take

water as they please; or to pasture their cattle as they please on common lands. But, as population grows, all these activities come under control; the resources in question become private property, or if they are recognized as public property, their use is carefully regulated by the state or other governing authority.

If it is necessary to protect public property from private abuse, it is just as necessary to protect private property from public abuse. The maintenance of law and order is one of the primary conditions of economic growth, and many communities have declined because the state was unwilling or too weak to protect the owners of property against the actions of bandits or of mobs. The instinct to invest can, indeed, survive considerable civil disturbance, and even revolution; but if the period of disturbance is long drawn out, dissaving takes the place of capital formation. Governments, too, can be as damaging to confidence as bandits or rioters. Investors may put up with a high level of taxation, if the nature and incidence of taxation are known in advance, but arbitrary taxation—such as when a ruler seizes a country house because he happens to like it, or when individuals are arbitrarily picked out and forced to pay—encourages men to conceal their wealth (usually in unproductive forms), to export it, or to consume it. (Taxation is discussed further in Chapter VII.)

Property is a recognized institution in every part of the world; without it the human race would have made no progress whatsoever, since there would have been no incentive to improve the environment in which one lived. There is, however, more to this institution than the fundamental right of exclusion, and societies differ widely in the complication of their laws and customs relating to property.

The fundamental requirement, from the angle of economic growth, is that a potential investor must believe that he is in a position to 'get his money back', plus some compensation for the act of making the investment instead of consuming his substance. This requirement applies whether the investor is a private person or a public authority, since even governments do not make investments unless they expect to get full value for their money. The investor may be wrong in his belief; the risks may be greater than he has estimated, and he may not in fact get his money back; but at the time of making the investment he must believe in his prospects. On the other hand 'getting one's money back' requires fuller elaboration. One may invest in a resource whose product is not to be sold, but is to be enjoyed with the passage of time—for example in the case of private persons, a house or other durable consumer good, in the case of governments, a school, a road or a block of government offices; or a private person may make loans out of sentiment, or a government out of political considerations, knowing that the money will not be repaid. These come within

'getting one's money back' in the sense that the investor is satisfied that the benefits he gets, whether material or sentimental or political, are worth the cost. Using the phrase in this wide sense, we may say that it is a condition of investment that the investor should believe that he is in a position to get his money back; plus some compensation for investing it instead of using it immediately for consumption purposes.

Now if the investor is investing in his own concern, without partners or employees, the problem is relatively simple. But if he has partners, or is hiring out his property, or employs people to manage it, or other people to work on it, complicated problems arise out of these relationships. For the joint product of his property and of other people's property has then to be shared out, and if the interests of those who share conflict, as will almost inevitably be the case, very strict rules have to be obeyed if all parties are to be satisfied.

Take first the relation of partnership. If joint property is shared equally between partners, each partner has an interest in putting in no more than his fellows put in, in trying to put in less, and in trying to take out more—whether what is put in be money, or effort, or thought. Family businesses also illustrate the point; where the members of the family are numerous or mutually antagonistic, the business often founders upon the fact that some members are more anxious to get what they can out of the joint property than they are to maintain it. Another example is provided by some of the early attempts of farmers to own farm machinery co-operatively; it was found that some farmers did not use the machinery as carefully as they would have done if it had been their own, and it became necessary to employ trained mechanics exclusively responsible for operation and maintenance, instead of allowing each farmer to operate the machines himself. The modern corporation also has its problems in the divergence of interests between different classes of shareholders. Or it may be the contingent interest of creditors which stands between the person who controls the property and his benefit; for if there is a fair prospect that the property may pass into the creditors' hands, the 'owners may be reluctant to improve it, and may deliberately encompass its decline. Economic growth requires that the person who is in a position to decide that the property be maintained or improved should have an interest in making the right decision.

Equally difficult problems arise if the person using property is not its owner. Thus the relationship between landlord and tenant has to be carefully regulated if the tenant is to have an interest in maintaining the fertility of the land and in making permanent improvements—we discuss this case in greater detail in a later section of this chapter.

Similar problems arise in all contracts of hiring.

Again, salaried managers or agents are notoriously unsatisfactory. It is not merely that they are tempted to keep for themselves some proceeds which legally belong to the owner; this may indeed reduce growth by reducing the reward for capital formation, but it may also merely involve a change in the distribution of income. More important, perhaps, from the angle of economic growth, is the fact that the agents may neglect the property, if their income does not vary directly with the care they take; or on the other hand may prolong its life improperly, in order to prolong their own employment, by re-investing in the property part of the owner's profits which could more profitably be invested elsewhere. These problems are specially acute in absentee ownership; but they are found even where the owner lives on the spot, if he does not bother to give serious attention to his property; and, of course, some agents are much better at managing the property than the owner could ever be, because of their greater knowledge or their natural flair for this kind of work. In any case, absentee ownership is now the rule rather than the exception in modern industrial communities. Most of our property belongs either to shareholders, who have entrusted its management to directors; or to the state or other public authorities, who also depend upon employees for its management. In both cases there are stringent and not altogether successful laws which seek to protect the owners' interest against the interest of those whom they employ. Some part of the case for private property, as against public property, used to rest on the argument that the private owner of property was likely to look after it better than the salaried employee of the state, but much of this argument has ceased to hold since the growth of large scale organization and of the joint stock company has caused the management of private property to pass largely from owners to salaried employees.

Finally, some of the most difficult problems of our society arise out of conflict between those who own property on the one hand, and those who are employed for wages to work with other people's property on the other hand. This conflict can be dramatized by stating it in terms of its extremist proponents on either side. On the one hand there are always some advocates of slavery, who hold that the worker should receive only the cost of his subsistence, and that all the surplus produce beyond this level belongs to the owners of property. On the other hand there are those who assert that only work creates produce, so that the worker is entitled to the 'whole produce of his labour'—whether this allows some deduction for depreciation of capital not even always being made clear. In between these extremes fit many different proposals for the division of the product.

This problem is different in kind from those we have so far considered in this section. Hitherto our concern has been that those who control property, whether as owners, as tenants, or as managers, should have an interest in maintaining and improving it. The share of the workers in the produce does not, however, necessarily raise problems of control, so we will consider it separately.

(c) The Reward for Work

We have said that men will not do their best work unless the fruit of their work is assured to themselves or to those whose claims they recognize. Problems arise so soon as it becomes difficult to distinguish the fruit of their work from other fruit, as is the case if they are working together on a joint enterprise, or if they are working with property which belongs to someone else.

Working together becomes necessary so soon as there are economies of scale. Since it has problems different from those which are due to the separation of work and ownership, we can best get it into perspective by considering the case where men work together with their own property, that is the case of co-operative enterprise. The word 'co-operative' is used by many different kinds of organization, but we are concerned in this context only with co-operatives in the literal sense, that is to say with organizations where the workers own the property, manage it themselves, and distribute the proceeds among themselves. (In other co-operatives the workers are employed for wages by consumers, or by farmers' marketing societies, or the like.) The need to work together arises as soon as the advantages of scale begin to be evident—either because of specialization, or because of the need to join together to work some piece of indivisible equipment.

Co-operative units have two major problems, namely incentives and authority. As for incentives, each partner has to rely on the good faith of the others, in a situation where any one partner can slacken off without correspondingly diminishing his share of the product. The system can work quite well if the partners are not numerous; especially if they are related to each other, or linked by mutual sympathy. Six or a dozen craftsmen or farmers can work together for decades without the partnership foundering on any major dispute. They do not always succeed; even family enterprises do not escape slackness, lack of incentive or dispute. However, once the partnership begins to involve larger numbers, it cannot be based exclusively on mutual trust and sympathy. It becomes necessary to pay each member according to what he does in terms of hours and of skill. The surplus profit can still be divided on some 'co-operative' principle—according to earnings, or equally, or according to capital contributed—but the emphasis has to be placed mainly on creating

a system of wage incentives—piece rates, bonuses and all the rest—which penalizes the partner who shirks and rewards the partner who gives superior effort.

This is not, however, the only problem presented by size: much more difficult is the problem of managing large co-operatives. A large body of people cannot work together efficiently without discipline and authority. Someone has to take decisions, and to enforce them. The members of a co-operative may be equal partners, but they cannot have equal authority. If they are numerous, they must delegate most of their authority to a committee, and no executive committee is effective which is not content in its turn to delegate most of its authority, and to put responsibility squarely on the shoulders of a small number of individuals. This means, however, that the great majority of the co-operators are removed from decision making, and have to carry out orders just like any paid employee. They become dissatisfied with this. They probably also become dissatisfied with the division of the proceeds; with their own pay relatively to others; or with the management's desire to put a large part of the surplus to reserve, for contingencies, or for expansion. Sooner or later they overthrow authority, and the organization is rent by internal dissension. Consequently it is virtually impossible for large scale organizations run as co-operatives to compete successfully against other large firms run without the co-operative principle. The exceptions prove the rule. The collective farms in the U.S.S.R. are co-operative only in name; the management is provided by members of the Communist party, who tell each member what he is to do, pay him according to what he does, and share out the surplus in proportion to earnings. The individual member has only theoretical power to change the management and alter its policy. In Israel the communal farms are genuinely democratic; they are, indeed, mostly indebted to and supervised by a central agency, but this does not seem to restrict their genuine powers of self-government. Membership averages around 250, and members are not even paid according to the work they do. Most observers seem to agree that the success of these collectives has depended so far upon the special emotions associated with immigrant Jewish agriculture in Israel, and upon the part played by collective organization in the military defence of isolated settlements. Sooner or later the special strains and emotions involved in creating a Jewish National Home will wear off, and if the collectives then retain their primitive communism, and succeed economically, they will be doing so contrary to all previous human experience.

Some form of co-operative is the primitive working unit of human beings. In the earliest societies we know, the working unit is the family, or the clan, or the guild of craftsmen, the priests, or other

E

grouping. Western industrial capitalism began in partnership units, with craftsmen working together; the employment of journeymen by master craftsmen seems to have arisen only in the later Middle Ages. Group work has its advantages, especially for people living on the margin of subsistence, or living in fear of attack or of recurrent natural disaster; for then each helps the other, and there may be mutual protection or insurance in working together. It is quite common for peasants to form working parties to work on each other's land, helping each other to build houses, or to clear the land, or to harvest. But this form of organization depends for its continuance on strong ties of group loyalty, resting in kinship, or in religious association. It breaks down as soon as more individualistic notions begin to spread, as soon as there are growing opportunities for trade or for innovation of which individuals become increasingly aware, and as soon as large scale organization begins to offer economies. The co-operative form of enterprise is excellent for stable societies, but it does not survive easily as a productive unit (as distinct from marketing or credit) once the lower levels of subsistence have been passed.

Problems of incentive and of authority are common to all large scale organizations, even when the workers own the property with which they work. The separation of ownership from work, however, introduces a third problem, namely that of the division of the proceeds between work and property. In co-operative organizations property has no separate share: the whole of the proceeds is divided amongst those who work with it and own it. But in capitalist and socialist societies property belongs either to the capitalist or to the state, and in either case the owner demands both some remuneration and also participation in controlling the operations. It should, in particular, be noted that the nationalization of property does not solve any of these problems. There was a stage in the development of socialist theory when socialists were proposing that property should belong to those who worked with it—in forms of syndicalism, or Guild socialism, or workers' control—in which case socialism would simply be co-operative enterprise, and would face only two problems instead of three. But in the event, whether in the U.S.S.R., or in Britain, or in the U.S.A. or elsewhere, socialism has taken the form of transferring property from private owners not to the workers but to the state or other public authority, which retains control and a share of the proceeds. How much difference this makes in the mind of the worker depends on his attitude to the state. He may well believe that it is more equitable to share with and be managed by the state than with or by a private owner; this depends very much on what he has been taught to believe. Some workers have grown up in fear of

their governments and in friendship with their employers, and would resist any such transition; whereas others have been taught to hate 'the employing class', and to respect 'the democratic state'. But in any case, even if the worker prefers the state boss to the private boss, and the state profiteer to the private profiteer, he is unlikely to prefer either to neither. That is to say, even in the best regulated form of state enterprise he is conscious of the fact that he does not get the whole produce of his labour (whatever this may mean), and of the fact that 'wage slaves' have to be at the beck and call of their supervisors. The problems of state-run enterprises have thus proved to be not essentially different from those of private enterprises, and if this is not as immediately obvious in the U.S.S.R. as it is in Britain or elsewhere, this is mainly because workers' attitudes are not easily expressed in non-democratic societies.

The right of property to a share in the proceeds has always excited men's minds. One school argues that wealth is created by work, and belongs only to those who work; from this stemmed a labour theory of value. Others have defended property's share on numerous grounds—on the natural right of men to own property; on the need to provide an incentive to improve property; on the Malthusian doctrine that the poor would waste the proceeds of property on having more children, while the rich would reinvest them; on the psychological cost of saving; on the right of each factor to earn its marginal productivity: and on numerous other defences. The state is no less ingenious than the private owner or his economic philosophers. If twenty per cent of the national income is needed for gross capital formation, and another twenty per cent for the current uses of government, even the most socialistic state has no difficulty in proving that the workers cannot expect to get the full produce of their labour; or to put it more prettily, that they must be satisfied with sixty per cent directly, and be pleased at having forty per cent spent on them indirectly in ways in which they could not or would not spend it themselves.

It is possible that these problems cannot be solved in large scale organizations. Piece rate and bonus systems of wage payment may succeed in stimulating effort, and profit-sharing arrangements may restore a little the atmosphere of co-operative enterprise, but the claimants to the produce are too many for the partners to trust each other implicitly without continually comparing input with reward. The workers will compare their own rewards, or their rewards with those of their supervisors and superior staff, or output in general with the share taken, if not by private capitalists, then by the state. The partners may quarrel more bitterly in some places or at some times than in other places or times; they cannot ever completely agree that

justice is being done to all since no one can say what justice is in terms which everyone else will always accept. So also the problem of authority is as insoluble as that of incentives; the psychological malaise of working in big institutions is incurable. The human mind revolts against discipline, and no big organization can be run successfully without discipline, obedience and loyalty. The workers may be given power to elect delegates to managerial committees, but if the organization is large, the delegates cannot be numerous, relatively to their constituents; and in any case once they become entrenched in managerial responsibilities, the delegates inevitably tend to side with the management, because they realize that a large organization cannot be run successfully from below. A sense of antagonism between management and worker is as inevitable in a large organization as is a sense of antagonism between clergy and laity, between government and subject, between father and family, or between general and private. It derives from the desire of each of us to have his own way, working in a situation where we have inevitably to accept countless decisions which we have no part in making, except remotely, and which are not tailored to each individual case. The situation provides a continuous challenge to managements—to win loyalty by the consideration which they show to those over whom they have authority (not less than by their efficiency), and to approximate their undertakings to the give and take and mutual respect which distinguish the happy family rather than to the reliance on hierarchy and sanctions which characterizes military groups. But conflict and frustration are inevitable accompaniments of large-scale organization.

Perhaps too much is made of the worker's desire for self-government, both by those who believe that democracy inside the factory is possible and also by those who fear that its impossibility must lead to the breakdown of the industrial system. Not all workers desire self-government in industry; probably a majority prefer to be given a job with limited terms of reference, and to be set free from responsibility for the affairs of the undertaking at large. In all human societies, whether factories or counties, trade unions, churches or states, it is observable that only a very small minority of people offer themselves as candidates for office, or take any continuous interest in the affairs of their organization. They may be very pleased to belong to the organization, and they may turn up to vote at elections—though the percentage voting is sometimes remarkably small—but it is exceedingly difficult to get members to keep themselves informed as to what is going on, let alone to participate actively in discussion or management. This being so, one might think that the desire of a minority for active participation could be met in industry by such persons drifting into the small firms, where

such participation is feasible, and leaving to the large establishments the people who prefer to have things run for them. But it does not work out in this way. The large establishments on the contrary frequently attract those workers who have an itch to organize and supervise, and these set about stimulating the rest to defend themselves and to participate (as they see it), or set about stirring up trouble (as the managements sometimes see it).

The role played by this active minority in indoctrinating and organizing other workers for wages also emphasizes the part played in human affairs by fashions in opinion. Although the success or failure of systems depends partly upon their intrinsic nature, it depends also partly upon what men choose to believe about them. The great industrial unrest through which the twentieth century is passing owes as much to propaganda as it does to anything else. The industrial worker in the U.S.S.R. has less freedom than his counterpart in the U.S.A., and receives a smaller share of what he produces, but it is conceivable that propaganda in favour of his situation may cause him to accept it much more than the U.S. worker, who is subjected to strong propaganda against a similar status, even though it is relatively superior. It is this which makes prediction impossible. An economist living in Rome at the time of Spartacus might have predicted confidently that slavery was so intolerable to the masses that it must soon fail; instead it was established more firmly than before. Similarly, one might now be tempted to predict that large scale organization, whether in co-operative, in private, or in state ownership, is proving so irksome to the workers that it must fail; and that there will soon come a time when only small establishments, based on personal relationships, will stay sufficiently free of strikes and of ca' canny to be successful in the market. But this prediction may be just as wrong, especially if the state increasingly takes over management, and lines up with the church and with trade union leaders to persuade the workers that this is a fundamental change which gives them the best of all possible worlds. To return to the point from which we started this section, 'men will not make effort unless the fruit of that effort is assured to themselves or to those whose claims they recognize', but what they consider to be their proper share of the fruit, and whose claims they recognize are largely subjective matters, which depend upon what they have been brought up to believe.

2. TRADE AND SPECIALIZATION

We turn next to consider the opportunities which institutions give for trade and specialization, since the extension of trade and of specialization are a vital part of economic growth.

(a) *Advantages*

Trade stimulates growth in many ways, of which its stimulus to specialization is only one. Trade stimulates demand, by introducing new goods to a community, and in doing so it may stimulate the desire to work more, or more effectively. Since limited wants, due to limited horizons, keep effort low in many primitive communities, the opening of trade may effect a revolutionary attitude towards the value of work. Trade also reduces the community's need for working capital. In the absence of trade each household must keep stocks of all it needs; when trade permits the stocks to be held by merchants in central reserves, the ratio of stocks to consumption is greatly reduced. Indeed these stocks may often mean the difference between life and death in countries which live on the margin of subsistence, since trade permits commodities to be moved from surplus to deficit areas in times of famine. Trade also brings new ideas—new patterns of consumption, new techniques, or new ideas of social relationships. Tales from foreign lands challenge established traditions, and allow individual members of the community to experiment in ways which would otherwise be prohibited. If in studying the history of any country we find that it is suddenly showing more rapid growth, or changes in beliefs, or changes in social relations, the explanation is almost always that there has been an increase in opportunities for trade.

Trade also stimulates specialization, since the division of labour depends upon the extent of the market. Adam Smith said of specialization that it owes its superior productivity 'first, to the increase of dexterity of every particular workman; secondly, to the saving of the time which is commonly lost in passing from one species of work to another; and lastly to the invention of a great number of machines which facilitate and abridge labour, and enable one man to do the work of many'. Smith attached so much importance to the division of labour that he made it seem even to be the cause of the growth of technology and of the application of capital. Later writers challenged this causation, and some even argued the other way—that specialization is not the cause but the result. In our day we are content to say that specialization, knowledge and capital grow together.

Increasing specialization seems to be as much a principle of economic as of biological evolution, and its association with economic growth is beyond all question. It has, nevertheless, its costs. Any specialist is likely to suffer if the demand for the service in which he specializes diminishes. Demands are altering all the time, because taste changes, or because new techniques or new goods render the old skill obsolete. If the specialist cannot turn his hand to something else, he may suffer a severe loss of income. This applies

also to a community as a whole: the greater the specialization, the greater the need for occupational mobility, which is the best insurance against changes in demand. The community may also suffer from specialization if trade breaks down, and if it is therefore unable to get essential supplies, as when a war interrupts trade, or when the usual sources of supply are cut off by earthquake or other disaster. Provision can be made for temporary interruptions of supply by carrying emergency stocks, like the stockpiles now being created by the U.S. government in case of war. But it may also be advisable to take the precaution of not specializing excessively—how far to go being a matter for subjective assessment of the risks.

Another cost of over-specialization is lack of balance. This can be seen clearly in agricultural operations. Excessive specialization on one crop may cause biological unbalance, showing itself in soil exhaustion, or in the spread of pests and diseases. It is open to the individual farmer to prevent soil exhaustion by having a suitable rotation of crops, and by mixed farming. But the individual cannot prevent the adoption of monoculture by the farmers in his region, and the dangers of pest and disease to which this gives rise. If monoculture is to be prevented, in a region where it is considered undesirable but is temporarily very profitable, there must be a group decision to prevent it, by prohibitions on planting, or by subsidization of other crops.

Specialization also causes lack of balance in the human mind. A people which specializes in mining does not see the world in the same way as a people which specializes in farming. Similarly, within the group people with different specialisms see things differently, and may clash irreconcilably in outlook as well as in material interests. These differences of outlook and of interest are often deplored; Speech Day orators denounce narrow specialization and urge that education should be broadly based. Nevertheless, this diversity may be thought to add something to the quality of human community life, which is missing in a community where everybody has the same occupation and experience. It poses greater problems of co-operation, but it also presents greater opportunities of intellectual progress, since it is in the clash of experiences that human ideas are refined.

In the same way, the clash of material interests at least causes society to change continuously. This is so whether we accept the view of those materialists who see all history as a succession of class struggles, or whether we reflect merely how little change there would be in society if each person were satisfied with his share of the national income. Some people regret that there is ceaseless change, and say that they would be glad to get back to a world in which each person grew his own food and spun his own cloth—if there

ever was such a world. We are not here concerned with the desirability of change or stability (we treat this matter in the Appendix); we note here merely that there is ceaseless change, and that specialization contributes towards it.

(b) The Extent of the Market

The greater the market the greater the possibilities of specialization. The size of the market depends upon the degree of household self-sufficiency, upon the size of the population, upon the cheapness of communications, upon the wealth of the community, upon the standardization of tastes, and upon the man-made barriers to trade.

The primitive household is almost completely self-sufficient. Every village has some specialist craftsmen, but they supply only a fraction of the villager's wants. The self-sufficiency of the village as a whole is associated mainly with its isolation, but the self-sufficiency of the individual household is associated mainly with the status of women. As economic development occurs, many of the jobs originally done by women in the household are transferred to external agencies, which do them more efficiently both because they are more specialized and also because they use more capital—fetching water, grinding grain, spinning, weaving and making clothes, teaching children, looking after the sick, and so on. This transfer of jobs is paralleled by a transfer of female labour out of the household to work in external establishments. In most primitive societies men object to their women working for wages. As the taboos break down, greater specialization becomes possible, and there is a substantial increase in national output—as well as a substantial increase in women's freedom.

The size of the market depends also upon the size of the population. There are substantial economies of scale in some kinds of production, especially in manufacturing, in public utilities, and in some kinds of service (education, public health, mass entertainment). Quite a few countries are under-populated, in the sense that if their populations were larger such products or services could be offered more cheaply on a mass produced basis, instead of being produced in smaller, less specialized establishments. The size of the population, however, is a concept which relates to space as well as to number, and which is therefore essentially a matter of communications. If transport costs were zero, even the smallest country could enjoy all the benefits of specialization, since the whole world would constitute a single market; even the smallest country could then specialize, and sell its surplus to others, in return for what it wished to consume. We discuss population questions more fully in Chapter VI.

The cost and extent of communications depends partly upon natural features, and partly upon the enterprise of transport under-

takings. Some governments are more alive to their responsibilities in this sphere than other governments. Indeed, in the history of most countries the good rulers are often marked out by the vigour with which they extend the system of roads, and the bad rulers by the poor state of the roads in their time. A cheap and extensive network of communications is the greatest blessing which any country can have, from the economic point of view. Before the invention of the railway, water transport was the only relatively cheap form of transport, and those countries which were easily accessible by sea or by river showed the greatest expansion of trade and of wealth. If we ask why some countries have played a more vigorous part in human history than other countries, greater accessibility by water is usually one of the answers.

That the size of the market for any commodity depends upon the wealth of those who buy it is obvious. Equally important is the degree of standardization of the demand. One reason which is sometimes adduced for the superior productivity of labour in the United States is the willingness of people to buy mass produced and standardized articles. This is partly a matter of the extent of social snobbery in the community; if snobbery demands that the individual show his superior status by buying commodities of individual design, or hand made commodities, or articles fashioned specially to his requirements, then the market for each type will be small. It may also be a matter of class structure; countries which have a well developed middle class may offer a better market for mass produced commodities than countries of equal wealth which have only rich and poor. Class considerations apart, the taste for artistic work of individual design may have been created merely by the excellence of a country's craftsmen, who, for decades or centuries before mass production became feasible, had specialized in producing work renowned for its high merit. Such may have been the position, for example, in France and in India. Then when mass production becomes possible the country may lag behind others which have not had these special skills, and in which therefore a mass demand proves easier to create. Much depends also upon the imagination and enterprise of business leaders. Nobody knew how large the demand for mass produced commodities could be until men like Ford and Woolworth showed the way.

Then there are the man-made barriers to trade—the tolls, the tariffs, the quotas and the prohibitions. The reduction of these barriers was one of the greatest achievements of the human race between the sixteenth and the nineteenth centuries A.D. The work began at home, with the removal of the internal barriers within political frontiers, and was associated with the creation of strong central governments in countries where previously local princes had

great power. The Mercantilist age is famous for its literature defending restrictions on foreign trade, but the most important work of the Mercantilist philosophers was their insistence on the advantages of internal unification, and the efforts that were made in their age to level the barriers to internal trade. Their work has never been undone; nobody today argues that subordinate political authorities—provincial governments, county councils or municipalities—ought to have the right to levy tariffs. The Mercantilist age passed imperceptibly into the age of free trade, which the nineteenth century was, *par excellence*. During that century barriers to international trade were reduced in almost every country of the world, and though the tide turned before the century's end, the level of trade restrictions was insignificant in 1900 compared with what it had been a century earlier. Nowadays opinions on international trade are again as sophisticated as they were in the Mercantilist age; we shall return to the subject in Chapter VI.

(c) Organization

As soon as men begin to specialize it is necessary to have some mechanism for co-ordinating their activities. On the smallest scale this can be done by administrative fiat. Inside a firm, or a government department, or an army unit, each specialist is told individually what to do, and it is the job of the management to have a mental picture of how the work of all the individuals fits together. This cannot, however, be done for a whole community, since the ends to be served and the means of serving them are too numerous for central co-ordination to work efficiently. Instead, the activities of individuals are co-ordinated by the market. Supply and demand determine prices, and each individual is able to suit his own purposes by responding to price incentives, while at the same time serving the wider ends of all individuals taken together. The price mechanism does not, indeed, resolve all social conflicts; it is an imperfect mechanism, like all other social institutions, and its operation is also affected by the efforts people make to prevent it from working freely. It is everywhere regulated, by private monopolists or by governments, but nowhere can it be dispensed with altogether, so long as there is specialization and trade. Even the government of the U.S.S.R., which regulates economic activity more than other governments, depends quite significantly on the price system to co-ordinate economic activities—to stimulate the supply of types of skill which are scarce, to stimulate agricultural output, to discourage consumption of scarce commodities, to enforce efficiency upon state-owned industries, and more or less for all the other purposes which prices serve also in less 'planned' economies.

Now, if the price mechanism is to serve as a regulator, people must be responsive to prices. They must be interested in prices, whether of the labour they can do, or of things they can make, or of commodities they may buy, or as the case may be; and they must be willing to respond to prices by altering their behaviour to take advantage of favourable changes in prices. A civilization in which people are responsive to prices may be referred to, contemptuously, as a 'pecuniary', or an 'acquisitive' civilization; our concern, however, is not with morality or contempt, but with the conditions of economic growth. Growth requires specialization, specialization requires co-ordination by a price mechanism, and this co-ordination is effective only in proportion to the response of individuals to changes in prices. Now the degree of this response is largely a matter of habit. When people who have hitherto produced only for their own subsistence are first introduced to a price economy, their response is both limited and unskilled. They neglect opportunities; they do not know how to choose; they are easily defrauded; they do not sense the difference between temporary and permanent price changes; they do not know about seasonal and cyclical variations, or about quantity discounts; and so on. One has to learn how to respond to market prices just as one learns any other part of one's culture. The performance improves as generations grow up who have always known and used the market, and who are experienced in its tricks.

Specialization requires also the use of money; barter is compatible only with the most rudimentary forms of specialization and of trade. The invention of money is one of the greater achievements of the human race, like the invention of the alphabet, or the discovery of how to make fire at will. Without money trade would be reduced to a trickle. Without money each household would have to store up all its possessions, instead of being able to buy from centralized reserves (shops) as required. And without money there could be very little lending and investment.

Despite its value, the invention of money has spread so slowly that there are large areas of the world where it is only just coming into general use. For example, in some of the great nations of Asia, where money has been used in one form or another throughout their recorded history, it is still the case that as much as forty per cent of their national output, on the standard definition, is not exchanged against money. The use of money is associated with specialization and trade; where people are so poor that they have little surplus to trade, they have little use for money.

The use of money alters social institutions by increasing the importance of the market; even more important, perhaps, it also

alters human attitudes. Once money begins to circulate in a community, and production for markets becomes common, economic relations move increasingly on to an impersonal basis. Status and kinship count for less, as money counts for more. Wealth is easier to accumulate in cash than in cows or in sacks of corn; the 'acquisitive' instincts—the desire for wealth—are therefore easier to exercise, and grow as they are exercised. The 'capitalist' relations of money-lending and of wage employment also spread more easily with money than without it. Hence, forms of organization which are feasible in societies which do not use money, such as the extended family system, or systems based largely on status, cease to work effectively when money comes to be widely used.

We note next that specialization and trade also require that market places should be organized. Lack of markets is one sign of the primitive community. There is almost always some meeting place where food, cloth, and the simpler consumer goods can be bought. But specialization requires a much greater range of markets than this: markets for labour, markets for houses, markets for land, markets for foreign currencies, markets for loans, markets for stocks and shares, and so on. These markets take different forms. It may pay an individual to become, as it were, the market, specializing in bringing prospective buyers and sellers together, just as a house agent's office is a market. Or the market may be merely a column of advertisements in a newspaper. The number and variety of the markets is a sign of the community's wealth. Sometimes wealth can be increased simply by opening a market, so that trade is facilitated, but it is also possible to open markets before the community is in a position to develop enough trade to justify them—as in the case of some of the poorer countries where there is talk of starting a stock exchange.

The relationship between specialization and the size of the economic unit is not simple. Some people believe that specialization increases the size of the firm, because the subdivision of jobs increases the number of jobs and therefore the size of the co-ordinated unit. But this is not necessarily so, since the activities of the specialists can also be co-ordinated by the market. When a new product first appears on the market, the firm introducing it has to make most of the component parts in its own workshop; but, as the demand grows, various firms specialize in making component parts. Thus the motor car is now produced by scores of different firms, each specializing in making chassis, or bodies, or windscreen wipers, or tyres, or scores of other accessories; whereas the so-called 'motor manufacturer' may not do much more than assemble parts most of which he has bought from other firms. Specialization increases the size of the firm in so far as it results in operations which have to be done on a large scale; but

it reduces the size of the firm every time that it splits an operation into component processes.

Large scale organization is thus one of the indirect results of specialization. Because people specialize, their activities have to be co-ordinated, and this co-ordination can be done either by market processes or within the firm. In this respect, the market and the firm pull in opposite directions. The more perfect the market, the less necessary it is to have co-ordination within the firm, whereas the less perfect the market, the greater is the opportunity for an entrepreneur to co-ordinate the activities of individual specialists. It is an error to think that the principle of specialization as such gives advantage to large scale organization. The small firm can survive easily if markets are well organized, so that it can buy cheaply such factors as specialist advice, engineering service, component parts, raw materials and the like, and can dispose easily of its product, whether to final or to intermediate buyers. The better organized the market, the less each firm needs to do for itself, and the smaller is the advantage of large scale organization.

The corollary of this is that if it is desired to favour small scale enterprise, the best way to proceed is to organize around the small firm specialist services and marketing agencies so efficient and cheap that the firm is not disadvantaged by being small. The large organization can conduct research, buy in bulk, sell in bulk, raise funds easily, produce a standardized article, advertise, hire the best specialist advice, and so on. The small organization can succeed just as well if it is surrounded by agencies—private, co-operative, or statutory—which will take over all that part of the work which needs to be done on a large scale, so that the small firm can concentrate on those activities which are adequately done on a small scale. Thus the small farm can get its specialist advice from an agricultural extension service, its standardized seeds from seed farms, or its tractors from the tractor hiring agency, and can dispose of its product to an agency which bulks it with that of other farms, and grades, processes, advertises and sells it in bulk. It is not true that the individual firm must be large in scale if there is to be efficiency or economic growth; but it is true that the advantages of specialization cannot be secured unless the economies of scale are available either within the firm or within the framework of well organized markets. All the same, the degree to which the well organized market can substitute for the large firm varies very much from industry to industry. It would be very hard to organize railway service, the manufacture of steel, or the assembly of motor cars efficiently on a small scale, whereas small scale enterprise can hold its own very well in road transport, in shop-keeping, in some forms of agriculture, and in a limited range of

manufacturing activities. Economic growth does demand some expansion of large scale production, however efficiently the market, the co-operative movement or the government may proceed in nurturing the smaller units.

The expansion of large scale organization depends on the availability of entrepreneurial skill, and on the access which this skill has to other factors of production. Entrepreneurship may be undertaken by private persons, or by government officials. In either case the size of undertaking which the entrepreneur can handle is a function of his ability, his experience and the techniques at his command. Taking first the techniques, large scale organization has progressed with the invention of means of communication—writing, telephones, wireless—of means of counting—statistical methods, accounting—and of administrative devices—hierarchies, committees, and so on. All such inventions increase the scale of efficient operation. In most under-developed countries there are very few people who have experience of large scale administration, or of its techniques. In such countries small scale organization is more appropriate than large, simply because of this lack of experience, and it is more economical to organize on a small scale operations which more advanced countries would find it more economic to organize on a large scale. As economic development proceeds, the country accumulates administrative experience, and can apply large scale methods more effectively and to a wider range of activities.

Because large scale organization involves great changes in attitudes and in social structures, and brings with it so much discontent, many people dislike it, and would prefer to have only so much economic growth as is possible without increasing the scale of organization. This attitude is feasible enough in a country whose natural resources are limited to cultivable soil, but if the country has considerable resources for mining or for manufacturing it will almost certainly restrict its opportunities unless the growth of large scale enterprise is permitted and encouraged.

3. ECONOMIC FREEDOM

(a) Individualism and Collective Action

The growth of income per head in Western Europe and North America in the last few centuries is very rightly associated with the growth of economic freedom—of freedom of the individual to change his social status or his occupation; freedom to hire resources and combine them in ways which increase output or lower costs; and freedom to enter trades in competition with others who are already established in those trades. In this section we shall be examining

the institutional obstacles to these freedoms, but we must first note that individualism is not necessarily the quickest road to economic development. Collective action is also necessary, and in certain circumstances may even have quicker results.

Collective action in the form of government action is necessary even if only to supplement private action. Governments have extensive functions in promoting economic development, to which we refer in more detail in Chapter VII. These range, even in private enterprise economies, from such obvious functions as maintaining roads or promoting research, to more sophisticated functions such as underwriting new enterprises or providing capital to private business. The role of government depends to some extent on the quantity and quality of private entrepreneurship; the less able the individuals to pioneer, the greater the burden that falls upon an enterprising public service.

Apart from government action, however, a strong sentiment of national cohesion may be helpful to economic development whether the pioneering is being done by individuals or by government. If the members of the nation are used to looking to and accepting leadership, the changes which economic growth requires are much easier to achieve than if each is a stubborn individualist. This may show itself in several ways. If the pioneering is in new techniques, the common people will change over more rapidly once innovators have shown that the new techniques are more productive. If it is necessary to arrange for work to be done in large scale establishments, where previously every man was his own master, a new discipline can be quickly established. If sacrifices have to be borne—for instance, if the government decides to launch upon a heavy programme of capital formation—they will be borne with less internal strife or less inflation than in communities whose members are less easily united by a common purpose. If habits and institutions must be changed—the status of women, the legal status of land, the attitude towards migration— the changes are more easily affected. And so on. Some historians contrasting the last hundred years of Chinese and of Japanese history lay great stress on the 'discipline' of Japanese social life, in contrast with the greater individualism of China. It is extremely difficult to give either precise meaning or precise weight to such concepts, but since it is clear that economic change is pioneered by the few and imitated by the many it seems plausible that the rate of change for society as a whole should depend on the willingness of the many to accept the leadership of the enterprising few.

Collective action and cohesive sentiment are not merely necessary to growth, they may also in certain circumstances achieve results superior to those achieved by individualism. A cohesive group,

organized on authoritarian lines is probably *better* able to attain *given* objectives than is a group more individualistically inclined. It is superior, presumably, for anything which has to be done according to a plan, where keeping together is of the essence of success—whether the objective is making war, or controlling the flow of some tremendous river which otherwise threatens destruction, or fighting forest fires, or any other activity where success is dependent on every person taking orders from the chief. The cohesive, authoritarian group will also have superior economic growth, *if the chief knows better than the individuals* the measures which growth requires. The chief can enforce education, or improved technologies, or the use of better seeds, or a higher level of capital formation, or changes in social relationships such as land tenure, or slavery, or monopoly. Hence it is not true to say that growth depends on the individual having freedom to manoeuvre, if the alternative is that the individual will be compelled to do things which lead to growth. The case for the superiority of individual freedom in economic matters rests on the belief that the chief has no superior source of knowledge, and that individuals seeking in many directions are more likely to discover open doors than a chief with a monopoly of manoeuvre. As we shall see in a moment, this belief is true enough in advanced societies, but it is not so obviously true of backward societies, which can grow simply by modelling themselves on the more dynamic features of the more advanced. Hence, given a government which has set itself to promote economic growth, and which has a reasonably competent understanding of the issues involved, a backward society on an authoritarian basis is almost certain to grow more rapidly than a backward society on an individualistic basis. The rub is in the provisos; governments can be intelligent, and they can be authoritarian, and they can have the interests of the common people primarily at heart; but to find these three features in combination seems to be the exception rather than the rule.

These considerations are more relevant to the current controversy about 'planning' than they are to the controversy about the operation of industry by public rather than private enterprise. These two issues are often confused in popular discussion, but they are quite separate. There can be centrally planned private or public economies; and a public enterprise economy can just as well be planned or unplanned. We say first of all a few words about public operation of industry, and then turn to the issue of planning.

The controversy between private and public operation of industries ranges over a great number of issues, most of which do not concern our present purpose. Much of the controversy is concerned with effects upon the distribution of income, in which this book is not

directly interested, the argument being whether state employees would absorb a larger part of the national income than private profit-making entrepreneurs. Another part of the controversy concerns the effects on individual liberty—on the freedom of the worker or of the consumer, or on political freedoms, in a society where property and initiative are concentrated in the hands of the state. Our present concern is only that part of the controversy which relates to effects on economic growth.

This resolves itself into questions of incentives and of access to resources. The entrepreneur, whether private individual or public official, must have the incentive to seek out ways of reducing cost, or of giving the public better service by introducing new or better commodities, or by improving distribution or service. He must also have access to labour, to capital and to materials; that is to say, he must not have too much difficulty in finding a backer who will provide the capital, or in persuading authorities of one kind or another to let him have the labour and materials which he requires.

In so far as it is a question of incentives, the private enterprise system relies, in the first instance, upon the lure of private profit. This incentive, however, operates more in small firms than it does in the large corporation, where entrepreneurship is exercised by directors and salaried managers whose remuneration in these days is not closely linked with profit. Entrepreneurship in large private corporations depends on much the same incentives as entrepreneurship in public corporations; in either case there may be a small bonus varying with profits, but the major incentives are ambition, desire to do one's job well, desire for promotion to a higher salary, and desire for recognition. Hence, as far as incentives are concerned, there is probably not much to choose between private and public enterprise in the sphere of large scale industry. There is much more to choose in small scale activities. The majority of small scale enterprises—the shops, the farms, the restaurants, the small factories, the professional services—are doing a routine job under routine management of men whose abilities are not above the average, and whose ambitions are not sufficiently strong to drive them to ever improved performance, if there were not also material incentives and the fear of bankruptcy. If private enterprise were entirely prohibited it is possible that the large enterprises could continue to maintain efficiency and drive, but it is highly probable that the smaller enterprises—which in any country account for more than half of industrial, commercial and agricultural employment—would sink to a pretty low level of efficiency.

Much the same distinction between large and small enterprises also applies to the question of access. In any system, private or public,

F

it is easier for large enterprises to raise the capital they need than for small enterprises. This difference would probably be increased if capital were available only from a state agency, because the political and other strength of large enterprises would make it easier for them to insist on getting the capital they required. The same strength might also give them more monopolistic power, to intrigue for capital and other resources to be denied to new and smaller rival industries or establishments or commodities. The small enterprises, and especially those which were anxious to experiment with untried ideas—new commodities, new inventions and so on—would probably find it even more difficult to get the necessary backing than they do in a system of private enterprise.

Much depends on how widely diffused is the control of resources. If no capital, labour, or materials can be obtained without a permit from a central authority, entrepreneurs have little room for man- oeuvre, whether in a private enterprise system or in a system of public ownership. The centrally planned economy, whether private or public, is then driven in directions determined by the plan- ners. Such an economy is superior to an unplanned economy in attaining a specific objective, since unplanned economies have no specific objectives. A planned economy is better at producing the sinews of war, and this is why all economies come to be highly planned in time of war. A planned economy is also better at imposing a high level of capital formation; or at creating a large industrial sector; or at any other single objective which planners set them- selves—whether it be irrigating deserts, or building houses, or what- ever it may be. Where the planned economy is inferior to the un- planned is if there is no single objective towards which effort must be concentrated. For then the judgement of individual entrepreneurs is as good as or superior to the judgement of the planners at the centre; there is no single direction in which the economy should go; and it is therefore best to leave each person free to make the best use of the resources available to him in the circumstances in which he finds himself. This applies equally whether the entrepreneurs are private persons or public officials. An economy in which all industrial capital is owned by the state need not for that reason alone also be a centrally planned economy; for the state can decide to confine its functions to those of a shareholder, and to leave its officials free to produce what they like, with what resources they can, subject only to the test of profitability in the market. Even if it is the sole source of capital, it may distribute capital through a multiplicity of agencies competing with each other, instead of through a single central con- trol; so that the firm in search of capital may have several chances of getting it. Planning and public ownership are not the same thing;

the world has had both unplanned public enterprise and also strictly planned private enterprise.

A corollary of the distinction between having a single objective and having no objective, or a multiplicity of objectives, is that planning is less harmful in countries which merely follow the leadership of others than it would be in countries which pioneer. In advanced industrial countries like Britain or the United States, nobody knows what the pattern of the economy will be or ought to be in fifty years' time; what new goods will dominate the market which have not yet even been invented; what new modes of transport will be important; what the shops will be like; and so on. If such economies were now put into the strait-jacket of central planning, and authority given to a small group of persons in a central office to decide what developments to encourage or to suppress, we can be fairly confident that growth would be retarded. That is to say, we cannot by any means be confident that output will not rise faster, since capital formation may be greater, but we can be confident that there will not be so many new goods or so many changes in the patterns of production and consumption. There may be more of the old, but there will be less of the new. The situation is very different if a backward country is merely following in the lead of the pioneers, ten or fifty or a hundred years after the pioneers have shown what is worth doing. Even in these circumstances strict central control may hamper those adjustments which are always necessary as techniques and institutions are transferred from one environment to another. But it is not as easy for the planners to go wrong as it is in the pioneering countries, because they have models which they can copy.

Much depends also on how much the particular community has learnt of the art of public administration. Most governments are, and always have been, corrupt and inefficient. The art of creating a public service relatively free from corruption, relatively efficient, and fairly anxious to maintain high standards in these matters, has been learnt only slowly, and only in a few countries. Hence in most countries of the world economic growth would certainly be impossible if the adoption of public ownership or of central planning were to put into the hands of present administrations the entire responsibility for economic affairs. In countries where government is corrupt and inefficient, *laissez faire, laissez passer* is the best recipe for economic growth. It is only as an efficient administration is built up that the relative merits of private enterprise and of public ownership or control merit serious debate.

In practice the real problem is not to choose between private initiative on the one hand and government action—whether planning or nationalization—on the other, but rather to combine these two in

the most fruitful proportions. Arguments for or against planning in general, or for or against public operation of industry in general are a hangover from the nineteenth century. In practice it is also clear that the role of governments in economic development is and ought to be much greater now than it has been in the past, if only because of the greater rate of growth which has now come to be generally expected. Much which developed only slowly over the centuries through individual effort in the countries which have pioneered in material advancement, may now be expected to happen in as many decades under government auspices in the more backward countries which have now started to tread the same road. The role of government in economic life is growing, and will continue to grow for some time yet. The problems which this creates we shall leave for more detailed consideration in Chapter VII.

(b) Vertical Mobility

Economic growth is usually associated with a high degree of vertical mobility, upward and downward. There are several reasons for this.

In the first place, if the upper classes—in business, government, science, and other spheres—are not continually refreshed from below, they degenerate, both biologically and culturally. Biological degeneration takes place because if a thousand intelligent men have a thousand sons, the sons will not all be intelligent. If we assume that at some point in the community's history a biologically superior group has taken over the upper class positions, and if this group henceforward never allows descendants of any but the original members to hold these positions, then we may fairly confidently expect a decline of biological vigour. A healthy upper class, biologically, is one which allows its weaker members to fall into the lower classes, and which in each generation recruits the more successful members of the lower classes into its own ranks. Similarly, it is necessary to have cultural fertilization. A closed upper class, based on family, usually tends to go in for some form of ancestor worship. Old ways of doing things become sacred, and there is too much looking backwards for success in a changing world. This is less likely to happen if there is constant recruitment of people who have no past to look back on, or who are anxious to forget their past. The case for recruitment from below, in the interests of growth, must not be confused with arguments for equality. There are always superior and inferior social classes, in the sense that there are always in any community, whether it be capitalist, socialist or communist, people set in authority over other people, whether in business, or in government, or in religion, or else. The point we are discussing is not

whether these divisions should disappear, for there is no doubt that growth would cease in a community if authority ceased; but what is the effect on growth of recruiting for superior positions by birth or by other tests. Again, those who are to exercise authority need special training for the purpose. They get longer education than the rest, and more privileges both during their training and afterwards. Some rich communities may be able to afford to give a long and expensive education to all children, but most communities cannot afford this, and so discriminate; the question is then who is to get the privileged education—whether the choice should depend upon birth or upon other tests.

If children could be selected for leadership solely on the basis of their biological inheritance, by intelligence tests and in other ways, no case at all could be made for associating growth with privileges of family status. The fact is, however, that a man's qualities depend also to a large extent on what he learns from his culture. Some part of this he learns in school, and in other institutions not connected with his family, but he also learns a good deal from his parents, and it does matter who his parents are. We can see this most clearly if the culture of the ruling class is quite different from that of the ruled. For example, in the West Indies in the nineteenth century the culture of the white ruling classes was quite different from that of the newly emancipated black slaves. The whites argued that all positions of importance should be reserved to their children, who had been brought up in their culture, and asserted that the islands would soon revert to barbarism if black people were allowed into positions of responsibility, however high their biological endowment might be, because of their inferior cultural inheritance. Nineteenth century white culture in the West Indies was not, as it happens, at a high level; it was generally despised by Englishmen for its immorality, and its lack of artistic achievement; and its backward techniques and lack of progressive business sense have bequeathed continuing poverty to the islands. All the same, it was superior to the black culture of the time, and the islands would probably have been even more backward today if universal adult suffrage had been established in 1838. The point at issue, however, is not equality, but the system of recruitment for privilege. If there could have been devised some system for recruiting the more intelligent blacks and giving them special training for their responsibilities it is not by any means clear that they would not have governed the islands better than they were actually governed. This policy was pursued by the Ottoman rulers, who recruited young Christian boys and trained them as Moslems for the major positions of responsibility; and most historians attribute the vigour of the Empire partly to this system. The French, also, have pursued similar

policies in parts of their African Empire, training selected Africans in French culture, and opening to them the highest posts. We may therefore conclude that, even when the culture of the ruled is quite different from that of the rulers, there may yet be advantage in opening the highest posts to the children of the ruled, provided that they get special training. It follows all the more that if we are dealing with homogeneous communities, where the cultural traditions of all the social classes are much the same, there is a case for restricting superior positions to people of superior training, but there is no case for restricting them to people of 'superior' birth.

When we say that the upper classes will degenerate if not refreshed from below, we are assuming that the upper classes are restricting recruitment to their own children. They may, however, be drawing a line which allows themselves considerable scope. For example, the white population of the Union of South Africa is about twenty per cent of the whole. If, therefore, superior positions are open only to whites, there is still considerable choice, providing that all the two million whites are eligible. Such a group can probably maintain its vigour indefinitely, new families coming to the top in each generation while others make way for them. In contrast the whites of the West Indies, who constitute less than three per cent of the population, could not possibly have maintained a vigorous monopoly of leadership, even if they had begun with superior biological endowment, since when one family produces duds there is no other family rising up out of obscurity to take its place.

Alternatively, a small ruling clique may well maintain itself by immigration. In the extreme case, such as those British colonies which are ruled but not settled, the ruling class is recruited afresh in each generation by immigration, and can remain vigorous so long as it can attract vigorous immigrants.

Subject to these qualifications we conclude that growth cannot be maintained through several generations if positions of responsibility are open only to members of a limited number of families. This is so even if the families are the best, from the point of view of growth, when they assume power. The position is even worse if these families are of poor biological endowment, or alternatively if their cultural traditions are not compatible with growth. It is often the case that the traditions of the upper classes are not compatible with economic growth. The top class in society tends to despise many things on which growth depends. It may despise work and the economising spirit, giving its time instead to hunting, shooting, and dancing, and living on its rents and dividends; it may despise learning, science and new techniques; and it may even despise merit, preferring birth. If superior positions may be filled only by persons raised in such

traditions, growth will not take place. Yet such are the traditions of the aristocracy in most pre-capitalist societies.

This brings us to the point that economic growth may require the displacement of the existing ruling class, and its replacement by another. The existing ruling class may be incompatible with growth because of its outlook and traditions. Or it may be incompatible because the bases of its economic power are due to be destroyed. Growth sometimes strengthens the existing bases, but it may also weaken them. We can see this clearly where the existing ruling class derives its wealth from land, or from serfdom. Economic development may raise the value of land, or it may reduce the value of land. The existing ruling class has no need to frustrate developments which will raise land values—such as working land for minerals, or putting in irrigation schemes, or making the area into a playground for rich tourists. But the existing class may be expected to frustrate plans for attracting labour away from the land into factories, or for reducing tariff barriers to the importation of cheap food, or for spreading education among the people (which usually makes them dissatisfied with the *status quo*). If the opportunities for growth happen to be such that they would reduce the wealth of the existing ruling class, this class will not be to the forefront in exploiting them, and will more probably be to the forefront in trying to prevent their exploitation. Growth will then depend upon the emergence of a new group, and there will be a struggle for power between this group and the old group, struggling for power to alter laws, or tariffs or systems of education, or systems of belief or other ways of living.

Because the development of new types of economic activity is so often pioneered by a rising social class, historians have always to look closely at class structure and class mobility when examining periods of rapid economic change. No simple historical pattern emerges, however. If one contrasts Britain and Russia in the eighteenth century, much emphasis can be laid upon the relatively more 'open' society of Britain, which gave to merchants and industrialists greater freedom of manoeuvre, and greater social status *vis-a-vis* the landed aristocracy than the commercial classes had in Russia. But if one contrasts nineteenth century China and Japan, it is not easy to establish that Japanese society was more open in this sense than Chinese society. There were some differences in the status and opportunities of the commercial classes in the two countries, but the differences were not great enough to account for the differences in development in the last third of the century. If the Japanese case is contrasted with the British, one observes that instead of a slow growth of the commercial classes through the centuries, to eventual domination, there is a revolutionary outburst by a lesser branch of

the aristocracy, which takes the commercial classes under its wing only after it has successfully made its revolution. This emphasizes that social changes which have economic consequences are not always made by the commercial classes—the respective roles of nationalist leaders and of commercial leaders in the contemporary anti-imperialists movements also stress the same point (see section 5(a) below); but it leaves untouched our main point, which is that it is easier for new economic classes to develop in an open than in a closed society.

Again, economic growth creates or expands the middle classes, mainly by recruitment from below, and is not to be expected in societies which place obstacles in the way of upward mobility. The middle classes grow because growth involves more use of knowledge in production, and greater co-ordination of resources. The accumulation and application of knowledge makes it necessary to have an increasing proportion of skilled persons in production—of engineers of all grades, of scientists and generally of people with several years of education and training—and a rising standard of life also creates demands for skilled services, for dentists, teachers, musicians and other purveyors of service. Growth also requires greater co-ordination because it is associated with greater specialization and with an increase in the skills of production; consequently it is necessary to have more foremen, more accountants, more managers and generally more people in supervisory positions. One of Karl Marx's most striking prophecies was that economic growth would be associated with the emergence of an ever widening gap between the capitalist employer and the worker, but exactly the opposite has happened, and we can see why it has happened. Karl Marx thought that social stratification depended entirely upon the distribution of ownership of the means of production, but we can see that the rise of the middle classes has followed from the accumulation of technical knowledge and from specialization, co-ordination and the increased scale of operations—factors which are independent of the ownership of the means of production, and which, operate equally in capitalist, socialist or other patterns of ownership.

We cannot therefore expect vigorous economic growth to occur in communities where social mobility is prevented by slavery, by caste, by race barriers, by social snobbery, by religious differentiation or the like—unless the privileged group is large relatively to the whole, or refreshes itself continually by immigration. And, in any case, even if the privileged group remains vigorous and enterprising, the community as a whole must lose because it is depriving itself of using the talents of members of the lower classes. Other things being equal, a community which is free from barriers to mobility must show more

rapid growth than a community which denies opportunity to the majority of its members.

In practice, the more 'sensible' aristocracies allow as much vertical mobility as is necessary for vigour, even when they are careful not to allow any more than this. Any class includes in its membership people of superior, of average and of inferior talent. The 'sensible' aristocracy permits people of superior talents to rise, and people of inferior talents to fall. This is all that the maintenance of its vigour requires. At the same time it protects its own average members against the average members of the lower classes. The class structure of society is thus upheld, since people of average talent in the lower classes are not allowed to displace people of average talent in the upper classes; while at the same time the aristocracy is continually refreshed. Since only a little vertical mobility is needed to keep the upper classes vigorous, a class structure and economic growth are not incompatible, provided that this minimum of mobility is allowed. At the same time, social peace is easier to maintain if it is clear that the most clever Jews or Negroes or working class boys will not be prevented from reaching the highest rungs of the ladder, even though they are only a negligible proportion of their class, and even though the great majority of average people in their class are kept firmly 'in their place'. Nevertheless however 'sensible' the aristocracy may be in tolerating these exceptions, a community must be depriving itself of opportunities for growth if it restricts the opportunities for vertical mobility.

One partial exception to this generalization is worth noting. In some circumstances discrimination against a group may cause that group to show vigorous development in directions other than those which interest the ruling class. Thus if the ruling class despises economic activity, and at the same time prevents some other group from expressing itself in the activities which the ruling class honours —such as the military professions, government, and the church— the despised group may cultivate instead the opportunities for economic activity, and may distinguish itself in this way. The position of the Jews in Western Europe springs at once to mind; they concentrated on money making in the days when this way of life was despised, and was almost the only one open to them. If discrimination against Jews disappeared, and Jews could distinguish themselves without hindrance in the professions, in science, in agriculture, in the military forces, and in all the more 'respectable' ways of life, they would probably cease to be better at making money than most other groups, and by reaction, might well grow to despise this way of life, and become inept at it. Similarly in India the Parsees, being ineligible, because of their religion, for joining the governing classes, concentrated on economic activity, and became more expert at it

than their hosts. This is a development we expect to see in small immigrant groups who, because of their religion or their race or some other difference merge neither with the upper nor with the lower classes, and concentrate on making a living for themselves—the Chinese in South-East Asia are another well known example. We shall have more to say about immigrants and their problems in Chapter VI.

(c) Freedom of Markets

Economic growth requires that men should be free to hire resources, and to enter trades—whether on private account or as public servants being a separate issue, which we have already considered in section 3(a) above. Here we discuss first difficulties in the way of access to resources, and secondly difficulties of access to markets.

By access to resources we mean that the entrepreneur should be able to buy, borrow, or hire factors of production, since if a person may use only his own labour, land and capital, the economies of specialization and of large scale enterprise are excluded. In this section we shall not say anything about capital, beyond noting that growth must be restricted if religion or custom frowns upon the lending of money at interest; institutional problems of capital are reserved to Chapter V. We discuss in this section the marketability of land and of labour.

There must be access to land. It is not always necessary to be able to buy land freehold, but at least it must be possible to get a secure lease with long tenure, especially if the enterprise involves making durable investment in the land, in the form of buildings or irrigation works or mining tunnels or other forms. Most systems of land tenure provide access to land, though usually with restrictions. Thus, land may be denied *de jure* or *de facto* to individuals and allowed only to collectives, as may be the case in the U.S.S.R. Or it may be denied to 'strangers', i.e. to immigrants, or to members of some particular race or creed, or, as in parts of India, to 'non-agriculturists' (a measure aimed at preventing moneylenders from buying out the farmers). There may also be restrictions on the uses to which land may be put, especially in these days of the geographical zoning of land use, under the name of 'town and country planning'. Or there may be restrictions on tenure; in some countries land cannot be bought freehold, but can only be leased; and the leases may not give sufficient security of tenure to justify making some kinds of long term investment. Difficulties also arise if there is uncertainty as to the ownership of land; modern countries have cadastral surveys and land registers, but there are many places where a person who purchases land may be harassed by litigation about the boundaries or about the title of those from whom

he bought. Clarification of titles is a necessary step in economic growth.

Though most systems provide that the owners of land can part with it if they desire to do so, communities nevertheless differ in their willingness to sell or to rent land. Ownership of land is frequently tied up with pride of family, and the latter may cause people to be unwilling to part with land which has been in their family for generations, and in which, sometimes, their ancestors are buried. Land ownership is also tied up with social and political status, so that some people regard land not primarily as a means of production, or as a source of wealth, but as a mark of status, and as something to be held on to even at a substantial cost of annual income. Such considerations are probably most powerful in countries where land is very unequally distributed, e.g. where all the land belongs to a small aristocracy; it is usually much easier to buy or rent land in countries where ownership is widely diffused. The attachment of familiar or political sentiments to land ownership reduces the mobility of land as a resource, and restricts economic growth. The existence of such sentiments has caused some governments to take powers to effect the compulsory sale of land, as for public purposes or for railways, or for transforming large estates into small farms or vice versa; or powers to effect the compulsory exchange of land, in consolidation schemes or in town planning schemes. There is probably no country in the world where land is bought and sold solely for its value as a factor of production, and no country where non-economic factors do not frustrate schemes which would otherwise increase output.

Access to land may also be denied in the social interest, where the effect of easy access would be to diminish natural resources. Some uses of land inevitably diminish natural resources. Of these the most important is mining; other examples are the building of aerodromes on fertile soil, or the erection of ugly structures in places where they spoil the view. Some other uses of land may but need not be destructive; agriculture can be done in ways which maintain soil fertility, and the cutting of timber can be done without destruction of forests; but users have not always the interest, or the sense, or the forethought to adopt the methods of conservation. It is not always in the public interest to deny access on these grounds. For example, it may be in the public interest to extract minerals, and to use the proceeds for creating other resources (including schools); or it may be more useful to have an aerodrome than to have its equivalent in cultivated land. But denial on these grounds is not necessarily incompatible with growth. On the contrary the control of land use may be fundamental to growth, since many communities have come to grief for no

better reason than that they have wasted their natural resources, perhaps by exhausting the soil, or by destroying their forests, or by working out their minerals without reinvesting the proceeds in creating other assets. (See Chapter VI, section 1(b).)

From land we turn to access to labour. If the economies of large scale production are to be enjoyed, it is necessary to be able to organize large numbers of workers under central control, whether in collective, in state or in private enterprises. And, because growth involves change, it is also necessary that labour should be mobile, leaving some enterprises and joining others. In authoritarian societies this mobility can be enforced by issuing administrative orders telling workers where they must work; even democratic societies resort to such compulsions in wartime. In peace time however, democratic societies rely on market processes; surplus labour is dismissed, and enterprises which want labour bid for it by offering wages.

In practice, labour is mobile only in so far as it is dependent on wage employment. It is very hard to get labour in a community where everybody has all the land he needs to satisfy his requirements. Hence one of the conditions of economic growth is the creation of a landless class. This may be done by depriving the farmers of land, as was to some extent the effect of the enclosure movement in Britain; or it may result from overpopulation. It is not a phenomenon confined to capitalism. Any system which is based on large scale organization, and which provides for change, must depend on a wage earning class, or economic growth would be impossible. In any case a high income per head and a population of which the majority are wedded to the soil are not compatible with each other on the side of the demand for labour, no less than on the side of supply. For a high income per head is associated with spending only a small proportion of income on food; or to put it differently, is associated with only a small proportion of the population being required on the land. In an efficient country like the U.S.A. the whole population can be fed if one-sixth of the population engages in agriculture. Even if a country makes its living by exporting agricultural products in exchange for manufactures, it will, at currently high standards of efficiency, require not more than one-third of its people in agriculture. Protest against the separation of the people from the soil has been a fruitful source both of political agitation and also of nostalgic poetic sentiments, but to the economic eye a community which needs to have the majority of its people working on the land is merely demonstrating its inefficiency. It must, however, be remembered that much of the protest against the separation of people from the land has been against compulsory proletarianization. If Africans are driven out of their reserves by high taxation to make them work in mines, there may be an enormous

increase in output, by any means of measuring output; and yet the majority of the people may be much worse off, their lands uncultivated, their wives and children left lonely and hungry for most of the year, and their tribal organization, with its ethical code, seriously disturbed. As we emphasize in the Appendix, growth of output is not synonymous with growth of happiness or with welfare. Fortunately they are also not always antagonistic.

Access to labour is restricted not only by widespread ownership of land but also by institutions which tie people to particular occupations or employers, such as slavery, serfdom, caste, racial prejudice, or religious discrimination; and by institutions which deprive the individual of the incentive to seek remunerative employment, such as the extended family system, or generous social security provisions. All such institutions reduce the mobility of labour, and make it less easy for new firms or new industries to establish themselves and to grow. This is why the promoters of new industries, whether they be governments or private persons, are usually hostile to such institutions. The serfs' best friend is always the employer in a new industry who cannot get the labour he wants: the status of Negroes in the Union of South Africa or in the southern states of the U.S.A. would be raised faster by a rapid growth of factory industries in those places than it could be raised by any other means. And this also is one of the reasons why there are always powerful classes opposed to economic growth, since it threatens to cut off the branch on which they sit.

In the early days of capitalism access to labour was not regulated by the state; employers and workmen were free to contract on any terms they pleased, short of slavery or its imitations. In these days, however, the contract to work is ringed with restrictions. The state forbids certain contracts, such as the employment of children, or the employment of women in mines. In some countries it stipulates maximum hours, or minimum wages. It may regulate apprenticeship. It protects the rights of trade unions; and so on. Some of its prohibitions restrict economic growth, but they are not, of course, necessarily bad because they do so.

We turn now to consider access to the consumer. Economic growth requires that men who have new ideas should be free to put them into effect, even though they may thereby do damage to their competitors. Growth requires freedom to compete; at the same time growth can be so damaging to competitors that it stimulates efforts to suppress competition. When we say that men should be free to put their ideas into effect we confine ourselves to ideas which increase competition; ideas for restraining competition, such as exclusive contracts, or market sharing arrangements are damaging to growth in so far as growth depends on competition.

The competition of new ideas—new products, new methods of production or distribution, new styles, new sources of supply—damages those whose fortunes are tied up with the old, and whose resources are 'immobile', in the sense that they cannot easily be adapted to the new ideas, or that they cannot be moved into some other occupation or trade without loss. Most resources are immobile in this sense. Labour is immobile as soon as it acquires a special skill; it may remain mobile between several industries while losing mobility as between occupations. So also land and reproducible capital are immobile in greater or less degree. Hence all men have some interest in restricting competition; our 'instinct' to compete with others has a counterpart 'instinct' to prevent others from competing with us. In the world of labour this reveals itself in the restrictive practices enforced by group sanctions—in the restrictive apprenticeship regulations of trade unions and professional associations; in resistance to 'dilution' and insistence on passing prescribed tests, which are sometimes necessary in the public interest, and sometimes not; in making it expensive to acquire skills; in rigid demarcations of jobs, as in the building trade, or in the line drawn between dentists and dental mechanics; and even, in some circumstances, in actual destruction of machinery and in murder or intimidation of rivals. Similarly, in the world of business, there are the market sharing arrangements, the price agreements, the amalgamations, the exclusive licences, and all the other tricks designed to reduce the market to 'order'.

Now though it is true that economic growth, by causing change, stimulates resistance to competition, it is probably nevertheless also true that competition is more acceptable in communities the more rapidly they are expanding. This is partly because loss is more easily avoided in expanding than in stagnant societies. If a person over-invests in an industry he will have to endure loss for some time, but, if there is a secular growth of income, demand will catch up with supply, and the period of loss will be the shorter the more rapidly income grows. Again, if a person becomes unemployed in one industry because of technological change, he will gain employment elsewhere the more easily if a general expansion of the economy is taking place all the time. So, while growth shakes people up more, and reduces the chance of staying in one place, it also at the same time creates so many new opportunities all the time that it seems less necessary to rely on monopolistic protections in growing than in relatively stable societies. Moreover, in societies where economic growth is taking place, the harm done by monopolies is more obvious, and there is greater resistance to them. Hence the public at large is more favourable to the idea of competition, and towards deliberate

efforts by the state to protect competition, if the community is where economic growth is rapid, than if there is relative stagnation.

The harm done by monopolies is more obvious in the sphere of economic growth than it is in other economic spheres. Most of the economists' writing on monopoly is about an abstruse topic the significance of which does not intrude itself obviously upon the public at large; for the economists' literature is concerned mainly with the effect of monopoly upon 'general welfare' by frustrating the 'marginal' proportionalities which 'ought' to determine the allocation of resources. The general public understands better, and is more interested in, the effect of monopoly on the distribution of income, a subject which it is not easy to separate from personal preferences for the individuals who suffer from monopoly, as compared with those who gain. Hence, if monopoly has to be discussed without reference to economic growth, the discussion is either abstruse and without meaning for the general public, or else it is real but incapable of solution except in terms of preferences for one group of people rather than another. Thus, according to personal inclinations, some people are for workers' monopolies, but against business men's monopolies; for retail traders' monopolies, but against manufacturers' monopolies; for farmers' monopolies, but against industrialists' monopolies; for booksellers' monopolies, but against doctors' monopolies; and so on. If the public has an attitude towards monopoly, it is probably merely that it is for good monopolies and against bad ones. The nearest translation of this seems to be that it favours monopolies of the weak, and not of the strong; though this is not always consistent with the rival translation which makes the public also favour monopolies of the efficient but not of the inefficient.

On the other hand, however diverse may be the attitudes to monopoly and its effect on the distribution of income, most people *in a society which is used to economic growth* would agree that monopolies are good in so far as they promote growth, and are bad in so far as they restrict growth. The reason for this is that the prospects opened up by growth are generally believed by most people who are accustomed to growth to be more important than the prospects opened up by redistributing national income. If income per head is growing by two per cent per annum, everyone can be twenty-two per cent better off in ten years, and this much exceeds any conceivable redistribution of income between classes, in the absence of economic growth. When we take account also of the fact that economic expansion itself also insures individuals against serious loss from competition, it is easy to see why competition is more favourably accepted in expanding than it is in stagnant societies.

This is not to say that monopoly is necessarily considered to be incompatible with economic growth. On the contrary, from the Mercantilist writers onwards, the most cogent supporters of monopoly have been those who have argued for it on the ground of its necessary part in economic expansion. Their argument has also been the more cogent because of its deliberate limitations. Their case for monopoly is twofold. First, that it is necessary to the efficient functioning of certain large scale operations. And secondly that it is necessary in some early stages of development.

If an industry is such that average costs of operation fall as output increases, up to the limits of what the market will absorb, because of economies *internal* to the firm, then it is cheaper to have one firm than several. This is not always a decisive argument for monopoly. For on the other side, we must take into account the fact that the existence of monopoly frequently stifles initiative and enterprise. So if the economies of scale are not substantial, it may well be cheaper *in the long run* to insist on competition, where competition is feasible, than to purchase temporary economy at the cost of ultimate stagnation behind the protection of monopoly. Balancing the pros and cons is a matter of judgement in each case.

If there are substantial economies of scale, monopoly will often be created by the competitive process. For the bigger firms will be able to drive the smaller out of the market, except in so far as the smaller specialize in types of the commodity or types of service for which there is a limited market. There are, however, cases where it is cheaper to have only one firm right from the start, as in planning the distribution of gas or electricity or water. There are also cases where the competitive process is brought to an end not by the emergence of a single large firm, but by agreement between two or more firms to cease competing with each other. Such agreements sometimes result in lower costs of production or distribution, but this is seldom either their main purpose or their main effect; their main purpose and effect being merely by raising prices, to redistribute income from consumers towards producers. These agreements do reduce costs in some cases, most notably when they result in standardization or in simplification. For sometimes in the absence of such agreements a firm will manufacture its commodity in a wide range of sizes or styles to ensure its standing in the market. The agreement may provide for each firm to specialize on a narrow range of styles, thus reducing costs of production; it may even also achieve a reduction in the total number of styles offered on the market; and it may sometimes, by sharing the market geographically, also reduce costs of marketing and of transportation. Agreements which aim at reducing costs and prices are the exception rather than the rule, but they do exist.

Another aspect of the advantages of large size is found in the argument that monopolies are essential to growth because only monopolies can afford to spend the large sums needed for research and development in these days. This argument has various strands, which have to be separated. In the first place, it is not true that all innovations require large expenditures. There is still a good deal of old-style application of ingenuity and adaptation by persons using quite small resources, and still a good deal of innovation by small firms. The costly discoveries are those which depend upon team work by highly trained chemists or physicists, and have therefore been most obvious in the chemical and the electrical engineering industries. Some other industries, such as steel manufacture, also have scope for the highly trained team, but in most other industries a mechanical flair and an ingenious and fertile mind are still the best equipment for invention. In the second place, monopoly is not the same as size. The cartel or market sharing type of monopolistic arrangement does not rest on the size of the individual firm, and seldom provides for joint research activity. It would therefore be more accurate to argue that in certain industries some types of research cannot be financed by small or medium sized firms, so that the large firms in these industries may have an innovating advantage. And in the third place this advantage can to some extent be offset if research is done co-operatively, or in government laboratories, as it is in some British manufacturing industries, and in the agriculture of most countries. It is true that the outside research organization is not a complete substitute for the research department inside the firm, which is in touch with the firm's daily problems, and able to adapt itself to them. On the other hand it is not the daily problems which require expensive research, but the fundamental long term work dependent on advancing the frontiers of science, and this can be done just as well in co-operative or government laboratories, with possibly the added advantage that results may be diffused more quickly through the industry. This is not, of course, to argue that research should be *confined* to laboratories working for the industry as a whole; on the contrary such laboratories are just as likely as the laboratories of the large firms to miss the more fruitful lines of enquiry. We are arguing only that the disadvantage of the small firms can be diminished through co-operative organization. Research cannot be adduced as an argument for monopoly since one of the surest ways of ending scientific progress would be to create a monopoly in research. (We discuss these problems more fully in Chapter IV, section 1(*b*).)

We have not, however, completely disposed of the argument for size, because of the difference between research and development. It is true that group research can have the same results as are produced

G

by the laboratory of the large firm. But it is also true that when the development stage is reached, the advantage may be with the firm which can put out large sums in carrying the innovation to the stage of commercial exploitation. The ability to finance expensive innovations is one of the undeniable advantages of the large firm, as is the ability to enjoy large scale economies of production. Sometimes these advantages result in monopoly, and sometimes they could not be enjoyed without first creating monopoly conditions. It is occasionally true in some industries that monopoly promotes growth, in the sense that size promotes growth, and that size and monopoly are related. But we must not exaggerate this into a general rule for all industries and situations.

Apart from these questions of economies of scale, it may be desirable to protect a new industry in the early stages of its development, provided that the protection is removed within a reasonably short period of years. This position first received legislative support in the Statute of Monopolies of 1624. In this statute, after two generations of heated controversy, it was enacted that the state could accord protection to new inventions, but that this protection must cease after a fixed period of years. This is the origin of our patent system. A new invention did not mean in those days only what it means today; it covered also new industries introduced to the country from other countries, however old and well established the techniques of the industry might be in other places. Hence the statute implicitly recognized what we now call the 'infant industries' argument, as well as the arguments which feature in current expositions of the patent controversy.

Despite centuries of disputation, nobody has improved upon the position the legislators took in 1624. Some new ideas need protection because of the cost of making them commercially profitable. This may be the cost of research, or of development; the cost of training workers; or the cost of familiarizing the public with a new commodity. And so governments have always been willing to grant protection to new industries, whether in the form of tariffs, of licences, of subsidies, or of patents. In some circumstances it is possible to examine each claim on its merits, and to adjust the type and duration of protection accordingly, as is being done at present in some underdeveloped countries which are giving encouragement to new manufacturing industries. In other circumstances, and especially in dealing with the new ideas which claim patent protection in industrial countries, individual treatment is out of the question; the law specifies the same number of years of protection for all cases, and leaves it to interested parties to determine in the courts what is and is not new. There is much to argue about in the details of patent legisla-

tion—how many years' protection should be given, who should be protected, from what date the protection should run, and so on—but the basic principle, that some new ideas require limited monopolistic protection if they are to be developed at all, is generally accepted.

It is also generally agreed that protection must be limited in time, or it will damage growth. This is based on the belief that men are more likely to make and utilize new discoveries if they are under pressure to do so than if they are not. It is also based on the belief that new firms are more likely to introduce revolutionary ideas than old firms—partly because old firms find it hard to keep vigorous, and partly because old firms are committed, both materially and intellectually to old techniques, and are not so likely to step out in quite new directions which might destroy their existing capital. These beliefs, like most generalizations about human behaviour, are clearly subject to exceptions. Some monopolists are most vigorous in introducing innovations, and some old firms do succeed in keeping remarkably young. All the same, a good proportion of innovation is done by new firms coming on to the market, and another good proportion of what the old firms do results from fear of losing in the competitive race. It is clear that the rate of innovation would be reduced if no new firms were ever allowed to enter the market. Freedom of entry is essential to economic growth. Hence, while it is important to protect the new against the newer, it is equally important to protect the new against the old. Patent protection serves the first purpose. Constant review of patent legislation to prevent its abuse serves the second purpose. And there is also need for general anti-monopoly legislation to prevent powerful firms, or combinations of firms, from using their power to deny new firms access to the market—by such devices as stop lists, exclusive dealing, price wars, price discrimination, the tying up of outlets, the monopolization of sources of supply, and the like. The drafting, the interpretation and the enforcement of such legislation calls for nice judgement, since monopoly is both needed for growth in certain circumstances, and inimical to growth in other circumstances. This branch of the law is therefore frequently among the more perplexing and obscure; but a task is not the less necessary because it is difficult.

Newly developing countries are particularly prone to monopoly because of their shortage of entrepreneurs. The risks of investment are greater in such countries than in the more advanced, since less is known of their problems and potentialities, and the less experienced and financially weaker entrepreneurs tend to be wiped out in recurring crises. One can see this very clearly in colonial trade, which tends to be concentrated in the hands of a few large and wealthy firms; or again in the history of Japan, whose economic life came

fairly quickly under the domination of a few trusts. The successful entrepreneurs tend also not only to dominate the industries in which they start, but also to spread their interests out from one branch of industry to another, partly because this may be less risky than having all one's eggs in one basket, and partly because each enterprise can help the other, either as a supplier or as a customer. Thus in the early stages of economic development it is not unusual to find close ownership links developing between the various sectors of the economy— between banking, insurance, commerce, transport, hotels, newspapers, manufacturing and so on. Doubtless this was the reason why Karl Marx, basing himself on earlier writers and upon his own observations of early nineteenth century capitalism, was convinced that the development of capitalism must be associated with increasing monopolization. The events have not borne out this prophecy (see Chapter V, section 3(*d*)). With the development of the economy there is also an increase in the supply of entrepreneurship, and in its average level of experience. The risk of investment also declines, since more knowledge about the economy accumulates, and since also the problems of the new industries become more generally familiar. It is then not so easy for a few clever minds to dominate the economic scene, and monopoly positions are harder to create and to maintain. In other words, there is an 'infant economy' argument for monopoly parallel to the 'infant industry' argument, but, like the latter, it is an argument of temporary significance only, and is subject to the same limitation that a prolongation of the monopoly may reduce the economy's vitality.

Finally, we should note an argument for monopoly which is based upon the high levels of savings and of profits required by a developing economy. According to this argument, it is desirable that a large share of the national income pass into the pockets of those who will save and invest, rather than of those who will spend it upon consumption. The argument is not, of course, meant to be taken to extremes; consumption is the reward for production, and is a spur to further effort; the point at issue is only one of degree. There has been much disputation about the effects on economic growth of the division of the national income between saving and consumption, springing from the proposition that if consumption is too large investment will be too small, whereas if consumption is too small investment will be discouraged; but there seems no reason to doubt that in the early stages of economic development, at least, very high rates of investment can be maintained for several decades without exhausting investment opportunities. Given that growth is not incompatible with a high level of savings, the next stage of the question is how far large profits are necessary in order to have large

savings. It is true that the non-capitalist classes tend to save very little, but it is not necessary for saving to depend entirely upon individual effort. It is feasible for the government also to act as saver, imposing taxes upon the public, which are used either for capital formation in public utilities, or else for lending to private producers. However, if the government cannot or will not be a productive saver, it is certainly true that a developing economy needs large profits if it is to have an adequate level of savings. Even so, the level of profits does not necessarily depend upon monopoly; monopoly may determine the distribution of profits as between one capitalist and another, rather than the share of profits as a whole in the economy. This was the opinion of most of the classical economists. In the early stages of capitalist development, there are usually large reserves of labour available for employment at a subsistence level of wages; it is only in economies where labour is scarce that the level of real wages depends upon competition. It is therefore possible to argue simultaneously in favour of profits being large in the interest of economic growth, while resisting monopolistic practices on the ground that they discourage innovation. (See Chapter V, sections 2(b) and 3(d) for further discussion of these issues.)

In sum, it is clear that the relationship between monopoly and economic growth does not lend itself to simple conclusions. We may perhaps say that monopoly is more likely to emerge, and more likely to be helpful, in the earlier than in the later stages of economic growth. At the same time, monopoly is dangerous at any stage, because of the cloak which it can throw over inefficiency, and because of the power with which it can resist or suppress innovation. Hence, whatever temporary advantages monopoly may have, it is a sound instinct that causes men everywhere to distrust monopoly, and to seek to restrict its powers.

4. SOME CASES

(a) Religion

We have made several references to religion in this and the preceding chapters; it may be helpful to draw them together in a brief summary of the relations between religion and economic growth.

There are two questions to ask in this context. First, how compatible is economic growth with various types of religious attitude? Secondly, do incompatible beliefs stifle growth, or is it merely that such beliefs flourish where the conditions for economic growth do not exist, and are rejected as soon as growth becomes possible? The first question is much easier to answer than the second; and we will take it first.

We have already discussed at some length the attitudes and institutions which favour growth, and need now only enumerate the main points. As we do this it will become clear that every one of them runs counter to the doctrines of one religion or another, though of course some religions are involved more comprehensively than others. First, growth requires that people should be willing to give their minds to ways of increasing productivity, whether because they desire goods, or because they would value additional leisure. The desire for goods may be due either to taking pleasure in the enjoyment of material things, or to the desire for the social prestige and power which go with wealth; and, correspondingly, growth is more rapid in those societies where wealth is an easy road to high social standing. Some religions do teach that salvation can be reached through the discipline of hard and conscientious work, and do elevate the pursuit of efficiency into a moral virtue. Some forms of Christianity also lay emphasis upon the virtues of thrift, and of productive investment. But most religions also teach that it is better to give the mind to spiritual contemplation than to the ceaseless search for ways of increasing income or reducing cost; and practically all religions discourage the desire for material things.

Next, economic growth demands a willingness to experiment. This is the main way that technology improves, and is also the way that changes are made in social relations and in social attitudes. Willingness to experiment is associated in its turn with a desire to discover the causes of things, and therefore with a belief in rationality. As has been pointed out, mediaeval Christian theologians made much of the doctrine that God Himself is rational, and thus helped in laying the foundations for the revival of scientific enquiry in Western Europe. Very few religions share this attitude to the nature of the universe.

Willingness to experiment involves also one's attitude to the sacredness of the universe. So long as it is sacrilegious to dissect the human body, medicine makes little progress. If animal life is sacred, man may have a hard time competing for existence with the cow, predatory monkeys, rabbits and squirrels, the snake, the insects and the microbes. Similarly, certain religious attitudes are opposed to deliberate family limitation and may result in overpopulation, famine and poverty. Much technological progress springs from an attitude that everything in this world is here for the convenience of man, and can be altered by man in his own interest. This is quite compatible with those religions which put man into the centre of the universe, but it is not compatible with religions in which man is merely one manifestation of the spirit of God—and a minor manifestation, at that.

Economic growth also involves the growth of impersonal economic relationships, in which people do business with other people irrespective of kinship, nationality, or creed. The attitude of a religion to strangers is therefore very important. If the religion encourages people to treat strangers fairly—to give honest service, to keep contracts faithfully, and so on—it will facilitate trade and specialization. Whereas if the religion is exclusive, encourages hatred of unbelievers, and divides people instead of bringing them together, it diminishes economic opportunities.

When we come to social institutions, the role of religion is almost always restrictive. This is because religion almost always puts the virtues of obedience, duty and obligation above all others, and especially above the virtue of justice, which sometimes conflicts with the others—and which is any case mainly a matter for the secular power. Hence religion leans heavily on the side of the *status quo*, in family relations, or in political or religious obligation. Now, as we have seen, economic growth flourishes best if the social institutions are such that men think that they are getting the fruit of their effort (and are not being exploited); if trade and specialization are possible (and economic relations are on an impersonal basis); and if there is freedom to manoeuvre economically (including vertical social mobility). None of these requirements is inconsistent with religious doctrines. Nevertheless, the tendency of religion to favour the *status quo* in social relations makes it usually an obstacle to change in any direction—whether leftwards or rightwards. Religion favours neither growth nor decay, but social stability. If the society is based on slavery, religion teaches the slaves to be obedient; but equally if the society is used to a high level of vertical mobility, the priests will be to the forefront in denouncing attempts to restrict opportunity. This generalization must not be pushed too far. Nearly every religion has its prophets, who from time to time arise and denounce the *status quo*. Their influence tends to be restricted, in comparison with that of the hierarchy, who are usually well in league with the secular power and with the aristocracy of the day; but the existence of the prophetic tradition cannot be ignored, and is sometimes decisive. It would also be a mistake to think of the authoritarian aspect of religion exclusively as hindering change, for it has also an important function of re-integration after change has occurred. Society cannot function without obedience, duty and obligation. As times change our obligations alter, and so do those to whom we owe them. Times of change are therefore frequently accompanied by moral disintegration, since the old duties disappear before the new duties are fully understood. It is the task of the guardians and teachers of morality to create and diffuse new codes appropriate to changed relationships.

This discussion so far has focused on antagonisms between religion and economic growth. The antagonism of religion and change, however, comes into focus only if we concentrate upon the religious views of those who are resisting change. If on the contrary we think of the religion of the people initiating change, religion sometimes appears instead as a strongly innovating force. In the first place, religious leaders are not opposed to every kind of change. It is possible sometimes to enlist their support for innovations which do not conflict with their religious principles—for new seeds, or artificial fertilizers, or community development, or co-operative societies— and then the fact that the innovation has religious support may help it to be adopted all the faster. Religion may appear also as an innovating force even if the old religious leaders oppose the innovation. For the innovators have frequently a new religion of their own, or a new version of an old religion, in which they find guidance, inspiration, or codes of conduct which distinguish them from the rest of the community, and which are linked in their own minds with the innovations they are introducing. Periods of rapid social change are often associated with religious ferment—whether we think of the rise of capitalism in Europe or of contemporary events in Africa—and if we are assessing the role of religion we must take account of the reforming zeal of the new religion just as much as of the resistance offered by the old.

Attention is also often drawn to the prominent role played by certain religious minorities in the development of the countries in which they live, e.g. the Jews, the Huguenots, the Quakers, or the Parsees. Several strands account for this. Members of a religious minority may have a peculiar biological toughness, mental or physical, because the troubles they have had to put up with have weeded out the weaker brethren. Those who are left are keen, alert, schooled in a tradition of industry and self-discipline and well versed in the tricks of self-preservation. They also tend to help each other; and though this would bring ruin to all if the group were below average in success, it brings advancement to all if the group has good fortune or ability above the average. The influence of biology in all this is doubtful, but not the influence of tradition. The religious minority may also be denied political advancement, or entry into some of the higher social professions (military, administration, science, etc.), and may thus have no better outlet for its energies than success in business. Again the religious taboos of the majority may prohibit members of the majority from pursuing certain activities (trade, moneylending) or from handling certain substances or creatures (compost, leather, pigs), or otherwise from exploiting profitable opportunities, and if the minority has different prejudices it may be

able to thrive on the opportunities from which the majority exclude themselves. It is not necessary that the religious precepts of the minority be more favourable to economic growth than those of the majority, at the time when the minority comes into existence, for time itself will effect the difference. As the minority adjusts itself to survival, its religious precepts will also change.

On the other hand, it is certainly not the case that all religious minorities thrive economically. For there are just as many religious minorities which, on the contrary, fall behind the majority in economic achievement, e.g. the Roman Catholics in Canada, or the Moslems in India. A religious minority turns to and shines in economic affairs only in those cases where the majority is more interested in other matters. But in those cases where the majority is materialistically inclined, the religious minority is just as likely to turn away from economic affairs, and in striving to keep its own way of life as distinct as possible, it may cultivate instead the professions or the arts, or may deliberately adopt precepts which are hostile to economic advancement.

This serves also to emphasize the fact that the phenomenon we are discussing is not essentially religious: it applies to minorities, whatever it may be that binds them together. Religion is usually much in evidence in these cases because religion is an important factor in binding minorities together. But the essential factor in the situation is that minorities, whether religious or not, tend to excel not in the matters which the majority choose to cultivate but in those to which they attach less importance.

We may therefore sum up the answers to the first question by saying that some religious codes are more compatible with economic growth than others. If a religion lays stress upon material values, upon work, upon thrift and productive investment, upon honesty in commercial relations, upon experimentation and risk bearing, and upon equality of opportunity, it will be helpful to growth, whereas in so far as it is hostile to these things, it tends to inhibit growth. Of course, the code may not be fully effective; people do not always act in accordance with the religion they profess. Priests are expected to be more strict in their behaviour, and, as was pointed out in the previous chapter, it has been suggested that religions which persuade a large proportion of the people to retire into religious orders (e.g. Tibet) impose a check on growth, whether by deflecting from economic pursuits too many of the more thoughtful people, or by reducing other output too much (assuming that the religious orders are not themselves engaged in agriculture, manufacture and other economic pursuits). Priests apart, people tend to ignore religious precepts which conflict with economic interests. However, religious

teaching is often strong enough to prevent people from doing what it would clearly be in their interest to do—e.g. from killing sacred cows or removing sanctified oppressors.

This brings us to the second question: does religion have an independent effect in shaping economic behaviour, or does religion merely reflect economic conditions? It is obvious that religious beliefs change as economic and social conditions change. Religious doctrines are continuously being re-interpreted, and adjusted to new situations. Hence some people go so far as to argue that religion is neither a hindrance nor a help to change. If the religious doctrines of the day are incompatible with certain changes, this is merely because the underlying economic and social conditions are not yet ready for such changes. When these conditions are ready, the change will be effected, and the religious teachings will be adapted to support the new *status quo*. According to this approach, almost any religion can adapt itself to almost any political or economic revolution. For there will always be among its priests some who are willing to re-interpret its doctrines, whether from conviction, or from frustration, or from ambition. These priests come into power after the revolution, remove their opponents from office, and swing the church into line. Or, in less extreme cases the dogma is modified either because the priests see that the people increasingly ignore it, or because they see for themselves its irrelevance to changing circumstances.

This seems too simple a view. In the first place, even if it were true that religious doctrines always gave way to economic interests, it would still not follow that they do not restrict change, for they might both slow down the rate of change, and also distort its effects. It may be that the doctrines will change in the end, but in the meantime they can hold up change for many decades, or even centuries. After all, social change results mainly from what people do, and this in turn is mainly the result of what they believe. Religion permeates our beliefs because religious instruction (whether formal or informal) begins while we are still on our mothers' knees. What we learn late in life for ourselves we can often unlearn by argument or demonstration, but what we have absorbed in childhood is much harder to cast out. Even if religion could not prevent change altogether, it could certainly reduce its rate and its effects.

More fundamentally we cannot accept the conclusion that it is always economic change which causes religious change, and never religious change that causes economic or social change. It is not true that if economic interest and religious doctrines conflict, the economic interest will always win. The Hindu cow has remained sacred for centuries, although this is plainly contrary to economic interests. Or, to take another example, the failure of Spain to seize

and exploit the economic opportunities presented by the discovery of the New World cannot be explained satisfactorily without taking into account religious beliefs and attitudes which hindered Spain in her competition with other countries. It is possible for a nation to stifle its economic growth by adopting passionately and intolerantly religious doctrines of a kind which are incompatible with growth. Or it is possible, alternatively, for conversion to a new faith to be the spark which sets off economic growth.

(b) Slavery.

The institution of slavery merits special consideration because it has existed through so much of human history. It has some obvious disadvantages, from the point of view of economic growth, but has nevertheless often been the basis of great prosperity. We can now examine this institution in the light of the principles which we have discussed in the preceding sections of this chapter.

Beginning with the counts against slavery, let us take the question of incentives. Slaves are notoriously inefficient and unwilling. A horse, if it is well treated and well cared for, will gladly give all the effort which a well loved master demands. Some slaves are like horses in this respect, but most are not. The difference arises in their humanity; their sense of justice revolts against a system which uses their labour to enrich others; and their sense of freedom chafes against restraint. Even if the majority of the slaves would rest content, there is always a minority who feel their humanity strongly, and who communicate these feelings to the others. If the slave is in close personal contact with a master, personal ties may smooth the relationship; but if slaves are employed in large scale enterprises, where they see much of each other, and little of the master, it is certain that they will resent their condition, and will react by doing as little as they can. There ensues a trial of strength between the masters and the slaves, in which each side probes to discover how far it can go. Out of this may come an 'equilibrium', in which it is tacitly agreed what are to be the 'traditional' rights and duties of each party. The slaves then do as little as they can, without incurring punishment, within the limits of this tradition, and no more.

In some systems all that the slave produces belongs to his master, whereas in other systems either law or custom allows the slave some free time and property which he may use on his own account. In the latter case the slave usually works much more diligently and effectively on his own account than he does when working in the master's time. Some masters, observing this, may restrict the slave's free time, alleging that the slave is exhausted by it, and unable to fulfil his duties. Others find it pays them to convert their right to

labour into a percentage of the slave's produce, so that slavery may shade, imperceptibly, into a system of metayage. Certainly slaves work more effectively if they have merely to pay a percentage to their masters than they do if all that they produce is on the master's account.

Secondly, slavery affects not only the slaves, but also the mentality of the slave-owners themselves. For the slave-owners are most likely to acquire an attitude towards work which is damaging to growth. Work is held in contempt, being fit only for slaves. Even the management of slaves is handed over to hired managers. The slave-owners, men and women, give themselves over to idleness, or to activities, however noble, which are not connected with making a living. They migrate from their estates to live in fashionable cities, and so on. They therefore lose the capacity to seek out new economic opportunities and to benefit from them; or even the capacity to adjust to changing conditions, so as to avoid disaster. The founders of the slave economy may have been men of vigour, who created a structure which produced great wealth in the conditions of their time; but their grandchildren are very different, and, as conditions change, the economy steadily decays.

The slave economy suffers also from lack of vertical mobility, and this is particularly damaging because of the effect which slavery has on reducing the will to work of the aristocracy. In a free economy the leading classes, in government, or business, or intellectual life, are constantly refreshing themselves by recruiting into their ranks clever people born in the lower classes. The slave economy deprives itself of this advantage unless it encourages manumission. Some slave societies do make it easy for slaves to buy their freedom, or encourage slave-owners to grant freedom; while others, especially if the supply of slaves is running short, are hostile to manumission. Slave societies differ also in the extent to which descent from slavery is a handicap to freedmen or to their descendants. If the slaves differ in race from their masters, it is difficult for their descendants, even after many generations, to be accepted at the highest social levels. The importance of vertical mobility depends on how numerous the slave-owners are, relatively to the number of leadership positions to be filled. For, if they are sufficiently numerous, they will provide their own layer of classes, with adequate mobility to keep the topmost classes vigorous, though of course the community as a whole will progress less rapidly if it is failing to make the best use of the talents of the great numbers kept in slavery.

Next, if slave labour is abundantly available, there is no incentive to invent or to use labour saving methods, and so we do not get economic growth, defined as growth of output per unit of work,

though of course total output will expand if more work is done. Thus it has been suggested that Greek science in its later phases invented toys rather than useful machines, and that this was because the existence of slavery removed the incentive to use machines. Both suggestions have been disputed. In any case, this line of reasoning does not work in a slave economy run on commercial lines, as were the plantations of the New World. For in those circumstances it pays just as much to economize slave labour as to economize any other cost of production. The incentive to adopt labour saving methods exists in slavery so long as one can sell the extra produce that results, or can consume it oneself, or can sell the slaves whose services are no longer required. These conditions are not fulfilled in economies where the slave-owners already have all the slaves they need for their purposes, or are not operating slavery on strictly commercial lines. The existence of domestic, as distinct from commercial slavery, probably discourages invention. In such societies the slaves, if they were free, might invent or adopt new techniques to ease their labour or increase their surplus; the difference, in slavery, is that new techniques are not adopted merely because they ease the labour or improve the lot of the worker.

Again, a slave society is less flexible than a free society, and is therefore less able to meet changing circumstances. For example a change in circumstances may make it necessary for a community to alter its way of earning a living; the demand for its major export may have altered, or the supply may be affected by the sudden onset of some new plant disease, so that new industries must be started, a new structure of production and distribution evolved, and new skills learnt. At first glance it may seem that the slave economy should be more flexible than the free, since the slave-owners have the legal power to effect large changes by command. The power of the slave-owners, however, is in fact restricted by the traditions which have grown up to regulate their relations with the slaves. For example, the tradition may stipulate that a house slave cannot be sent to work in the fields, or that a slave trained as a carpenter must not be asked to work in a quarry. Precisely because slavery does not rest on contract it comes to rest instead on concepts involving what is fair as between master and slave; it is a status economy, and is accordingly less flexible than an economy based on terminable contracts. Again, flexibility is reduced by the ties between master and slave. In a changing economy different enterprises are affected differently; some should contract, and others expand. If there are good slave markets it is possible for the expanding enterprises to buy slaves from those which are contracting, but this process is hindered by the personal ties between the slaves and their masters, and also by the

fact that since the ownership of slaves carries social and political prestige and privilege, masters are reluctant to part with their slaves. The difference in flexibility is only a difference of degree. All economies are inflexible, and slow to react to changing conditions. There seems however some ground for thinking that a free economy will react more quickly than a slave economy, and if this is so the slave economy is less likely to survive and to grow, if conditions are changing all the time.

On the other hand, to say that slavery is inefficient is not to deny that it may be the only way of developing certain industries in particular places. What we are comparing is the work of free men and of slaves in the same place at the same time. The comparison is not, however, valid if slaves can be made available at that place while free men cannot. The huge sugar industry of the West Indies could not have been developed in the seventeenth and eighteenth centuries without slavery, since free men were not available. And even if free men are available, in the sense that they exist in the country, they may not be available, in the sense of being willing to work in sufficient numbers in the proposed industry, at the wages proposed—particularly if they have all the land they want, and get from it a standard of living which they consider to be sufficient. Slavery is essentially appropriate to conditions of labour scarcity; if labour is plentiful in relation to resources, it is usually cheaper to hire free and willing labour for wages. And even where the scarcity of free labour makes slavery profitable, some types of production are much more appropriate for slavery than others. Because slave labour is unwilling, it is appropriate only where it can be easily supervised. In agriculture, for example, it is appropriate only to those crops which have a relatively high labour requirement per acre, such that a single overseer can keep his eye on a large number of slaves—to sugar, or cotton, or tobacco, or tea, but not to wheat or coffee or cattle ranching. This is also the reason why mines and factories and ships propelled by oars have been associated with slavery even in circumstances where other occupations were left to free labour; the fact that large numbers of persons are concentrated in a small space facilitates supervision in these occupations. Another consequence of the unwillingness of slave labour is that it is inappropriate to occupations where the worker has to exercise a craft skill responsibly. Some domestic slaves, well treated by their masters, have been superb craftsmen. It will often be found that where slaves are practising a craft the master is careful to share the slave's earnings with him on a proportionate basis, or even to allow the slave to keep everything earned over a stipulated sum, so that he shall have an economic incentive to work well at his craft. In general, because slave

labour is inefficient, it cannot compete with free labour except in conditions where free labour is scarce.

To say that slavery is inefficient is also not to deny that a high level of civilization can be erected on this basis. The produce of the slaves can maintain a leisure class, which, as in Ancient Greece, may give itself to philosophy, to sculpture, and to the other liberal arts, and which may paradoxically pioneer in freeing the human spirit and the human mind. Slavery does not always have this effect; the planter civilization in the West Indies was universally despised, and though the culture of the Southern States was at a higher level, in general the riches produced by slavery in the New World were frittered away in luxurious idleness, without contributing to human progress. Moreover, even where slavery is the basis of a vigorous civilization, the benefits of this civilization are narrowly restricted; the slavers benefit, but not the slaves. There are always those who argue that most men are better off if they are well cared for as slaves than they would be if left to their own ill-directed devices; just as some argue that the domestic horse is better off than the wild horse. We need not pursue the argument here, since our interest is not in the desirability of one way of life rather than another, but in the mechanism of economic growth.

It should be noted, finally, that a slave economy, however prosperous it may be for a time, is usually threatened with decline because a slave population usually does not replace itself. A slave economy prospers so long as a cheap source of slaves is available from outside, and it begins to decline as soon as this source is cut off. Slavery flourishes, therefore, so long as there are continuous wars or slave raids, in which large numbers are captured and sold into slavery. But the system declines when peace is established, or the slave trade abolished. This was alike the experience of Rome, whose slave economy began to decline as soon as peace was established on the frontiers, and also of Jamaica, whose decline began not with the abolition of slavery in 1834, but with the abolition of the slave trade nearly thirty years earlier.

The cutting off of the stream of slaves must at once cause the slave population to decline. For, since more men are enslaved than women, even if the women had enough girl children to replace themselves (which they do not), the slave population must decline as the surplus men die off. Then after a generation a new equilibrium becomes possible based upon natural reproduction, with male and female numbers roughly equal, but even then the slave population does not reproduce itself.

If we take a country which has had no immigration of slaves for such a long time that all its slaves were born within the country, only about a third of the slave population will be available for work. This

is about the proportion which the West Indian sugar planters reported just before slavery was abolished there. The rest of the slaves are children and mothers looking after their children and their husbands; and there is also usually a large number claiming to be sick or otherwise taking advantage of loopholes which the system has for avoiding work. This low proportion should not occasion surprise when we remember that even in free societies, the 'gainfully occupied', as defined by the census, are usually only thirty-five to forty per cent of the population.

Now, if the slaves were allowed to live together in families, they would have as much chance of replacing themselves as would a free population—possibly more chance, since they might get better medical care, and would probably also work less. Slaves are not, however, usually allowed to live together in families, for this imposes upon the slave-owner the necessity of maintaining two ineffectives for every effective slave. Many slave-owners therefore keep only adult male slaves, who are not encouraged to marry. Women slaves are unpopular; they are not encouraged to have children, and if they do have children they are not allowed enough time to look after them. So the birth rate is low, and infant and child mortality are high; thus the slave population fails to reproduce itself. Naturally the big plantations fare better than the small ones, since it is easier to maintain a proper balance of men, women and children in a large establishment than in a small one. The smaller establishments therefore die out before the larger ones, and, as in the later Roman Empire, inequality increases. But even the big establishments will die out unless they approach the problem of breeding new slaves from its commercial angle.

Exactly the same fate would befall an economy based on the labour of horses if each owner of horses were expected to keep horses in the right balance of male and female, adult and child. This does not happen because in a horse economy it pays to specialize in breeding horses for sale. So also a slave economy maintains itself without immigration only if some slave-owners specialize in breeding slaves for sale. This system was adopted in the Southern United States after the abolition of the slave trade, but it is the least popular aspect of slavery, since it involves separating wives and husbands, and children and parents, and denying all the emotional attachments which we consider to be proper to sexual relations between human beings. Slave farms are not therefore usual in slave economies, or if they exist, are usually not numerous enough to cope with the problem of maintaining the supply of slaves. Accordingly, in most slave societies the economy is doomed as soon as the external supply of slaves is cut off.

In this respect serfdom is much superior to slavery, and this is no doubt one of the main reasons why slavery gives place to serfdom when the external source of slaves dries up. Serfs have the right to marry, and they live in this respect much as free men do. Serfs have also usually the right to some free time, and also to some land to cultivate on their own. Some serfs are also on a share-cropping or metayer basis. In the most advanced stage of serfdom, the serf is tied to the soil in the sense that he cannot move to some other place without the lord's permission; but his obligation may be only to pay a fixed rent, and he has then every incentive to produce more than this on his own account. A society based on serfdom can last for centuries, but a society based on slavery must begin to decline as soon as its external source of slaves is extinguished.

(c) The Family

The family is such an important social institution that it is not surprising that it raises nearly all the problems we have already discussed. There are questions of incentive, of specialization, of vertical mobility and of access to resources. We shall begin by considering the family so to speak horizontally, that is to say, the relationship between one branch and another, then we shall consider the status of women, and finally we shall come to the generations. We are leaving population problems for Chapter VI.

In primitive society the concept of the family is usually very wide. A man acknowledges ties not only with his parents and his wife and children, but also with a wide range of cousins, who may number as many as five hundred. Within this group varying degrees of communism may be practised; land may be jointly owned and operated; and all members of the family have recognized claims upon the family for subsistence.

It seems to be the case that as a community grows more wealthy, its family concept narrows. The extended family is essentially a means of social security, appropriate to a society living on a low subsistence level. At low levels, members of the family must rally round to help those in distress; and the wider the family circle, the more effective is is the insurance system. As the standard of income rises, however, individuals are better able to save and to provide for themselves against misfortune. There is also greater difference in wealth and income between the various members of the family. Government is better organized, and is beginning to assume responsibility for helping the aged or the destitute. And social relations are founded more on the idea of contract than that of status, so that men in wealthier societies are more prone to deny that they have moral obligations to distant relatives. So, in general, the more advanced the society is

H

materially, the smaller the number of persons whom the income earner will recognize as belonging to his family, in the sense of benefiting automatically from increases in his income, or even in the narrower sense of having some claim on his income if they fall destitute. Family claims are also easier to press in small communities, where everybody knows everybody else, and where therefore public opinion may force the richer to help the poorer members of the family. Whereas in the largest communities, where men do not know their next door neighbour, one can ignore one's family and live without caring what their friends think about it. This also is related to the average income of the society, since the size of towns and villages is related to the wealth of the country.

The extended family system has tremendous advantages in societies living at a subsistence level, but it seems not to be appropriate to societies where economic growth is occurring. In such societies it is almost certainly a drag on effort. For growth depends on initiative, and initiative is likely to be stifled if the individual who makes the effort is required to share the reward with many others whose claims he does not recognize. Where the extended family exists, any member of the family whose income increases may be besieged by correspondingly increased demands for support from a large number of distant relations. This is at any time a deterrent to making superior effort, and it is especially so at times when the family concept is narrowing, and the community is passing from wider to narrower recognition, since it is then that men are least likely to accept claims which they would previously have taken for granted. There are many reports from Asia and from Africa of able men who have refused promotion because the material benefit would accrue mostly to relatives whose moral claims they do not recognize. Or, if we look at the matter from the other angle, the system is a drag on initiative because it provides everyone with automatic insurance against want, thereby diminishing mobility, thrift and enterprise.

A strong sense of family obligation, even when genuinely felt, may also be a bar to success in other ways. It may cause a man to appoint relatives to jobs for which they are unsuited, and it may even happen that others refrain from appointing him to positions which he could well serve, because they know that he will thereupon appoint unsuitable relatives to posts at his command. In primitive societies men fear the effects of witchcraft if they offend their families, and it may be fear, rather than affection, which drives them to nepotism. Sometimes, of course, a member of one's family is the best person to appoint, either because of his talents, or even merely because one is certain of his upbringing and can have confidence in him. But this

is not always so. Another difficulty is that of managing family businesses, where several members are involved. If they have confidence
in each other, and each pulls his weight, the family sentiment may be
a source of strength; but it is frequently a source of weakness. Often
in countries where family ties are strong, the most enterprising and
successful individuals are those who have no family obligations, and
who are therefore able to stand by themselves.

Against these deficiencies of the family sentiment in business one
must set its strength. In societies where men cannot rely on strangers
to give faithful service, the family may be the most appropriate unit
for large scale enterprise. For example, in some kinds of business it is
useful to be able to set up branches in many towns, or suburbs, or
countries, e.g. in banking, in the chain store type of retail trade, in
wholesale distribution, etc. In these circumstances a family which has
many brothers, or closely related cousins, may be at a considerable
advantage, since the brothers can trust each other more than they
could trust branch managers who were not related; and since, even if
there is dishonesty, the money will remain in the family. Or the inter-
dependence may be not of branches in the same trade, but of different
trades and professions, each brother being able to support the others'
businesses to some extent. In much the same way closely knit groups
of immigrants or religious minorities can, by putting business in each
other's way, and by lending each other support in time of crisis,
strengthen the position of the group as a whole, and help its members
to make greater economic advancement than they would if their
special relationship to each other was not allowed to influence their
business. Of course these kinship or other obligations are not specially
helpful if the group is not on the average better favoured economically
than the rest of the community, and they may even drag the group
down if members are below the average in competitive ability, since
the more fortunate members will be put at a disadvantage by their
obligation to carry the more than average burdens and defections of
the rest. On the other hand a talented family may be greatly advantaged by sticking together. When one reads accounts of the early
economic development of any community, there are always a few
talented families who stand out by the wide range of their activities—
whether one thinks of Italian bankers in the fourteenth century or of
Indian or Japanese industrialists in the twentieth century. In these
early conditions it is possible for a talented family to conduct
business on a scale which is not open to any other kind of organization. This advantage is lessened as administrative techniques improve, and as it becomes easier to appoint strangers to managerial
positions in fair confidence that they will not simply embezzle the
funds.

We turn next to consider the part of women in economic activities. The attitude of men towards women's work varies from community to community. In some communities men try to assure recognition of their social status by withdrawing their women from working; they deliberately keep their wives and daughters idle, and surrounded by servants, to show that they are men of substance. Some of these women do useful unpaid social work; otherwise this form of snobbery lowers the output of women, even though it may raise the output of some men who have to work harder in order to foot the bill. In modern western societies middle and upper class women have had to fight a 'battle' in order to get the right to work. But in many other communities it is men who have lived in relative idleness, while women have had to work very hard, often in cultivating the ground as well as in preparing food and weaving clothes for their husbands.

Restrictions on the work women may do are also everywhere a barrier to economic growth. In some primitive communities women are not allowed to work except within the household or on its farm. This increases the degree of self-sufficiency of each household, and so reduces trade and the opportunities for specialization. It is indeed, very marked that economic growth and a transference of women's work from the household to the market go closely hand in hand. As income per head grows there is an even more rapid growth of such industries as dressmaking, hairdressing and catering, not to speak of the education of the young in schools, which is a substitute for education at home. The association is not to be explained away simply by the refusal of statisticians to include housework in calculating the national income, for there is also a real increase both in the quantity and in the quality of the output, which results from specialization. Growth is restricted if custom requires that women may work only at home; or that if they work outside their homes they may only be domestic servants, or typists, or crowded into some other narrow range of jobs. Often one of the quickest ways of increasing the national output is to open factories offering light jobs of the kind which women do most easily; many communities that are short of male labour have found in this a chance for further expansion. This may increase output not only directly but also indirectly. For example, some farmers, e.g. in Africa, insist on processing badly at home crops which could be processed more efficiently in central factories, because their women folk would have too little to do if the processing were transferred to the factory. Creating more outside jobs for women would thus help to improve the processing of crops. Or, again, in some African communities women spend hours pounding grain by hand. If more paid jobs were available to them outside their households they would soon insist that the grinding of grain should hence-

forth be done mechanically. To create more paid jobs for women is the surest way simultaneously to raise their status, to reduce their drudgery, and to raise the national output.

In some communities the sense of the continuity of the family through the generations is very strong, even, in extreme cases, to the point of ancestor worship. It is arguable whether this is good or bad for economic growth. It has certain advantages. Presumably one acquires a certain sense of confidence from knowing that one belongs to a family which can be traced back through several generations. The family tradition is also emphasized in one's youth, and if this includes some special skill, or adventurousness or character trait, it may be preserved and developed to a greater extent than if family traditions did not exist. Thus the British Navy believes that sons of 'naval families' make better sailors, on the average, than do other recruits, and there may well be professions where the young person who grows up in their atmosphere from birth is better qualified than the person whose parents belong to some other profession. The sense of belonging to a line of generations may also affect one's sense of property. One may feel that one is merely a temporary trustee for what one has inherited, and may be careful to preserve it, and even to improve it through one's own effort and saving.

But there are also disadvantages. Too much looking backwards upon history is bad for a community which has new challenges to meet, different from those which faced its fathers. The traditional patterns may have been excellent for their times, but may be most unsuitable for the present, with its different problems. When a community becomes more conscious of its past than anxious to experiment with its future, it is doomed. A strong sense of family tradition also interferes with social mobility. People of 'no family' do not get chances commensurate with their talents, and people of 'good family' but no talent get too much chance of making a mess. Occupational mobility also is diminished if tradition insists that sons must follow in their father's footsteps. The disadvantages of too close a tie between generations show themselves in their extreme form in the caste system, which prevents vertical and social mobility by requiring each individual to follow in his father's footsteps, or else to become a farmer. This is one of the surest ways of preventing change, and therefore economic growth.

When we were analysing the extended family horizontally, we saw it mainly as a drag upon effort, at any rate in so far as men are called upon to meet claims of distant relations for whom they have no affection. When we come, however, to the claims of children upon their parents, we may take it for granted that the family serves to some extent as a spur to greater effort. This spur is at its most effect-

ive when men are ambitious for their families, desiring that their descendants should have a higher social status than that into which they themselves were born.

The desire to raise one's family's social status feeds upon the opportunity to do so. This desire cannot exist in impoverished villages where every farmer lives at subsistence level, since the chance of raising one's material status is small. It cannot exist if legal or customary barriers, caste or colour, prevent men from rising from one class into another. And it cannot mean much in a stagnant or declining economy. Some social mobility is found even in stagnant economies, but the greatest mobility is found where output is growing rapidly. For these are the circumstances in which a middle class grows most rapidly, recruiting people from below to be administrators or technicians or business or professional men. And it is these circumstances which provide the greatest opportunities, whether for making money, or for success in other directions. The desire to 'found a family' is thus strongest and most effective in economies where growth is taking place; it is least felt in stagnant economies. This is just another of the many respects in which the forces which make for growth feed upon each other. Once growth has begun men become more ambitious for their families, and may even adopt family limitation in order to have no more children than they can afford to establish well in life. Then the spread of this outlook itself speeds up the rate of growth.

The concept of founding a family has meaning only in communities where the family is elementary and patrilineal, and not in communities where it is extended or matrilineal. Since what is implied is raising the social status of the next generation above the social status of the present generation, one cannot think in these terms unless one means by the next generation only a few direct descendants and not all the hundreds of cousins who can make claim to family relationship. The extended family is thus ruled out. As for the matrilineal family, it is possible to conceive of a man working very hard in order to make his sister's children rich rather than his own. But the matrilineal family does not survive easily in conditions of rapid economic or other change, since change usually implies mobility, and mobility usually strengthens the conjugal and patrilineal ties. A man who moves takes with him his wife and his children, not his sister and her children, and so the matrilineal ties are weakened in any society where men begin to move about in search of fortune.

It is not clear how important the right to bequeath one's property is as a spur to effort even in elementary patrilineal families. Ambition to found a family varies in different communities, and is not always greatest in those which display the greatest rate of growth. For

example, many rich Americans use their money not to endow their families but to found educational trusts, or for other charitable purposes; a few even deliberately leave little to their sons so as not to spoil their characters. It is probably true that rich Englishmen, when disposing of their wealth, leave a greater proportion to their families, on the average, and a smaller proportion to philanthropic bodies. This is because the institution of the family counts for more in England than it does in the great American cities. All the same, Americans find quite enough spurs to effort in other directions, including their desire to enjoy a high standard of living, and their desire to have power and prestige for themselves.

However, even though the importance of the right to bequeath as a spur cannot be exactly assessed, there can be no doubt that it is a spur, and that the restrictions which modern states are increasingly putting upon this right—and especially the high death duties—somewhat diminish the incentive to make a fortune. On the other hand, we must at the same time consider the effect of the inheritance of wealth upon the property inherited, upon the heirs, and upon the rest of the community.

One of the disputed points is the effect of inheritance upon the care of property. The son of the founder of a business or an estate is not necessarily the best person to look after the property. On the contrary, institutions founded on inheritance do not survive as long, or show as much vitality, as those which recruit their leaders afresh in each generation. Some of the vitality of the Roman Catholic Church is no doubt due to the fact that its bishops are made, not born. And the strength of the Ottoman Empire is often traced to the system of Janissaries, recruited afresh in each generation. Some people regret that in modern large business corporations the family connection is often small, but it may well be a source of strength that business corporations increasingly recruit their leaders without reference to family connections. On the other hand, the system by which property passes automatically to the next generation has also its advantages; it is more certain; it therefore permits the successor to be trained in anticipation; and it is simple.

The effect of inheritance depends also on whether property passes exclusively to the eldest son, or on how it is divided up between the members of the family. Primogeniture keeps the property intact, and this is specially important where there are economies of scale, or in those farming communities where holdings are already so small that further fragmentation would be uneconomic; but the point is not so important if it is possible for the property to be operated jointly by the heirs without subdivision. On the other hand, primogeniture helps to maintain an unequal distribution of property, and may also

be unfair to the rest of the family. The eldest son is also not always the most competent son, and this is recognized in systems (political more usually than economic) where the heir is not the eldest son but the son designated for the purpose. Some economists have argued for primogeniture on the ground that the system forces younger sons to be industrious; and others on the ground that by driving younger sons of the nobility down into the middle class it prevents the classes from despising each other, and thus assures greater social cohesion and mobility; but if these arguments were pushed to their logical conclusions, they would support the abolition of property inheritance altogether.

Against the incentive which the right to bequeath is to the maker of the fortune we must also set the extent to which the effort of the heirs is diminished. Heirs are sometimes inspired by the example of their forefathers; and may treat their inheritance as a trust which they are challenged not only to maintain but also to increase. But they more often react in the opposite way. Taking them on the average, heirs would almost certainly lead more useful lives if their inheritances did not shield them from the necessity for hard work.

The inheritance of property also diminishes vertical mobility and enterprise. This can be seen very clearly in those agricultural communities where all the land belongs to a few families, and where all the remaining families are condemned from one generation to another to remain at the bottom of the social scale. The effect of the inheritance of property is that each generation starts with the dice loaded heavily in favour of a few of its members, whose own abilities are not necessarily superior, and are often not as well cultivated because inheritance removes the need to make the best use of one's talents. There would probably be greater economic growth in a community where all started equal, and greater growth still in a community where the dice were loaded deliberately in favour of those with superior talents.

(d) The Organization of Agriculture

The laws and customs governing the ownership and use of land are of the greatest economic importance, especially in the poorer communities, where agriculture is the principal form of activity. At the same time, land plays a large part in determining political and social status, and so the rules and customs are seldom framed with economic considerations primarily in view. From the point of view of economic growth, we are interested in the tenure of agricultural land, in the size of farms, and in the relationship between these matters and incentives, capital formation, and technical innovation.

Take first the question of communal tenure of land. This term is

used in three distinct senses. The first sense, in which it is used here, is the case where several people have the right to use the same piece of land, each on his own account—e.g. to pasture his cattle upon it, or to cut firewood. This is to be distinguished from the second sense, where people work together on the same land, under a single authority, and pool the proceeds. This is co-operative or collective farming; we have discussed its main problems earlier in this chapter (section 1(c)), and shall revert to them at the end of this sub-section. Thirdly, there is the case where each person has a right to exclusive use of a particular piece of land, but where his rights to dispose of the land are restricted on the theory that the land belongs to the chief or to the tribe. Since the use and disposal of land is subject to restriction in practically every community, the differences between 'communal' tenure in this sense and 'freehold' tenure are differences only of degree. If we treat as 'individual' tenure (using the word individual to represent the family) all those cases where the individual has exclusive *use* of the land, then individual tenure of land may be said to be almost universal outside Soviet Russia, and what we have to say will relate mainly to this form of tenure. But first we must say a word about communal tenure in the first sense distinguished above, where there is communal use without collective management or pooling of the proceeds.

There can be no doubt as to the superiority of individual over communal tenure. This shows itself in its effects both on investment and on innovation. If large numbers of people are free to use the same piece of land, each for his own purposes, each has an incentive to take what he can out of the land without putting anything back. In these conditions, as soon as land begins to be scarce, it begins also to deteriorate through over-cropping, or excessive pasturage, or failure to take appropriate measures for soil conservation. It pays no individual to invest in improving the land, in fertilizers, in drainage, or in improved grasses. Trees will be planted if the rights of individuals to their fruit is recognized, as it usually is, but trees will not be planted for general purposes, such as for shade or for afforestation. Communal tenures worked passably in Africa so long as populations were very small in relation to land, but population pressure everywhere causes such tenures to destroy the land. Investment apart, communal tenure is a handicap to innovation. Livestock cannot be bred selectively unless they are segregated and their mating controlled; neither is it convenient to experiment with new agricultural methods in circumstances where communal activity imposes its own routines. These are the reasons why communal tenures are disappearing rapidly in places where they flourished fifty years ago. Many people regret their passing for sentimental reasons, but there is no reason to doubt their incompatibility with economic development.

When we turn to individual tenure, we find that throughout most of recorded history most farmers have held their land under a contract of tenancy. We begin therefore with the tenant's relationship with his landlord, which involves questions of compensation for displacement, of rights of tenure, and of the form and amount of rent to be paid.

The need for compensation arises out of the principle that the tenant must be assured the produce of his effort. If the tenant is to make any investment in the land he must be assured that in case of dispossession he will be compensated for all improvements he has made whose benefit is not yet exhausted. Otherwise he will not plant trees, or construct substantial buildings, or make improvements in drainage, or effect any other investment. The corollary of such protection is that the landlord must give his prior assent to improvements for which protection is claimed. In most advanced countries the law ensures this protection, but in primitive countries such provision is the exception rather than the rule, with the effect that tenants are careful not to invest in improving the land, and will even permit it to lose fertility, if the landlord allows them to get away with this.

Many countries are not content to protect unexhausted improvements; they also give legal security of tenure. At the least they prescribe minimum periods of notice, while in more extreme cases the law gives the tenant a right to remain on the land so long as he maintains good husbandry (e.g. in the United Kingdom), and may even ensure to his heir a right of succeeding to the tenancy, if reasonably competent. The way such legislation works depends very much upon the complexion of the tribunals established to administer it; in 'democratic' countries it becomes almost impossible to get rid even of a bad tenant, unless he is obviously ruining the land, whereas in 'reactionary' countries the law is operated to afford little protection even to the best tenants. The point of such legislation is to give tenants sufficient security to justify their investing in long-term improvements. There is also an argument against giving too much security, based upon the desire to ensure mobility of land, but we shall take this up later when we discuss freehold tenure by farmers, to which it also applies.

By the form of the rent we mean whether it is a fixed or a proportional payment. A fixed payment may bear heavily on small farmers in years when conditions are bad, even if the rent is quite bearable when good and bad years are taken together. The rent may be fixed in money or in kind. A rent fixed in kind bears more heavily if bad conditions are due to poor harvests, and a rent fixed in money bears more heavily if bad conditions are due to low prices; since farmers suffer from both, there is not much to choose between money rents

and rents in kind, except in time of war, when farmers whose rents are fixed in money gain handsomely, at least for the time being. If we take the world as a whole, however, most rents are not fixed, but proportional, the farmer paying the landlord a proportion of his crop (or receipts) which may vary from one quarter to one half, according to the scarcity of land.

Proportional rents are popular with poor farmers because they are less burdensome than fixed rents when conditions are bad. They also give more to the landlord when conditions are good—but one can afford to give him more then, and in any case the amount evens out over good and bad years. Proportional rents, however, are usually attacked by economists because they lessen the incentive of the farmer to adopt improvements. For a given improvement to be worth while at the margin to the farmer it must yield twice as much if the rent is one half as it would have to yield if the rent were a fixed amount. This pre-supposes that the farmer bears all the cost of the improvement. In more advanced systems of metayage or sharecropping (as proportional rents are called), the landlord bears part of the cost of improvements; or the contract provides that the rent is to be adjusted if the tenant undertakes improvements. But in less advanced countries there is usually no such provision, and the system of proportional rents certainly diminishes the farmers' incentive to adopt improvements.

The amount of the rent is in most countries a source of great complaint and agitation. What the landlord gives in return varies from country to country. In England the contract usually imposes upon the landlord the duty to provide the permanent buildings, and to maintain the fixed capital; it may even require him to provide some of the working capital as well. At one time English rents were high enough to compensate the landlord for the cost of these duties, and also to leave him a surplus, which was the 'pure' rent due to the scarcity of good land, but in these days rents are so low that there is seldom any surplus above the cost of maintaining the fixed capital of the farm. At the other extreme we find that in most primitive countries the landlord has no duties whatever to the land; he merely collects rents. He may of course perform some social functions—he may be the equivalent of a magistrate, or a policeman, or a district administrator, or a priest—and if he were not remunerated out of rents, he or someone else might have to be remunerated out of taxes or in some other way. But as far as the land is concerned, its productive capacity would not be reduced if the rent were kept by the farmer (i.e. if the landlords were 'liquidated' and the land passed into the freehold ownership of the farmers), or if the rent were paid instead to the state (the state often collects a rent anyway in the form

of direct taxes levied on the land or on the farmer). Indeed, if rents were reduced, or abolished, the productive capacity of the land might be increased, since the farmer could now afford to save more, and to invest more in the improvement of the land. In those countries where landlords take fifty per cent of the farmers' output and do nothing for them in return, it is hard to believe that agricultural productivity would not be greatly increased if this incubus were removed from the farmers' backs.

In many countries there is a demand that landlordism be abolished altogether, and that farmers should own the land they work. This demand should not be confused with other demands for altering the size of farms. Some reformers want to increase the number of farms, by breaking up large estates and distributing the land as small farms; others wish to do the opposite, namely to reduce the number of small farms, by persuading or compelling the farmers to join collective farms. We shall discuss later problems of size. Our present concern is simply with freehold ownership on the one hand, as against tenancy on the other. Though much of the demand for land reform is associated with demands for changing the number of farms, there is also, especially in Asia, a considerable land reform movement which is confined to a demand for abolishing landlords and converting tenancy into ownership.

The effects of this conversion depend to some extent on the payment terms on which it is done; on the amount of compensation received by the landlords, and on the size of the payments which the farmers are required to make for the land which they now acquire. Apart from the question of compensation, however, there are many other issues involved in comparing tenancy and ownership. In fact, many people argue that a system of peasant ownership of land is not in the interest of economic growth. They consider that it reduces the the mobility of land, and that it is associated with bad husbandry, with fragmentation and with excessive indebtedness. They therefore prefer that small farmers should be tenants only, and should be subject to controls, whether the landlord be a private owner, or a government agency. In fact, as we shall see, most of the desired controls can be exercised just as well over owners as over tenants: in fact, if controls are adequately applied, on the one hand to give the tenant security, or on the other hand to enforce good husbandry upon the proprietor, the economic distinctions between tenancy and ownership largely disappear.

Let us begin with the mobility of land. As we saw earlier, some people object to legislation giving security of tenure to tenants whose husbandry is good on the ground that this makes the agricultural economy less flexible. They argue that the landlord, who is presumed

to be interested in seeing the land put to its most profitable use, should be able to change tenants freely as conditions change. Conditions may make it desirable to change from arable to livestock; or to alter the size of the farming unit; or for some other reason to change over to a new tenant more capable of coping with the new situation, and this may be frustrated if the sitting tenant is protected. For the same reason the same people object to freehold tenure of land by small farmers, because they believe that such farmers are slow to react to changing conditions, and believe that response would be quicker if landlords could bring it about by changing tenants. The argument depends for its validity first of all on the assumption that landlords are keen and knowledgeable agriculturists, always looking out for better ways of using the land, and while this may be true of some, it is probably true of most that they are absentees knowing not much more about the land than the amount of rent it yields. And, in any case, the argument could be extended to say that no one should ever own the resource he uses, since resources are more likely to move into the hands most capable of using them if the resources are owned by people who specialize in moving them from hirer to hirer at short notice. One should not even own one's house, presumably, since there is always someone else who could make better use of it. The answer is surely that the owner is always open to receive offers. If someone else thinks he can make better use of the resource, let him offer an attractive price for it. Our experience is, indeed, that land changes hands much more easily if the ownership of land is widely diffused than if land is owned by a few powerful families who regard it as a source of political power and of prestige rather than just as a source of income. Easy access to land requires wide distribution of land ownership.

There is more substance in the claim that freehold owners may exhaust the soil if not controlled. In many parts of the world small farmers are engaged in practices which impoverish the soil. This is not usual in those parts of Asia which have been so thickly populated for so many centuries that the farmers have an acute sense of the importance of soil fertility. But it is common in places where the transition is being made from abundance of land to scarcity of land, especially in North America and in Africa, and where the farmers have not yet been forced into permanent settlement on the same area of land, with the maintenance of soil fertility as a prime condition of existence. In these conditions reformers are particularly keen to be able to control the farmers' practices, especially with regard to soil conservation, and to crop rotations and fallows. They are aware that the landlord exercises such controls in the more advanced leasehold systems, and they therefore hanker after such systems. It is doubtful how far it is

desirable to try to improve farming practices by compulsion rather than by education. But, in so far as it is practicable it can be done as well by law as by trying to introduce a highly advanced type of leasehold contract into conditions to which it is foreign. Bad farming can be made an offence, punishable by fine or by dispossession, and agricultural officers, or tribunals, can be established in each district to lay down standards and to try cases, much as the landlord would do, but with greater knowledge (in most cases) and impartiality. Also good farmers can be rewarded, e.g. with prizes or with bonuses.

Fragmentation results usually from a system of inheritance which allows each of the farmers' sons (or daughters) to receive a piece of the farm when the farmer dies. To ensure fairness when the farm is being broken up, each son receives several pieces, such as a piece near the river and a piece far from the river, a fertile piece and a piece useful only for grazing, a wooded piece and a barren piece. After this has gone on for some generations each farmer's holding of land is in several small pieces, which may be widely distant from each other. Fragmentation causes waste in several ways. A lot of labour time is wasted in travelling from one plot to another. Secondly, distant plots cannot be supervised as easily as the nearer plots; they may therefore be less productive because of greater liability to disease, or less care, or greater liability to theft, and because they are less productive may receive still less care. Thirdly it may be necessary to duplicate capital on some of the holdings, e.g. equipment, or cattle stalls, or water troughs, because of the distances between the holdings. And fourthly if the plots are very small it may be difficult to work them with ploughs, difficult to protect them from one's neighbours' weeds, difficult to make experiments which one's neighbours distrust, and impracticable to provide space for wells, buildings, or other capital. Much land may also be wasted in boundaries. The major loss, however, is in time. Hence, where labour time is scarce, the farmers are glad to effect an exchange of pieces, which consolidates each farmer's holding into a single piece. Many countries have passed legislation to effect such transfers compulsorily in areas where a majority of farmers indicate their desire for consolidation. On the other hand, if labour time is abundant, as in over-populated countries, consolidation adds much less to output, and the farmers are usually unwilling to bother with a consolidation scheme.

It is possible to prevent fragmentation without resorting to leasehold tenure. Fragmentation does not occur under a system of primogeniture. But even without primogeniture fragmentation does not occur if it is the practice for the heirs to administer their inheritance jointly, and without breaking up the unit. It is no more difficult to administer a farm jointly than it is to administer a shop, or a manu-

facturing business, or any other inheritance which it would be un-economic or even impossible to break up into pieces. If fragmenta-tion is taking place, and is causing significant waste, a law can be passed to prevent agricultural land from being broken up into units of less than a stipulated minimum size (say five acres), without the permission of an agricultural tribunal constituted for the purpose. In this, as in other matters, if it is desirable to restrict the farmer's rights over his land, this can be done by establishing impartial tribunals, and without resort to landlordism.

Debt affects output adversely when it is so heavy that the farmer is virtually working for the moneylender. There are many countries where the farmers are so heavily in debt that they cannot afford to make the annual interest payment and repayment of principal which are due. The moneylender then takes from the farmer whatever the farmer produces, less the bare subsistence needed by the farmer. Farmers in this position have no interest in adopting improved practices, for the whole or most of the benefit would go to the money-lender. When this situation becomes widespread, as it often has, the government may have to step in and reduce the debts within manage-able limits, in order to give the farmer some incentive. Many countries have established tribunals for this purpose. It is not enough, however, merely to reduce the debt, if the farmer will promptly get himself back into his previous thraldom. Small farmers have a very high propen-sity to get into burdensome debt. This is mainly due to the risks to which they are subject—of flood, drought, low prices, epidemic disease, and whatnot. It is also partly due to their own improvidence, but it is often just as much due to the deliberate policy of the money-lender. If the farmer owes more than he can pay, he is ripe for ex-ploitation: the moneylender may compel him to sell all his market-able produce through the moneylender's agents, or to buy all his requirements in the moneylender's shop, in either case at unfavour-able prices. Or the moneylender may drive the farmers bankrupt, buy their land cheaply, and take extortionate rents. To some extent, therefore, farmers get into debt because moneylenders deliberately make it easy to get into debt, so as to exploit them, and a government may well think it necessary to take counter measures to prevent the farmers from getting into debt.

The only way to prevent small farmers from getting excessively into debt is to make it difficult to borrow, by denying the protection of the law to the security on which farmers would otherwise borrow. Thus, in several countries a farmer's land cannot be sold for debt; it is thus not a marketable security, and moneylenders will not advance money on it. Other countries will not give legal recog-nition to crop liens; for example, in Uganda the law says that an

African's cotton must be sold in a licensed market, at not less than the price stipulated by the market authorities, and that cash for the full amount must pass from the buyer to the seller at the time of the transaction—provisions which make it dangerous to advance money to a farmer, unless you can stand over him on market day, and extract the cash from him as he sells his cotton. The Bechuana-land Protectorate goes even further; the courts will not enforce shop-keepers' debts against Africans—so the shopkeepers do not get African farmers into debt.

It is not enough, however, to prevent the farmers from borrowing from moneylenders, since farmers have legitimate needs for loans. If the private moneylender is going to be excluded, it is necessary that other institutions be created to meet legitimate needs. Actually, the farmer probably needs insurance, even more than loans. Much debt is due to misfortunes of a statistically foreseeable nature—to sickness, or the cost of a wedding or a funeral, or fire, drought or hurricane, or accident to livestock. Such events happen regularly, and are not really suitable for loans, since if a poor farmer has to borrow to pay off the cost of an illness, or to replace crops lost in a hurricane, it is most unlikely that he will be able to save enough out of future harvests to be able to pay off the debt. All such statistically foreseeable events should be covered by insurance. The obstacle to this is the cost of insuring large numbers of people for small sums of money. Some governments of under-developed countries are nevertheless starting compulsory insurance schemes, e.g. hurricane insurance in Jamaica. Where the farmers to be insured are all liable to much the same risks, the cost of administering the insurance is minimized by raising the revenue out of general taxes on farmers, instead of making an individual assessment of each farmer.

Besides insurance, the farmer also needs credit. The cost of lending to small farmers has been greatly reduced by the invention of the village co-operative society. The cost of lending lies in the cost of acquiring information about the borrower's credit status, in the cost of collecting instalments, and in the cost of keeping an eye on his movements. If a commercial bank were lending money to farmers, in sums of fifty pounds or less, these costs might easily amount to the equivalent of a rate of interest of twenty per cent per annum. To the members of the village, however, these costs are very small; they have known the borrower and his character all his life, and he lives among them so that they are able to follow all his fortunes—which they do anyway for their own pleasure, whether he borrows money or not; hence village societies are able to lend at a cost of five to eight per cent above the rate at which they borrow. Such societies need to be small: a unit such that every member knows every other, or else

the main advantage, of costless information, is lost. And they also usually need some supervision by government officers, since the members have usually inadequate experience of running the affairs of an organization and looking after its money. Moreover, the society runs with the least bad debts when it is tied in with the agency which markets the farmer's crop; for arrears and bad debts are avoided when the sums due from the farmer can be debited automatically against his crop.

Co-operative credit societies have had great success in most of the under-developed countries of the world. Their emphasis, however, has primarily been upon encouraging small farmers to save, and providing a cheap banking mechanism. Farmers, however, need much more capital than they can afford to save. If funds can be obtained, whether from taxing the farmers themselves or from other sectors of the economy, or from external sources, the co-operative credit society is an excellent channel through which to make them available to small farmers. There is a world of difference between the attitude of farmers who are heavily indebted to moneylenders, and that of farmers whose debt is kept within manageable limits by a credit system which they help to manage for themselves.

We come now to the question of the scale of farming operations. This question is much debated by land reformers. There are countries where large estates, worked by paid labour under direction, are being broken up, and converted into small farms And there are other countries where the small farmers are being compelled to join their lands together to form big estates, operated as collectives.

Large scale agricultural operations are more efficient, and show more rapid economic growth than small scale operations, if there is economy in mechanical cultivation, or in large scale control of irrigation, of seeds, of disease precautions, of processing, or of marketing. There is almost always some difference in favour of large size—interpreting this to mean say units of not less than 300 acres of arable land or its equivalent (beyond say 1,000 arable acres the diseconomies of management soon show up)—but the extent of the difference depends partly upon the nature of the crop and the land, and partly upon the amount of effort which is made to organize around the small scale farmer services which maintain his efficiency.

Let us deal first with mechanical cultivation. In the first place, mechanical cultivation is not economic unless there is a shortage of labour relatively to capital. If labour is super-abundant, as it is in India or in China, the main effect of introducing mechanization is to create still more unemployment, at the cost of using up scarce foreign exchange to import the mechanical equipment and its fuel. In such a situation the objective of economic policy is to maximize

I

output per acre, and not output per worker. Mechanization will increase output if it enables land to be brought into cultivation which could not be cultivated by hand methods, because the soil is too heavy, or because weather or climate leave too little time to get the work done by hand. This is a valuable contribution, but apart from this it is more usually the case that hand cultivation is more productive per acre than mechanical cultivation because it is done with greater care. Mechanical cultivation is also economic in surplus labour countries in so far as it releases for human use land which is otherwise required for feeding draught animals; this depends on the cost of machinery and fuel on the one hand (which probably have also to be imported) and on the value of the crop released in this way on the other hand. It also depends on whether the peasants would in fact keep fewer animals if they were no longer required for work. It is difficult to be certain how this calculation would work out for China, but it seems fairly clear that in India, where cattle play also a religious role, mechanization should at present be only marginal to agricultural policy. The reverse is the case where land is super-abundant, as in some parts of West Africa. Here the objective of policy should be to maximize net output per worker, and not per acre. In general, economic growth creates new demands for labour outside agriculture, and reduces the proportion of the population which can be spared for agriculture. Mechanization simultaneously reduces the demand for labour in agriculture, and increases output per worker, by enabling each worker to cultivate more acres. It is a necessary part of economic growth where labour is scarce, but is only marginally relevant where labour is abundant.

Given that the relative scarcities of labour, land, and capital are such as to justify mechanization, the feasibility of mechanization depends next upon the land and the crop. Mechanical cultivation is appropriate if the land is flat, is used for annual crops, and is not easily leached. Hilly land is not suitable for mechanical cultivation, and might from this point of view just as well be in the hands of small farmers. Land planted permanently to grass, or to trees, also does not require mechanical cultivation. There is also doubt about the wisdom of mechanical cultivation in countries which are subject to extremes of heat or of rainfall. These qualifications restrict the area to which mechanical cultivation applies. In this area there is advantage in having farms of such a size that it pays the farmer to keep mechanical equipment; that is to say, it seems that in arable cultivation in temperate climates farms of less than 100 acres are at a disadvantage, and arable farms of 300 or 400 acres are often the most economic in Western Europe.

Mechanical cultivation can in any case be combined with small

farming if the machinery is owned by a central agency which cultivates the land for the farmers in return for a fee, while leaving each farmer to plant, weed and reap on his own account; the performance of mechanical operations by central machinery owning agencies has been successful in many parts of the world. The condition for success is that the farms be neither too small nor too big, say between twelve and fifty acres. For if they are too small, the machine does most of the work that the farmer would otherwise do for himself, and it is cheaper for him to do the operations for himself than to pay for the machine. While if the farm is large enough, there is enough work to justify the farmer in having his own machines. It is particularly convenient for the farm to have its own machines available just when it wants them, instead of having to wait in a queue. This has been one of the major obstacles to the success of co-operative ownership of machinery by farmers: the difficulty the farmers have in agreeing on who gets the machinery when—a difficulty which is perhaps more acute in countries where the weather is changeable and unreliable, as in Western Europe, than it is in some other parts of the world. Many governments have taken the initiative in organizing machinery pools under government or co-operative ownership, or in encouraging private entrepreneurs or large farms with surplus machinery to provide small farmers with machinery service, in return for a fee. These schemes have had reasonable success, in areas where the farms are of appropriate size; but the cost of cultivating a large fertile plain mechanically is almost always lower if the plain is operated in farms large enough to own their own machinery, than if it is split up into small farms, however efficiently one may try to organize the operations of a central machinery agency.

Much the same sort of analysis applies to marketing operations, though it is in practice much easier to disintegrate marketing than to disintegrate mechanical operations. For there are always middlemen willing to buy produce from the farmer in small quantities, and to bulk the produce of several farms in order to perform such processing or marketing operations as are most economically performed on a large scale. However, though middlemen are always available, their services are everywhere complained against, and investigated, on the grounds that they are inefficient, or too numerous or monopolistic. Inefficient service, where it exists, can usually be prevented by a system of inspection, such as is involved in compulsory grading. Excessive numbers result usually from imperfect competition; excessive numbers may be able to make a living under the shelter of a minimum margin, which they agree tacitly or openly not to undercut; or again excessive numbers may survive if each has his own area—his particular group of farmers tied to him by debt, or by sentiment, or by zoning

regulations enforced by law. The simplest remedy in this situation is usually the enforcement of competition—by cleaning up the debt situation, or by ending the zoning, or by prohibiting price and market sharing arrangements. But there are also cases where monopolistic organization is genuinely more efficient than the competition of many small middlemen, as for instance where processing is most economically done in large factories. Here the remedy lies in co-operative marketing, or in price and profit controls on private middlemen, or in state marketing agencies.

The success of co-operative marketing depends upon the quality of the private entrepreneurship with which it competes. The co-operative is sometimes able to sell a better product than the middlemen do, but this is only if the middlemen are unusually inefficient in arranging the bulking and grading of the crop, or in offering adequately differentiated prices for superior grades. This in turn would probably be a sign of lack of competition amongst them. Conditions are most favourable to the success of co-operatives if lack of competition between middlemen is causing them to be inefficient, or to be excessively numerous, or to take too high a margin; for if the middlemen are efficient and competitive they can usually outbid the co-operative organization because of their greater flexibility. This is not to say that co-operatives must succeed in monopolistic conditions. In such conditions the middlemen may 'gang up' against them and use all the usual tricks of would be monopolists—the price war, exclusive dealing arrangements, and so on; and the co-operatives may not be able to survive these tricks unless their members are men of sufficient education and substance to be able to hold on. Or the scale on which the marketing has to be done may be beyond the control of co-operatives; small farmers can run a small cotton ginnery for themselves, but it is not easy for them to run a large modern rice mill or sugar factory as a co-operative. This is why co-operative marketing has succeeded best of all among farmers operating on a fair scale—say farms of thirty acres or more. When the farmers are on the three to twenty acre level, the range of what they can co-operatively do is limited—eggs, milk, and a few other crops not requiring elaborate processing. Outside that range their protection from monopolistic practices among middlemen rests either on legal controls or upon the creation of statutory marketing agencies.

Other operations can also be disintegrated, besides mechanical cultivation, and marketing, with greater or less success. Irrigation can be controlled by a separate water agency. Seed control is harder to effect, but can be ensured if a co-operative or state agency maintains pure seed farms, and if the farmers are persuaded or compelled (as they are e.g. in Uganda) to plant only seeds supplied by

these farms. Precautions against infectious diseases of plants and animals are harder still; but these also can be enforced by law or by persuasion. It is too much to expect the small farm to be as efficient as the large, but it can hold its own provided that it is buttressed by a network of other agencies, responsible for machinery, or seeds, or credit, or water, or marketing, or control of infectious diseases, or research, or whatever else it may be that needs to be done on a large scale: merely to recite the network is to explain why small farmers are not competitive in many fields of agriculture, since there are so many fields where the necessary network is simply not provided. And even where the network is provided, the small farm is almost certain to be slower in adopting improved techniques than is the well run estate. Some estates are run badly, especially if they have been in the same family for generations, and are regarded as a mark of status rather than as commercial enterprises. But the well run estate will adopt new types of crop, or livestock or fertilizers or disease controls in a fraction of the time which it takes to persuade or bludgeon small farmers into widespread acceptance.

This analysis so far has thrown up the weaknesses of small scale agriculture, but there are also some substantial points in its favour which in appropriate circumstances make it more efficient than large scale agriculture, even on the economic tests.

First comes the fact that small farmers cultivate the land more intensively than large farmers. There are a number of cases where product per acre is higher on the large farms, e.g. sugar; especially where new varieties, new methods or new fertilizers are being adopted more rapidly by the larger farmers. But there are also many other cases where product per acre is higher on the smaller farms, mainly because the small farmer, having a small area to handle, cultivates it more intensively. This is almost universally the case in European agriculture, and similar results are reported from other continents. If labour is much more scarce than land, the object of policy is to use a system which maximizes output per head, rather than output per acre, so full employment industrial countries which are in a position to import food cheaply are better served by large scale agriculture, using machines, and maximizing output per man, than by small scale agriculture with its low output per man and high output per acre. On the other hand, in those Asian economies where labour is abundant, small scale agriculture has the advantage of using most intensively what is most scarce, namely land. A good deal of emphasis in the land reform movements, whether in Latin America or in Asia, is upon the more intensive use of land which would result if some of the large estates were broken up and converted to small family farms.

Next, the family size farm has over large scale farming the advantage that the farmer works harder and more carefully than the hired agricultural worker. As Arthur Young said, after observing the operations of the French peasantry 'the magic of property turns sand into gold'. This may appear to conflict with what we have said earlier on the danger of peasants impoverishing their soils, but as we pointed out there, this danger is found only in places which are in transition from abundance to scarcity of land. In countries where land has been scarce for many centuries, e.g. in China or Java or for that matter in parts of Africa, the farmers have learnt to treat their soil lovingly, and to maintain its fertility. The superiority of peasant farmers' work over hired labourers' work is greatest in types of agriculture which are not labour intensive, since types which use a great amount of labour per acre can afford to pay for adequate supervision (this difference is much the same as the difference between free and slave labour to which we referred in an earlier part of this chapter).

This brings us to the third advantage of small scale farming, which is that it does not make large demands upon supervisory staff. If such staff is available, and can be used in an agricultural extension service it will yield plentiful results, but if such staff is difficult to recruit and expensive, as is the case in most under-developed countries, peasant agriculture can get along with whatever is available. This is not the case with large scale agriculture, whose efficiency stands or falls by the quality of its management. The managerial problem is so severe that it puts sharp limits upon the economic size of the farm; though, as we have said, a European farm of 300 arable acres is more efficient than one of forty acres, a farm of 1,000 arable acres is not noticeably more efficient than one of 300 acres, and efficiency may fall sharply as size rises beyond these limits. Most of the attempts to establish giant farms, whether to grow grain in Russia, or to grow groundnuts in Tanganyika, have failed for this simple reason. In countries where superior agricultural skills are scarce it is often more effective to use what there is in schemes for improving peasant production than to use it for launching new large scale agricultural enterprises.

Beyond these economic considerations lie also social considerations which would make many people prefer the family size farm even if larger operations could be proved to be more economic. As we have seen in an earlier section, large scale enterprise tends to bring with it disputes between employer and employed; moreover, land ownership carries with it such political and social prestige or power that the concentration of land ownership in a few hands is deplored by most people. There is a school which sees the way out of

these difficulties in collective ownership of the land, either by the state, or by farmers' co-operative societies. We have already discussed these forms of organization in section 1(c) of this chapter. State farms exist in some countries, but the substitution of the state for the private employer has not noticeably diminished industrial disputes. Collective farming, if run on a democratic basis by the farmers themselves, has greater attractions as a social form, but large scale co-operative enterprises run by the workers themselves have seldom been successful in history, for reasons which we have already seen. There is everything to be said for persuading small groups of farmers to experiment in collective management, and if the groups are kept small—to say not more than five or six families—many of them will prove successful. But it seems improbable that there is much future in democratic countries for large collective farms involving whole villages of say a hundred families or more.

The desire to combine individual enterprise with large scale efficiency has led to experiments in tenures involving some forms of compulsion. In the classical example, which is the Gezira cotton plantations in the Sudan, the land is split into small units which each farmer cultivates on his own account; but the farmer is subjected to various controls. His land is ploughed for him mechanically; he has to plant the seed he is given in the rotations he is told, to fertilize and cultivate as recommended, and to hand over the crop for processing and marketing by the central agency which runs the scheme. The case for compulsion is that it ensures ever-increasing efficiency, whereas if the services offered by the agency were voluntary many farmers would plant inferior seeds, or would cultivate or market in ways which forfeited the advantages of large scale organization. Compulsion combines the advantages of plantation size with the advantages of family size; on the other hand it does this only by partly reducing the status of the cultivator from that of independent farmer towards that of labourer acting under orders.

Gezira is only the extreme case of a range. It is not unusual for farmers to hold their land on condition that they observe certain covenants. Probably the best line of approach in countries based on peasant agriculture is to begin by offering a network of voluntary services, and to convert such services from a voluntary to a compulsory basis (compulsory use of improved seeds, compulsory collective marketing, compulsory soil conservation) only when the majority of the farmers having grown used to the central agencies, the coercion of the dissident minority is possible without alienating general farm support.

So much emphasis is laid in contemporary literature upon ques-

tions of agricultural organization that it may be as well to end upon a dissenting note. It is of the greatest importance everywhere that farmers should hold their lands on terms which give them security and incentive, and it is also of the greatest importance to have adequate institutions for making capital available. These questions apart, far too much emphasis is placed in current discussion on other institutional matters—especially fragmentation, size and marketing— and much too little upon other means of increasing efficiency— especially water supplies, seed farms for improved seed, fertilizers, and agricultural extension services. One gets the impression from much of the discussion that not much can be done to increase agricultural productivity without vast institutional changes in the countryside. This is not so. The typical farm in Japan is still only between two and three acres in size; nevertheless productivity per acre on these farms is two to three times as great as in other parts of Asia. Productivity per acre in Japan increased by nearly fifty per cent in the thirty years before the first World War, and had doubled by the middle 1930's, without significant changes in the size of farm. The secret of rapid agricultural progress in the under-developed countries is to be found much more in agricultural extension, in fertilizers, in new seeds, in pesticides and in water supplies than in altering the size of the farm, in introducing machinery, or in getting rid of middlemen in the marketing process. (In any case increasing farm size and introducing machinery are doubtful policies for over-populated countries.) The present institutional framework is in most under-developed countries (but not all) quite adequate for an enormous advance in productivity by means of the introduction of improved technology. Indeed the best hope of raising the standard of living in most of these countries lies in the fact that the backwardness of their agricultural techniques makes possible spectacular advances in production at relatively low cost. We shall come to these matters in Chapter IV.

(e) Cottage Industry

Every community has some part of its population specializing in producing manufactured articles as independent producers. The proportion seldom falls below five per cent, even in the poorest economies, unless the economy becomes very dependent on foreign trade. These craftsmen are engaged first and foremost in making cloth, which is everywhere man's next requirement after food; and there may also be workers in wood, in leather, in metal, in raffia, in clay, and in such other materials as are available. Some of the work may be of exquisite craftsmanship, for use by princes or by rich men, but most of it is just ordinary work for ordinary people.

In Western Europe, where the industrial system began, the factory system sometimes grew out of cottage industry. The crafts sometimes provided a reservoir of skill. And the domestic or 'putting-out' system was sometimes a stage between the individual's workshop and the factory. This was not always so. For sometimes the factory was based upon a machine which rendered the old skills obsolete. And sometimes its owners deliberately looked for labour in places where they could avoid the high wages or the restrictive practices associated with the craft. There is no necessary evolution from workshop to factory. The new as often challenges the old, and destroys it altogether.

Many people are anxious to preserve the independent craftsman from destruction by the modern factory for the same reasons that they prefer small scale proprietorship to large scale systems of farming. Looking at the matter in economic terms, there is also a striking similarity in the conditions of survival. That is to say, in industry as in agriculture, there are some technical conditions which favour large scale more than others; these apart, the survival of small scale efforts also depends upon surrounding the producer with a well organized network of services, operating on a large scale. Whether we are interested in agriculture, or in industry, in mining, in transportation or in retailing, we shall always find that some spheres offer more scope than others to small scale enterprise, and that in addition the success of small scale operations even in these spheres depends upon a proper organization of marketing, of credit, of research, and of education, all of which need usually to be done on a large scale.

Cottage industries are most likely to survive, in the first instance, to the extent to which they are a part-time occupation. Farmers and their wives are fully occupied in agriculture only for a part of the year. If they spend the rest of the year manufacturing in their own homes, largely for themselves, their costs of production, in terms of alternatives foregone, are so low that they can stand very severe competition. In practice, the greater part of the output of cottage industries is produced by full-time specialists, and not by agriculturists in their spare time. However, some social workers in the village improvement campaigns are persuading farmers' wives to take up handicrafts in their spare time.

All handicraft production has the advantage, compared with factory production, that it economizes two scarce factors, capital and supervisory skill. Capital is very scarce in under-developed countries, and so those which have abundant resources of labour, relatively to land and other resources, are wise to develop methods of production which use labour rather than capital. Factory production also calls for a great deal of supervisory skill, in the shape of

foremen, engineers, accountants and the like, and such skill is also in short supply. These disadvantages of factory production may be offset by the superiority of machine production. The machine may be superior either in terms of the quality of the work, or in terms of the quantity of labour required. Quality superiority shows where the product has to be standardized, and made in precise sizes, or shapes or patterns. Here the machine is often more precise than human hands and eyes, and in such work it quickly supplants the handicraft worker. If on the other hand questions of precision do not arise, the competition is then mainly in terms of labour cost. Some machines are much more productive than others in this relative sense. Thus the loom used for weaving in factories is not essentially different from the loom used in the home, but the factory machine used for spinning is immensely more productive than the spinning wheel used in the home. Accordingly, home weaving continues to be economic long after spinning has disappeared into the factories.

Small scale production, whether in the home, or in the small work-shop, is best able to survive in industries where there is no mass standardized demand. Once there is mass demand it is profitable to invent highly specialized machines to do the work, and the dis-appearance of the smallest units is then only a matter of time. Besides, as we have just seen, if standardization is a condition of purchase, the handicraft worker is at a disadvantage, compared with the machine, either because he cannot control his own output exactly, or because of the difficulty of getting other handicraft workers to produce exactly the same article as himself, so that their output may be bulked and sold in quantity. Lack of standardization is one draw-back to the marketing of handicraft products, as has been found by those who have tried to sell such products in the markets of Britain or the United States. The chance of survival is greatest where the commodity is bought in small numbers; and where there is advan-tage in the fact that no two pieces are exactly alike. The consequence is that the sphere for individual production is very narrow. There is room for artistic work in textiles, in wood, and in precious metals, but the mass demand for textiles, for footwear and for metal goods must be expected to pass to the factories.

The prospect of small scale industry depends, next, upon improve-ment of its techniques. Often the tools in use have not changed for centuries, and it is possible to improve them very substantially, in the light of modern experience, without altering the basic skills required by the craftsman. Just as in small scale agriculture, there is room for a government research agency, to experiment in improving techniques, and for an advisory service to spread the new knowledge among pro-ducers, so also, in small scale industry, efficiency and the prospect of

survival are much enhanced if there are agencies charged with experimenting in improving the craftsmen's tools and techniques, and with spreading the new knowledge amongst them. Improvements in technique are not confined to equipment; the craftsman can be introduced to better materials, e.g. for dyeing; or to ways of testing his materials; or of ensuring greater accuracy or standardization. Of course, the greatest revolution which has been made in techniques is to attach small electric motors to the craftsman's tools, and to connect them to electricity; this alone multiplies output per man. But in most under-developed countries it is simply out of the question to carry electricity into many villages.

Next comes the organization of marketing and of finance. The craftsman cannot afford to hold stocks of materials, or to produce finished articles for stock. If he works to customers' orders only, he will as likely as not be subject to much irregular unemployment. Production is most economically organized if there is a middleman between the craftsman and the final consumer. The middleman can carry stocks; can arrange for bulk display in shops, in order to widen the market; can arrange to have several craftsmen producing identical articles, if the market requires standardization; and can arrange for the work of different craftsmen to be assembled, if the article is one which lends itself to specialization and assembly. Such work is often done by private middlemen, but it is generally thought that the middlemen are able to take advantage of the craftsmen, by getting them into debt. In these days, therefore, governments are creating agencies to perform these functions, sometimes in conjunction with the functions of research into new techniques, and advice. Probably the best results have been achieved in Indonesia, where successive governments have put considerable effort into improving and organizing the handicraft trades, through agencies specially created for the purpose.

Indonesia has excelled in reorganizing old trades, but Japan has excelled in organizing new trades on a cottage industry basis, without, indeed, the government having much to do with the matter. In that country the 'putting out' system seems to have taken firm root, private merchants supplying materials to craftsmen to be worked up in their homes, or in small workshops. The system is specially famous for its extension into trades where a commodity has to be made in several parts; the parts are put out to individual craftsmen, or to small workshops, working to detailed specifications, whereafter the assembly is done in central factories. Thus, many commodities are being made by Japanese craftsmen today which were totally unknown to their forefathers. The survival of small scale production depends upon continuous enterprise of this sort, bringing new commodities

within the range of the system, for small scale industry must contract if it depends only upon age old products, since most of these will disappear into factories sooner or later.

The measures we have discussed so far have been for making cottage industry more efficient, rather than for protecting it against factory competition. Most people would agree that cottage industry should survive in so far as it can be made to compete on an economic basis with factory industry, and this is the case for having a systematic programme for research into techniques, for the improvement of raw materials, for capital, and for superior marketing arrangements. Protecting cottage industry is quite a different question; some governments have embarked on this, and it merits special consideration.

The problem has significance only in those countries where there is surplus labour in agriculture and in cottage industry which cannot be found full employment for lack of land or capital resources. It is then arguable that the real cost of using labour in cottage industry is zero, whereas factory production uses scarce capital and supervisory skills. If the cottage workers were willing to work for whatever money income they could get, however low, competition on the basis of price would yield the right result. In practice, however, they hold out for a subsistence income, and the prices they charge may exceed the real social cost. Hence whatever the difference in money cost may be, the difference in real cost favours the cottage industry. Obviously no such argument can be applied in countries where labour is relatively scarce. If this argument has validity, it is an argument for the more crowded parts of Asia, and not an argument for Africa or for Latin America.

Let us now consider the validity of the argument in countries where there is surplus labour. The point can be illustrated by a numerical example. Suppose that there are 100 cottage workers. And suppose that large scale industry could produce the same output by having ten persons continuously engaged in making, maintaining and replacing machinery, and thirty persons using it in factories. (There is also an interest cost on the capital involved, but this does not come into the argument of this paragraph.) Then, if the demand is the same, the establishment of factories would mean that forty people would do the work formerly done by 100, and that sixty would be reduced to destitution. The validity of the conclusion depends upon the assumption that the demand is the same. If, on the contrary, the demand increases by sixty per cent, there will be work for everybody if forty work in factories and sixty in cottages; and if the demand increases by 150 per cent, there will be work for everybody in factories. The cottage industry argument is therefore just a part of the general argument

about technological progress. If productivity increases faster than demand, unemployment is created; but if demand increases faster than productivity there is either inflation or increased employment.

The moral is simply that measures to increase the productivity of manufacturing industry (whether cottage or factory) must be paralleled by measures to increase the demand for manufactured products. This demand comes only to a small extent from industrial producers themselves, who are only a small proportion of the population of such countries. It comes to a greater extent from all other classes, of whom the farmers are far and away the largest category. If capital is being put into developing manufacturing industry while a country's agriculture remains stagnant, the result is bound to be distress in the manufacturing sector, as factory and cottage workers compete for a limited demand. But if there is balanced development, with the productivity of the farmers growing rapidly, and the demand for manufactures correspondingly increasing, there is ample scope for investment in industry. Moreover, in over-populated countries industrialization to some extent depends upon developing an international trade in manufactures. The secret of most development problems is to maintain a proper balance between sectors, and we shall have more to say on this subject in later chapters (Chapter V, section 3(*b*), Chapter VI, section 2(*a*), Chapter VII, section 1(*b*)).

When all this is said, it remains true that in countries which have surplus labour, capital can be put to better advantage in the early stages of development by using it to expand transport and other public utilities, irrigation and other agricultural requirements, and those forms of manufacturing where the advantages of large scale production are greatest—especially metals, chemicals, engineering, building materials—than by using it to compete with what the cottage workers can do fairly well—especially the weaving industry. This is only a temporary phenomenon. If development is taking place the demand for cottage products will soon catch up with the supply, and there will be room for an expansion of factories without significant unemployment resulting. Whether in the meantime the establishment of factories in spheres where cottage production is most likely to be able to hold its own should be restrictively licensed is a moot point, depending on how effective the price mechanism is in reflecting the true social costs, and on how much confidence one can have in the way in which licensing is likely to be administered in the particular country. An economic case can be made for temporary protection of certain cottage industries, as a measure to prevent capital from being used wastefully, but not all economic cases deserve to have administrative support.

5. INSTITUTIONAL CHANGE

(a) *The Process of Change*

So far we have considered social institutions solely from the point of view of their compatibility with economic growth. Now it is time to consider how institutions change, and whether change follows pre-determined paths.

Perhaps it is as well to remind ourselves at the outset that economic change does not result exclusively from changes in institutions. Economic growth may occur because of an increase in capital formation, or because new technological knowledge becomes available, or for other reasons not originating in institutional change; a clear example of this occurs when foreigners bring new knowledge or new capital. Growth originating in one of these factors is almost certain to cause institutional change. Alternatively, there may be institutional changes which do not originate in economic change, such as changes produced by religious, political or natural upheavals—the idea that all social upheavals have an economic origin amounts to thinking that men are motivated by economic interest only, and is palpably false. This section is confined to studying the nature, the causes and the effects of institutional change; but there is no suggestion that this is the primary or exclusive cause of economic change.

Our enquiry into the compatibility of institutions and economic growth led to the conclusion that institutions promote growth according to the extent that they associate effort with reward, according to the scope which they allow for specialization and for trade, and according to the freedom they permit for seeking out and seizing economic opportunities. Now the institutions of different countries differ greatly in these respects. Also the institutions of any one country are changing all the time however slowly or rapidly. They may be changing in ways which are favourable to growth, but they may also be changing in ways which restrict growth.

Probably the most important characteristic of institutions, from the angle of economic growth, is the amount of freedom to manoeuvre which they permit. Once it is possible for people to seize economic opportunities, growth will occur, and as it occurs institutions will accommodate themselves so as to protect incentives and to encourage trade. Conversely, if opportunities are reduced, growth will decline and institutions will begin to be adjusted towards stagnation. Suppose, for example, that gold is discovered in a community where all the institutions are unfavourable to growth—where there are only rudimentary conceptions of property, where families are self-sufficient, and where new activities cannot be started except under the strictest licence, which is seldom given. Then suppose that some

person—whether private individual or public official—is given a licence to mine the gold, to hire labour, and to import materials and staff from abroad. This is all that is needed to revolutionize institutions. The families will cease to be self-sufficient; there will be an immense growth of internal and external trade; property relations will become subtle and complex; and so on. Given the chance to seize opportunities, men will in due course alter all their institutions accordingly.

It follows that change reinforces itself cumulatively. Once economic growth has begun, institutions change more and more in directions favourable to growth, and so strengthen the forces making for growth. Alternatively, if the rate of economic growth begins to decline, institutions become less favourable to growth; monopolies are more acceptable and more easily maintained, families become more self-sufficient, vertical mobility is reduced, and social status plays a larger economic role, even to the extent of a movement towards feudalism.

It is easy to see why there are these cumulative processes. The continuance of a social institution in a particular form depends upon its convenience, upon belief in its rectitude, and upon force. If growth begins to occur, all these sanctions are eroded. The institution ceases to be convenient, because it stands in the way of opportunities for economic advancement. People then cease to believe in it. Priests, lawyers, economists, and other philosophers, who used to justify it in terms of their various dogmas, begin to reject the old dogmas, and to replace them by new dogmas more appropriate to the changing situation. The balance of political power also alters. For new men are raised up by economic growth into positions of wealth and status; they challenge the old ruling classes; acquire political power slowly or in more revolutionary ways; and throw force behind the new instead of the ancient institutions. Once economic growth begins it will certainly erode the old institutions, and create new ones more compatible with further growth. In the same way, when growth stops, the institutions which suited an expanding economy are no longer appropriate. People cease to believe in them; the priests, the lawyers, the economists and the philosophers turn against them, and the powerful groups who favour the *status quo* are able to enforce changes unfavourable to economic growth.

These cumulative forces work in the same way if the change starts not in the economic opportunities but in the institutions themselves. For then the very fact that people become more willing or have more chance to seize opportunities will itself either create or reveal new opportunities to be seized; and the emergence of new opportunities will in turn reinforce the changes in beliefs and institutions. It is

because of this cumulative interaction of economic opportunities and of beliefs and institutions upon each other that it is usually so difficult to lay one's finger on the 'fundamental' cause of change—to say, for example whether in Western Europe in the thirteenth to sixteenth centuries it was growing economic opportunities which brought theological changes, culminating in Reformation and Counter-Reformation, or whether it was changing theological conceptions that permitted people to make use of opportunities which would have existed in any case. All such questions are usually unanswerable.

The adjustment of institutions to changing economic circumstances may be a painful process. It is neither balanced nor complete. Change begins at some spot in the web of beliefs and relationships, and spreads outwards from there. Consequently some beliefs or habits in the culture are changed completely, while others continue to be held firmly. The new and the old are mixed illogically and in curious proportions, which differ widely from society to society. The transformation is never complete. This is why western capitalist countries differ so much from each other even today. They retain pre-capitalist ideas in different proportions, and differ in such matters as the closeness of kinship ties, equality of opportunity, attitudes to private entrepreneurship, attitudes to private wealth, and many other matters. A society in which the acceleration of growth has occurred only in very recent decades always displays many incongruities. People take a long time to adjust themselves to a money economy; to learn to take advantage of opportunities expressed in money terms; and to learn how to spend or how to keep money when they get it. They need a new pattern of morality, which may take a long time to be created; for they cease to live in a community where obligations are based upon status, and move into one where obligations are based upon contract, and generally upon market relationships with people with whom there are no kinship ties. Thus a community which has hitherto been extremely honest may become extremely dishonest, until people learn that honest service in labour or in goods has to be given even to perfect strangers in fulfilment of contracts expressed in terms of money. There has to be also a new sense of values; people no longer respect the old superior status; chiefs, grand-uncles and elders no longer command automatic obedience. Leadership shifts to other directions, and much time may pass before the new leaders either command or deserve to command the same sort of respect as the old. The decline of the old morality is one of the more painful aspects of economic change, and it is one reason why the moralists and anthropologists are usually opposed to change, or at any rate, to rapid change, since they know that rapid change causes old beliefs

and institutions to disintegrate more rapidly than new beliefs and institutions can be integrated in their place. Another example of incongruity which excites much attention in these days is the lack of balance between birth and death rates which occurs shortly after the start of economic growth, causing the population to increase. (There is similar excitement when economic decline is accompanied by falling population.) In a stagnant society birth and death rates are roughly equal at high levels. Then when economic growth begins, the death rate begins to fall; at first merely because the growth of communications and trade puts an end to local famines; later because of improvements in public health measures and in medical treatment. The death rate falls long before the birth rate starts to fall, and in the interval population may double in anything from sixty to thirty years. It takes some time for people to realize that if they are going to control death rates they must also control birth rates. (We return to this subject in Chapter VI.)

Faced with the incongruities of change, many people have wondered whether social change could not be regulated in a 'balanced' way, i.e. by preventing some beliefs and institutions from changing, more rapidly than others. The answer seems to be that this is impossible. A culture cannot be changed in all its myriad aspects simultaneously and in equal proportions. Some parts feel the strain more than others, and give way, pulling others with them in differing degrees. We cannot always predict what will give way first, because this varies in societies according to their history and traditions; neither can we predict what parts of the culture will be pulled along, or in what proportions. The only way to prevent unbalanced change would be to prevent all change, and this no one can do.

Of course, while it is true that we cannot foresee all the changes which will result from any particular event, it does not follow that we can have no influence whatever upon the course of change. For example, we know that industrialization has resulted in the creation of urban slums in many countries in the past, but we also know that it is possible to have industrialization without slums if appropriate town planning measures are adopted. We know that in some other places it has been accompanied by vast migrations of labour from village to town and back, and we know that this also can be controlled and eliminated (Chapter IV, section 3(c)). What is more difficult is to foresee how human attitudes will change, on such matters as family relations, or respect for tribal authority, or religious observance, or the sanctity of contractual obligations. What some people fear is the disintegration of the old moral values as the new wine of economic growth pours into the old bottles of social stability. Presumably the extent to which old relationships disintegrate de-

K

pends partly upon how development is sponsored. If it is sponsored by foreign capitalists and governments, who show their contempt for the old political, religious and family leaders, it will erode established authority more quickly and effectively than if it is sponsored under established leadership. The Japanese are sometimes said to have adapted Western capitalism to suit their own way of life, but it is doubtful whether this was a conscious process. The fact is rather that the sponsorship of capitalism by already existing Japanese leadership groups reduced to a minimum the conflict between new ways and old authority. Economic growth has its least revolutionary consequences—in terms of its impact upon attitudes and social relations—when it is also least revolutionary in the class sense; that is to say when the new entrepreneurial leaders are accepted and sponsored by the old political, religious and social hierarchies. This is also the great difference between Asian and African reactions to economic growth. In Asia the old religious and political systems were tougher than in Africa, and were not competely destroyed by the Western impact. Whereas, in Africa the European capitalists and governments have acted in opposition to, and with contempt for the established customs, religions and ways of life, wherever these conflicted with European interests, with the result of more extensive disintegration.

Once institutions begin to change, they change in ways which are self-reinforcing. The old beliefs and relationships are altered, and the new beliefs and institutions gradually become more consistent with each other and with further change in the same direction. Nevertheless, it is not the case that growth, once started, will go on forever, or that decline, once started, is never arrested.

In the first place, all growth tends to be logistic in character, that is to say it starts slowly, accelerates, and then slows down again. This is because each stimulus to growth eventually nears the limit of its possibilities. A hypothetical example may illustrate. When radio sets are first introduced, the public is ignorant of their possibilities, and rather sceptical; at first only a few sets sell, but gradually radios become popular, and soon they start to sell like hot cakes. Something like a limit is reached, however, when every household has a radio set. As this limit is approached, the rate of growth of sales declines sharply. Sales may double in the second year, treble in the third, and quadruple in the fourth; but they cannot double every year for ever, because there just are not so many people. The same may apply to institutional change. When some new principle is introduced it is at first resisted. After a while, however, it takes on, and begins to be applied with enthusiasm to a widening range of social relations. But there must come a time when it has conquered nearly all the

ground where it is relevant. Growth is a response to successive
stimuli, each of which ultimately reaches its limit. Continuous growth
at a steady rate would therefore occur only if by some accident the
new stimulus always arrived just as its predecessor was beginning to
flag. In practice, the most we can expect is not a steady rate of growth,
but successive surges of expansion, separated by periods of relative
calm.

Experience shows, however, that even rhythmical growth may
come to an end. Some societies have shown vigorous economic
expansion, followed by stagnation and decline—even to the point
of leaving nothing but ruins behind. Growth may be followed by
stagnation, just as stagnation may be followed by growth. History
shows turning points of acceleration and of deceleration. In all
enquiries into dynamic processes, it is the turning points which are
most interesting, since the cumulative processes which follow
immediately after the turning point are relatively easy to understand.
We must therefore give most of our attention to studying these
turning points.

Let us take first the accelerations. We have already made the point
that what is fundamental to growth is the seizing of opportunities.
Thus growth may accelerate either because new opportunities come
into existence, or because institutional changes now permit opportunities to be seized which already existed, or for both reasons.

The new opportunities may be of many kinds. New inventions may
create new commodities, or reduce the cost of producing old commodities. New roads, new shipping routes, or other improvements in
communications may open up new opportunities for trade. War or
inflation may create new demands. Foreigners may arrive in the
country, bringing new trades, investing new capital, or offering new
chances of employment. Such new opportunities are to a large extent
independent of current institutions. This is not entirely so, and we
shall be investigating in subsequent chapters the effects of institutions
upon such matters as the rate of invention or the inflow of foreign
investment. However, to the extent that such matters are not
dependent upon a country's institutions, there may be an acceleration of opportunities, for reasons not connected with any change of
institutions, and this acceleration of opportunities will be followed by
institutional change.

It is also possible that there may be institutional changes permitting
greater freedom of manoeuvre, without the underlying economic
factors having changed. A possible case, but rare, is a change of heart
on the part of the ruler, permitting people to manoeuvre in ways
which were previously prohibited. A more likely case is a change of
political regime, following upon some shock to the country, such as

is administered by war, famine, hurricane, earthquake, plague, or other disaster. Such shocks, sometimes weaken the grip of the ruling cliques, who favour the *status quo*, and allow power to pass into the hands of other persons who have an interest in change.

Thus acceleration may be due either to a change in the economic situation, creating opportunities which did not exist before, or to institutional changes which give greater freedom to seize opportunities. In practice, a turning point of acceleration is usually associated with both types of change. The economic situation has become more favourable to growth, perhaps because of increasing opportunities for foreign trade, and this has strengthened the hands of those people who wish to change the institutions in the direction of permitting greater freedom.

These innovators are always a minority. New ideas are first put into practice by one or two or very few persons, whether they be new ideas in technology, or new forms of organization, new commodities, or other novelties. These ideas may be accepted rapidly by the rest of the population. More probably they are received with scepticism and unbelief, and make their way only very slowly at first if at all. After a while the new ideas are seen to be successful, and are then accepted by increasing numbers. Thus it is often said that change is the work of an elite, or that the amount of change depends on the quality of leadership in a community. This is true enough if it implies no more than that the majority of people are not innovators, but merely imitate what others do. It is, however, somewhat misleading if it is taken to imply that some specific class or group of people get all the new ideas. For each innovator is an individual person, who may be advanced in some things, and just as reactionary in others; and who has no necessary connection with other innovators, either of class, of kinship or other connection. Nevertheless it is sometimes the case that the innovators constitute a separate group, or at least are forced to become a group, conscious of sharing the same interests, because barriers to their advancement force them to band together in self-defence or in attack. New ideas are not originated in any single class, but the originators may well find themselves moulded into a new class by the resistance which society makes to their innovations.

One of the more fruitful observations in the theory of economic growth is the generalization that it is 'new men' who play the most prominent part in effecting change at this turning point. This means that the ruling classes in the previous situation of relative stagnation are seldom to be found among those who are seizing the new opportunities, or effecting institutional changes which increase freedom to manoeuvre. In the first place, the ruling classes are usually satisfied with the *status quo;* they have no need to seek

new opportunities. It is people who are frustrated by the current set-up who seek other ways of using their energies and of realizing their ambitions. At the same time, while it is not those at the top of the social structure who initiate change, neither is it those who are at the bottom. Those who are at the bottom may be caught in the toils of slavery, or of serfdom, or of caste, and may not be able to seize new opportunities; or they may just be too poor, too uneducated, or lacking in courage or in traditions of enterprise. The new men thus come from intermediate social classes, probably near enough to the top to have some resources, some personal freedom, and some tradition of action. In Japan the new men of 1868 belonged to a lower order of the nobility, who were chafing at the loss of former privileges. In Western Europe in the thirteenth and fourteenth centuries the new men were former serfs or their descendants who had escaped into the protection of towns. In Africa the new men are the detribalized, who have some smattering of western education, and who can no longer fit into the old tribal patterns. Needless to say, this generalization is not absolutely rigid. The new men may include among their number one or two of the old aristocrats, and one or two from the lowest classes, since there are always individual exceptions to the class patterns. The generalization states only that the great majority of the new men will be drawn from an intermediate station.

The new opportunities, in the second place, may challenge the economic power of the existing ruling class. They may alter the value of land, on which the wealth of that class is based. Or they may challenge serfdom, or slavery, or by providing new opportunities for employment, may raise wages to the discomfiture of the ruling class. Then this class will be hostile to the new opportunities, and there may be a struggle for power, even to the point of civil war. Alternatively it is possible that the new opportunities do not menace the ruling class economically, in the sense of reducing their wealth, but are an ultimate menace politically, in the sense that as the new men grow rich they will demand an equal share of prestige and of political power. In this case compromise is possible, for the ruling class may follow the example of the new men in exploiting the new opportunities (consider, for example, the role of the old landed aristocracy in the early development of the British coal and iron industries), and may agree to receive some of the new men into their ranks by inter-marriage or by ennobling them. Thus the development of new opportunities may in extreme cases require a civil war; but it may also be achieved by compromises after struggles of less intensity and bitterness.

The 'Whig' historians have tended to dramatize the role of revolution in effecting change, while the 'Tory' historians have played it

down. To the Whigs, revolution has seemed to be the necessary climax of change—like the bursting of the egg to release the chicken, or of the chrysalis to release the butterfly. The Tory, on the other hand, has pointed out that much fundamental change takes place without civil war. The old ruling classes may adopt the new ideas, and may thus become part of the new ruling class; or they may compromise with the new men and incorporate them into the old ruling class. If revolution comes, it comes long after the new men first appeared— perhaps even centuries later; for it comes only when they have been so successful and so well established for so long that they are in a position to command enough armed forces to challenge and to defeat the government. By this time most of the rights they seek have long been conceded. These generalizations, however, go too far. They apply well enough to the English Civil War, or to the French Revolution, or to the wars of independence in North and South America, in the sense that the propositions established by these revolutions might have been accepted in any case in another generation or two even without war. But they do not apply to the Haitian Revolution, to the Restoration in Japan, to the Chinese Revolution (1912) or to the Russian Revolution, or to the succession of uprisings in twentieth century Europe and Latin America which have brought the dictators into power. Some revolutions may have been 'unnecessary', in the sense that history seems to have been going their way in any case; but others have created a sharp break with the past, and even a reversal of previous trends.

Another suggestion is that the decisive role in the acceleration of economic growth is always played by townsmen. It is probably true that townsmen contribute more towards change than do people living in the country, not because of their biological superiority, but for reasons of environment or opportunity. Thus, the towns led the struggle for greater economic freedom in the closing centuries of the Middle Ages in Europe; but then townsmen tend to be prominent in organizing most political movements, whether their aim is greater freedom or less, if only because government is usually done from cities, to which the politically ambitious are attracted. It is also natural that townsmen should take the lead in the advancement of trade, of manufactures, and in these days of invention; and natural that the advancement of agricultural techniques has depended, until the scientific revolution of recent decades, mainly upon the countrymen. The atmosphere of towns is also alleged to be more favourable to the attitudes and beliefs which favour growth. The fact that large numbers of people are thrown together in towns, in a competitive struggle for existence, weakens kinship ties and excessive respect for status; encourages impersonal economic relations and a willingness

to trade wherever opportunities are favourable; and sharpens the wits. Though, presumably in these and other respects one should distinguish between commercial towns, on the one hand, and military, cathedral, or political towns on the other. In addition, the fact that towns develop a great range of arts and entertainments means that the opportunities for spending money are virtually unlimited, that wealth tends to acquire as much prestige as birth, and that ambition is stimulated. Townsmen are also alleged to be more open minded and less superstitious than countrymen, and therefore to be better placed to pursue those scientific enquiries which result in improved techniques. The countryman is impressed by the power of nature, since nature so often frustrates all his work, with its droughts, its floods, its storms, its epidemic diseases of crops, and other signs of its strength. The town, on the other hand, is created by man, who has learnt enough of the secrets of nature to be able to erect great buildings, to trap water in great reservoirs and transport it where he wants it, to summon electricity out of the skies to be his servant, and so forth. So the townsman is more easily tempted to believe that man can do anything he wants to do, if he tries hard enough. There is no doubt that the attitudes of townsmen differ in many respects from those of countrymen simply because the town throws large numbers of people together. There is also no doubt that some of the results are specially favourable to growth. But towns have also played their part at the turning points of deceleration. For the town is the home of the mob, and mobs are as prone to sweep tyrants into power, who reduce the opportunities for economic freedom, as they are to take part in liberating movements. The town is also the home of the monopolists —the traders' associations, the guilds, the workers' combinations— whose aim is to restrict opportunities and to keep out new men. The town takes the lead in restricting the size of families, which is sometimes good for growth of income per head, and sometimes bad. And the town takes the lead in movements for reducing the amount of work done, and for working sullenly or resentfully, instead of doing the best one can with the job in hand. If therefore a case can be made for saying that towns lead out of stagnation into growth, as good a case can be made for saying that they lead out of growth into stagnation.

An alternative, and somewhat opposed suggestion, expects economic growth to be most vigorous along economic 'frontiers'. 'Frontier' in this sense is hard to define: it combines the idea of a place which is geographically remote from the commercial capital of a country, with the idea of a frontier between man and nature, that is to say a place which is still settled rather sparsely. Frontiers are expected to promote growth both because the opportunities for

settlement attract immigration, and also because their distance from the capital prevents them from being easily controlled, whether by law, by convention, or by the pressure of organized groups. Their institutions are therefore free, and easily adaptable. This combination of opportunity and of freedom attracts from more settled areas some men of energy who find themselves frustrated in more hide-bound conditions. The generalization is of doubtful historical validity. If a country has rich resources, whether on its frontiers or not, it will attract immigrants; and if a country is attracting a lot of immigrants its social institutions will be flexible. As its resources begin to be exhausted, or all its lands are taken up, or its differential advantages are reduced, immigration will be reduced, and its institutions will tend to be more stable. This much seems true. But there is no particular reason to associate it with frontiers. Frontiers sometimes contain attractive resources, and sometimes do not. Every country of the world has had frontiers in this sense throughout its thousands of years of history, but there are extremely few where these frontiers have played a significant role in setting the pace of economic growth.

There is much more in the suggestion that frontiers are significant in the ordinary political or cultural sense of the place where two nations or two cultures meet. This is because of the decisive role which foreigners usually play in economic growth. Indeed we know of very few countries where an acceleration of growth can be attributed exclusively to domestic evolution. This seems to have happened in the Fertile Crescent, five thousand years ago, in China, and in Renaissance Italy. Most other countries owe a large part of their acceleration to foreign contacts. Foreigners bring new ideas of social behaviour and social relationships, which challenge established patterns, and weaken faith in their moral sanctions. Foreigners also bring new opportunities for trade, or for employment. Or it may be foreigners who loosen the grip of the existing ruling class, so that the new men get their chance to manoeuvre economically, or to make their *coup d'etat* politically. Foreigners may do this by threatening war, or by making war, or by conquering the country and in the extreme case deposing the existing ruling class. The behaviour of conquerors differs, and may make a great difference to the prospects for change. Some conquerors come to terms with the existing rulers, and support these rulers against dissident groups; while other conquerors back the dissident and overthrow the ruling class. Recent centuries have shown interesting differences in this respect between the British and the French. The British in India and in those parts of Africa which had strong ruling classes, such as Northern Nigeria, have made it their habit to back the ruling classes, and have always

been on very bad terms with the new men, who have therefore identified imperialism with reaction and stagnation—an identification which
is certainly not true of imperialisms in general. The French, on the
other hand, have believed in coming to terms with the new men, and
have gone out of their way to try to turn Africans or Asians into
Frenchmen, and to use them as a part of the French imperial system,
even in the very highest positions. We must not, however, be thought
to be putting an emphasis upon conquerors, for foreign traders, with
or without war, play as important or more important a role.

There is also an indirect effect of the foreign impact, namely the *nat'lism*
growth of nationalism, which tends in these days to have important
economic consequences. We associate nationalist political movements
with countries which are or have recently been in colonial status, but
nationalist feeling is by no means confined to such countries. Nowadays nearly all 'backward' countries resent their backwardness, and
are anxious to stimulate growth, and since backward is a purely
relative term, the desire that one's country should not fall behind
others in economic growth plays its part in the economic policies of
countries as widely different as Britain and China.

Strong nationalist feelings sometimes promote growth, but this is
not always the case. For the 'new men' in politics and the 'new men'
in economic activity are not the same, do not necessarily spring from
the same class, and are not always in sympathy with each other. In
the first place, not all nationalist politicians favour economic growth.
Some, like Gandhi, have reacted against 'westernism', and desire on
the contrary, to return to old ways. These however are in the
minority among nationalist leaders. In the second place, many of the
new men in economic activity are foreigners, and are therefore suspected or disliked by the nationalist leaders, who put obstacles in
their way, instead of encouraging them. Again, many nationalist
leaders are socialistically inclined; they are therefore suspicious even
of their own native *bourgeoisie*, and tend to restrict their activities.
All the same, nationalist governments tend in the direction of wanting to 'modernize' their economies; some of them extend educational
facilities, or protect the peasants from rapacious landlords, or embark on schemes of capital formation in roads, water or other public
services, or attack caste and other obstacles to vertical mobility, or
reduce the power of superstitious priesthoods, or in other ways seek
to promote change. Nationalism is a dangerous force, because it is
so often based upon stirring the passions of envy and of hatred in
great mobs of people; but it is also sometimes a constructive force,
and it is playing a part in effecting institutional changes favourable
to economic growth.

This brings us back to a point which we have made before, namely

that economic growth results not only from the manoeuvres of individuals, but also from the actions of governments. The turning point of acceleration may therefore in some cases be associated with the coming to power of a group of men—nationalists, for example—who are determined to promote economic growth, and who take positive measures for this purpose. In the materialistic conception of these matters, the new private entrepreneurs come first, capture the state, and use it to promote their ends. It may however happen that there is not much connection between the new private entrepreneurs and the new masters of the state; either may precede the other; and they may be hostile or indifferent to each other. If the government is both determined and intelligent it can do a great deal to advance economic growth, whether by the improvement of public services, by education, by the reform of institutions, by the encouragement of new industries, or by pioneering with new technologies. We shall be returning to these matters in detail in our final chapter.

We turn next to consider the turning points marking deceleration of the rate of economic growth. Here again we distinguish between deceleration due to reduced opportunities, and deceleration due to institutional changes which restrict freedom to manoeuvre while the economic opportunities have not lessened. A reduction of opportunities may well result in unfavourable institutional change, but we wish to distinguish this from institutional change which occurs through the evolution of institutions, and not as a result of changing economic circumstances.

Economic circumstances may change unfavourably from a variety of causes. Natural resources may be exhausted, or population may grow too large, or too small. Other countries, with better resources, may develop as strong competitors in international trade. There may be a great outflow of capital, or of skilled talent, to newly developing countries. There may be natural disaster—earthquake or hurricane, for example—or war may have similar effects. Some people have suggested that there may be unfavourable genetic change, due to the best types emigrating, or to unfavourable types immigrating, or to dilution of the superior types by intermarriage with the inferior, but we do not know enough about this subject to know how seriously the suggestion should be taken. Still others have suggested that there are natural tendencies towards stagnation involved in the way people spend their money as they grow richer; some say they spend too much, and others that they save too much; or that too much goes into tombs and monumental buildings; or that a voracious bureaucracy swells up; and so forth. In later chapters we shall be considering all these matters, both in terms of whether they are inevitable, and also in terms of their likely effects. It is sufficient for our present purpose to note

that economies can decline for one or other of these reasons, and have frequently declined in the past.

Our present interest is rather to enquire into the decline of economies on account of institutional change alone, not due to any of the matters mentioned in the preceding paragraph. This could occur because of increasing divergence between effort and reward, or because the channels of trade were increasingly restricted, or because of increasing limitations on economic freedom. There are always people who have an interest in furthering such developments. There are the people who might gain by having an increased share of the product of other people's labour, such as landowners, and would-be owners of serfs or slaves; it is not impossible for such people to gain political power, even by counter-revolution, and to use it to bring about a return to economic exploitation. Then there are the people who wish to retain an aristocracy by birth, and who resent the measures which aim at increasing equality of opportunity, such as progressive taxation, free schooling, or death duties; these also may acquire power. There are also the would-be monopolists, who are potentially any persons whose interests are damaged by competition; this means nearly everybody, since competition damages us in our individual capacities as producers, and benefits us only as consumers of other people's products; and so the political left and right may easily find common ground in restricting competition, trade, change and growth. And finally there are the planners, left and right, who dislike the results of economic freedom, and who may succeed in subjecting managers, workers, and controllers of resources to such extensive regulation that the pace of change is reduced. It is by no means inevitable that economic growth will continue once it has started.

It is necessary to emphasize that institutional change does not depend exclusively upon changes in physical environment, in technology, or otherwise in material conditions. Changes in these factors do often give rise to accommodating changes in institutions, but it is also possible that institutions may change so to speak on their own, without material conditions changing. Thus the Haitian Revolution, which destroyed a prosperity based upon slavery, and substituted for it poverty and freedom, cannot be attributed to technological or environmental change. The opposing view springs from excessive emphasis on the power of the economic trend to dominate political and other social beliefs and relations. The economic trend may be in favour of developing this or that line of activity, but the political trend, or the trend in social attitudes, or the trend in customs and taboos, may be all the other way. Prosperity can be destroyed merely because people adopt habits or beliefs which are inconsistent with

economic expansion, or because groups come into power who impose unfavourable institutional changes.

Whether a society will permit groups to use political power for restrictive purposes depends very much on how well educated people are in political and economic matters. If enough people value the free economy, and are vigilant in preserving it, the economy will remain free. To explain why some peoples achieve and preserve freedom more easily than others would start a long enquiry, probably without conclusive results. It is sufficient for our purposes to observe that some communities have freedom in their history and traditions, while others have instead a long history and tradition of authoritarian regulation. A country which has a long tradition of freedom will be vigilant in keeping its institutions free, and if they succumb, we may surmise that it has run into serious troubles, such as war, or the reduction of its economic resources, which have shaken confidence in freedom. Whereas, a country which has a long tradition of illiberal institutions finds its freedom hard to win, and hard to keep.

These differences of history and tradition can sometimes be explained by geography. For, just as foreign influences play a great part in helping to start growth, so also they play a great part in helping to stave off decline. A country is most likely to retain free institutions if it is easily accessible. For it is then hard for the social structure to ossify. There is a coming and going of people, of goods and of ideas. New opportunities create new rich and new poor, and preserve vertical social mobility. New ideas prevent the more dusty superstitions from taking hold. The constant meeting of strangers makes it necessary to take men on their merits, rather than by reference to their status. And so on. Accessibility does not guarantee freedom; it may even increase the risk of foreign conquest. But it makes it harder for the enemies of freedom to prevail; and even the foreign conqueror may find it profitable not to stand in the way of economic growth.

(b) The Cycle of Change

This chapter is concerned with institutions from a particular angle, namely their evolution in the direction of stimulating or restricting growth, through the association of effort and reward, through facilitating specialization, or through increasing economic freedom. We have studied acceleration of this evolution, and the cumulative processes which are then set in motion; and we have also seen that deceleration can occur, and has its own cumulatve downward impetus. We have next to consider theories of social evolution. Is there a path which institutional change inevitably follows? Is there a succession of stages? Is there inevitable 'progress'? Or is the

movement of history along some cyclical curve?

Many people have interpreted history as showing that each community must pass through certain specified stages of evolution. Such stages are defined differently, according to the writer's interest. If he is interested in the way people earn their living, he may see the community passing inevitably from nomadism, through settled agriculture, to trade and then to industry; and may expect its institutions to change in ways appropriate to each of these ways of making a living. If he is interested in class relations, he may see instead some such succession as primitive communism, slavery, serfdom, proletarianization, and 'socialism'. He may study religious change, from animism and ancestor worship to monotheism and rationalism. Or, in the sphere of political ideas, he may profess to see an ever widening allegiance, from the family, to the village, the nation, the empire, and finally to the United Nations.

Inevitable successions of stages are no longer a popular idea. Even the Communists have abandoned the idea that a country must pass through capitalism before reaching socialism or—since the arrival of communism in China—that communism can be made only by an urban proletariat and not by a peasantry. It is now clear that a community can bye-pass one or more of these stages, 'jumping' say from 'serfdom' to 'socialism', and equally clear that it may move 'backwards' as well as 'forwards', say from imperial to racial or to national or to provincial allegiance in politics. One reason why stages are no longer considered inevitable is that we have become more aware of the impact of one community upon another. Perhaps in former times, when communities were more isolated, each community could go through a series of stages without reference to what was happening in the outside world; but in these days the influence of a few powerful states stretches all over the world, and even the most primitive communities find themselves imitating the most advanced, without reference to the difference in their 'stages'. At the same time, those people who believe themselves to be bearers of the most advanced ideas, usually also consider their missionary techniques to be invincible; the Communists believe that they can turn any society communist, whatever its stage; the rationalists think rationalism is good for everyone; the internationalists carry their gospel into the most remote and self-sufficient villages. The idea that the stages are inevitable is resisted most by those who consider themselves to have reached the highest stage.

The idea of stages was also bound up, to some extent, with belief in the inevitability of progress, and it has therefore receded with this belief. The idea of progress is rather new in human history. Before the eighteenth century mankind more usually believed that there had

been a Golden Age in the past, and that history recorded the fall of man. Then for two centuries belief in the inevitability of progress seized men's imaginations, reaching its height when the theories of biological evolution arrived on the scene to complete the trilogy of body, mind and spirit—the mind evolving towards rationalism, and the spirit towards liberalism. Nowadays hardly anybody believes that progress is inevitable, and many dispute even that progress is a meaningful concept. Certainly, to bring the matter down to the plane of our restricted interest, it is not possible to hold that institutions evolve cumulatively in directions favourable to growth, since it is clear that there have been many periods in the past when the opposite has happened—when slavery has succeeded freedom, or increasing obstacles to trade have reduced specialization, or increasing rigidity of social classes and castes has reduced the opportunity to man-oeuvre. Economic growth is not inevitable; and even the most vigorous growth can be stifled.

The nineteenth century optimists were of course aware that growth had often been stifled in the past; their belief in progress was founded on the idea that men—or at least men of European stock—had 'escaped from history', through the accumulation of knowledge. The most plausible defence of the proposition would be to say that it was possible for growth to be stifled in the past because men did not know enough about it, or about the ways in which it was stifled. They lost their freedom because they did not know enough political science to recognize attacks on freedom and to create invincible defences. Or they permitted measures which stifled growth because they did not know enough political economy. With the accumulation of know-ledge of the social sciences, its diffusion among the people, and the increased application of reason in human relations, growth might hereinafter be secure. It is precisely this belief in the power of reason in human affairs which the twentieth century has lost. We know that human affairs are governed by men's desires, and that these cannot be proved to be right or wrong by reason, or be resisted exclusively by rational demonstrations.

To reject inevitable growth or decline is not necessarily to accept the cyclical conceptions. One may instead take a neutral position, denying both that growth is inevitable and also that a cyclical move-ment is inevitable. For changes in the rate of growth are not ex-clusively due to the evolution of institutions. Once more we make the distinction between changes which are due to changing economic opportunities, and changes which are due to the evolution of institu-tions. Thus the rate of growth may slacken because population over-takes resources; or because of natural disaster; or because of a shift in the world's trade routes; or because of a decline of world demand

for the products in which the country specializes; or for many other reasons not originating in internal institutional change. One may even believe that growth is bound to end sooner or later—for one or other of such reasons—without believing that there is necessarily a cycle of institutional change. The present chapter, however, is concerned only with changes due to the evolution of institutions; changes due to other causes are discussed in later chapters.

Cyclical theories of institutional change assert that growth promotes contraction, and *vice versa*. It is not thereby asserted that the long run effect of this cycle is to leave the standard of living unaltered. For cyclical movement is quite consistent with long run growth or decline. It is not asserted that the upward and downward movements must be of equal magnitude. All that is required is that growth and decline should alternate.

There are three classes of cyclical theories of institutional change, operating respectively in terms of biology, of social attitudes, and of social groupings.

Biological theories associate movements in one direction with one biological type, and movements in another with a different biological type. Men of one biological type exert influence in favour of institutions of the kind that promote growth, whereas men of the opposite type are disposed towards institutions of the kind that restrict growth. Then, according to such theories, these biological types alternate with each other. When the 'progressives' are in power, they promote growth. Inevitably, however, the ruling class comes to be diluted with 'non-progressives'. Why this is so is not clear. Perhaps the 'progressives' fail to reproduce themselves adequately—the ruling classes in society usually have fewer children than the rest. Or perhaps they inter-marry with the 'non-progressives'. We do not know enough about the relations between human biology and social behaviour to pursue this line of thought profitably.

The cycle in social attitudes corresponds not to biological differences, but to opposed longings in the breast of each of us. Each of us sees the advantages of growth and the advantages of stability; each of us wants freedom and control; each of us wants material goods, and at the same time realizes that material goods are worthless in comparison with spiritual values; and so on. When growth begins, we are enthusiastic for it; but after a while it palls. We begin to long for stability; we reject materialism and return to spiritual preoccupations; and so on. Thus social attitudes alternate between favouring growth, and reacting against it, and social institutions alter in the same way. Such a theory does not, however, explain social change until it provides the link between changes in attitudes and changes in institutions. For institutions are changed by the efforts of groups of

individuals, usually because they have an interest in changing them (material, political, religious), and the change is resisted by other groups, whose interest is tied up with the *status quo*. Hence any theory of social change has to be translatable into terms of social groups with conflicting interests (not necessarily material).

Cyclical theories in terms of social groups may be idealistic or materialistic. The idealistic theories assert, like that which we have just considered, that men's beliefs swing between opposing poles. We are for change, or for stability; for freedom, or for authority; for the things of this world, or for a passionate concern with God; and so on. Whichever is the prevailing mood at the time establishes itself; the persons so disposed acquire influence and power, and institutions are moulded to their mood. After a while, however, people begin to revolt against their way of life. Their outlook has lost the fire which it had when it was being established; corruption has crept in; and the inadequacies of the philosophy are more obvious. So opposing schools are created, and it is only a matter of time before some individual of fiery personality founds a 'new' faith which sweeps the masses in behind him. Then we get a religious reformation, or a political revolution, or whatever it may be. These idealistic theories presuppose that men are moved by ideas of what life should be—in political or religious or romantic terms—and that these ideas by themselves, unidentified with material interests are capable of effecting social change; or that if they are identified with material interests, the ideas are primary and the interests they attract are secondary forces in social change (e.g. that it was Hitler who attracted financial backers, and not financial backers who made Hitler).

The materialistic theories, on the other hand, see social change in terms primarily of changing economic interest. These theories may take two lines. They may assert that the new economic class which has started the acceleration in the rate of growth—the 'new' men—in due course turns against further change. Or they may assert that growth stimulates resistance among those who lose by it, and that these in due course organize themselves to restrict further growth.

The first line may be elaborated as follows. While the new men are acquiring power and influence, they favour aggressively the 'open door'. They support competition, increased trade, vertical mobility, and the like. However, once they have established themselves, they begin to be more interested in protecting their own position than in assuring an open door for others. Former free traders now advocate tariffs. Former believers in competition now seek to build up monopolies. Former social climbers now send their own children to exclusive schools, and try to assure them a privileged entry into the world of economic affairs. The Radicals become Conservatives. Thus

the social system begins to ossify. Besides, economic conditions change. The opportunities which brought the new class into wealth and power tend to disappear; for there are changes in technology, or in demand, or in the sources of supply. Growth is a response to a succession of stimuli, each of which may require different treatment from the last. This class may not be able to adapt itself to these successive changes; it may feel its wealth threatened, and may take steps to prevent unfavourable changes. A ruling class tends to lose its adaptability because it is hamstrung by its own traditions; there is a tendency to glorify the precepts and techniques which brought it into power, to look backwards, and to idealize the ways of pioneering forefathers. Hence, as conditions change, demanding new techniques, the class ceases to be able to cope, and becomes a drag on progress. When this class was new, its new men had to challenge an existing ruling group before they could make the fullest use of their opportunities; now they in turn may become like the old group, anxious to protect themselves from a new generation of new men.

The second line follows the behaviour of people who are hurt by accelerated growth. To begin with, there are people whose skills relate to the old technologies or demands, and who cannot adjust to changing conditions. There are the craftsmen who build up unions to protect themselves, and who impose restrictions on apprenticeship or on dilution, and insist on strict demarcation of the jobs which they alone may do. There are the small shopkeepers who resent the growth of large retailing; they band together to assure themselves protection, by exerting pressure on manufacturers, or by lobbying for legislation to control the chains. Many different groups are affected by change, and many of these groups form associations and bring pressure to stop or slow down the changes from which they are suffering. Since each of us is likely to suffer from change, in our capacity as producers, economic growth makes as many enemies as friends. When the social system was young, and demonstrating its power to deliver the goods, it commanded the enthusiasm of the people. But, as the number of dissidents grows, the ruling class ceases to command the allegiance of those over whom they rule. The society is divided against itself. There is a new struggle for power, in the course of which the ruling class tends to lose confidence in itself, and to compromise with the principles on which it came into existence. Barriers are erected to protect those whom change would hurt, and economic growth is slowed down.

There is no doubt that these things may happen. Equally we cannot say that they are inevitable. If there is a cycle, it completes itself more rapidly in some communities than in others, for reasons which we cannot fully explain. If we ask why community 'A' has remained

L

free for so long, while community 'B' has lost its liberty so easily, we are often driven to such explanations as, 'these people are less given to extremes', or 'these people have a better political sense' or some other mere restatement of the question. But if 'A' can hold out longer than 'B', perhaps it might hold out indefinitely, learning from experience what the pitfalls are? Perhaps 'indefinitely' is too long; but at any rate we clearly cannot predict how long or how short the cycle will be, and if the institutional changes are postponed long enough, economic growth may accelerate or decelerate for one or other of the many reasons not arising from institutional change itself. In sum, institutions may change in ways favourable or unfavourable to growth. The change may be a reaction against what has gone before, or it may not. If it is a reaction, it may have set in early or it may be long delayed. This is about all that we can say on the direction change may take.

BIBLIOGRAPHICAL NOTE

There is a large literature on the subject of property, corporate enterprise, and the control of business. See for example, A. A. Berle and G. L. Means, *The Modern Corporation and Private Property*, New York, 1932; P. T. Bauer, 'Concentration in Tropical Trade', *Economica*, November, 1953; N. S. Buchanan, *The Economics of Corporate Enterprise*, New York, 1940; J. Burnham, *The Managerial Revolution*, New York, 1941; J. M. Clark, *The Social Control of Business*, 2nd Edn., New York, 1939; W. A. Lewis, *Overhead Costs*, London, 1950; E. A. G. Robinson, *Monopoly*, London, 1943; J. A. Schumpeter, *Socialism, Capitalism and Democracy*, New York, 1923; T. Veblen, *Absentee Ownership*, New York, 1923.

On the relations between social mobility and economic growth see J. Wedgewood, *The Economics of Inheritance*, London, 1929; H. Pirenne, *Economic and Social History of Mediaeval Europe*, London, 1936; M. J. Levy, 'Contrasting Factors in the Modernization of China and Japan', *Economic Development and Cultural Change*, October 1953.

For problems of agriculture consult P. T. Bauer, *The Rubber Industry*, London, 1948; Food and Agriculture Organization, *The Consolidation of Fragmented Agricultural Holdings*, Washington, 1950, and *Cadastral Surveys and Records of Rights in Lands*, Rome, 1953; W. A. Lewis, 'Thoughts on Land Settlement', *Journal of Agricultural Economics*, June 1954; C. K. Meek, *Land Law and Custom in the Colonies*, London, 1946; A. Pim, *Colonial Agricultural Production*, London, 1946; P. Ruoff, ed., *Approaches to Community Development*, The Hague, 1953; United Nations, *Land Reform: Defects of Agrarian Structure*, New York, 1951, and *Rural Progress through Co-operatives*, New York, 1954.

On religion, see references at the end of Chapter II. On slavery, B. Farrington, *Greek Science*, London, 1944; J. E. Cairnes, *The Slave Power*, London, 1863; Eric Williams, *Capitalism and Slavery*, Chapel Hill, 1945.

BIBLIOGRAPHICAL NOTE

On small industries there is an informative article by E. Reubens, 'Small Scale Industry in Japan', *Quarterly Journal of Economics*, August 1947; also useful is J. Stepanek and C. Prien, 'The Role of Rural Industries in Under-developed Areas', *Pacific Affairs*, March 1950.

For theories of social change see references at the end of Chapter I. Also J. J. Spengler, 'Theories of Socio-Economic Growth', in National Bureau of Economic Research, *Problems in the Study of Economic Growth*, New York, 1949, which has extensive references to the literature.

CHAPTER IV

KNOWLEDGE

THE proximate causes of economic growth are the effort to economize, the accumulation of knowledge, and the accumulation of capital. In the two preceding chapters we have examined the effort to economize, in terms both of the values which make economy seem worth while, and also of the institutions which encourage or frustrate economizing effort. In this chapter we consider the accumulation and application of knowledge, while the following chapter will deal with the accumulation of capital. We have already emphasized, in our introductory chapter, that these three factors are separated only for analytical purposes; they are equally important, and mutually inter-dependent.

Economic growth depends both upon technological knowledge about things and living creatures, and also upon social knowledge about man and his relations with his fellowmen. The former is often emphasized in this context, but the latter is just as important since growth depends as much upon such matters as learning how to administer large scale organizations, or creating institutions which favour economizing effort, as it does upon breeding new seeds or learning how to build bigger dams.

This chapter is divided into three parts. In the first part we examine the process by which knowledge grows; the second part deals with the application of knowledge to production; and the third part deals with training. Once more the division is analytical only. The growth and the application of knowledge stimulate each other, and where one lags behind the other is certain to lag as well.

1. THE GROWTH OF KNOWLEDGE

Knowledge grows because man is by nature curious and experimental. His curiosity causes him to enquire into things because they attract his attention, even though they may not be immediately relevant to his practical problems. And his desire to experiment is also greatly stimulated by the practical tasks in hand, and the problems they pose for solution.

Because each generation builds upon the knowledge of its forefathers the most important invention which has helped the accumulation of knowledge is the invention of writing. Until writing was invented each generation could pass on only what it could remember in the head—and how little this is we can discover if we compare

how much history the illiterate historians have passed on, in those
primitive societies which have a specially appointed class of historians, with the amount of history passed on in literate societies—
say comparing the history of the nineteenth century in both cases.
Even more important is the difference which the art of writing makes
to the handling of abstract ideas. Progress in mathematics, for
example, is impossible without writing (many illiterate societies do
not even have words to describe more than the first dozen numerals),
and in every other field of study the knowledge of illiterates must end
in the earliest stages of abstraction.

The second invention which has made all the difference to the rate
of growth of knowledge is the invention of scientific method. This is
really the work of the philosophers. It began in Ancient Greece, with
the invention of logic and of metaphysics, but it did not come to
flower until nearly two thousand years later, when the Renaissance
reopened these fields of enquiry. Since that time the rate of growth of
knowledge has been phenomenal compared with anything that went
before.

Accordingly, in considering the growth of knowledge one must
distinguish three eras, the pre-literate, the era of writing without
scientific method, and the era of scientific method. In the same way
we must distinguish between societies according to whether they are
illiterate, and according to whether their culture and philosophy are
imbued with the scientific outlook.

Much of the discussion of the conditions appropriate to the growth
of knowledge relates to societies in the second stage—literate, but
pre-scientific. It is fascinating to ask why there was greater progress
in some countries than in others during this stage, or in some
centuries than in others, within the same country. Similar questions
might be asked about countries in the pre-literate stage, though we
do not get very far with such questions both because the pre-literate
peoples do not differ so widely in their technical attainments (they
had invented the same tools, agriculture, smelting, and other technical processes, the major differences being whether or not they used
the wheel, and whether they were capable of building in stone), and
also because the evidence is so scanty. There are greater differences
and more evidence in the literate but pre-scientific societies. The
questions are not, however, any more answerable, and since they
have little bearing upon the practical problems of our time (all
countries now having available to them the results of the scientific
revolution), we shall not spend a great deal of time upon them.

(a) Pre-scientific Societies

Broadly speaking, the rate of growth of knowledge in literate,

pre-scientific societies seems to have depended upon their philosophical attitudes, and upon their class structure.

The growth of knowledge requires a reasoning, questioning, experimental mind. This attitude presumably flourished best in certain environments, but we can only speculate as to which environments were most favourable, and cannot hope to reach firm conclusions on this subject. Presumably the questing mind flourished better in countries where religion was competitive, in the sense that there were many religious cults, between which the citizen was free to choose, than in countries where religion was authoritarian and monopolized. Similarly, the enquiring mind would flourish best in societies where political and economic power were widely diffused, and liberally exercised; this is indeed an indispensable condition for free speculation in the field of social institutions. The mind would also retain and develop the habit of questioning in an environment where it constantly encountered diversity of experience; in the town, where visitors come from all over the country, with different ways, rather than in the country; in the community engaging in foreign trade, and hearing constantly of different modes of living and doing; or in the area with many diverse resources, giving rise to great differentiation of occupations, which in turn produces different outlooks upon the world. Knowledge grows considerably through the cross-fertilization of cultures, so we should expect geographical situation to play an important role. There may also have been a secular pattern; a young and ambitious nation, it has been suggested, would be experimental; whereas, as the nation grew successful it would set in its ways, take pride in its past, its race, its religions and its institutions, and lose its faith in the virtues of free enquiry. We do not know what were the conditions for the questing mind in the pre-scientific societies, and we are not now ever likely to find out.

The same goes for the effect of class structure upon the growth of knowledge. Here one gets different results according to whether one considers the invention and application of new processes by the upper classes, or invention by peasants and artisans. As for the upper classes, it has been argued that the growth of science depended on the existence of a leisure class, with the time to think abstractly and to experiment, but this is a dubious proposition, partly because in such societies nearly everybody has leisure for half the year, when agricultural work has ceased, and partly because at this level of technology progress comes more from observing and experimenting in the course of doing one's job than it does from abstract thinking. It has also been argued that the upper classes are less likely to be interested in the adoption of labour saving devices in slave societies than in free societies, but we have already suggested (Chapter III, section 4(*b*))

that this argument fails in commercial slavery. As for the attitude of peasants and of artisans, it seems likely that much depends on the extent to which they are allowed to keep the produce of their labour. If landlords and princes are sure to take from them all but the cost of subsistence, however much they may produce, they will have little incentive to invent or to adopt ways of increasing output. This is perhaps the greatest single social factor affecting technological progress in such societies, since in such societies the attitude of the man on the job is probably much more important than the theoretical speculations of gentlemen of leisure. Another 'class' factor which may have been important in these societies was the extent to which knowledge was monopolized. Though we call them literate societies, in fact only a tiny proportion of the people were literate, mostly priests, administrators, and business men. In many societies the literate guarded their secrets jealously. The illiterate also formed themselves into guilds, and made a mystery of their crafts. Knowledge does not grow rapidly if it is kept a secret for the few.

Whatever the reasons may have been, communities have differed widely in the status they accorded to scholars, and in the respect and affection in which they were held—e.g. consider the favourable status of scholars in China or in Renaissance Europe. It seems most doubtful, however, whether these differences in the status of scholarship have had much bearing upon technological progress, both because few scholars were interested in science, and also because the science in which they were interested was remote from technology. During most of the written history of man, the growth of technology has owed very little to science as we now understand the term, that is to the application of an existing body of abstract principles. Invention has been done by two classes of people, by the worker at the job, and by the professional inventor. The former class includes all those who, in the course of their daily activities, observed ways of improving their methods, or experimented with ideas which came to them. The latter consisted at any time of a few individuals, usually gentlemen of leisure, who were interested in the science of their day. For the most part their interests were metaphysical, theological, or astrological, and if they turned their minds towards invention the results were only occasionally of practical importance, if only because their isolation from the practical tasks of daily life prevented them from knowing in what fields the most fruitful practical contributions could be made. In the earliest days these 'scientists' gave extremely little thought to technological questions, However, with the passage of time, the accumulation of technical knowledge, and the writing of the first treatises on the subject, an increasing proportion gave their minds to such matters. There was a comparative outburst of mechanical

invention in the Greek world, during the five centuries before the birth of Christ. Thereafter, so far as we know, the interest of scholars in these matters was subordinated to theological and other speculations, and there is no similar outburst until after the Renaissance.

It is just as difficult to account for a decline in the rate of growth of technical knowledge in one country as it is to account for differences between countries. Presumably one has to seek the reasons which cause scholars to disinterest themselves in technology, investors to lose interest in labour saving, or the common people to lose interest in increasing output. One has for this the same range of explanations as we saw in Chapter III, section 5, when we were dealing with the general problem of institutional change. One can invoke biological factors, or changes in the valuation placed upon material things, or changes in political or religious attitudes which make free enquiry dangerous, or checks to investment resulting from monopoly or from insecurity, or increasing pressures upon the common people which deprive peasants and artisans of the incentive to increase their output, or excessive war or civil strife. The most interesting case for study is the apparent decline of technological progress in the Greek world after about the first century B.C., for which no fully convincing explanations exist as yet. There is also considerable discussion of the possibilities of technical stagnation in our own day, to which we shall refer in Chapter V (section 3(*d*)).

(b) Invention and Research

The third stage in the history of technology begins with the Renaissance, which stimulated the growth of knowledge in every field. In so far as relates to economic growth, the most important results of the intellectual activity of the Renaissance occurred in the philosophy of knowledge, in mathematics, in social science and in mechanical invention. In the philosophy of knowledge the foundation was laid for the development of pure science which, though it did not begin to flower for some time, in due course proved of such fundamental importance. Mathematics gained immediately, though the consequences of this were also postponed. The social sciences also gained immediately, for there were set in train at once political speculations out of which the modern studies of economics, politics, psychology, jurisprudence and sociology have grown. There was also a revival of interest in mechanical inventions, which gained momentum in the sixteenth, seventeenth and eighteenth centuries, until the nineteenth century saw the emergence, among the class of inventors, of people who engaged in invention not as an offshoot of their daily labour, or as gentlemen of leisure seeking knowledge, but as a full time occupation, at which they hoped to make their fortunes.

Pure science made its contribution to technology first of all through chemistry, starting slowly in the seventeenth century, and not achieving spectacular effects until the nineteenth. Then came also the applications of electricity, and in our own century the spectacular contributions of other branches of physics.

This background is necessary if we are to understand the curious relationship which now exists between science and industry. The layman thinks of the world in which he lives—at any rate the manipulated part of it—as having been created by science, and is often astounded to learn that over large realms of industry the practical men have no use (or have even contempt) for scientists. The fact is that the great inventions of the eighteenth and nineteenth centuries were not made by scientists—the steam engine, the inventions in weaving and spinning, the new system of agricultural rotations, the new ways of smelting ores, the machine tools—these were all invented by practical people who knew no science, or very little. It is only in the twentieth century that a scientific education has become essential for the would-be inventor, or that the discoveries of science have become the major source of further technological progress.

Science has affected invention in the twentieth century in more ways than one. Not only has it become necessary to be a scientist in order to be an inventor, but a good deal of invention has now passed beyond the individual working on his own, into the laboratory staffed by a team of scientists. These transitions are by no means complete. It is still possible for the worker at the bench, using his machine, to notice ways in which performance could be improved, and to suggest useful modifications. Progress is still made in these ways, though it is not great in relation to the total stream of invention. It is also still possible for the lone inventor, with some scientfic knowledge combined with a mechanical flair, to make quite important inventions. Probably the greatest number of inventions in the fields of mechanical engineering, as well as of animal or plant genetics, are still the work of a single mind. Team work has its best use in the chemistry of materials and in the physics of radio and of nuclear fission.

Much is now said and written about the organization of technological research, meaning by this the kind of research which is done by teams in expensive laboratories. It is still, however, necessary to take account of the work of the lone inventor. His position seems also to have been transformed. A few still work on their own, at home or in their laboratories, in their spare time, or even full time, but most have found invention too risky a source of full time income. The majority seek employment by others, who will provide a laboratory and a salary, with perhaps also a share of royalties. They may share

the laboratory with other inventors, each pursuing his own line. And they may be restricted by their employers as to the subject on which they may work. Conditions range all the way from freedom to working in a team. The number of gentlemen of leisure, who invent for pleasure, is insignificant (it always was).

The growing importance of team research presents new problems of organization. Such research is very expensive, and is therefore beyond the reach of individual small firms. It is therefore the very largest firms which have pioneered this kind of research and this in turn gives them a very substantial competitive advantage over their small and medium size competitors. This advantage, however, is reduced if research is disintegrated from other activities of the firm, and done collectively for a group of firms or for an industry as a whole. This line of development has been pursued in the United Kingdom. On the one hand there have been created, with some financial help from the government, a large number of co-operative research institutions, owned and controlled by such firms as care voluntarily to join and to subscribe to the institution. And on the other hand there are also a number of government research institutions, wholly financed and controlled by the government, whose discoveries and inventions are open to all, such as the institutions controlled by the Department of Scientific and Industrial Research. Besides these institutions, the government also makes grants to private institutions, including university departments, to conduct particular researches; this is the principal way in which bodies like the Agricultural Research Council or the Medical Research Council discharge the duties laid upon them. This disintegration of team research is not complete, since in addition to what is done collectively or under government auspices, large firms continue to finance their own private teams and laboratories.

Another effect of science upon the growth of technical knowledge has been to divide the process into three separate stages, namely the formulation of scientific principles, the application of these principles to given technical problems, and the development of technical inventions to the point where they are ready for commercial exploitation. The first of these stages, the advancement of pure science, is now almost entirely left to the universities and to other noncommercial organizations. Now and then an industrial firm may permit a scientist in its laboratories to pursue researches which have no immediate relevance to its technical problems, but this is rare. The second stage, the stage of technological research, applying known scientific principles to the solution of commercial problems, is the point where the inventors and industrial research teams, private, co-operative, and public, take over from the universities (some such

work is done in universities and technical colleges also, but for these it is a lesser occupation). The result of the work done at this stage is a formula, a blueprint, or a model. Then comes the problem of translating this result into something which can be manufactured cheaply, in large quantities, and at standard quality. This production problem, known as the development stage, is often as difficult and as costly as anything that has gone before. For example, the idea of an aeroplane driven by jet propulsion preceded by many years the first flight of such a plane; vast time and money went into such problems as choosing metals able to stand the heat, or designing fuselages appropriate to the speed. The development stage cannot always be distinguished sharply from technical research, either because some of the development problems are technical, or because the same people engage in research and development. A line of principle can however be drawn.

In its effects upon the structure of industry the development stage presents the same problem as research, namely that in some instances only the biggest firms can afford to undertake the development work, and this gives them an advantage over their smaller rivals. Could this problem be tackled in the same way, namely by disintegrating development from the other responsibilities of the firm? The obstacle to doing this lies in the fact that the decision whether development should go forward is essentially a commercial decision, to be made in the light of estimates of the potential demand for the commodity, while the decisions which are made at the previous stages are more of the nature of scientific decisions. The advancement of pure science is in the hands of scientists, who go more or less by the principle that all knowledge is worth having for its own sake, a principle which is fortunately but only secondarily supported by the belief that all scientific knowledge becomes useful in due course in one way or another. At the stage of technological research, the decisions are not so exclusively scientific; some commercial judgement is also needed in choosing the problems which it is worth trying to solve; all the same, the scientific element is still of great importance, and not much is lost by disintegrating these decisions to institutions ruled jointly by scientists and by business men. It is quite appropriate at this stage that time and money should be spent on demonstrating a much larger number of possibilities than will in fact be taken up. However, once the scientists have demonstrated at the research level what is possible, their role is largely ended. The decision which of these possibilities is worth exploiting, and which should be neglected, is a commercial decision, to be made by people whose expertise is rather in the field of production costs and of potential sales.

In a private enterprise economy, this decision is left to the individual firm, which must make its own estimates and lose or gain according as the estimates are right or wrong. Alternatively, the decision could be entrusted to a committee of all the business men in the industry concerned, in which case the industry as a whole would decide which inventions to develop, and the industry as a whole would pay the cost. Apart from the difficulty of defining an industry for this purpose, many people believe that the effect of this would be to hold up progress, either because the industry acting collectively would also act monopolistically, to protect existing investments against technical change, or else because the collective judgement of new ideas is so often wrong that it is arguable that progress depends on individuals being free to back their own judgement despite collective disapproval. The decision might also be entrusted to a government committee created for this purpose, and given funds for developing new inventions. Such an agency has been created in the United Kingdom, but it has no monopoly of development, and can make decisions only about such inventions as are offered to it. To give a monopoly of decision to a government committee would seem to have the disadvantage of both worlds; because the decision would have to be made collectively the individual initiative would be suppressed; and because the decision makers were not using their own money they would have no pecuniary motive to take care that their decisions were commercially sound. We may therefore conclude as follows. We are likely to get best results at the development stage if any person who thinks that an invention will pay is free to back it with his own resources or with those of others who are willing to share the risk. In those cases where the development is very costly, this gives an advantage to those who command large resources. If, to avoid this differential advantage, development were made a collective responsibility, other disadvantages would follow. There is no perfect solution for any social problem. In any case, the advantage of large scale organization in some fields is one of the facts of life; we cannot always escape it, however much we try.

The division of the process of invention into the three stages of pure science, technical research, and development helps to throw light on the problem of patents. Discoveries in pure science cannot be patented. They are also not usually kept secret, not because the discoverer could not sometimes make a fortune by applying his discovery secretly, but mainly because it is contrary to the professional code of scientists to keep their discoveries secret. The advancement of science requires that many minds should work at the same problems, each fertilized by the thought of the others, and science would certainly suffer if the freer exchange of ideas were

substantially restricted. There are such restrictions today, on the movement of scientists across frontiers for international discussion, and on the publication of results in fields closely related to national defence; the restrictions are still small, but many people fear them because they fear that once the principle of free exchange of ideas is violated, restrictions may spread more widely. Since scientific ideas do not become private property, scientists cannot live by selling them. Hence the advancement of pure science is largely a charge upon the public funds.

When we pass to the stage of technical research, the results are patentable. This follows from the fact that technical research is financed mainly by people who expect to make a profit from it, and who must therefore obtain private property in the ideas derived therefrom. In the nineteenth century, when invention was done mainly by lone inventors, it used sometimes to be argued that the flow of inventions would not be significantly reduced even if the ideas could not become private property; either because the number of inventors inventing for the love of the thing was enough to keep up an adequate flow of inventions; or else because the inventor who kept his invention secret and exploited it commercially could make enough monopoly profit out of his invention in the early stages to reimburse himself for the expenses of invention. Neither of these arguments was accepted universally in the nineteenth century, and their chance of acceptance is even smaller today. Inventions must become private property if invention is to be financed by private interests. If technical research were financed out of public or non-commercial funds, the argument for private property would disappear; inventions could then be freely available to all. So long as invention is financed by interested parties, however, the results must become private property. The advantage of the patent system at this stage is that it not only protects the owner, but also encourages him to disclose his invention, and so maintains the free flow of scientific ideas.

Our patent system, however, conveys monopolies not only upon the inventor but also upon the developer, and later upon the commercial producer. The developer claims his monopoly on two separate grounds; he claims a monopoly of development, and also a monopoly of subsequent production. The inventor is free to license as many developers as he chooses, but in the vast majority of cases developers undertake to develop only if they are given an exclusive licence. The case for a monopoly of production is, however, sounder than the case for a monopoly of development. The monopoly of production rests on the same argument as the inventor's monopoly, namely, that since development is expensive those who are to finance it require some assurance that they will be able to

reimburse themselves by having a monopoly of production once they have solved the development problems. This is no reason, however, for giving a monopoly of development. For just as all inventors freely use the principles of science, in a race which gives the patent to the first successful inventor, so also there might be a race in which many developers worked on the invention, with the monopoly of production going to the first successful developer. This monopoly would follow automatically if development resulted in patentable processes, on the present definitions used by patent law, but the protection could also be widened to include the protection of all new industries, as the law was originally intended to do (and as is now done in those under-developed countries which accord 'pioneer status' to new industries). There are still many people who argue that neither development nor production needs protection. Essentially they argue that the advantages to be derived from priority are such that there would be an adequate flow of risk-bearers even without protection. This is certainly true of a number of industries; but it is equally true that there are other industries where priority confers little advantage, compared with the cost of development, and where the rate of progress might therefore be reduced if developers were not given exclusive rights.

The three-fold division of the process of invention into pure science, technical research, and development is important also in assessing where different countries should lay their emphasis. For example, it has now become popular to say that the United Kingdom, when compared with the United States, spends very adequately upon pure science, but falls behind in the later stages. It is doubtful whether Britain falls behind in the stage of technical research, in the sense that fewer inventions per head of the population are produced in the United Kingdom than in the United States; on the contrary, if we consider recent technological advances—artificial fibres, jet engines, television and the like, the United Kingdom seems to be well to the forefront of invention. Where she lags behind is in bringing new inventions to the point of commercial mass production. This leads to the conclusion that the deficiency is not in research or invention in any sense, but in the incentives for the exploitation of new knowledge; we shall therefore return to her case in the second part of this chapter.

The poorer countries differ from the developed in that they have no real need to spend significantly on the advancement of pure science. For the most part, they can leave this to the advanced industrial nations, whose results are freely available to all. There may be exceptions in the sense that some parts of science are of greater interest to them than are other parts of science, but it is very hard to

think of examples in the realm of pure science. In any case, the growth of pure science is somewhat like the wind, 'which bloweth whither it listeth', and it is doubtful whether any good would come out of expenditures by the poorer countries which were designed to affect the discovery of new scientific principles. Technical research is quite a different matter. Much of the technical research and invention done in the developed countries applies equally to the under-developed countries, and can be borrowed wholesale. The developed countries, however, have concentrated on applying scientific principles to their own problems, which are not the same as those of the under-developed countries. For example, the principles of thermodynamics have been applied to inventing ways of maximizing the heat utilized in the burning of coal, in which many of the poorer countries are deficient, rather than the heat utilized in the burning of wood, which some of these countries have abundantly. The principles of genetics have been applied to improving the varieties of wheat, rather than to improving the varieties of yam. The principles of physiology have been employed to devising ways of living in temperate zones, rather than ways of living in the tropics, and so on. Hence there is very great need for technical research in the under-developed countries, in all matters where they are situated differently from the developed countries. Finally, even where the results of technical research are applicable, the development problems are different. For methods of production which are economic in countries which have abundant coal, iron ore, capital and skilled labour, may be totally uneconomic in some other countries, whose problem is rather to devise means which use mostly the available surplus of unskilled labour, and such materials as can be had cheaply on the spot.

There is no doubt that one of the main deficiencies of under-developed countries is their failure to spend adequately upon research, and upon the development of new processes and materials appropriate to their circumstances. Part of the reason for this is institutional. In industrial countries private entrepreneurs spend great sums on industrial research, because they hope it will pay them to do so. The under-developed countries, on the other hand, are agricultural. Where their agriculture includes large commercial companies, these companies have invested in research (e.g. rubber, bananas, sugar) either individually or collectively, but, in all that part of their agriculture (the major part) which is not organized on this basis, there are no private interests financing research. It follows that almost the whole of the research expenditures needed in these countries (i.e. excluding mining and commercial agriculture) has to fall upon the public purse. Whereas in industrial countries research can be thought of primarily as a matter for private interests, with the

government plugging gaps, in under-developed countries research is primarily a matter for governments, and ought to be one of their major fields of activity.

How much ought they to spend? This is of course an unanswerable question. Current expenditure on industrial research and development in the United Kingdom is estimated at a little under one per cent of the income generated in industry. In the United States industrial research is at a similar level, while agricultural research is a little less than one half of one per cent of the net value of agricultural output. On the same basis it would not be unreasonable if the under-developed countries were to spend on research of all sorts (technical, social, health, etc.) a sum equal to between ½ and 1 per cent of their national incomes (not to be confused with government expenditure). There is no firm basis for such a suggestion. All the same, current expenditures, which do not reach a fraction of this level, are clearly too low.

So far we have discussed mainly technological knowledge; a word must now be said about social relations. Man has been no less inventive in this than in the technological field. The process of invention, however, is rather different. In the first place, many important social inventions were not made by individuals; society, in the process of adjusting itself to changing situations, imperceptibly creates new social institutions, which are often not recognized as such until long after they have been in operation. Yet, there are also cases where we can spot the individual inventor and even name the date—e.g., wherever the invention is created by the process of legislation, or by administrative action (unemployment insurance, the collective farm, central banking, government by parliament, to name a few instances). In the second place, the stages in the process are different. We can think of a stage of enunciating general principles, and a stage of applying these principles to problems if we like, but the relationship is more often the other way, namely that people who have a practical social problem to solve are often led by this to theorize about society, so that social theory is much more the result of social 'research', than research is the application of theory. The development process is also very different. Interested persons unite to make propaganda for their idea, so that it is either gradually accepted, or imposed by force. In other words, social knowledge grows through a political process, which throws up particular problems for attention, and the sponsoring of proposed solutions also depends upon political support. This differentiates social knowledge from technological knowledge only superficially, in the sense that both depend upon interested support. All the same the difference is not without importance. For, if the technological scientist sells his interested supporter a formula which

is false, in the sense that it will not do technically what it is required to do, he is soon found out. Whereas the social scientist can get away with selling formulae which are false in the sense that they give an untrue picture of the world, but which are nevertheless highly successful in the sense that they enable the interested supporter to fulfil his political ambitions. The moral is that while it may be safe to leave the promotion of technological knowledge to interested parties, it cannot be safe to leave the extension of social knowledge primarily to interested parties. Each one of us has a personal interest in the structure of society, which colours our approach to its problems. This is as true of social scientists as of anyone else. Social scientists, however, have their code of professional integrity, which makes them strive to be as objective as they can be in the presentation and analysis of facts. The truth about society is therefore most likely to be ascertained and promoted by those social scientists who work in institutions financed in such ways that scientific freedom is preserved.

The under-developed societies have as much to gain from borrowing social inventions as they have from borrowing technological inventions from the developed societies. To name just a few—the invention of an efficient administrative service, relatively free from corruption; the invention of free compulsory education; the invention of a system of land tenure which stimulates investment and preserves soil fertility—in fact this book itself may be thought of in one sense as a catalogue of useful social inventions. And, again in the social as in the technological field, there must be care in borrowing. Some of the inventions are inappropriate at current levels of development (e.g. Tibet does not need universal insurance against unemployment); others need modification (e.g. reliance on private enterprise in spheres where private enterprise has not developed); and still others would be dangerous (e.g. payment of family allowances in countries where the population is already doubling every twenty-five years). One is often impressed in these countries by the fact that they are as short of ideas in the social field (and of people to carry them out) as they are of capital or of natural resources. Expenditure on the study of society deserves therefore as high a priority as does expenditure on other branches of knowledge.

2. THE APPLICATION OF NEW IDEAS

There is always a gap between what is known to the experts to be the most effective way of doing things, and what is actually done by the great majority of people. It is not enough that knowledge should grow; it should also be diffused, and applied in practice. The rate at which knowledge is taken up depends partly on the receptiveness of

M

the people to new ideas, and partly on the extent to which institutions make it profitable to acquire and apply new ideas. We shall consider each of these in turn.

(a) The Attitude towards Innovation

New ideas will be accepted most rapidly in those societies where people are accustomed to variety of opinion, or to change, and are therefore pragmatic in their outlook. We have already considered the main factors which create such a situation, when we were considering the conditions which favour scientific enquiry (section 1(a) of this chapter). The main ingredients we stressed there were political and religious variety, and a geographical situation which brings together people of many different occupations, or from many different parts of the world. A country which is isolated, homogeneous, proud, and authoritarian is by contrast unlikely to absorb new ideas quickly when it meets them.

Apart from this general background, the rate at which a new idea is received depends also partly upon the idea itself. In the first place, not all new ideas are appropriate, however useful they may be in some other country. For example a new seed may yield abundantly in good weather, but if it is also exceptionally sensitive to drought, it is not appropriate to a locality where the rainfall varies widely from year to year. A new idea may also be inappropriate because the technological level of the society is not yet ready for it. For example, a new tool may not be acceptable unless the local blacksmiths or mechanics can make it, or at least can repair it when it breaks down. Or the new idea may require considerable changes in capital equipment. For example the adoption of a new high yielding seed may require that improved mills be built for grinding it, new barns for storing it, or new transport facilities for carrying it. Or the use of new fertilizers may have to wait upon the provision of irrigation facilities, if the land is otherwise too dry for fertilizers to be productive. It is not often that a new idea fits into an old technology without at the same time requiring a range of other changes of skill, or of capital formation, in order to accommodate itself. This is one of the main reasons why there is so often a gap between the expert who arrives from another country, and the people whom he is advising. The expert takes for granted a whole set of conditions upon which his innovation depends, but which are no part of his expertise, and are not present in his mind. The person advised, however, may see at once that the idea will not work in his conditions; of if he does not see this at once, may in due course be frustrated when one unforeseen obstacle after another prevents him from getting the results which are obtained elsewhere. The only remedies for the situation are humility

on the part of experts, combined with willingness to make pilot experiments on the part of those whom they advise.

In addition to technological readjustments the new idea may also involve social changes, and may be resisted on this account. For example, the introduction of central mills for extracting oil from the oil palm fruit doubles the yield of oil, but it also deprives the wives of West African farmers of the perquisites they get when they extract the oil for their husbands, and is therefore strongly and effectively resisted by them; it also alters the division of labour between husband and wife, and anything which does this has far-reaching and unforeseeable consequences. Or the innovation may damage whole classes of people who earn their living in particular ways, and who therefore resist its introduction. Such were the Luddites, whose behaviour is repeated daily in every community, by workers or capitalists or landowners who lobby to prevent changes which would damage their particular interests. Innovations are not therefore easily introduced in communities where there is tenderness towards established expectations; it flourishes better in places where competition is well regarded, and where attempts to create or preserve monopoly positions are ruthlessly suppressed.

The innovation will also have a hard time making its way if it conflicts directly with current taboos or religious doctrines. In such circumstances a new idea is frequently championed first of all by minority groups, such as religious, racial or political minorities, with whose creed it does not conflict; or by frustrated or dissident members of the majority group, who take it up as a way of expressing their dissidence. This is one reason why progress so often comes not through the efforts of those who are in authority, but in opposition to their efforts.

Much depends also on who are the first sponsors of an idea. If the idea is sponsored by influential members of the society, it is likely to be accepted more rapidly than if it is introduced by people whose opinions carry no weight. In some societies influence is wielded by persons in authority—by chiefs, elders, priests, magistrates and rich men, and the effort of the innovator has to be directed in the first instance to persuading people in authority. This is one of the advantages claimed by the British for 'indirect rule' in Africa; once the chief and elders were persuaded, they told the people what to do, and the new idea was universally applied; whereas in more democratic societies it is much harder to get new ideas accepted. In some societies there is tension between those in authority and those whom they govern; the old rulers may be on their way out, and real influence is centred elsewhere. Finding the point at which to begin is the first task of would-be disseminators of new ideas. The influence

of foreigners also varies very much. If they establish themselves as a rich and powerful ruling class, people will probably want to imitate them, and their ways will spread. But foreigners may also be hated, for anti-imperialist reasons, or despised, because of their lowly origins, and some or all their ways may be deliberately rejected. In practice, foreigners are the greatest vehicle of new ideas today, whether their influence is exercised in person on the spot, or through their writings, their films, or their radio programmes, or through students and visitors from the home country visiting foreign lands.

(b) Knowledge and Profit

If new knowledge is to be accepted and applied to production, it must be profitable as well as new. It takes effort to acquire knowledge, and to apply it may require both extra resources and also extra willingness to bear risks. The application of knowledge therefore demands an institutional pattern which associates differential effort with differential reward. We have already discussed this matter in Chapter III in general terms. It remains here only to say a few words with special reference to the institutional requirements for the acceptance of knowledge.

Essentially the point is that there must be adequate differentials in the rewards for skill, for responsibility, and for risk-bearing. The extent of differentiation for these factors seems in practice to vary with the degree and the rate of economic development. In societies where output per head is not growing, the supply of skill often exceeds the demand; it is hard to find work for all the people who qualify, and the differential payment for skill is small. This situation ceases when growth begins. Economic growth makes enormous demands for skills of many kinds. It is associated with a great increase in specialization, and therefore in the range of skills. This in turn increases the need for co-ordination, increases the average size of firm or other economic unit, and increases the demand for supervisory and administrative staff. The 'middle' classes thus grow rapidly, relatively to all others. In this process the differentials between skilled and unskilled, literate and illiterate, supervisory and supervised, tend to widen. And this process is especially helped if, in order to meet the demand for skills, it is necessary to recruit skilled people from more advanced countries; for such people have to be paid salaries higher even than they could earn at home, and this enables their native counterparts also to demand incomes which are disproportionately high when compared with the incomes of farmers or of unskilled workers. Accordingly, in societies at this stage, differentials are wider than they are both in less developed and in more developed societies.

The currently high differentials in the U.S.S.R. are an excellent example of the point.

This situation rights itself as the spread of educational facilities begins to increase the flow of people with superior training. Compulsory education comes into force, so that mere literacy ceases too command a premium. Technical schools and apprenticeship arrangements multiply the supply of carpenters, mechanics, builders, and other grades of skilled artisan. Secondary schools produce an outflow of typists, clerks, teachers, and personal assistants of various kinds. And universities begin to pour out the people needed at higher levels. As the supply increases, the differentials are reduced. High differentials also stimulate the substitution of machinery; machines are introduced to do work for which manual skill was formerly required, and these machines are manned by people with little skill, at lower levels of wages. There may also be significant institutional changes. In the beginning it is the skilled workers who most easily organize themselves into trade unions and professional associations, for the purpose of raising earnings. But in due course all are unionized, and if the skilled feel themselves menaced by the unskilled with new machines, they may take particular care themselves to organize the unskilled and to keep the differential between skilled and unskilled from being substantial. All these factors cause differentials to narrow in advanced economies, with well developed educational facilities. And they also of course create social tensions, since the 'middle' classes resent the fact that they are losing their place on the economic ladder.

It seems that much the same happens to entrepreneurial incomes. In the early stages of development there is a marked reluctance to take the risk of branching out in new lines. Money goes easily into land, into trade, into moneylending, and into urban housing, but the native capitalists will not venture into mining, into public utilities, into commercial agriculture or into manufacturing unless they see chances of exceptional profits. Besides, they have little knowledge of such matters. These fields are therefore left to foreigners, who bring with them new techniques, both of production and also of organization, and who in turn are attracted only because they believe that they can make much larger profits than they would if they invested their money at home. In the early stages of development, profits grow as a proportion of the national income, and so do savings (the process is described in Chapter V). The foreign entrepreneurs are also widely imitated, to the point where eventually native entrepreneurs are so numerous that the economy ceases to depend upon foreign entrepreneurship. It grows up into economic independence, and may even in due course begin to export capital and entrepreneurs itself.

Outside the sphere of agriculture, which can be conducted on a family size basis, economic growth is bound to be slow unless there is an adequate supply of entrepreneurs looking out for new ideas, and willing to take the risk of introducing them. Thus a private enterprise economy will be retarded if it has not enough business men, or if its business men are reluctant to take risks, whether because they cannot raise the capital, or because they are timid by nature, or because the differentials for risk-taking are inadequate. For example, we saw earlier in this chapter that many people compare the United Kingdom with the United States, and say that the adoption of innovations is slower in the former. We pointed out that this is not due to any deficiency of invention, for the United Kingdom has been well to the fore in inventing new commodities and processes, If there is a deficiency, it is a difference in the rate of bringing new commodities to the stage of mass production. This is a deficiency not of research, but of entrepreneurship, suggesting that, for one reason or another, British entrepreneurs are not as quick to exploit new inventions as are their American counterparts.

Entrepreneurs are stimulated to innovate by the desire for social success, by the hope of big profits, or by the fear of great losses if they fail to innovate. The first of these motives is weak in societies where business success is not highly regarded; the second has no point in societies which tax profits and capital gains heavily; and the third disappears if the general atmosphere of the economy becomes monopolistic rather than competitive. If it is true that British entrepreneurs are less enterprising than American entrepreneurs—and not every one accepts this as a fact—the explanation is probably to be found in one or other of these factors.

Many under-developed countries, awakening in the middle of the twentieth century to a strong desire for economic development, are embarrassed by what it seems to require in terms of inequality of income, whether as between the 'middle' classes and the farmers, as between foreigners and natives, or as between profits and other incomes. For the climate of our day is hostile to income differentials in general, to foreign differentials in particular, and to handsome profits in the extreme. These, however, are part of the cost of development. One way to respond to this situation is to hold up development, keeping it in step with the supply of native skills, and with the capacity of the public service to substitute for private entrepreneurship. An alternative response is to accept these differentials as a temporary cost of more rapid growth. In either case the most effective remedy is to multiply as rapidly as possible the skills on which development makes acute demands, since this both hastens the possibilities of development and also keeps at a minimum its cost in inequality.

3. TRAINING PROGRAMMES

(a) Priorities

Economic development makes tremendous demands on educational facilities at every level. There is a greater demand for primary education, culminating in the demand that every child of school age should have compulsory education. More secondary schools are needed, either to supply more secondary education for its own sake, or else to provide material for the universities, or for further training as secretaries, teachers, or technical assistants. A whole range of training facilities is required, for artisans, agricultural assistants, teachers, nurses, secretaries, mechanics. Outside the range of these institutions there is the field of adult education, extending from literacy campaigns or agricultural extension to literary classes. And crowning the whole system is the need for training at university level in almost every branch of knowledge.

The cost of providing all these services 'properly' is beyond the budget of any low income country. Hence choice has to be exercised. Shall there be a few well trained, or a much larger number half-trained? Or what priorities shall there be as between technical and secondary, adult and primary or humanistic and technological?

Take first the question of priorities. The difficulty education raises is that it is both a consumer and an investment service. In so far as it is an investment, it contributes directly towards increasing output. There are countries where all education is suspect because of its potential damage to current authority, whether political, religious, racial or caste. But most countries have no difficulty in deciding that all educational facilities which directly increase output are worth expanding to the limit, in the sense that the money spent on these facilities is a capital investment just like money spent on irrigation. The difficulty is where to draw the line with those types of education which contribute more to enjoyment than to output—literacy for example. Some members of the community must be literate, otherwise they cannot do their jobs. But it is not arguable that the majority of peasants, porters, barbers or domestic servants will be so much more productive if they are literate as to cover more than the cost of educating them. We want education for all these people not as an investment, but as a consumer good, because we think it will help them to enjoy some things more (books, newspapers), or to understand some things better. (Not that they will necessarily be any the happier for this: they will only be more human.) In economic terms, such part of education as is not a profitable investment is on a par with other consumer goods, like clothes, houses or gramophones.

National income is not large enough for every person in the community to have his fill.

In the days before education was free, compulsory, and nationalized, each family solved these problems for itself, buying as much education from private teachers as it could afford, having regard to its income, its investment programme, and its other needs. Since the uneducated are not really in a position to judge correctly the advantages and disadvantages of education, the decisions made were incorrect, erring presumably on the side of under-valuing education—at any rate, in such communities the demand for education is extremely small, in relation to the population as a whole. Nowadays however, education is a public service, and therefore most of the decisions which have to be made are matters of political controversy.

Political views on educational priorities are changing. Fifty years ago most nationalist politicians nailed their flag to the mast of literacy; the supreme objective of educational policy was thought to be to get all the children into school. The emphasis was primarily on education as a consumer service; some of it would also yield dividends in the form of increased output, but it was a matter of national pride that the community should be literate, whatever the effect on output might be. In these days priorities are changing, and the investment types of education are receiving a stress which they never had before. For example the financial provision for agricultural extension services and for technical institutes is expanding rapidly in many countries. And adult education is coming to the fore. There are even education theorists who say that it is more valuable to teach the parents than the children at this stage. What the children learn in school, it is argued, they forget or ignore when they return home to their unenlightened families; and after five or six years of compulsory learning to read, many have forgotten how to read within three years of leaving school. Whereas, if the parents are taught to read and write, their children will learn too, in one way or another; and the parents can also be taught, at their own workplaces or farms, how to improve their productive skills. There are even extremists who say that too much is claimed for literacy; people should be taught to make more of their environments—taught ways of increasing yields per acre, or artisan skills, or child care, or dressmaking, most of which can be done without teaching literacy, and is more useful.

The same sort of ferment engulfs attitudes towards higher education. Education at university level is primarily seen as an investment, by those who submit themselves to it; it is a means of ensuring superior social status and superior income. The status of lawyers being what it is, and the income of the most successful lawyers being very attractive, this branch of learning has always been dispropor-

tionately cultivated. This is one reason why there are too many law-yers in most low income countries, and why it is believed that some lawyers are tempted into trickery in order to make a living. In countries where university facilities are provided extensively, the number of lawyers is so obviously superfluous that many students have to look to other faculties. If at the same time the community is not undergoing economic development, so that there is not an ex-panding market for engineers, scientists or doctors, the country is flooded with arts graduates, who have to take any jobs that they can get, and who are extremely dissatisfied and first class material for political agitation because they cannot get the salaries or even the social status which they think their superior education deserves.

Looked at from the social point of view, the question whether university education is a consumer or an investment service depends simply on the supply in relation to demand. In those low income coun-tries where large number of unemployable arts graduates are turned out every year it is primarily a consumer service, and is indefensible. It is indefensible because the cost of training a university graduate is so high that if education is only a consumer service it would be much fairer to spend the taxpayers' money on providing more primary schools, or on giving more children a secondary education, rather than to spend it on giving a relatively small number education to university level. But the situation is quite different in a community in which economic development is occuring fairly rapidly. Here there is an ever expanding demand for doctors, engineers, biologists, administrators, and all the other products of the university. Even the demand for more primary education also puts its strain upon the university; for, to have more primary students you must have more primary teachers; more primary teachers means more secondary students; this means more secondary teachers; which means more university students; primary, secondary and university education constitute a pyramid, where all levels must expand in step. The 'anomaly' of a poor country spending a lot of money to build a university when only ten per cent of its children are receiving primary education is no anomaly at all.

The general effect of changing opinions is to change the emphasis of educational budgets. Fifty years ago the main emphasis was on primary education, but today in many budgets much greater em-phasis is given to higher education, to technical education, or to adult education (including agricultural extension). The tendency is to agree to regard these others as investment expenditure, and to give them absolute priority, while leaving the extension of primary education to fight for its place in public expenditure with roads, health, and all the other services which governments have to provide.

Apart from the question of priorities of different types, there is also the question of the quality of each type. Should primary education be provided for all children for five years, or for half the children for ten years? Must all primary school teachers have a secondary education followed by two years special training—in which case their numbers will be small—or should there be a rapid multiplication of teachers on short courses, who know little themselves beyond the three R's, but who can then be used for a rapid extension of the primary school system? The U.S.S.R. chose numbers rather than quality, and set about rapidly multiplying the numbers of half-trained teachers, agricultural assistants, dental assistants, medical assistants, and the like. There are two arguments for doing this. The compelling argument is speed. It takes time, and costs a lot of money, to train people to the highest standards of their craft. Hence if only the fully qualified are allowed to practise, most of the population are left without any dental, medical, agricultural or educational facilities, when they would be much better off if they could have the services of the half-trained. The other argument is that most of the work done by the fully trained can be done just as well by the half-trained. Hence it is a waste of skill to insist that only the skilled should practise. On the other hand, the main political argument against this 'dilution' of skills is national pride. In several countries where the proposal has been made it has been rejected by the press and by the nationalist politicians on the ground that national pride demands that 'our doctors (teachers, etc.) should be as good as those in England'— or whichever advanced country is the local model. There is also the resistance of professional associations, but this would probably not be effective if national pride could not also be enlisted on its side.

Opinion is also changing on the subject of how long it takes to teach a skill. Under the influence of professional associations and of trade unions the emphasis has hitherto been upon long periods of apprenticeship and training. During the second world war, however, when speed was of the essence of success, it was conceded that people could learn the essentials of a job sometimes in as little as a quarter of the time which had hitherto been required. New techniques were worked out for giving rapid training, with perhaps the most spectacular results in the fields of teaching literacy, and teaching foreign languages, but also with specially useful results in shortening the time required for training artisans and mechanics. These methods can play a major role in places where a shortage of skills is holding up development.

Yet another result of breaking the hold of the professional upon training programmes is the realization that education need not primarily wait upon professionals. 'Mass education' programmes act

upon the principle that each person who learns should teach, and new techniques have been worked out for mass adult literacy campaigns which do indeed make it possible for a relatively small number of trained teachers to achieve astonishing results, on the basis of students passing on their knowledge. The secret of success in any adult education campaign—whether in literacy, in agriculture, in child care or in Chinese literature—is to win the enthusiasm of the students, who not only therefore give their time and their minds to the subject, but also infect others with their enthusiasm and pass their knowledge on. This enthusiasm is all the more likely when the programme takes the student into itself to the extent of giving him also a missionary role, than it is in programmes where there is a professional barrier between student and teacher.

The dilution of skills is a perennial problem, since technological progress is always rendering established skills useless and creating new skills. It would do this in any case, but does this all the more because each skill, as it is established, begins to be monopolized by people who draw up codes of demarcation and rules of apprenticeship, desiring to secure superior status and remuneration for their skill, by limiting the numbers who are permitted to practise it. Monopoly always presents a challenge to new invention, so that its toll may be evaded. Hence every skill has a sort of life history; it is born, recognizes itself, becomes subject to a host of regulations, excites hostility and evasion, fights a rearguard action against new skills which are invading its province, and either compromises or dies; all this to the accompaniment of much pride, anger, sweat and tears.

There are now a number of countries (e.g. the Gold Coast) where the funds available for development cannot all be spent because of a shortage of required skills. Political factors will determine whether in these circumstances the rate of growth will be held up in the interest of quality and propriety, or whether there will be a rapid multiplication of the partially trained.

(b) Agricultural Extension

Agricultural education illustrates very well several points which we have just discussed, namely the problem of priority, the role of the partially trained, and the importance of enthusiasm.

As for priority, expenditure on bringing new knowledge to peasant farmers is probably the most productive investment which can be made in any of the poorer agricultural economies. For raising the productivity of the soil is in most places the surest and quickest way now available of increasing the national income substantially. For example, some agricultural experts assert that agricultural yields per acre could be doubled in India, by the application of techniques

now known—the most important sources of gain being better seed selection and control, more use of artificial fertilizers, greater use of pesticides, and better conservation and utilization of water supplies. Such striking possibilities are not open everywhere, because the gap between what is known to the experts and what is done by the farmers is not everywhere as great as this. In many places, however, this is merely because there has been failure to do necessary research on food production. For reasons already mentioned, agricultural research in the tropics has concentrated upon the commercial crops which are exported to industrial countries (sugar, cocoa, rubber, tea, etc.), and has almost wholly neglected what is produced for home consumption (yams, cassava, sorghums and the like) despite the fact that in nearly all these economies the manpower and acreage devoted to food production is four or more times as great as that which is devoted to commercial crops.

Research is a pre-requisite to extension, so where the basic research has still to be done, there is not yet scope for agricultural extension. However, once the knowledge becomes available, the need for extension workers is tremendous. If we assume that there should be one extension worker to every thousand persons gainfully employed in peasant agriculture, that two-thirds of the population are so employed, and that to maintain an extension worker costs four or five times as much as a farmer receives, then the cost of the service, including supervisory staff works out at more than a quarter of one per cent of the national income. Add to this the desirable cost of agricultural research (this chapter, section 1(b)), and we arrive at the conclusion that the Department of Agriculture should be spending on research and education somewhere between three-quarters and one per cent of the national income. The United States of America maintains something like this ratio of service expenditures to agricultural income; it has one extension worker to every 700 persons gainfully occupied in agriculture, and it spends upon agricultural extension and research about three-quarters of one per cent of net agricultural output. The United Kingdom also has a ratio of 1 to 700, but among the poorer countries of the world the only country which spends at this level upon agricultural services is Japan (it is also the only one which has had spectacular increases in peasant productivity).

If an annual expenditure of one per cent of national income per annum could increase agricultural productivity by one per cent per annum (equivalent to one half of one per cent of national income) this would be an extremely productive investment, since it is equivalent to a return of fifty per cent per annum. The increase in productivity cannot be credited exclusively to agricultural extension, since capital has also to be provided, for water supplies, tools, fertilizers,

etc. However, even when allowance is made for other needs, this complex of investments is the most profitable that agricultural countries can make. The rates we have used are well within the bounds of possibility. In Japan between 1880 and 1920 productivity per acre grew at a cumulative annual rate of 1 3 per cent per annum. Rates of one per cent have been attained also by England and by the United States. Countries which start with a much wider gap between what is known and what is done should have no difficulty in achieving spectacular yields from what they spend on agricultural services.

In order to provide agricultural service at this rate there would have to be a tremendous expansion in the number of agricultural officers. Many very highly trained people would be needed for research, and also to supervise the extension service, but the biggest expansion of all would be among the extension workers themselves, since one is needed for every five to ten villages. It would be impossible to provide these numbers if each had to be given a full university education in agriculture. But it is also unnecessary and undesirable to have university graduates for this work. It is unnecessary because the extension worker's job is only to transmit to the farmers techniques which have been thoroughly tried elsewhere. He needs to have his wits about him, and to know a good deal about practical agriculture, since he will otherwise be ineffective with the farmers. The best training for this is to have worked on a farm himself, doing all the farm jobs, and then to have spent a year or at most two being trained in the new techniques. It is also undesirable that the officer be a university graduate since his main problem is to make contact with the farmers and be accepted by them, and this is much more difficult for a university graduate than it is for someone whose background is not far removed from that of the farmers themselves.

The extension officer's main problem is to make contact; not just social contact, which is easy enough in village communities, but that contact of minds which results in imitation. For example, the main work of extension officers used at one time to be done on demonstration farms, owned and operated by the agricultural service. These farms cultivated the best plants in the best ways, and farmers were invited to visit them and to see the results for themselves. Even when yields were very high the farmers did not always imitate what they were shown. They argued that the results achieved on the demonstration farm would not necessarily be achieved on their own holdings. Perhaps the farm had been specially selected for soil or other qualities; perhaps equipment was being used, which the ordinary farmer did not possess; or perhaps the workers on the farm had had special training, or were receiving special supervision which would not be

available on the peasants' holdings. To get round these difficulties, modern extension techniques supplement the demonstration farm by persuading a few farmers to try out the innovation themselves on their own holdings. It is then clear to the remainder that good results have been achieved by farmers just like themselves on holdings just like their own. The success is no longer the success of a remotely controlled institution; it is the success of their neighbours, and hence it calls for gossip, interest, investigation, discussion, and emulation. One of the first tasks of the newly arrived extension officer is now to find out which farmers are most respected in the district, and most likely to be imitated, and to try to enlist their co-operation in the campaign he has in hand.

There is a world of difference between doing extension work in a community where the farmers are not used to the idea of technical change, and doing it in an environment where farmers look naturally to the scientist to solve their problems. In an advanced community like England or the United States the farmers know that the geneticists are breeding better varieties, that the entomologists and the pathologists are producing ways of controlling pests and diseases, and that manufacturers of machinery are constantly introducing improved equipment. They are keen to hear about these things, and so they subscribe to farm journals, they listen to radio programmes for farmers, and they attend meetings of farmers' clubs. In these ways new ideas are disseminated rapidly. The extension problem in backward communities is to create a similar atmosphere, in which the farmers look upon the agricultural officers as an essential part of the agricultural community, existing in order to make life easier for the farmer. Part of the secret of this consists in getting the farmers to form agricultural societies, for discussion, for visiting each other's farms, and for demonstrations. The other part consists in really having something to offer. If the extension officer succeeds in solving some problem which has worried the farmers—some disease for example—he will gain their confidence; whereas if nothing comes from taking his advice, the farmers will not take him seriously.

The background to farmers' enthusiasm is sometimes political. In a world in which farmers have been exploited for generations by landlords, moneylenders and traders it is difficult for them to work up enthusiasm for new techniques, especially if they suspect that the main result may be to increase the takings of their oppressors. Land reform is therefore often a necessary prelude to successful agricultural extension. If the country's political leaders begin to take a real interest in the farmers' problems—which most often they do not— and show by their deeds as well as their words that they are out to help the farmers, then the farmers are likely to respond. Agricultural

extension without the political changes and political enthusiasm which it requires may just fall flat.

We have observed before that the introduction of new techniques requires a great number of changes, not only in economic and social structure, but also in the provision of capital, and the acquisition of new skills. Agricultural extension must therefore be seen only as one part in a wider programme of agricultural improvement, which includes such other things as roads, agricultural credit, water supplies, efficient marketing, land reform, the development of new industries to absorb surplus labour, co-operatives, and so on. Economic growth always involves change on a wide front, and of no sector is this more true than it is of rural life.

(c) Industrial Aptitudes

Economic growth results in a continuous decline of the importance of agriculture relatively to other sources of employment. Hence other industries are continuously recruiting labour from the agricultural sector (absolutely, if population is stable, and relatively if population is growing rapidly).

It is universal experience that when labour first comes into industry (or mining) from the countryside its productivity is very low, compared with that of labour which has been working in industry for a very long time. There are several reasons for this. First of all, the industrial way of life is quite different from the agricultural. In agriculture one has short bursts of intense activity, from dawn till dusk, associated with planting or with harvesting, followed by long periods of idleness or leisurely activity in the seasons unfavourable to agriculture. In industry, on the other hand, one is expected to work at an even pace for eight or nine hours of every day, five or six days a week, throughout the year. In peasant agriculture again, one works as one's master, plying a craft familiar from birth, and making numerous decisions all the time. In the factory one is plying a new craft, under supervision, doing exactly what one is told, and acting merely as a cog in some very complicated mechanism, making perhaps one knows not what, to sell to almost certainly one knows not whom. The community is also different. In the fields one works alone, or with a few chosen friends. Whereas in a factory one works with a large crowd of people whom one has no part in choosing. It takes a long time to grow accustomed to these new ways of living, and to settle down into the kind of regularity industrial life demands. It is said that women and children make the adjustment more easily than adult men, and that this is one reason why industrial revolutions tend to rely so much upon child and female labour in their early stages, if not controlled in this respect. The transition is also easier where the

philosophy of the people already includes a great respect for discipline, for system, and for order in community relations, since this prepares them for the highly regulated life which they will have to live in large industrial undertakings. Some historians, for example, believe that the Germans and the Japanese took easily to industrialization for this sort of reason.

The differences of background between rural and industrial life also explain why new recruits are much better at some jobs than at others. For example, however knowledgeable and responsible a person may be on a farm, the knowledge required for exercising responsibility in a factory is quite different. Instead of having well developed instincts for rain and animal or plant behaviour, he must have well developed instincts for mechanical processes, which alert him to error or to opportunities of improvement. Lacking these, the recruit has to be taught one operation at a time, leaving the minimum to his discretion; he cannot do jobs where several different operations have to be performed and co-ordinated. The division of labour has to be all the greater the less skilled is the labour one is using. Correspondingly one needs to have a greater proportion of supervisors, to co-ordinate what is subdivided. The need for a high ratio of supervisory staff is a mark of all countries where industrialization is new, and, when these supervisors have to be imported from abroad, this is also one reason why costs in these countries are not as low as one might expect them to be, having regard to the low level of wages. Alternatively the use of very unskilled labour stimulates mechanization, since jobs are subdivided into the simplest processes, and also since the machine brings greater precision to some operations than unskilled workers can be relied on to have. This, it is sometimes thought, may be one reason why mechanization proceeded more rapidly in the United States of America in the second half of the nineteenth century than it did in England.

These differences of background explain also why discipline tends to be so strict and irksome in the early stages of industrialization. Many of the things which rural workers have a natural inclination to do are incompatible with efficient industry, and the task of forming different natural inclinations is no easier than is the task of preparing children for life as adults. Much of this discipline is crude and self-defeating, because it is exercised by persons who do not understand the problem or the people with whom they are dealing, but irksome forms of discipline cannot be escaped entirely in the early stages of industrialization.

With the passage of time, workers adjust themselves to their new environment, and acquire a new range of knowledge and of instincts. They become more skilled, not only in the sense that they know more

operations, but also in the sense that their discretion can be left to operate over a wider range of problems—they recognize what is wrong as they did not before. Productivity grows with special rapidity as between the first generation of urban workers and the second. The process is hastened if the newcomers are allowed and encouraged to settle down to urban life, making a complete break with agricultural employment, and it is least rapid where industry recruits workers who remain with it for a year or so, and then return to their villages.

The use of migrant labour in industry is not a simple issue. There are some special cases. For example, Japanese girls leave the village to work in the cotton industry, and in due course return to the village to marry. Female labour has everywhere a similarly high rate of turnover whether migration is involved or not. Temporary mining communities are another special case; if the industry itself is only temporary, it obviously cannot build up a permanent labour force. Apart from these special cases, some industrialists believe that they get labour more cheaply in this way. They believe that young men who are leaving the village for a year only will do so partly out of a spirit of adventure, and will therefore come for lower wages; that they will put up with cheap and uncomfortable bachelor's barracks, since the period of occupation is short; that a high turnover makes impossible the creation of a strong trade union movement; and that if it becomes necessary to reduce the labour force, men can be returned to their villages without bothering about unemployment pay. It is most doubtful whether this reasoning is correct. Certainly the mining companies of Central Africa, which started operations on the basis of migrant labour, are now all abandoning it in favour of creating permanent labour forces. Money spent on purchasing an experienced and settled labour force is often the best investment. If the industry is subject to sharp cyclical or other fluctuations it may seem an advantage to be able to return the unemployed to their villages, but it is hopeless to expect continuously improving productivity on this basis.

Whether permanent or migrant, the new industrial force is too often crowded into unpleasant slums, without the amenities or advantages of town life. In this environment the incentive to break one's links with the village is at its minimum. There is no reason why new industrial towns should not be well planned, and equipped with family size houses, schools, parks, churches, cinemas and all those other amenities which make a good town a much more attractive place to live in (for most people) than a village. Neither is there any excuse for not developing a proper range of social services—medical services, unemployment pay, pensions and the like—in the absence of which the industrial worker is forced to keep one foot in

N

the village, so that he can return to it in case of need. The effect would be a healthier labour force, more settled, and more anxious for improvement on the job. These things cost more, but they also pay off in extra productivity, as well as in human happiness.

Of particular importance to the productivity of newly recruited workers are health and diet. In the poorer countries most people are infected by parasites of one kind or another, such as malaria or hookworm, which sap their energy and reduce productivity without preventing people from turning up for work. It pays industrial companies to provide free medical services, to see that their workers are well housed, and even to have the houses sprayed regularly with DDT. It also pays to provide free or cheap meals in canteens, to ensure that the workers are properly fed. Good welfare services inside the factory are even more necessary in these countries than they are in Europe or North America. Much of the difference in productivity is due just to unhealthy and malnourished bodies.

The productivity of labour depends also upon the training it receives. Much money is now being spent on building new technical institutes in the poorer countries, for a whole range of artisan skills—building workers, mechanics, electricians and the like. These institutes meet a great need, since economic development creates a great shortage of all these skills.

Most of the industrial labour force, however, consists of skilled and unskilled workers who learn their work not in an institute but on the job. Much of this training is done badly, since the newcomer is merely allocated to some other worker who is supposed to teach him the job; not many people, however good they may be at their own job, are also good at teaching it to somebody else, unless they have also received some instruction in teaching, or take a special interest in the problem. The more efficient firms select for the purpose workers who have proved to have a special aptitude and liking for teaching. And they may also create special courses for newcomers, and appoint a special officer to run them.

These strictures on training apply equally to organized systems of apprenticeship. A system of apprenticeship is necessary in all those trades where experience is necessary to craftsmanship. All the same, most apprenticeship systems degenerate into a racket. Interested unions or associations prolong the period of apprenticeship, so as to reduce the inflow to the trade, and maintain scarcity earnings. The apprentice's time is then misused, since he is expected to spend his early months sweeping floors, carrying tools, making tea, or in equivalent pursuits. And the journeyman to whom he is attached may be a good, bad or indifferent teacher. It is therefore very desirable that apprenticeship systems be reviewed from time to time, that they

be associated with part-time or evening instruction, and that the
firms which participate should give special attention to the selection
of those workers to whom the apprentices are assigned.

Productivity depends, finally, on the worker's interest in his job.
This is partly a matter of pay, partly a matter of the prospects of promotion, and partly a matter of the social atmosphere of the factory.
In so far as it is a matter of pay, what is required is mainly that there *incentive*
should be adequate differentials for skill, for superior output, and for
responsibility, so that the worker should be encouraged to give of
his best, and should feel rewarded for doing so. Whether these
incentives should be individual or based on group performance is a
subsidiary matter, to be decided according to circumstances. As for
promotion, this concerns relatively few, unless large classes are
affected by some mass discrimination such as a colour bar, or discriminations based on religion, sex, nationality or the like. Such
mass discriminations reduce the rate of economic growth, apart from
their effects on social relations, if only because they deprive society
of the superior talents of some of those against whom the bar is
operated. In any case, even if promotion concerns only a few, these
are a very significant minority, since their performance in positions of
responsibility may make a substantial difference to the quantity and
quality of output; it is therefore important that workers should feel
that there is a clear road open to all who deserve it. As for the social
atmosphere inside the factory, this is a complicated matter to which
we made extended reference in Chapter III. It is a matter partly of
size of firm, of amenities inside the factory, of opportunities for
consultation, and of a free flow of confidence between workers and
their supervisors. All industrial communities are wrestling with this
problem, and we cannot yet be sure that it has any universal solution.
One point on which most observers agree is the crucial position of
the factory foreman, whether in maintaining good human relations,
or in ensuring a high level of productivity. The system of selection
and promotion must therefore be such that men who have the right
qualities for foremanship are spotted quickly, and given training
adequate for their important role.

Behind many of the problems of adjustment to industrial life lies
the greater problem of the adjustment of ethical codes. The recruit
to industry from tribal conditions has a very highly developed
ethical code, which lays down for him patterns of obligation to a wide
range of persons in relationships of kinship, age, political or religious
status. If he comes from a non-pecuniary society, his code may contain no rules governing relations between employer and employed,
buyer and seller, or workman and his mates; such precepts as 'a fair
day's work for a fair day's pay', or 'a fair day's pay for a fair day's

work' are foreign to his code, and come to have meaning only as he acquires a new code appropriate to his new conditions. Even more foreign to his experience is the idea of nine hours continuous work every day for six days every week under strict supervision. The clash of moral codes is painful, and what emerges is often not recognizable by any person who was brought up in either of the conflicting codes. This makes it all the more desirable that very special efforts should be made to create a new and meaningful community life in areas of new industrial growth. Otherwise, what might be a disciplined, happy and productive community may instead become a spiritual, political and industrial sore. Historically, the establishment of a new way of life is often associated also with a new religious ferment. The spread of Methodism in the new industrial towns of England and Wales during the industrial revolution did much to integrate these new communities, and to provide newcomers to urban life with a system of ideas which suited their new lives and made them meaningful. Religious innovation has no doubt a similar role to play in most other industrial revolutions.

(d) Business Administration

Economic development creates a very great demand for competent administrators, whether in business or in public service. The poorer countries frequently have a multitude of business men—small traders especially—with a well developed passion for making money by buying in the cheapest and selling in the dearest market, or by lending money at the highest rates which the traffic will bear. What is deficient is not the spirit of enterprise, but the experience of administration. The economies of large scale production make possible a considerable increase in income if only people can be found capable of managing large undertakings efficiently, including managing large numbers of men and great quantities of physical resources; and it is in knowledge and experience of the problems of large scale administration that the deficiency of these countries is most evident.

The great entrepreneurs are born, not made. The men who introduce new commodities or new systems of organization—the Fords or the Woolworths—are few in number, and cannot be made to order. Most business men, however, have only to do a fairly routine job, for which they can be fitted by acquiring knowledge and experience.

Some of this knowledge can be learnt in business schools, but an important part can be learnt only by experience of the job, and the rest depends on personal qualities of temperament and character. Business schools can teach the tricks of keeping records (of stocks, orders, credits, debits, etc.), some of the tricks in the handling of physical resources (factory layout, care of machinery, the smooth

flow of work through the factory), and some of the tricks in the management of men (selection of staff, delegation of duties, methods of training and so forth). But they cannot teach a business man how to get on with his staff, so that he combines their loyalty with their efficiency—this he must learn in practice, if indeed his temperament permits it. Neither can they impart that commercial sense, which cuts out waste, adjusts the use of resources to the flow of output, knows what prices to pay or to charge, and knows how to buy and sell and how much credit to give. And it is quite beyond them to instil the sense of integrity, without which a firm cannot acquire reputation or goodwill, and without which it cannot therefore last.

In practice much of the experience required for competence in administration is gained by working in foreign firms at home or abroad, after which the employee becomes a manager on his own account. Hence perhaps the most serious indictment which can be levied against some foreign firms is their reluctance to employ the native people in any but inferior positions—usually because of racial, religious, or other prejudice. If no one will employ the local people above the level of clerks, they cannot learn how to manage industrial businesses for themselves; their economic affairs will then always be dominated by foreigners, and economic growth will be held up by the costs and shortages involved in dependence upon foreign enterprise. This is one reason why most colonial countries, as soon as they become independent, pass legislation or take other steps to compel foreign firms to open up managerial positions to local people. But even non-colonial countries have taken such measures; thus, when foreigners brought new trades to England in the sixteenth and seventeenth centuries, the patents of monopoly which they were granted often included the condition that the foreigner must train a number of Englishmen in his craft within a stipulated period.

At the same time, countries in the initial stages of development find it profitable to send some of their young people abroad, to gain experience in foreign firms. Thus the Germans sent large numbers of their young people to work in England in the last quarter of the nineteenth century, and their example was followed a little later by Japan, whose people were sent to Germany and to the United States. On their return a few go into business on their own; but most of them find employment in existing firms, domestic or foreign; or else in the ever expanding government service, which also demands knowledge and experience of administration. It may not be so easy for the coloured nations of the world to carry out this policy as it was for the white, since colour prejudice in the advanced countries may make it difficult to find firms willing to accept coloured trainees, but there are more opportunities than are in fact exploited. One favourable

circumstance is the fact that some of the industrial countries are anxious to extend their personal relations with the poorer countries, in order to divert orders to themselves away from other industrial countries; and for this reason they may welcome the opportunity to meet and train the men who will be giving the orders when they return home.

The main school of business experience, however, consists of the little men engaged in trading, in operating a lorry or two, in running a small workshop, and in similar small commercial enterprises. Many of these go bankrupt. A few go from strength to strength, and gaining experience, ultimately flower into the management of large undertakings. Frequently the numbers in these trades are excessive, and there is substantial waste of capital. It is therefore sometimes argued that entry into such trades should be regulated, either to ensure adequate incomes, or else to reduce the waste of resources. Looked at as a means of securing immediate output the over-development of these trades may be wasteful; but if one looks at it as a means of giving people experience of business management, the waste may be a training cost well met.

In some of the under-developed countries it is felt that the growth of the native small business class is menaced by the competition of immigrants in similar trades. The great European concerns tend to confine themselves to large scale activities, but the Indians and Arabs in East Africa, the Syrians in West Africa, the Chinese in Jamaica and the Chinese in South East Asia are to be found competing even in the smallest trades, and because they have a longer commercial tradition than the native peoples amongst whom they live, they tend to be more successful. Besides, immigrants tend to stick together, and to help each other, and this promotes the prosperity of the group as a whole. In such countries there is often a demand that native business men should be protected from the competition of immigrants in certain lines. This raises awkward problems of racial discrimination, and in addition, since imitation and competition are the two roads to learning, it is not clear that native business men would progress more rapidly, or the community as a whole benefit, if the activities of immigrants were restricted. It seems a better policy to insist on immigrants taking native apprentices (as Tudor Britain did) and to create other opportunities for native business men to improve their abilities. (Migration is further discussed in Chapter VI.)

In their anxiety to develop local sources of enterprise, some governments create special financial institutions to lend money to small business men. This is helpful in so far as the deficiency of local enterprise is simply shortage of capital. However, this is seldom the case. The local capitalists are deficient in the skills of management,

and lending money to inexperienced small business people without supervision is often equivalent to pouring it down the drain. What these people need is first supervision and advice, and only secondarily capital. Their position is much like that of the peasant farmers. Special financial institutions ought therefore to regard their main duty as being to have a staff of experienced business administrators who can give advice to small business people who ask for it (just as industrial consultants do in advanced industrial countries, or agricultural extension workers in the countryside). And when money is lent, its use should be supervised carefully; the officers of the institution should have power to enforce changes in managerial practice, as a prior condition of the loan, and to check unprofitable practices at least until the loan has been repaid. There is just as much scope for a commercial advisory service as there is for the parallel service in agriculture.

The most difficult problem in lending to small business men in these countries is the small importance which so many attach to business reputation. In the advanced countries 'goodwill' is regarded as one of the most valuable assets of a business. Firms are anxious to protect their reputation for honouring their contracts— by delivering according to specification, by delivering promptly, by accepting what has been ordered, and by paying promptly. There are, however, many under-developed countries where the buyer, the seller or the lender who relies mainly upon the honesty of the business man with whom he is dealing is certain to be deceived in nine cases out of ten. Indeed, one reason why immigrant business men tend to be more successful in such countries is precisely the fact that foreign suppliers, banks and even the public at home have found from experience that they are more reliable. Presumably the importance of 'goodwill' (or of the fact that 'honesty is the best policy') is something that can be learnt with time, and which competition, and the growth of a new code of commercial morality in due course incorporate into the community's traditions. Meanwhile the relative absence of this sense makes it necessary for government institutions to tread with great care when they are trying to help small business men with loans, with contracts, or in other ways involving personal reliability.

Another training ground for business management is the co-operative movement which, when it is run on a democratic basis, gives large numbers of people an insight into business problems, and some experience of commercial management. This is probably the most valuable aspect of the co-operative movement; the jobs it does, the marketing of produce, the channelling of savings, the purchasing of supplies and so on could in many cases be done just as efficiently by private enterprise or by public agencies, but the educational value of

these other agencies is not comparable. Viewed in its wider perspective, this is just another illustration of the fact that administrative capacity and enterprise are likely to be more widely diffused in countries where decision making is decentralized than in countries run on an oligarchic basis. This is one of the great arguments for democracy, and it applies just as much in commercial life as it does in public administration. Indeed commercial life itself will probably be more vigorous in countries where public administration is decentralized and democratic, where the people are used to managing their own affairs at every level, from the village upward, than in countries where political power vests in an oligarchy. This is also one of the greatest arguments for competition, which similarly diffuses decision making and administrative experience in economic life.

Competition is in any case also vital to business efficiency for another reason. In the last analysis, business men are most likely to make use of the facilities for training and advice, and to seek out all ways of improving their own competence, if they have incentives to do so. The most powerful of the positive incentives is the prospect of success, while the most powerful of the negative incentives is the fear of bankruptcy. Both these incentives depend upon the existence of competition. Competition by itself will not ensure the efficiency of business, but neither will any other factor if competition is not also preserved.

BIBLIOGRAPHICAL NOTE

On the social background of invention see H. G. Barnett, *Innovation, The Basis of Cultural Change*, New York, 1953; J. D. Bernal, *Science and Industry in the Nineteenth Century*, London, 1953; H. Butterfield, *The Origins of Modern Science*, London, 1950; B. Farrington, *Greek Science*, London, 1944; S. C. Gilfillan, *The Sociology of Invention*, Chicago, 1936; H. S. Hatfield, *The Inventor and His World*, London, 1953; S. Lilley, *Men, Machines and History*, London, 1948; A. P. Usher, *A History of Mechanical Invention*, New York, 1929. The best introduction to the discussion of patents is an article by F. Machlup and E. F. Penrose, 'The Patent Controversy in the Nineteenth Century', *Journal of Economic History*, May 1950. On mass education consult *Fundamental Education, A Quarterly Bulletin*, published by the United Nations Educational, Scientific and Cultural Organization, Paris, 1949 to date. On agricultural extension see E. S. Brunner, I. T. Sanders, and D. Ensminger, eds., *Farmers of the World*, New York, 1945; *Agricultural Extension and Advisory Work, with Special Reference to the Colonies*, His Majesty's Stationery Office, London, 1949. The adaptation of labour attitudes is discussed in W. E. Moore, *Industrialization and Labour*, New York, 1951. A case history of helping small business men will be found in my official report, *Industrialization and the Gold Coast*, Accra, 1953.[*]

CHAPTER V

CAPITAL

In this chapter we shall consider separately how much capital is required for economic growth, the main sources of saving, and the process of investment.

1. CAPITAL REQUIREMENTS

Economic growth is associated with an increase in capital per head. It is, as we have seen, also associated with much else: with institutions which give incentive to effort, with attitudes which value economic efficiency, with growing technical knowledge, and so on. Capital is not the only requirement for growth, and if capital is made available without at the same time providing a fruitful framework for its use, it will be wasted. In what follows in this chapter we take for granted all that has already been said about these other matters. We are thus able to concentrate upon studying the fruitfulness of capital when conditions are appropriate to its use.

How fruitful is capital? The question is extremely difficult to answer, for lack of recorded evidence. We have only informed guesses about the growth of capital and of income over past decades, and these guesses only for a few of the advanced industrial countries. Practically all our knowledge of the quantitative relationship between income and capital is due to the pioneering work of Professor Simon Kuznets, and of Dr. Colin Clark, and what follows in this section draws heavily on their calculations.

The estimates of the growth of capital and of income, for what they are worth, show remarkable agreement on two propositions; first, that in the industrial countries the ratio of the value of capital to the value of output seems to be pretty constant at the margin, when capital-intensive and capital-sparse industries are taken together; and secondly that this marginal ratio lies between 3 to 1, and 4 to 1, when the value of land and other natural resources is excluded from capital and the value of external assets from both capital and income. This result can be expressed in different ways, such as by saying that on the average an investment of £100 is associated with an increase of national income by between £25 and £33 per year; or that raising national income by 3 per cent per annum cumulatively is associated with an annual net investment of between 9 per cent and 12 per cent of national income. The industrial countries

do indeed tend to invest between 10 per cent and 15 per cent of their national incomes, net of depreciation, and their incomes do tend to grow by between 3 per cent and 4 per cent per annum.

In the mathematical sense the ratio of the existing stock of capital to income (i.e. the average as distinct from the marginal ratio) is simply a function of the proportion of national income invested, the average life of investments, and the rate of growth of income. Thus if gross income were constant, and 12 per cent gross were invested annually in structures with a life of fifty years, and 8 per cent in equipment with a life of ten years, the average capital-income ratio would be 3·4 after fifty years. (The original cost of the structures existing at any time would be 6·0 times the national income, and the original cost of equipment would be 0·8 times the national income; assuming the capital to be on the average half worn out, its average value would be 3·4 times the national income.) Add say 0·5 for stocks held, and this brings the ratio to 3·9. Changing the rate of growth of income does not make as much difference as one might expect; for example, if we now assume national income to grow by 3 per cent per annum, and keep the other assumptions, the capital-income ratio including stocks falls only to 3·0. (It doesn't make so much difference because the earlier capital, which is now more than half worn out, is very much smaller than the later capital which is less than half worn out, because of the cumulative growth.) Given the average life of capital, the principal determinant of the capital-income ratio is the proportion of national income annually invested. So it is not surprising that countries which invest much the same proportion of national income have much the same capital-income ratio.

For the same reason the ratio of capital in existence to annual income is much lower in undeveloped countries (nearer 1 to 1), because their rate of accumulation has been much smaller. We do not, however, know how the *marginal* capital-income ratios compare in industrial and in the less developed countries (using for this purpose capital per head as the index of development). There are many reasons for not expecting the capital-income ratio to be the same at the margin. The same proportion of national income invested may not be associated with the same rate of growth of national income, and the average life of capital may not be the same. Some people are convinced that the capital-income ratio is higher at the margin in the less developed countries, relying for their conviction upon relative inefficiency of the industries which make capital, upon greater waste of capital, and upon slower growth of technical knowledge, as factors which make capital less productive. Other people expect the ratio to be lower, and these rely on the opening up of new natural resources, on more rapid growth of population, on the different relative impor-

tance of the agricultural, the industrial and the public utility sectors of the economy, and on the greater incentive to use the less capitalistic methods of production. A word may be said on each of these points.

The first of these propositions contends that, when compared with the developed countries, the less developed are relatively more efficient at making consumer goods than at making capital goods. If this is so, it raises the cost of capital in these countries relatively to income. To tackle this problem we have to divide capital formation into its two main component parts, namely the work of building and construction, and the manufacture of equipment. As to building costs, we have no conclusive evidence as to whether they are higher, relatively to consumer good costs, in less or in more developed countries. There is certainly evidence that they rise steeply if the building industry is overloaded, since this is an industry where work is easily disorganized if it is not properly planned or supervised, but this is as likely to happen in the developed as in the less developed countries. There is more evidence relating to machinery; fairly clear evidence, for example, for the U.S.S.R. when compared with the U.S.A., of relative disadvantage in engineering production, at any rate in the nineteen thirties. On the other hand, while construction has to be done at home, machinery can be imported, so that the comparative disadvantage of domestic production can be escaped. All told, it is plausible to expect capital cost to be higher relatively to income in the less developed countries, but there is probably not a great deal in it.

Next, the capital-income ratio is expected to be higher because of greater waste of capital. Of this there cannot be much doubt. There is waste in the sense that capital goods are not handled with as much care as they are in more developed countries. Workmen are less skilled, and handle their tools less carefully; chauffeurs and engine drivers drive their machines beyond the breaking point; and roads, buildings and other equipment are not so carefully maintained; hence depreciation rates are much higher in the less developed countries. There is also waste, it is thought, because there is more mal-investment, due to greater ignorance of what is possible. The resources of the less developed countries, in soil, rainfall, minerals and so on, are less well mapped, and less is known about potential markets, at home or abroad. Hence great blunders are made, and experience is bought at great cost (the classic example of the attempt to grow groundnuts in Tanganyika being only the best publicized of thousands of similar cases, involving private entrepreneurs even more than governments). And there is also waste because, for this very reason, capital tends to stick to the beaten tracks, with the result that

there is over-investment in some activities and under-investment in others. It is true that these wastes are relative, in the sense that capital is wasted in the developed countries also; for example, in that if their rate of physical deterioration is lower, their rate of obsolescence tends to be greater. Even so it seems almost inevitable that we must expect waste to be relatively greater in the countries with least experience.

Thirdly, it can be argued that capital will be less productive in the less developed countries because fruitful use of capital depends on ever improving technology, and the growth of knowledge is slower in the less developed countries. The argument may be put in different ways. One way of putting it is to say that in the developed countries income tends to grow because of growing knowledge, and would grow even if capital ceased to grow; whereas, in the less developed, technology advances more slowly and contributes less to the growth of income. Or an alternative way of putting it would be to say that capital is often used to introduce new technologies, so that where technology grows slowly capital is less fruitful. On the other hand it is equally arguable that the very backwardness of technology makes possible spectacular advances, so that if capital were invested in the more backward countries, and the necessary expenditures on education and training were undertaken at the same time, they might show much more rapid rates of growth than the more developed can show. Many thinkers believe that for this reason it is much easier to get high rates of economic growth in countries which are starting from a low level than it is in countries which are already at a very high level, and they adduce in support of their claims the relatively high rates of growth of output in the U.S.S.R. and in Japan.

The argument about resources leads in the same way to no demonstrable conclusion. Just as capital is particularly fruitful when it is used to introduce new techniques much superior to those prevailing, so also it is more fruitful when used to open up new rich natural resources than when it merely assists in better exploitation of resources which are already in use. Hence it is sometimes argued that the less developed countries can make more fruitful use of capital than the more developed. This is not however by any means necessarily the case. In the first place, the resources of the less developed countries are not by any means necessarily richer than those of the more developed. Asia and Africa have not yet demonstrated themselves to be particulary rich in soil, in fuel, or in other minerals, and it is by no means clear that capital invested in Asia or in Africa will cause resources to fructify more than will capital added to the already known resources of North America. In this context we must not use such large categories as continental areas, but must speak instead of

particular projects in limited areas. In some parts of the under-developed world there are rich resources still waiting to be opened up, whereas in other parts the contribution of capital will be con-fined mainly to making it possible to exploit better techniques. Then, in the second place, it may even be that capital has an affinity for the already capitalized. Any new enterprise has to depend for its productiveness on using the services of many other enterprises (public utilities, engineering service, raw material suppliers, etc.). Hence in many cases it is more economic to make new investments in places where a lot of capital has already been invested than in places which are not yet developed. To this extent, the developed have an advantage over the less developed, and there is no natural tendency for the productivity of capital to be higher in less developed countries. All the same, if the difference is mainly a matter of how much capital has already been invested, then the disadvantages of the less developed are reduced as they accelerate their own invest-ment. We know unfortunately too little about the resources of the less developed, or about the importance of increasing or decreasing returns to capital to generalize confidently on these subjects.

Next, we should expect the capital-income ratio to be higher in countries where population is increasing slowly than in countries where population is increasing rapidly, on the 'law of diminishing returns' ground that capital is likely to yield more if used with a greater rather than with a smaller increase of labour. Here again it must not be assumed that all the less developed countries have rapid population growth; for instance, the population of North America is growing much more rapidly than the population of Asia. On the other hand, if population is growing slowly, as in France, less capi-tal is needed for housing, which has a high capital-income ratio, and this is probably more important.

We can be a little more confident in dealing with arguments based upon the relative importance of different sectors in the economy. The capital-income ratios differ widely as between the different sectors of the economy. Thus the ratio is very much higher in public utilities than it is in manufacturing; even in an advanced industrial country it is five or six times as high, and it seems to be even higher in the earlier stages of economic development because the sub-stantial economies of scale which this sector enjoys lower the ratio rapidly as economic development proceeds. On the other hand, when capital is invested in a public utility it may increase productivity not only in that utility but also in the rest of the economy; so the net result for the economy as a whole may be a low capital-income ratio. There are also substantial differences between the capital requirements of agriculture and of manufacturing. In the more developed countries

the ratio is higher for agriculture than it is for manufacturing, but it seems probable that in the less developed countries the lesser mechanization of agriculture should put its ratio lower than that of manufacturing, at any rate apart from handicraft industries. Now when we take account of the different ratios of different sectors, and of the fact that the sectors combine in very different proportions in more and in less developed countries, we should expect to get very different ratios for the economy as a whole. In the less developed countries agriculture is much more important, relatively to manufacturing, than in the developed. At low levels of productivity 60 to 70 per cent of the gainfully occupied population is needed in agriculture in order to feed the people, compared with the 12 to 15 per cent that suffices in developed countries for the same purpose. (But all such comparisons are subject to the difficulties inherent in census classifications, to which we refer in Chapter VI, section 1 (c).) At low levels, also, agriculture is not very capital intensive (excluding land from consideration). Heavy expenditures may be needed in connection with water, for drainage, reclamation, irrigation or flood control. Those less developed countries which are sparsely populated may also gain by using machinery to increase the area cultivated per head, but the densely populated countries stand to gain only marginally from mechanizing operations, since widespread use of machinery would do much more to increase unemployment than it would do to raise output (see Chapter III, Section 3 (d)). Apart from the contribution of capital to water conservation, raising productivity in agriculture in the less developed countries depends more upon new techniques (fertilizers, seeds, pesticides, rotations and so on) than it does upon capital. The development of manufacturing industry is much more capital intensive. It is true that the development of cottage industries where this is appropriate does not call for large sums of capital, but the development of factory industry also cannot be avoided, and this is very capital intensive when compared with agriculture at these levels of development. Since agriculture is so large relatively to manufacturing (from 6 to 1 to 10 to 1 in terms of employment), and since progress in agriculture depends on annual expenditures on agricultural extension and research much more than it does on capital, it seems legitimate to conclude that a given increase in income can be secured for a smaller increase in capital than in industrial countries. On the other hand, the less developed countries need very heavy expenditure on public works and public utilities (harbours, railways, roads, electricity, schools, etc.), probably higher in relation to income than in industrial countries, so over all there may not be much difference in the capital-income ratio, as far as it is influenced by the relative importance of different sectors.

Lastly we come to differences resulting from the relative shortage of capital. In the less developed countries it is economical to use capital more sparingly than in the developed. Thus, if it is possible to use a process which requires heavy capital investment associated with low running costs, or alternatively to choose methods associating lower initial investment with higher annual cost, the latter methods are often more appropriate. It is better to build for twenty years than for fifty years; to use processes involving hand labour rather than machinery; and generally to economize capital relatively to labour. All this, of course, must be taken relatively rather than absolutely; the argument is not that capital should not be used at all, but that since it is scarcer than in more developed countries, it should be used more sparingly. The argument applies to all the less developed countries, but it applies with particular force to those countries which have surplus labour relatively to their physical resources, in the sense that the current output could be produced by a smaller labour force without any increase in capital or improvement of technique. Some countries in the Middle East and in South Asia are in this position, for example India, where it is thought that the cultivable land is carrying about a quarter more people engaged in agriculture than are required for its cultivation with current equipment and techniques. In such countries it is wasteful to use capital as a substitute for labour, and the use of machinery in agriculture, in manufacturing activities, in building and construction or in other activities should be confined to cases where machinery makes possible an increase in output which could not be achieved instead merely by using more labour. The corollary of this proposition is that we should expect the amount of capital associated with each increase in income to be lower in the less developed countries than in the more developed.

We have now considered half-a-dozen reasons why the marginal capital-income ratio should be different in developed and less developed countries. The upshot of the analysis is that we do not know what the marginal capital-income ratio is in any underdeveloped country, and can only hazard guesses as to whether it is likely to be higher or lower than in the United States of America. All the same, if for want of anything better we use the ratio which has been found for industrial countries, it is easy enough to see why income grows so slowly in the less developed countries. A country such as India is estimated to be investing about 4 or 5 per cent of its national income annually. It is dangerous to compare such figures with the figures for investment in industrial countries, because we are less certain of the estimates for the less developed countries. For example, we do not know how much capital formation the sub-

sistence farmers do for themselves on their farms, in opening up new lands, in drainage or soil conservation, in improving their houses, etc., so it is conceivable that capital formation in rural areas is underestimated. However, if we accept the figures, annual net investment of 4 or 5 per cent might raise national income by just about the $1\frac{1}{4}$ per cent which is the rate at which India's population is currently increasing—or even by less than this if, as is possibly the case, investment in housing is a larger proportion of investment when investment is small, and productive investment a smaller part of investment. At best, then, current investment is only enough to keep up with population growth; there is nothing to spare for raising the standard of living. For India to raise her standard of living by 1 per cent annually she would have nearly to double her current rate of investment. Every year the gap between the Indian and the U.S. standard of living widens; to hold this gap constant, India's standard of living would have to rise at the same rate as the American standard, say by about $1\frac{1}{2}$ to 2 per cent per annum. For this to happen net investment in India would have to rise from its current level of 4 or 5 per cent to say 12 per cent of national income.

   This in turn raises the question how rapidly capital formation can be accelerated without reducing the fruitfulness of capital. All the countries which are now relatively developed have at some time in the past gone through a period of rapid acceleration, in the course of which their rate of annual net investment has moved from 5 per cent or less to 12 per cent or more. This is what we mean by an Industrial Revolution. Unfortunately figures do not exist which would enable us to say for any particular case either how long the transition took, or how the productivity of capital was affected during the transition. We have seen some very swift transitions (i.e. within a decade or so) in such countries as Japan, Germany, Northern Rhodesia, and the U.S.S.R., but we cannot say whether the speed of the change reduced the productiveness of the effort. All the same, it is arguable on *a priori* grounds that there are limits to the rate at which a country can fruitfully step up its capital formation. Of these, the two most important limits (given finance, suitable natural resources and appropriate institutions) are shortage of skill, and inadequacy of public utilities.

   Shortage of skill not only prevents people from using capital fruitfully, but may prevent them from using it at all. As we shall see in a moment, more than half of capital formation consists of work in building and construction. Hence the expansion of capital is a function of the rate at which the building and construction industry can be expanded. Plans cannot be executed if there are not the carpenters, the masons the electricians and the engineers to do the necessary

construction, whether it be of roads, bridges, dams, factories, power plants, houses or the rest. Hence the question how rapidly capital formation can be accelerated resolves itself first into the question how rapidly the building industry can be expanded. The other limit, the inadequacy of public utilities, operates because new enterprises need communications, dock facilities, water supplies, electric power and other such services. The expansion of public utilities, however, (given finance) again resolves itself into a question of the rate at which these things can be constructed, which is the same question as to the rate at which the building industry can be expanded. So the most important bottleneck which restricts the rate at which capital can be absorbed is shortage of skill.

Now skill can be imported, or it can be trained. In Northern Rhodesia it was imported as required, and so capital formation expanded rapidly without physical restraints. Elsewhere the expansion of skill depends to a greater extent upon training, though in every case the importation of skilled people, even if only for training purposes, makes capital formation much easier. The training of building workers and supervisors looms large in any training programme, but of course many other skills are also needed, including the skills of the people who are to use the capital when it is installed. Failure to put training into the foreground of development programmes accounts for much of the frustration occasioned by such programmes, which, though they are seldom large in relation to national income, almost always lag behind in performance because of the physical difficulty of carrying them out. If, on the contrary, a great training programme is launched, as in the U.S.S.R., or as when armies are rapidly expanded on the outbreak of war, there seems no reason why lack of skill should be an obstacle to doubling the rate of capital formation within ten years. A building industry can be doubled in ten years if the training facilities are provided, and if the precaution is also taken of importing experienced supervisors from other countries. Productivity will of course be low initially; but then, the productivity of workers drawn into new employments is always low, whether the rate of expansion is great or small.

We turn next to consider the composition of capital, which can be looked at from three angles: the ratio of net to gross capital formation, the industries in which the capital is used, and what the capital consists of.

We know very little about the ratio of gross to net investment. Even in the industrial economies the division raises intractable theoretical difficulties, and the figures used in practice are only informed guesses, based, like the capital-income ratio, on estimates of past investment and of the average life of capital. On this basis it

o

is usually estimated that the replacement of obsolete or worn out capital requires about five to ten per cent of gross national output in industrial countries. In the United States, for example, over long decades up to the great slump, net investment averaged about 13 per cent, and replacement about 7 per cent, making gross investment about 20 per cent of gross national output. It is thought, in the U.S. case, that there is evidence of a tendency for replacement expenditures to grow relatively to net investment. This is very plausible having regard to the fact that public utilities make heavy demands on new capital in the initial stages of economic development, whereas in the later stages, thanks to the economies of scale which they enjoy, their demand is more for maintenance expenditures and less for new extension. We cannot be too confident of this since technical progress from time to time renders some public utilities obsolete, and calls for vast new expenditures on others, and since in addition, our standards of the service we expect are rising all the time. The available figures cannot be taken as conclusive since the concepts are not sufficiently precise, or the figures sufficiently accurate. All that we need note for the present is that a large part of economic activity is needed just to keep the capital stock intact.

The proportion of national income required for replacement is much smaller in the less developed economies since their stock of capital is much smaller in relation to income. In the industrial countries the stock of reproducible capital is more than three times as great as national income, whereas in the poorest countries the stock of capital, excluding land, is smaller than or not much greater than national income. Depreciation therefore requires only 2 or 3 per cent of national income, compared with 7 to 10 per cent in the richest countries. The stock of capital and the depreciation ratio both rise rapidly as net investment rises.

Next we come to the division of capital investment between the various sectors of the economy. We have data only for advanced industrial countries, where gross investment is around 20 per cent of gross national output. These countries show differences between themselves, but if we care to think of a 'typical' programme, gross fixed investment (i.e. excluding stocks) might divide like this:

Housing	about	25 per cent
Public works and utilities	,,	35 per cent
Manufacturing and agriculture	,,	30 per cent
Other commerce	,,	10 per cent
		100 per cent

These figures are averages over long periods; there are marked fluctuations from year to year into which we need not at present enter.

There is much to be said about these figures. Take first housing. It usually surprises people to discover how large a part of gross investment is required merely to house the population, but this is in fact typical, at any rate of industrial countries. The proportion varies according to the rate of growth of population. It is probably also particularly high in countries where a transfer of population from agriculture to industry is still taking place, since this requires a rapid expansion of the towns. These are probably the reasons why the proportion has been nearer 20 per cent in Great Britain and nearer 30 per cent in the U.S.A. The need for this great expenditure on housing is easily overlooked; it seems to have been overlooked in the U.S.S.R. when the first five year plan was being drafted. Probably the less developed countries need more than 25 per cent of their investment to be in housing if the towns into which their people will move as development gets under way are not to repeat one of the worst features of most industrial revolutions.

The figures also bring out the great importance of public works and public utilities (roads, docks, transport, water, electricity, schools, hospitals, government buildings). Even in industrial countries this item always uses up more capital than goes into manufacturing activity. We would like to know more about how this proportion varies in the course of economic development, but the figures available do not permit confident generalizations. There is reason to believe that the proportion is particularly high in the first decades of development, and declines thereafter. This is because initial development calls for the establishment of a framework of utilities, and though it is also necessary to spend money on maintaining, improving and extending the framework, it is possible that these later expenditures are relatively not so heavy as those which have initially to be made. This is the same proposition which we encountered earlier on, as an explanation of a suspected tendency for net investment to fall relatively to gross investment. We shall meet it again in a moment explaining a tendency for construction expenditures to fall relatively to expenditures on equipment, within the total of gross investment. And later still we shall meet it again as one of the reasons advanced by those economists who expect that the well developed countries will have increasing difficulty in finding enough outlets for their savings as they 'mature'.

Another interesting corollary of the importance of investment in public works and utilities is the importance of public investment in relation to private investment. In those countries where the government leaves public utilities to private enterprise, government investment is only a small part of total investment—10 per cent or less. The proportion rises sharply, however, as public utilities are nationa-

lized, and more sharply still if the government takes on responsibilities for housing expenditures, not to speak of investment in mining and manufacturing. Many of the less developed countries have resolved to take over responsibility for these investments, only to discover that the sums involved mean an enormous expansion of government expenditure beyond what they are in a position to finance.

The division of investment between manufacturing and agriculture depends on the relative importance of these two activities in the economy. In Great Britain agriculture takes only 5 per cent of gross investment, but then it employs only 5 per cent of the people. In the United States the proportion of investment is more like 8 to 10 per cent. In every country the growth of national income per head expands manufacturing relatively to agriculture, since, as people grow richer, they increase their purchases of manufactures more rapidly than their consumption of food. There must therefore be a natural trend for the proportion invested in manufactures to rise, and the proportion invested in agriculture to fall. Apart from this, the relative proportions depend on the natural resources of a country relatively to its population, since this in turn determines whether it is overpopulated, and must export manufactures in exchange for food, or whether it can prosper by exporting primary products in exchange for manufactures. In overpopulated countries like Japan or India one expects a development programme to include a relatively large investment in manufacturing, since there is no other way of employing all the people, or of paying for imports of food. Whereas in countries with ample fertile soil, such as Burma or Siam, one expects rather a preponderance of investments of the sort which raise agricultural output per head.

Lastly we come to the division of capital formation between construction, equipment and adding to stocks. Let us take stocks first, since this item is often neglected. Stocks in existence at any time are between one-third and one-half of national income. Hence if national income is increasing by 3 per cent annually, one needs to add to stocks about 1 to $1\frac{1}{2}$ per cent of national income, which may be as much as 12 per cent of net investment. The need for this large item is frequently overlooked in development planning, with the result that the economy develops shortages of raw materials and of consumer goods, and the expansion of output is thus held up.

The relative shares of construction and of equipment in gross fixed capital formation depend upon how well endowed the country already is with roads, railways, houses, and public utilities generally. The share of construction in 1952 was in the United Kingdom 48 per cent, in the U.S.A. 56 per cent, in the Gold Coast 59 per cent and

in Nigeria 61 per cent. The figures we have for the U.S.A., stretching back to 1870, reveal the same trend: construction has fallen steadily from its initial level of about two-thirds. The abnormally low proportion in the U.K. is partly due to the deliberate restriction of investment in the public services in recent years, as an anti-inflationary measure; this is most obvious in the very low expenditure on roads. Public investment (excluding public corporations and utilities) in the U.K. was only 9 per cent of gross fixed investment in 1952, compared with 16 per cent in the U.S.A.

The great importance of construction is not generally realized; many people think of capital formation mainly in terms of installing machinery, while in truth it consists to a greater extent of building structures of one sort or another; civil engineering is the key industry in capital formation, with mechanical engineering following some distance behind. This has its corollaries. One is the point we have already made that, given finance, the real bottleneck which holds up a rapid acceleration of investment is the capacity of the building industry to extend itself. Another corollary is that in the earlier stages of economic development the greatest need for capital is for public works and public utilities, which in these days are not directly open to private foreign investors; so private foreign investment is of limited relevance to the capital needs of the less developed countries. But we shall come back to this in section 2(c).

Enough has already been said to indicate that any figures which appear in this section are highly speculative, and that there is no typical pattern of capital investment to which any particular country should be expected to conform. All the same, even when allowing for the wide differences which rightly exist between countries, and which can be explained, the figures nevertheless also throw light on some typical misconceptions, and for this reason alone have value. They bring out, for example, the importance of building in capital formation, the importance of stocks, and the importance of housing, for neglect of which many development programmes have come to grief. In each country there is no substitute for a detailed survey of resources and potentialities if one sets out to make an investment programme; but it is also helpful to glance at what has happened elsewhere, if only to make certain that some major item has not been overlooked.

2. SAVINGS

(a) The Need for Savings

The proposition which we have established in the preceding section is that investment is necessary to economic growth. From this it

follows, in a passive sense, that saving is necessary to growth, because investment has to be matched by saving. It nevertheless remains open to ask whether the process of investment will not automatically create all the saving that is required, so that we need not worry about the level of savings, and can concentrate on investment. We can also go further and ask whether saving may not discourage investment, by destroying the market for goods, so that it is better to encourage people to spend than to save. These questions have been asked for a long time, and we have to deal with them before we begin to analyse the sources of saving in detail.

At any level of income, people can consume only the quantity of consumer goods which exists. Since their incomes derive from producing consumer goods and investment goods, and since they can buy only the consumer goods, it follows that they must save a part of their income equal to the value of the investment goods which have been produced. In this sense people must always save as much as has been invested. What they are thus forced to save may not, however, correspond to what they would like to save at that level of income. If they would like to save more, they will reduce their expenditure on consumer goods; and if they would like to save less, they will increase their expenditure on consumer goods. In either case, their expenditure will not exactly correspond with the value of the consumer goods produced. If people want to save more than is being invested, the producers of consumer goods will make losses, since part of the incomes they have paid out as costs are not returning to them as sales; and if people want to save less than is being invested, the producers will make unexpected profits. Either of these disequilibria sets off a corrective movement. If people wish to save more than is being invested, the producers who are making losses will reduce their outlays, and income and employment will contract. If on the other hand investment exceeds saving, producers will increase their outlays and income will expand. This expansion of income will be reflected also in an expansion of real output and of employment if there are idle resources of labour, land and capital which can be absorbed; but if there is a shortage of some or all of the resources needed for expanding output, the expansion of income will show itself instead merely in an inflationary rise of prices.

This, then, is the answer to the question whether saving matters. It does matter. Given the level of investment, if people's desire to save is excessive there will be deflation, and if their desire to save is inadequate there will be either expansion of output if this is possible, or else inflation of prices. Given the level of investment, it is equally possible for people to want to save too much or too little.

In the popular thinking of the Victorian age these problems did

not arise because people were not used to thinking of the level of investment as something which could be 'given' independently of the level of saving. In their way of looking at the matter, entrepreneurs invested their own or borrowed savings. They could not invest savings which did not exist, and all savings automatically got invested. Hence saving and investment were always equal, the level of investment being determined by the level of savings. Since the Victorians wished to increase investment, they could concentrate their minds on ways of stimulating saving. In our day, however, we recognize both that saving is not necessarily always invested (some may be hoarded), and also that some investment may not be matched by current saving (it may be financed by dishoarding or by the creation of additional money). We have therefore come to analyse separately the forces determining saving, and the forces determining investment, and to recognize that there may well be at any time either too much or too little saving for the level of investment then prevailing.

Moreover, when we examine the forces determining investment, we see another possibility which most of the Victorians overlooked, namely the theoretical possibility that an increase in saving may discourage investment rather than lead automatically to increasing investment, as they thought it would. This theoretical argument depends upon the assumption that the ratio between the community's capital and its consumption is fixed, since if this is not so, capital accumulation may be proceeding faster than consumption is growing, and a decline in the rate of growth of consumption will not necessarily check the rate of growth of capital. Is the ratio of capital to consumption fixed? Not necessarily so. In the first place, consumer goods can be made by processes which are more capital-intensive or less capital-intensive, the choice depending to some extent on how cheap capital is relatively to other resources—that is to say upon the level of the rate of interest. Now an increase in thrift tends to lower the rate of interest, not by very much if the rate is already very low, but substantially if the rate is high. Hence an increase in thrift may encourage producers to use more capital-intensive processes, and may therefore stimulate the production of capital for producing consumer goods even though the demand for consumer goods is growing more slowly. This is a theoretical possibility; the check to consumption pulls in one direction and the fall in the rate of interest in the other, so we cannot be certain what the net result will be. More important, perhaps, is what emerges when we ask what is meant by consumption. As we have seen in the preceding section, even in rich industrial communities only about 30 per cent of gross fixed investment goes into manufacturing industry and agriculture, and is thus, directly

tied to the consumption of these things in the shops. Some 60 per cent is absorbed by houses, public utilities and public works, the demand for which—or at any rate the demand for investment in which—is not very closely geared to current levels of consumer spending in shops, if only because these are very long-lived investments geared as much to expectations of demand in the longer run. These investments are also very highly capital-intensive, with capital-income ratios five or six times as high as the ratios in manufacturing and agriculture; and they are for this reason particularly sensitive to changes in interest rates. It is therefore quite plausible for an increase in thrift to diminish investment in manufacturing while more than correspondingly increasing investment in housing, public utilities and public works. It is theoretically possible that increasing thrift will discourage investment, but it is equally possible that it will stimulate investment.

The possibility that the level of saving may be too high has to be taken into account by countries which are already so well stocked with capital that the incentive to invest is weak, and there is danger of a chronic shortage of investment opportunities. It is arguable whether any such countries exist, since even the richest countries are constantly raising the standards they expect in housing, communications, hospitals and so on, as well as inventing new consumer goods and new methods of production which demand new capital. We shall come to the problems of these countries later (this Chapter, Section 3(d)). In the less developed countries there is no such danger. On the contrary, quite apart from the willingness of private persons to make investments if they could find the finance, governments are overwhelmed with projects for spending on roads, water supplies, flood control, irrigation, electric power, factories, schools, houses, hospitals, and on and on. What restrains this investment is not lack of demand, but simply the lack of saving to finance it. In these countries it would be possible for decades to maintain fruitful programmes of public investment of say 12 per cent net of the national income, but the people are willing to save only 4 or 5 per cent. Hence, if the money were created to finance the difference between saving and investment, people who received it would spend too much of it in the consumer markets, and there would be an inflationary trend. If, on the other hand, people would save more voluntarily, larger investment would be possible without inflation. Whatever may be the case in the more developed countries, the obstacle to greater investment in the less developed countries is that the current propensity to save is too low.

Now some people hold the view that investment is so necessary in these countries in order to raise living standards that it should be

undertaken even at the cost of generating inflation. It is therefore necessary to pursue the analysis to see what happens if investment is undertaken at a level which exceeds voluntary savings.

The answer, in general terms, is that money income will expand continuously until it reaches a level where savings equal investment. The point of the analysis is to discover how this equilibrium is reached, how long it takes, and what happens in the interim to prices and to output.

Let us begin with output. We must distinguish what happens to output immediately from what happens to output in due course when the new capital goods created by the process begin to bear fruit. The output created by the new capital goods is the same whether these are financed out of savings or out of creating new money. Its effect on prices is also the same; namely, it causes them to fall. In this respect, there is an important distinction to be made between inflations whose purpose is the creation of useful capital goods and other inflations. Most of us associate inflation with war, when its purpose is to withdraw goods for destructive purposes. Such inflations can get cumulatively worse, since an ever-increasing supply of money may face an ever-dwindling supply of goods. Inflations for the purpose of creating useful capital are on the contrary self-destructive, since sooner or later they result in an increased supply of goods to the market. How soon and how large an output depends on the nature of the enterprises financed in this way. If a school building programme is financed in this way, prices will rise for a very long time, and when the effect begins to show in the increased output of the school-leavers, prices may not fall very much. But if new money were spent in the countryside to conserve water supplies on schemes which took only a few months to build, cost very little, and doubled the output of the lands supplied with water, prices would rise very little, and would quickly fall much more.

It is important to bear in mind that inflation for creating useful capital is ultimately self-destructive. All the same, it is also important to analyse what happens in the interim before the new capital begins to bear fruit. What happens in the interim to output, and therefore to prices, depends upon whether the economy has idle resources which are easily absorbed into increasing output. In the industrial countries in the middle of a slump there are factories closed and labour idle. When investment is increased, the people who are thus employed spend part of their incomes on buying consumer goods, and this encourages producers of consumer goods to produce more. This in its turn gives more employment, and so the spiral continues upward. The picture is however different in the less developed countries. They have no factories full of useful equipment standing idle—or in

so far as they have they are very few and even the smallest pressure of demand would soon reach the limits of output. Some of them—especially in Africa—also have very little unemployment, in the sense of people standing ready to work if offered employment at the current wage. Others—especially in Asia—have surplus populations, especially in the countryside, but do not have the equipment to match these populations. If extra money were put into circulation it would expand a little the output of agriculture, and of handicraft industries, but very soon these would be working to the limits of their capacity, and further increases in money income would serve only to raise prices rather than to increase the output of consumer goods.

All the same, even in economies where the output of consumer goods cannot be increased, for want of land to produce food, or machinery to produce manufactures, it may nevertheless be possible to use surplus labour to produce certain forms of capital, without withdrawing land or equipment from other purposes. We have already seen that some 50 to 60 per cent of fixed capital formation is in construction work. Now many forms of construction can be done by hand, using virtually no scarce equipment—witness the achievements of man from the building of the Pyramids to the construction of the great railway tunnels in the middle of the nineteenth century. Surplus labour can be used for building roads, irrigation channels, water tanks, houses and many other kinds of works, without reducing the output of anything else, and some of these works, especially those connected with water for farms, or with land clearance, fructify both quickly and bountifully. In one sense the countries which have surplus labour have therefore an advantage over those countries which have not. For the latter countries cannot increase their capital formation without withdrawing labour from producing consumer goods, whereas the countries which have surplus labour can increase capital formation at zero cost in other goods.

What holds back the use of such surplus labour is not the lack of fixed capital, but the lack of working capital. If labour employed to dig an irrigation canal is paid, the workers will take their wages to the markets. The stream of money demand will be increased, without a corresponding increase in the output of consumer goods. Hence prices will tend to rise. This, plus the increase in demand, will also stimulate imports of consumer goods, with unfortunate effects upon the balance of payments, and if these effects are prevented by strict control of imports and of exports, the effect is merely to swell the sum of money circulating at home, and so to put greater pressure on domestic prices.

The cause and effect of this increase of prices is a redistribution of

consumer goods towards the newly employed away from the rest of the economy. These newly employed were previously managing to scrape a living somehow, presumably at the expense of their relations. Now they are better off (or presumably they would not accept employment) and other people must therefore be worse off, since there has been no increase in consumer good output. The rise of prices is therefore just a substitute for taxation, since exactly the same result would be achieved, without the rise of prices, if the government levied a tax on the community at large, and used the proceeds to pay the workers on the irrigation canal. The choice between inflation and taxation is largely political. Governments are driven to inflation when they think the political difficulties of raising resources in this way are less than the political difficulties in the way of raising the same sum in taxes.

An alternative way of getting capital works done, without inflation or taxation, is to persuade people to work on them without payment. We have already seen (Chapter III, section 1(a)) that this is indeed feasible in rural areas, if the works in question are of strictly local interest, and if they are likely to benefit nearly everyone in the village. Such activities are not without cost to the government. In the first place, it has to create an administrative service to make propaganda for this kind of activity in the villages, to organize the villagers so that they can discuss and plan what they want to do, to supervise its execution, and generally to act in liaison with all the other government departments which are affected by these activities (attempts to organize 'community development' without special staff for the purpose never achieve much). And in the second place the government has usually to provide such raw materials as are not easily to be had locally, and also to pay for skilled labour or other technical help. It has been found that the government has to supply from 30 to 50 per cent of the cost of the works done in this way; the remaining 50 to 70 per cent being the value of the labour freely contributed. Such efforts are valuable for many reasons beyond the output which the capital will contribute, or the fact that the method avoids both inflation and taxation. They are valuable also because they stimulate the communal spirit in the countryside, and because they encourage the villagers to feel that they can help themselves—a sentiment which may yield dividends in many other directions once it is aroused. This is also the best kind of planning: since the villagers are not compelled to work communally, they work only on projects which they want; whereas works planned and paid for at the centre of government frequently do not meet the real needs of the people, if they do not, indeed, forget the remote rural areas altogether. There is everything to be said for putting into 'community development' all

the resources which it can take. On the other hand, it must be realized that the contribution which this can make to capital formation is strictly limited by the fact that people will work only on projects of strictly local interest. This cannot therefore be seen as a substitute for other methods of capital formation on any substantial scale. Unpaid labour may be very important in countries which resort to compulsory labour, but its scope in other countries is restricted.

Let us continue to assume that capital formation is being financed by creating money, and pursue the inflation to see what happens. First we must get the balance of payments out of the way. If inflation were carried on without control of imports, foreign exchange reserves would disappear very rapidly. It may also be necessary to control exports, otherwise the increase in domestic demand will cause the public to consume at home goods which might otherwise be exported. This difficulty does not arise if the exports consist of goods which are not consumed at home (rubber, cocoa), but it may be very important if the exports are also consumable at home (rice, cotton, oilseeds). Control of exports is not easy, since it involves some kind of licensing or of requisitioning, which is easier to apply to large factories or plantations than to handicraft workers or peasants. Then there are the difficulties created in export markets by rising prices at home. If the country is exporting competitively, in the sense that its output is merely a fraction of world output, the world price will be unaffected by its inflation, and its exports may drop as domestic costs rise relatively to world prices. Various devices may be adopted, of the nature of export subsidies, but the final outcome of any substantial inflation is inevitably devaluation of the currency. This is of no adverse significance to a small country, since its terms of trade are not adversely affected by devaluation, and since its external assets and liabilities are usually fixed in terms of foreign currency; but it may be of greater importance to a large country. To these difficulties with exports we must add again the need to control the flight of capital overseas; inflation encourages people to hold foreign currency instead of domestic currency, especially in anticipation of devaluation. When all this is taken into account, it is obvious that it is extremely difficult to have such perfect control of the foreign exchange situation that inflation does not have some adverse effect on the balance of payments—but some countries find these things easier to manage than others.

We assume that the balance of payments is not allowed to deteriorate, and continue the analysis. We note next that even with output constant some creation of money is possible in some of the less developed countries without pressure on prices. This is the case where the economy is being increasingly monetized, in the sense that

the use of money is growing relatively to production for subsistence or for barter. To the extent to which people need more money for transactions, more money can be put into circulation without pressure on prices. Similarly, more money can be put into circulation without increasing prices in any economy where output is growing, whether because population is growing, or because more land is coming under cultivation, or because of increases in productivity. In every economy where economic growth is occurring, people need to hold more money, and so the government can create more money without causing prices to rise. Unfortunately, this source of finance is not really very large. The ratio of money in active circulation to the national income is always much less than one. So, even if the output exchanged against money is increasing by 2 per cent per annum, this hardly permits of financing investment beyond about 1 per cent of national income without creating pressure.

Beyond this level, if more money is created to finance investment, investment will exceed saving. Money income will then rise continuously until saving catches up with investment. How long it takes to reach this new equilibrium depends on whether the level of saving is a function of money income, or of real income only. If saving is a function of real income only, then saving cannot be increased by inflating money income; so equilibrium cannot be reached until after the new capital goods have begun to increase the output of consumer goods. Whereas, if inflation redistributes income from non-saving towards the saving classes, equilibrium may be attainable without any increase in real income, and before the new consumer goods reach the market.

Let us explore more fully what chance there is of the inflation petering out even without taking into account the increased output of consumer goods which it ultimately brings into the market. The most favourable case, from this angle, can be constructed as follows. Assume that the government employs the unemployed to dam up a river and construct irrigation channels. These unemployed take their wages into the markets, where the effect is to raise prices. If we assume that this results exclusively in an increase of profits, and that these profits are all hoarded, or used to buy government bonds, then the inflation is over. Prices have risen by the amount invested, but so also have savings, and so prices will not rise any more although the investing process goes on. This is one extreme case. We can also see the other extreme case from the same example if we assume that as soon as prices rise all members of the community demand and receive higher wages, salaries, and interest payments in order to keep their real incomes and consumption unchanged. On this assumption equilibrium cannot be reached until the new output of consumer

goods becomes available, because the inflationary process is not allowed to redistribute income in favour of the classes that might save and hoard.

It follows that in practice the chance of an inflation being held within narrow limits depends (a) on whether the inflation redistributes income towards the classes who save, (b) on what they do with these savings and (c) on how soon the new output of consumer goods becomes available.

As to (a) the classes who normally benefit from inflation are entrepreneurs, peasants, and in some cases the government. Entrepreneurs benefit because of the tendency of the prices of what they sell to rise faster than wages, salaries, rents, debenture interest, pensions and some of their other expenses. Peasants benefit because food prices usually rise more sharply than other prices, because of the inelastic demand for food. Now peasants and entrepreneurs are both more thrifty than other classes of the community, so an inflation almost certainly increases savings. The contrary view is a sectional view. Inflation reduces the savings of the salary earning middle classes, because it reduces their real incomes; for this reason, and because the middle classes speak and write more than the other classes, it is frequently asserted that inflation reduces savings. This is not however the case. The fall in middle class real incomes is matched by a rise in entrepreneurial and peasant real incomes, and both of these classes have a higher propensity to save than the middle classes have. It is also important to consider the effect of the inflation upon government savings. The effect of inflation upon the government's revenue differs from case to case, according to whether the proportion of income taken in taxes is larger or smaller at the margin than it is on the average. If marginal taxation exceeds average taxation, a rise in money incomes raises the share of the national income taken in taxes, so that ultimately the government, which begins by creating money to finance its expenditures, reaches a point where its revenues have risen so much that the new levels of expenditure can now be maintained without any further creation of money. Many modern governments are in this position (e.g. the U.K., the U.S.A., and the U.S.S.R.); whereas on the contrary in many other countries government receipts lag behind money incomes in inflation, with the effect that inflation increases the government's deficit instead of reducing it.

As to (b), even if inflation increases savings, this will not bring the inflation to an end unless the savings are hoarded, or used in place of more new money to finance the investment which has been causing the inflation. Thus, if the entrepreneurs use their new profits to finance more new investment, as they are prone to do, this is excellent

for capital formation, but it serves also to keep the inflation going. If on the other hand they use their profits to buy government bonds, the government will be able to cease creating new money to finance its programme. (Alternatively, if the inflation has been created by entrepreneurs borrowing from the banks, it will be stopped if those entrepreneurs who now make profits use them to pay off bank advances, or hoard them, or buy the securities of the entrepreneurs who are making the new investments.) Peasants use their profits to pay off debt, and to buy more land, and the effect of this depends on what is done with the money by moneylenders and by the vendors of land. The moneylenders probably hoard it, waiting for 'better' days (i.e. for days when the peasants are again short of money), while the vendors of land may react in different ways. If the government wishes the inflation to peter out as soon as possible, while maintaining its new higher levels of expenditure (in real terms), and if it cannot rely on the savers hoarding their savings, then it must get hold of the savings in some way, either by taxing them away, or by offering favourable terms for government bonds.

The chance that savings will be hoarded or invested in government bonds itself depends on the rate of inflation, and on how long inflation lasts. If prices rise rapidly, or for a considerable period of time, people lose confidence in money, and will hold neither money nor government bonds. They then prefer to hold real assets, whose prices rise with the inflation, and the general movement out of money into goods itself exacerbates the inflation. Whether people move out of money into stocks of commodities or into fixed assets is partly a matter of temperament; there is always some movement in both directions. The movement into stock speculation is damaging to the economy because it aggravates the shortage of raw materials, and may even cause production to slow down, thereby raising prices even faster. The movement into fixed assets results in some creation of new assets—houses are built, farms are improved, and there is a spate of new factories as well. Inflation increases fixed capital formation; even hyper-inflations, like the German inflation of 1919—1923 have this effect. In the long run it is an excellent effect, since it increases real output and the standard of living. But at the time when it is happening, this capital creation carries on the inflation, and may even, like the movement into stocks, temporarily reduce the output of consumer goods by drawing resources away from the consumer good industries, and so cause prices to rise even more.

If a government has an efficient administrative service, it can try to prevent inflation from getting out of hand by fixing maximum prices, by rationing essential consumer goods, and by licensing new investment. If these policies are successful, they also strike inflation

at the root, because people will tend to save the money which they cannot spend on rationed commodities, and so saving will be brought into equilibrium with investment. This is one of the secrets of successful war finance in the United Kingdom and the United States during the second world war, during which prices rose only by about 50 per cent in spite of the magnitude of the war effort. (The other important weapon was a very high marginal rate of taxation, which sucked up 50 per cent or more of expenditure as fast as it generated incomes.) In these days the techniques of managing an inflation, so that it does not get out of hand, are much better understood than they were twenty years ago. These techniques, however, can be operated only by governments which have efficient administrations, and these are mainly the governments of advanced industrial countries. The less developed countries have rather inefficient administrations, and their attempts to control inflations often do as much harm as good, especially if their main effect is to make it more profitable to produce uncontrolled inessential articles, or to create a network of black markets and to encourage bribery and corruption.

The worst consequences of inflation occur when prices have risen so much or for so long that people lose confidence in money. This does not happen in short, mild inflations. People do not panic if prices rise 5 per cent per annum for two or three years, because they believe that prices will soon fall again. This confidence is maintained by the monetary authorities in the better run countries, whose habit it is not to increase the supply of money continually from one year to the next, but rather to alternate short periods of monetary expansion with sharp periods of restriction. Bank credit moves three steps up and one step down, instead of moving upwards continuously. In this way the creation of new money contributes towards capital formation without provoking runaway inflations, and without seriously affecting people's confidence in money and in government bonds. The moral is that if inflation is to be used for capital formation, it is best done in small doses at a time, rather than continuously.

As to (c) we have already seen that in any case inflations which are used to create useful capital are self-destructive, in the sense that in due course the new capital produces a new stream of consumer goods which either checks the rise of prices, or even brings prices down. In addition, this rise in real output may also bring about an increase in saving, and so provide the savings that maintain investment at its higher level. Higher saving does not necessarily go with higher real output, since the level of saving is a function of the distribution of income rather than of the level of real income per head; we need not however pursue this point immediately, since we are coming to the determinants of saving in a moment.

To the moral that if inflation is to be used for capital formation it should be used only intermittently and in small doses, we may add the moral that it should be used only for investments which can be completed quickly and which are then very productive. It is relatively easy to make out a case for financing with new money an agricultural extension service, to spread knowledge of new high-yielding techniques; or those measures of making more water available to farmers which do not involve long and costly work on rivers; or schemes of land clearance, drainage or reclamation which rapidly bring new fertile areas under cultivation. Whereas schemes which demand considerable foreign exchange (e.g. to buy machinery for factories), or which take a long time to execute (e.g. multi-purpose river valley projects), or which have a high ratio of capital to output (e.g. building kindergartens) are not suitably financed by creating new money. It may be thought that this 'moral' is not particularly meaningful because, since all investment as a whole is financed by all saving as a whole, it is not useful to pick out some schemes in a programme which are described as being financed by voluntary saving while others are described as being financed by creating new money. Hence it may also be thought that the better 'moral' would be to avoid all schemes which are costly in relation to output, or take a long time to execute, or require much foreign exchange, in which case the marginal schemes will be those which are least desirable from these points of view, and in a sense it will always be these marginal schemes which are being financed by new money. In practice, however, this is not so. Many schemes find a place in an investment programme irrespective of these criteria (e.g. public health schemes, or industrialization schemes), and it is by no means true that the excluded schemes are always potentially more inflationary than the schemes which are included. It is therefore meaningful to think of an investment programme being drawn up first on the assumption that there is to be no creation of money; and then to add that if some inflation is permitted, the schemes now added to the programme should be the least inflationary of those which would otherwise have been excluded. (Inflation apart, investments which take a long time to bear fruit should not be ruled out if the ultimate harvest is bountiful; the choice between these and other investments depends simply on the rate of interest.

(b) Domestic Sources

We have seen in the first section of this chapter that communities in which the national income per head is not increasing invest 4 or 5 per cent of their national incomes per annum or less, whilst progressive economies invest 12 per cent per annum or more. The central

P

problem in the theory of economic growth is to understand the process by which a community is converted from being a 5 per cent to a 12 per cent saver—with all the changes in attitudes, in institutions and in techniques which accompany this conversion.

It is customary to account for this conversion in terms of increasing thrift, and of better use of savings. That thrift increases is true, but it is also very misleading if it suggests that the essential change is that all classes of society become more thrifty or less wasteful. For the essential change is rather the emergence of a new class in society—the profit making entrepreneurs—which is more thrifty than all the other classes (the landlords, the wage-earners, the peasants, the salaried middle-classes), and whose share of the national income increases relatively to that of all others. In private capitalism these entrepreneurs have made private profits, and have reinvested on private account; whereas in the U.S.S.R. the great increase in profits has been concealed as a 'turnover tax', which the planners have reinvested on public account. But, in either case, the essential feature of the conversion from 5 to 12 per cent saving is an enormous increase in the share of profits in the national income.

A relative increase in profits is not necessarily the same as an increase in the inequality of income distribution, since this increase may be associated with a corresponding decline in the relative importance of income from rent. In fact, the communities in which income is most unevenly divided are not those wealthy economies where profits are large, but rather those impoverished, overpopulated economies where rents are large. In Ceylon or Puerto Rico the top 10 per cent of income receivers get about 40 per cent of the total of personal incomes, whereas in the United Kingdom or the United States of America the top 10 per cent receives, before taxation, nearer 30 per cent. These figures are somewhat misleading, since the undistributed profits of companies are not included in the assessment of personal incomes; when account is taken of undistributed profits there may not be much difference either way. In any case, it is not possible to make a general comparison between more and less developed economies, in the matter of inequality. The less developed differ amongst themselves, according to whether land is scarce or plentiful, and widely distributed or concentrated in ownership; and also according to whether there has been considerable development of capitalist enterprises within them, such as mines or plantations. The more developed also differ amongst themselves, and their distribution of personal income is also less unequal (before taxation) today than it was twenty years ago (though this is mainly because of the increase of undistributed relatively to distributed profits). The fact that there is no unique difference between more and less

developed economies in this respect serves, however, only to reinforce our conclusion. The ratio of savings to national income is a function not just of inequality, but more precisely, of the ratio of profits to national income.

Large rent incomes do not result in saving because a landed aristocracy does not think in terms of using its income for productive investment—at any rate did not think in these terms until there was a capitalist example to imitate. Traditionally rent incomes are used to buy more land, to carry a large number of retainers (including a private army if the central government is weak), to build churches, temples, tombs and monuments, to extend charity, and to entertain lavishly. With the passage of time these habits change under capitalist pressure; the combination of taxation of rents and the example of profitable capitalist investment tends to make landlords more thrifty, and in advanced capitalist societies rent may even be a source (a minor source) of saving for productive investment. This, however, happens after the event; so an increase in the thriftiness of landlords cannot be used to explain why the community changes from a 5 to a 12 per cent saver.

The same goes for the peasant class. The peasants are a class who paradoxically combine a thrifty temperament with a high propensity to be burdened by debt. Peasants learn to be thrifty because they know how near they live to the brink of disaster. In some communities hardly a year passes without flood, or drought, or locusts, or cattle plague or some other Act of God which reduces to destitution all the peasants except those who have some savings to fall back on. These recurrent disasters are part of the explanation of the propensity to incur debt. At the same time, those peasants who save tend to invest either in lending to less fortunate peasants, or else in buying land, and in neither case is the result an increase in capital formation. Buying land raises the price and alters the distribution of land, but it does not make land more productive. If the peasants own the land, they may invest in improving it, but most of the techniques of improving land involve a temporary reduction in its yield (fallows, rotations, afforestation, grass strips, erosion control), and are not popular in areas where the pressure on the land is considerable. Peasants also like to invest in cattle, but the attitude of many peasants in Asia and in Africa to cattle is not commercial, so that in many cases this investment is a burden rather than a source of profit. Considering the precarious life of the peasant, and his non-commercial attitude towards his land and his cattle, it is not surprising that net capital formation by peasants is only a very small part of the national income.

The wage and salary earning classes have a more regular income

than the peasants, and usually also even the unskilled urban worker earns more than the average peasant. Yet these classes save very little because their mentality is directed towards spending rather than towards saving. Workers' savings are very small. The salaried middle classes save a little, but in practically every community the savings of the middle classes out of their salaries are of little consequence for productive investment. This is especially so in countries where the ruling class differs in race from the middle and lower classes, since the middle classes then seem to distinguish themselves in conspicuous consumption, in their zeal to demonstrate that they are as good as their foreign rulers (Chapter II, section 1(b)). Low savings out of salaries are in any case almost universal. Most members of the middle class are engaged in the perpetual struggle to keep up with the Jones's; if they manage to save enough to buy the house in which they live, they are doing well. They may save to educate their children, or to subsist in their old age, but this saving is virtually offset by the savings being used up for the same purposes. The offset is not complete if income or population is growing, since the amount set aside by each generation is then larger than the amount set aside by the previous generation and now being consumed. These savings are of course very important to the individual saver. It is important to have something put by for a rainy day, even in a welfare state, and social reformers have always been right to urge people to save. However, the very fact that these savings are merely a postponement of future consumption, and are thus largely offset by other postponed consumption, means that they are not important in the context of productive investment.

The low level of savings of the salaried middle classes also bears out the point that saving and inequality of income are not directly related. Middle class earnings are much higher in relation to average earnings, or to the earnings of small farmers or unskilled workers, in the less developed than they are in the industrial countries. This is partly due to the greater shortage of middle class skills, but it is also due to the greater mobility of the middle classes, as between richer and poorer countries, which enables them to demand in poorer countries as high a standard of living as they could get in richer countries; in fact, because the poor countries have to attract middle class skills from the rich, the middle classes tend even to have a higher standard of living in the poor than they do in the rich countries. Thus the greater inequality of income is associated with a larger proportion of national income going into middle class consumption.

There is very little evidence on savings out of wages, salaries and peasant incomes. Such evidence as there is suggests that even in the

richest countries these savings seldom exceed 4 per cent of the national income. Japan is a notable exception; figures as high as 8 or 10 per cent have been quoted in her case. In the less developed countries small savings seem to be much nearer 1 per cent of national income, according to the best calculations so far made. Needless to say, even 1 or 2 or 3 per cent of the national income is not to be despised: it is well worth while pursuing measures designed to push small savings up from 1 to 2 or 3 per cent. These measures lie in the directions of institutions, of propaganda, and of financial incentives. There is a whole range of savings institutions that can be developed— post office savings, friendly societies, co-operative credit societies, co-operative retail societies, insurance policies, building societies and the like. Experience shows that the amount of saving depends partly on how widespread these facilities are; if they are pushed right under the individual's nose, to the extent of having street savings groups, or factory groups, or even deductions from earnings at source, people save more than if the nearest savings institution is some distance away. Saving is also a habit, which can to some extent be created by propaganda. People save more if they are given some acceptable reason for saving. They save more in wartime partly because they are persuaded that this is the patriotic thing to do; they might also save more in countries launching upon develop-ment programmes if these programmes caught their imagination, and if they were persuaded that this is a way of making their contri-bution. In addition people can be persuaded to save in their own individual or family interest, for education, for old age, for house purchase, for weddings or funerals, or as a safeguard against sickness or disaster. Even if these savings are largely offset by consumption, the habit of self-reliance and the avoidance of destitution are com-pelling reasons for doing all that we can to stimulate them. The principle of insurance appeals easily, and a cheap well advertised system of personal insurance stimulates saving. In addition, the financial incentives for saving should be adequate, in the sense that the rate of interest should be attractive. It is customary to pay only rates of 2 to 3 per cent on small savings, partly because the cost of collecting and using small savings tend to be high; but there may well be a case for subsidising the rate of interest offered on small savings, so that more attractive rates can be offered. If the community is also using inflation for the purpose of capital formation, with the result that the value of money is falling, there is something to be said for guaranteeing the real value of small savings; otherwise small savers are discriminated against (since the value of other assets rises as prices rise), and small savings are discouraged.

It is particularly important to stimulate saving among the peasants,

because of the role which agriculture has to play in economic development. Economic growth results in the expansion of all other activities relatively to agriculture—because the income elasticity of demand for food is less than one. Relatively speaking, therefore, other occupations are growing all the time, and the people in these occupations have to be fed out of the produce of the farmers remaining in agriculture. Hence economic growth requires that the produce of farmers per head must increase, to provide a growing surplus per head from which to feed the non-farmers. At the lowest levels of productivity each farm family is producing food for itself and half a non-farm family; whereas at the highest contemporary levels each farm family feeds itself and seven other families.

Savings enter into this process at two points. In the first place, the required growth of productivity in agriculture usually means that more capital must be invested in agriculture. Sums of money can be set aside for this purpose by the government, and lent to the farmers through rural banks or credit societies. This involves, however, an absorption of capital into agriculture from other sectors of the economy (unless the money comes from taxes on landlords), and since all other sectors are simultaneously clamouring for capital, the more the farmers can finance themselves the better. This gives special point to savings campaigns and savings institutions in rural areas.

Saving may also be involved in the process in another way. If agricultural productivity is rising, and providing a larger surplus which can be used to feed the towns, governments are frequently tempted to tax this surplus away from the peasants, and to use it to finance expansion in other sectors, including capital formation in public utilities or in manufacturing. There is a double temptation, since taxing the farmers opens up one opportunity of finding resources sorely needed, and since also, if the farmers are not taxed, the rise in their real incomes may make it necessary to raise real wages and salaries in the cities and in other occupations, so as to continue to attract labour from agriculture, and this increase in real wages and salaries reduces the share of profits and therefore of saving in the national income. Hence in a number of cases an increase in the productivity of farming has been accompanied by heavy taxation of farmers, which has been used to finance capital formation in other sectors, and it has been true to say in these cases that, far from agriculture absorbing capital from other sectors, it has been the farmers who have been forced to finance the industrial revolution. Japan is a case in point. In that country productivity per person engaged in agriculture doubled between 1885 and 1915, but much of the increase was taken from the farmers in higher rents or taxes, and

used to finance the rest of the economy, as Mr. B. F. Johnston has admirably described (see the Bibliographical Note to this Chapter). The U.S.S.R. is another case where farm incomes per head were kept down, between the world wars, in spite of farm mechanization and the considerable release of labour to the towns. This was done jointly by raising the prices of manufactures relatively to farm products, and by levying heavy taxes upon the collective farms. Current examples are provided also by the Gold Coast, Burma, and Uganda, three countries whose governments have withheld from their farmers a very large part of the increase in the price of farm produce since 1945, and who are using part of the proceeds to finance economic development in other sectors of the economy.

Economic development can take place without levying upon the peasants to finance capital formation if the necessary savings are forthcoming from some other group. In practice the only other major source of savings in the past has been the profits of business enterprise, which, as we shall see in a moment, tend to grow relatively to national income in less developed countries if circumstances are favourable. If it is desired to accelerate capital formation at a time when profits are still a small proportion of national income there is in practice no other way of doing this than to levy substantially upon agriculture, both because agriculture constitutes 50 to 60 per cent or more of the national income, and also because levying upon other sectors is handicapped by the fact that it is desirable to have these other sectors expand as part of the process of economic growth. Levying on agriculture is in turn politically very difficult to do, as the U.S.S.R. discovered, unless the productivity of agriculture is rising rapidly so that the levy can be effected without reducing the standard of living of the peasants. The model of how it can be done is provided not by the U.S.S.R. but by Japan, and the moral is that any programme for industrialization and heavy capital formation should have as its counterpart measures for increasing agricultural productivity rapidly—not mainly with tractors or with new economic structures, but mainly with new seeds, fertilizers, pesticides and water. Behind this again lies a political problem of whether countries in which the peasants have political power are capable of launching upon programmes of this sort; but to this we shall return in Chapter VII.

Apart from the cases where the farmers are squeezed to provide for capital formation, the main source of savings in any economy is profits, distributed or undistributed. If one enquires why the profit making class is more prone to thrift and to productive investment than all other classes, the answer is probably to be found in its place in the social hierarchy. Unlike the salaried middle classes, capitalists

do not have to engage in conspicuous consumption in order to impress upon other people their social importance, since the mere fact of their independent status as profit makers and as employers of other people, combined with their known wealth, assures them some social prestige; the middle and lower classes can never save much, no matter how high their real incomes may rise, since they are always imitating the consumption standards of those richer than themselves, whereas the rich can save because their incomes are more than adequate for their accepted standards of consumption. The profit makers have lower social status than the landed aristocracy, but they know that they cannot attain the prestige of the aristocracy simply by spending conspicuously, and so only a few of them try to do this. Like the aristocracy, they are ambitious for power, but their road to power lies in a different direction. The aristocracy achieve power by increasing the size of their estates, and (in feudal and early capitalist stages) by monopolizing the highest political, military and religious offices. The profit maker, on the other hand, knows that his power lies in his money; he therefore saves, and invests his money as profitably as he can. Some of his money is invested, as the peasant invests money, simply in financing other people's consumption, or in buying land, two forms of 'investment' which do not increase capital formation. But the profit maker knows that the most profitable investments are those which exploit new techniques, or open up new resources, and these also pander to his ambition for power because the greater his productive investments, the larger the number of people he has working under him. The capitalist is therefore the only person whose ambition drives in the direction of using his income to create an empire of bricks and steel; all other classes fulfil their ambitions in other ways—the salaried middle classes by conspicuous consumption, and the agricultural classes by buying land, or by holding office. In the later stages of capitalism these distinctions are blurred; capitalists buy or marry their way into the landed aristocracy and make a bid for political office; landowners go into the City, and invest their rents productively; and even peasants get the idea that it is just as good to use money to improve the land one has already, as to use it to buy still more land. In the later stages thrift and productive investment spread to all classes of the community, but in origin productive investment is essentially the mark of the capitalist class.

It is for this reason that it has sometimes been asserted that thrift is essentially a capitalist virtue, and some historians, associating the accelerated spread of capitalism with the Reformation, have sought to explain an increasing propensity to save in terms of Calvinist doctrine. This is much too simple an association. There are three

strands in the capitalist philosophy, namely restraint in consumption, willingness to produce as much as possible, and a preference for productive investment. The first of these, namely restraint in consumption, has been recognized as a virtue in all ages and by nearly all religions. However, many philosophies which recommend restraint in consumption also associate this with discouraging attention to production and to the material things of life; these philosophies encourage men instead to take life easily, or to spend their time rather in spiritual exercise, or in practising such other arts as war, love, sport, chivalry, learning, poetry or conversation. The capitalist philosophy is distinguished from this group by its second strand which makes a virtue of work and of efficiency, and which holds that a man has a moral duty to make the best use of the talents and resources which God has given him. If we have a moral duty to produce as much as possible, combined with a moral duty to exercise restraint in consumption, it follows that we have a moral duty to produce a surplus. Even this concept however, is not confined to Protestant theology. The distinctive feature of capitalist philosophy is its third strand, which prescribes a particular use for this surplus, namely productive investment. Other philosophies have prescribed other uses—the surplus should be used for charity, or to keep a horde of retainers, or to make war, or to build pyramids or tombs or country houses or temples or churches, or to found universities. The capitalist philosophy is not alone in recommending restraint in consumption, or diligence in labour, but it is alone in combining these recommendations with the sentiment that the right use for a surplus is productive investment. These recommendations eventually adopt a religious cloak, in which thrift is a virtue and charity a means of ruining the characters of one's fellows, but the true explanation of the crucial recommendation, namely the recommendation to invest productively, is probably sought more usefully in analysing the place and ambitions of capitalists in the social hierarchy than in interpreting religious texts.

If profit is the major source of saving, the conversion of an economy from a 5 to a 12 per cent saver must be explained by an increase of the share of profits in the national income. How does this come about?

One obvious answer is: by the growth of the capitalist sector of the economy, relatively to the rest, resulting from the continuous reinvestment of capitalist profits. In the less developed economies very little capital exists, and there is very little employment offered by capitalists. As the capitalist sector expands, it draws on many sources. The peasant sector of the economy usually has surplus labour, in the sense that the family is not fully occupied in working

its holding, and there is a drift into the towns to work in capitalist enterprises. There is a similar drift from handicraft industry, especially if the capitalists are exploiting new techniques which undermine the handicraft producers. The capitalists also attract workers out of domestic service, and also provide work which attracts wives and daughters out of the household, and so increases the proportion of adult women who are 'gainfully occupied' in the census sense. If the community is overpopulated, it has also probably much surplus labour in casual employment, and in petty retail trade, which is glad to secure regular employment even at a bare subsistence wage. In addition, if the population is increasing, some part of the increase can be absorbed into capitalist employment even without drawing people from other sectors. The classical economists, from Adam Smith onwards, used to emphasize that economic development involved a transfer of workers from non-capitalist to capitalist employment—they called it from 'unproductive' to 'productive' employment—and that the rate of this transfer depended on the extent of saving and on the rate of growth of capital. If there is any productive investment at all, the capitalist sector of the economy must grow. Whether it grows relatively to the economy as a whole therefore depends on the rate at which the rest of the economy is growing—on the rate of growth of population, and more especially on whether productivity is also growing in the peasant sector of the economy. It is not inevitable that the capitalist sector will grow faster than the rest of the economy.

In the first place, much depends on the political security of capital investments. In most pre-capitalist civilizations capitalists are at the mercy of the political aristocracy. They are expected to invest their wealth in lending for consumption purposes to aristocratic spendthrifts, and for military purposes to princely adventurers; and if they make outstandingly successful investments they are liable to be faced with sudden and arbitrary levies. In such circumstances capitalists tread carefully; they seek first of all the protection of powerful lords, by tying up much of their wealth in personal loans; and they also invest in forms of wealth which are easily hidden and easily transported, such as gold and jewels, rather than offering hostages to fortune in the shape of fixed capital formation. Rapid expansion of the capitalist sector of the economy cannot therefore begin until productive investment is reasonably safe from arbitrary depredations.

Given political security, the capitalist sector is most likely to grow rapidly if the opportunities for investment are very profitable. In the early stages of capitalist development an unlimited supply of labour is available at a subsistence wage from the sources already mentioned, if only because capitalist employment is small relatively to the total

population, but even more so if the economy is overpopulated, or if the population is growing rapidly. In such a situation practically the whole benefit of increases in productivity in the capitalist sector goes into profits. These increases may be associated with technological progress, or they may be due to the widening of opportunities for trade, owing to improvement of communications or to geographical discovery. The more rapidly the opportunities for productive investment expand, the faster profits grow, and the greater is capital accumulation. In a community which is not undergoing technological change or geographical discovery, profits grow slowly, capital grows slowly, and it is possible that these grow no faster than the rest of economy. But, once there are fruitful opportunities for investment it is almost certain that profits will grow relatively to national income, and therefore that the share of national income reinvested will rise continuously.

This means that the fundamental explanation of any 'industrial revolution', that is to say, of any sudden acceleration of the rate of capital formation, is a sudden increase in the opportunities for making money; whether the new opportunities are new inventions, or institutional changes which make possible the exploitation of existing possibilities. The British, the Japanese and the Russian industrial revolutions all fit into this pattern. In each case the immediate result is that the benefits of rising productivity go not to the classes who would increase their consumption—peasants, wage earners—but into private profits or public taxation, where the proceeds are used for further capital formation. More and more labour is taken into wage employment, but real wages are not allowed to rise as fast as productivity.

This increase in capitalist profits is also accelerated by the inflations which occur regularly in all capitalist economies, either in the mild form associated with the expansionary phase of the trade cycle, or in the more virulent form associated with wars and with the extravagance of governments. Inflation raises profits relatively to other incomes, and also stimulates a flight out of money into bricks and steel. Every inflation is followed by deflation, when profits are low and investment is checked. But the periods of deflation are seldom as long as the periods of inflation. The long run tendency is for the supply of money to increase, and for prices to rise, or at least to fall less rapidly than increasing productivity would require. Most of the historical periods which are associated with rapidly increasing production and with investment rising rapidly relatively to national income are also associated with rising prices and profits— for example, the British Industrial Revolution after 1780, or the higher ratio of investment (home plus foreign) in Britain from 1890

to 1913 than from 1870 to 1890, or the relatively high level of investment during the French and German inflations after the first World War, or the swift upward turn in the Japanese economy from 1870 to 1913, or the first, second and third five-year plans in Russia; or for that matter, the expansion phase of the trade cycle compared with its stable or declining phases. Inflation is not an essential explanation of economic growth. Profits could grow and investment would occur even if there were no inflations. On the other hand, a little inflation from time to time increases profits, and speeds up the rate of capital formation.

If the process of converting an economy from a 5 to a 12 per cent saver is essentially dependent upon the rise of profits relatively to national income, it follows that the correct explanation of why poor countries save so little is not because they are poor, but because their capitalistic sectors are so small. No nation is so poor that it could not save 12 per cent of its national income if it wanted to; poverty has never prevented nations from launching upon wars, or from wasting their substance in other ways. Least of all can those nations plead poverty as an excuse for not saving, in which 40 per cent or so of the national income is squandered by the top 10 per cent of income receivers, living luxuriously on rents. In such countries productive investment is not small because there is no surplus; it is small because the surplus is used to maintain unproductive hordes of retainers, and to build pyramids, temples and other durable consumer goods, instead of to create productive capital. If this surplus were going instead as profits to capitalists, or as taxes to productivity-inclined governments, much higher levels of investment would be possible without inflation. It should also be noted that when we say that saving is low because the capitalist sector is small, we do not refer only to private capitalists, but use the term also to refer to state capitalism, or to any other form of economic organization where capital is used to employ people, and where, after payment of wages and salaries, a substantial surplus remains of which a large part is reinvested productively. In practice, judging by the U.S.S.R., the state capitalist can accumulate capital even faster than the private capitalist, since he can use for the purpose not only the profits of the capitalist sector (disguised as taxation) but also what he can force or tax out of the peasants, or squeeze out of the economy as a whole by inflation.

Behind this economic analysis of the growth of capitalist profits lies also the sociological problem of the emergence of a capitalist class, that is to say of a group of men who think in terms of reinvesting income productively. The dominant classes in pre-capitalist economies—landlords, traders, moneylenders, priests, soldiers,

princes—do not normally think in these terms. What causes a society to grow a capitalist class is a very difficult question, to which, probably, there is no general answer. Most countries seem to begin by importing their capitalists from abroad. Foreign traders or foreign investors open up new opportunities, make profits, and re-invest part of them in the country; whereupon their example is imitated. The emergence of indigenous capitalists is associated with the emergence of new opportunities, whether demonstrated from abroad, or discovered autonomously at home. These opportunities may be new techniques, or may result merely from a widening of the market, due to new opportunities for foreign trade, or to better communications or peace at home. If the opportunities are for trade only, the new class will be primarily commercial in its outlook; but if there are also new techniques or new resources which would fructify with capital, there will also be a group of capitalists thinking primarily in terms of fixed capital formation. We have already seen, in Chapter III, the importance of institutions, political, religious and caste, in helping or stifling the growth of an entrepreneurial class; opportunities and institutions play upon each other, and jointly determine the rate of growth of this class, and the scope allowed to its activities.

The Japanese case is particularly interesting, since it involved a swift transformation of landowners and nobles into capitalists, as Mr. I. I. Kramer has recently pointed out (see Bibliographical Note). This resulted from the state buying out the feudal rights of the nobility, and depriving them of their administrative functions; at the same time it also took over the debts of the feudal lords. Finding themselves with plenty of money (or rather government bonds), and no duties, some of the lords turned in the first place to banking, and when in 1880 the government decided that it was ready to sell some of the factories which it had established for pioneering purposes, it found a ready market. This swift transformation of an old-type aristocracy into a new-type capitalist class was profoundly important in increas-ing the supply of entrepreneurship in Japan in the crucial last quarter of the nineteenth century. At the same time, whereas the feudal aristocracy had previously battened upon the commercial classes, and diverted commercial capital into consumption loans, the com-mercial classes now found a new freedom to invest productively, and were powerfully reinforced by the entry into their ranks of some of the richest and most powerful families in the country.

We have also noted the growth in the modern world of a new class of state capitalists (e.g. U.S.S.R., India), who for one reason or another are determined to create capital rapidly on public account. These state capitalists are just as relevant as private capitalists in so

far as they hold similar views on the importance of saving and of productive investment. The growth of nationalism, of the desire for military strength, and of the urge to make an all-out attack on the poverty of the masses of the common people, will powerfully reinforce this trend.

So far we have been examining the process by which an economy is moved upward from the 5 per cent saving level. It should now also be noted that the capitalist sector cannot continue to expand rapidly relatively to national income, since if it expands rapidly it must sooner or later come to include the whole economy. When there is enough capital to provide capitalist employment for everyone, this relative expansion ceases. Moreover, as the capitalist sector takes in more people and ceases to be small relatively to the rest, it ceases to be possible to expand at a constant real wage equal to a low subsistence level. This may happen relatively early, as in France, if agriculture remains organized on peasant lines, and if special measures are not taken to increase its productivity. There comes therefore a point where further capital accumulation raises real wages. It ceases also to be the case that all the benefit of technical progress accrues to profits, for the increased profitability of investment increases the demand for labour, and so raises real wages. There comes therefore a time when it is an open question whether further capital accumulation and further technical progress will raise wages, or will raise profits; or, if both increase, which will increase faster than the other. Most economists in the past have expected the rate of profit to fall in this later stage of capitalism; that is to say, they have expected wages to get the lion's share of the benefit of further progress. But in fact what seems to have happened in advanced industrial economies during the past eighty years is rather that the rate of profit has remained constant, and that wages and profits have grown in the same proportion. In the early stages of capitalism profits grow relatively to national income; but in the later stages profits are a constant proportion of national income (subject to cyclical and secular swings). Correspondingly, in the earlier stages the rate of saving rises relatively to national income, but in the later stages net saving becomes a constant proportion of national income —how high a proportion depending on how much the capitalist sector has been able to expand before coming up against labour shortage or an inefficient peasantry. Thus is explained a former paradox. Because the rich save more than the poor, it used to be expected that every country must save more as income per head rises. It was found however that in the wealthier countries real income per head doubled in fifty to seventy years without any increase in the savings ratio. The explanation is that the rate of saving is

determined not by whether countries are rich or poor, but by the ratio of profits to national income, and both these ratios cease to increase once a certain stage of development has been reached. It must not, of course, be concluded that this is an eternal law. We do not know exactly what determines the ratio of profits to national income in advanced capitalist societies, and so we certainly cannot predict how this ratio will behave in the future.

To complete the analysis of saving we must now also take account of government saving. We saw in section 1 of this chapter that in advanced industrial economies 35 per cent or so of gross fixed investment is in public works and public utilities—say about 7 per cent of gross national income. Of this, about 2 to 3 per cent of national income is in public works, strictly defined (roads, harbours, schools, hospitals, public buildings, etc.) and the remaining 4 to 5 per cent is in the public utilities which may or may not be publicly administered (railways, road transport, telephones, electricity, gas, etc.). The share of the government in gross investment therefore depends partly on the extent to which it leaves public utilities to private enterprise. In many countries it is as high as 7 per cent of national income (e.g. in New Zealand), whereas in very few does it fall below 2 per cent.

If only because of the need for public works, all governments have to save. They may spend first and save afterwards, or they may spend only out of savings, but the result is the same. That is to say, some governments prefer to pay for capital formation out of loans in the first instance, rather than out of current taxation, but the result is the same, since the treasury has to open a sinking fund to repay the loan, and the finance for this comes out of current taxes. If a government spent on capital formation at a steady annual rate, borrowing the money, its sinking fund payments would soon equal its annual borrowing.

One of the inexorable features of economic growth seems to be a rise in the share of the government in the national income. At the lowest levels of national income per head, the share of the government may be as little as 5 per cent; whereas modern industrial-governments use up to 10 per cent or so of real resources for current purposes, apart from what they use for military purposes (which is currently even more than this), and in addition to this use from 2 to 7 per cent of real resources for capital formation, plus another 10 per cent or so for transfers (pensions, insurance payments, interest payments, etc.). It is therefore necessary that the marginal rate of taxation should exceed the average rate, so that tax receipts grow faster than national income. This is particularly necessary where a government is using inflation as one of the means of increas-

ing rapidly its share of the national income, since a high marginal rate of taxation is one of the ways of preventing prices from rising fast as more money is put into circulation.

As the government's needs increase it levies higher and higher taxes upon the larger incomes. As we have seen, in backward economies taxes levied upon rent incomes probably have little effect on saving, since such incomes are not a source of saving. Such taxes force landowners to reduce their retinues, to live in smaller houses, and to cut their contributions to charities, churches, etc., but they have probably very little effect on saving. It is quite different when taxes are levied upon profits; these fall almost wholly upon saving rather than upon consumption. Hence taxes upon profits discourage economic growth, unless the proceeds are used productively.

In one sense, if a government is not acting wastefully, all its expenditures are 'productive'. Its bills for education and for public health—two of the largest in modern governments—contribute in different degrees to output, and even defensive military expenditure may in some circumstances be a cost of maintaining the national income from predators. It is a truism that governments should indulge only in useful expenditure. All the resources used by a government are a deduction from the resources available to its citizens in their private capacities, and waste occurs if the government uses them in ways which are less valuable than the ways in which the citizens would have used them. This is equally true whether the resources have been levied at the expense of consumption, or at the expense of investment; but if one takes the view that a cut in investment is more dangerous than a cut in consumption (a view which not everyone accepts), then the government ought to be all the more careful in assessing its marginal expenditures if these are financed by reducing private saving.

In recent years in advanced industrial countries taxes on profits have been so heavy that dividends net of taxes have been reduced substantially, and private savings out of disposable incomes have fallen to low levels. The fall in dividends net of tax has not been due entirely to taxation; it has also been due to the fact that the amount declared in dividends has not risen in proportion to the national income. Profits have risen more or less in proportion to national income, but companies have also been retaining a larger share of undistributed profits in the business, and distributing a much smaller proportion as dividends. In turn the price of equity shares has not risen in proportion to the value of the assets which they represent. This is possibly only a temporary phenomenon, since, as fresh capital is raised for industry in shares to create new physical assets,

the value of shares and the value of assets must come together again
—the present divergence results from the war and post-war policies
of keeping dividend rates low. The effect of taxes in keeping dividends
low is likely to be more permanent since all modern governments
have developed the practice of taxing profits heavily, if only because
they regard this as desirable for equalitarian reasons.

This fall in personal savings has not had the effect of reducing
investment in manufacturing industry, because it has been associated
with a rise in the proportion of profits not distributed to shareholders,
and these profits have been adequate to maintain and extend the
capital of existing manufacturing business. The main effect of the
fall of personal saving has been to reduce the amount of disposable
savings outside the control of corporate enterprise, and this reacts
very much upon the prospects of various classes of borrowers.
Traditionally the manufacturing and commercial sectors of the
economy finance nearly all their new investment out of their own
profits, and have in addition a surplus which they distribute as dividends, and which is used partly to finance borrowing by new business,
by foreign borrowers, by agriculture, by public utilities, and by the
government. But, according to recent calculations by Mr. C. T.
Saunders (see Bibliographical Note) the amount of personal saving
left over after deducting the amount invested in unincorporated
business, in farms and in housing, was in 1952 only 1·8 per cent of
personal income in the U.K., and only 2·0 per cent of personal income in the U.S.A. This drying up of dividends net of tax, even if it is
offset in total by the growth of other forms of saving, hits some types
of investment hard. How hard it hits new business is not very clear.
Established manufacturing business has always financed itself
largely out of its own undistributed profits, but new business must
start by raising capital from some external source, and as the funds
outside the control of other business contract, it is harder for new
business to find private backers. It is hard to say how important
this is. There are still plenty of wealthy men who own assets which
they can sell (e.g. government bonds) if they want to back some new
enterprise. Some people fear that the effect is considerable, and that
it strengthens monopolistic tendencies in the economy, and tendencies towards technological stagnation, by reducing the opportunity
for new business to challenge and to replace old business. Such
people suggest that the government should place part of the proceeds
of taxation at the disposal of an agency or agencies which would
specialize in financing new business. The position is, however,
obscure, for lack of information.

Much the same problems are created for agriculture, for foreign
investment, for public utilities, and for the government itself. If

Q

the government is taking in taxes the savings on which these borrowers previously relied, it is up to the government to use part of its taxes to finance capital formation in these sectors. Agriculture has always had difficulty in raising finance. In the United Kingdom the provision of finance is traditionally divided between a landlord and the tenant farmer, the landlord financing land improvement and buildings out of rent, while the farmer finances machinery and other working capital out of profits. In practice both parties have tended not to save enough to finance all their net investment, and agriculture has been a net borrower from the rest of the economy. In recent years landowners have been more embarrassed than ever, by a combination of high taxes and inflexible rents, though farmers have been better placed to finance additions to capital out of profits, which have been high. Foreign investment has also become more difficult to finance as disposable savings have shrunk. Corporate business is well placed to finance extensions of its overseas assets, but direct investment in mines or plantations or factories has always been the smallest part of foreign investment. There has also, from time to time, been some capital flight to the outer sterling area, which Central Banks have used to pay for imports. But the major part of foreign investment consists of lending to governments or to public utilities (now mostly in government ownership) and the prospects of such lending are adversely affected by shortage of disposable savings. This is one reason why, as we shall see in a later section, foreign investment has now become much more dependent upon inter-governmental transfers, and much less on private lending. As for public utilities at home, for a long time it has been the practice to control their prices and profits at such low levels that these undertakings have not been able to put much to reserve, and have had to finance their extensions by fresh borrowing. In the new situation, either they must charge higher prices, and earn large undistributed profits, as manufacturing business does, or else they must turn increasingly to government for finance. The political atmosphere seems hardly favourable to the first of these courses.

As the government taxes profits more heavily, and so reduces private saving, it is inevitable that it must save more itself, if total saving is not to fall, and also that it must create machinery for supplying savings to some classes of borrowers who hitherto relied on disposable private savings. Hence in the United Kingdom in the years immediately after the war the Central Government, in sharp contrast with pre-war practice, financed from taxes not only the whole of its own capital formation, but also all the borrowing of the local authorities. More recently it has receded from this position; it does so correctly if its purpose is to reduce taxes on profits and so to

stimulate private saving, but not if its purpose or effect is to stimulate consumption, unless it is now desired to reduce the rate of capital formation in favour of a higher ratio of personal consumption. If taxes on profits remain at their present levels it is hard to see how the United Kingdom government can escape an obligation not only to finance all central and local capital expenditure out of taxes, but also to be a source of savings for new business, for agriculture, for foreign investment and for public utilities.

The fact that high taxation on profit incomes eats into private savings pleases those people who object to economic growth occurring through private investment and the growth of private fortunes. They prefer that the state should be the major source of finance, and the only large owner of wealth. Something like this is indeed achieved if the state siphons off into its own coffers the larger share of profits, which it in turn uses for further investment, but how far it can go in this direction without diminishing the incentive to invest is an open question. Many people in the United Kingdom are convinced that the limit has already been reached and passed; others point out that in fact, despite the level of taxation, gross investment in the United Kingdom is currently higher than it has been for many decades. Presumably even if the state took nearly all the profits, investment could still be kept at a high level provided that the state left enough incentives to the managerial classes to keep them willing to go on working for the state investor. High taxes on profits will destroy development if the proceeds of the taxes are spent by the state on current purposes, instead of being saved and invested productively; and if the managerial classes are not rewarded both financially and socially; but the disappearance of the private investor need not hold up development if other agencies take over his functions.

Quite apart from problems of profit taxation, many people take the view that in the less developed countries a special duty lies upon governments to levy taxes as a source of saving, with a view to raising the rate of investment above the levels it would otherwise attain. Since in these societies profits are only a small part of the national income, this is largely a question of taxing wages and salaries, peasants' incomes, and rents. The rent incomes of large landowners are in these societies used largely to maintain retinues, and to support local charities, rather than saved, and taxes on these incomes force landlords to reduce their 'consumption' mainly by cutting down the number of people who depend on them for support. It is in these days politically easier to tax large landlords than to tax workers or peasants, but it is generally not possible to raise a substantial sum in taxes without extending some way down the scale of incomes. Perhaps the least painful way of getting the required

sums is to tax increases in income, but this is practicable only in societies where income per head is in fact increasing. It has been achieved in such countries as Burma and the Gold Coast, where the government has impounded much of the improvement in the terms of trade since the war; and it was also achieved in Japan before 1914, when vigorous measures designed to increase peasant yields per acre were associated with equally firm taxation, which siphoned off a good deal of the increase into the coffers of the government.

It is probably true that any country can save 12 per cent of its national income without hardship if it wants to. It seems also to be true that it can save that amount voluntarily only when profits have become a sufficiently large part of its national income. If it does not wish its development to depend upon private profits, or if, alternatively, it does not wish to wait for a slow growth of private profits to that level, it can force itself to save through inflation or through taxation. It is only comparatively recently that we have come to think of the government as a potentially large source of saving. It seems likely that in the twentieth century it may come to exceed all other sources in importance, even in countries where the economy is left mostly to private enterprise. The problems which this creates we take up again in section 3(a) of this chapter, and in section 2(b) of Chapter VII.

(c) External Finance

Nearly every developed state has had the assistance of foreign finance to supplement its own meagre savings during the early stages of its development. England borrowed from Holland in the seventeenth and eighteenth centuries, and in turn came to lend to almost every other country in the world in the nineteenth and twentieth centuries. The United States of America, now the richest country in the world, borrowed heavily in the nineteenth century, and is in turn called upon to become the major lender of the twentieth.

A developing country would find difficulty in supporting its capital programme exclusively from domestic savings even if it wanted to, in so far as development programmes usually involve importing some capital goods from abroad. For example, suppose that a government plans to spend £x on importing capital goods, and £y on wages and salaries, and that for this purpose it levies in taxes £$x+y$. On the face of the matter this act should seem neither deflationary nor inflationary, since expenditure and taxes exactly offset each other, but in practice it is deflationary, and strains the balance of payments. The £y paid out locally is more or less offset by the £y of taxation, in its effects both on local purchasing power and on the balance of payemnts. But the £x spent abroad cannot be financed

by taxing away £x of local purchasing power, which releases foreign exchange only to the extent of £mx, where m is the marginal propensity to import. Moreover the £x spent abroad also takes some purchasing power out of domestic circulation, without putting anything in its place, and so sets deflation in motion. These unpleasant consequences are avoided if exports and home consumption substitute for each other, so that as home consumption falls more goods are automatically exported, since this both provides foreign exchange and also maintains home income. This happens to some extent, but not completely. In due course balance of payments equilibrium is reached, the deflation at home causing imports to contract, and the fall in prices causing exports to expand. Once the necessary adjustments have been made, a country can maintain a given level of capital formation without foreign aid. But the impact effect of stepping up the rate of capital formation is almost certainly to cause a shortage of foreign exchange, which has to be met by running down foreign assets, if any, by foreign exchange control, or by foreign assistance.

If a programme financed by taxation or by domestic savings imposes a strain on the balance of payments it may be surmised that an even greater strain is imposed by a programme which puts the unemployed to create capital and uses new money for the purpose. If such a programme is not to cause inflation at home, almost the whole of it must be covered by foreign exchange, part to pay for capital goods imported for the programme, and part to pay for imports of consumer goods to set against the money paid out locally. If imports and home goods do not quite substitute for each other, there will still be a minor amount of local inflation, which will facilitate the absorption of the imports. In practice, not quite the whole of the local expenditure needs to be covered by foreign exchange, since some part of the money spent locally will be hoarded, and need not be matched by consumer goods. On the other hand one act of investment usually sets off others, so that any foreign exchange saved in this way will almost certainly be used up in further expansion.

We are here at the core of the dispute between the United Nations International Bank for Reconstruction and Development on the one hand, and would-be borrower nations on the other, when the Bank, at its inception, interpreted its terms of reference to mean that it should lend only the foreign exchange required to pay for capital goods imported abroad for development projects, and should not lend to finance wages or salaries paid locally. This interpretation provided all the foreign exchange that was required if the local wages and salaries were paid out of taxes, or out of borrowing of a kind

that reduced other domestic outlays correspondingly; but it was inadequate if the object was to use surplus labour to create capital goods without reducing other domestic outlays. Given the level of saving in the less developed countries, if they are to step up domestic capital formation without taxes or inflation, they will need additional foreign exchange equal almost to the whole cost of their additional programmes.

Given the level of domestic savings, additional foreign exchange may become available through mobilizing existing hoards, or through receiving foreign assistance in the shape of loans or of grants.

The quantity of gold, jewellery and foreign exchange privately owned varies widely from country to country. In the countries of South and South-East Asia and of the Middle East it is customary for people to hoard gold and jewellery; in other countries existing hoards are relatively insignificant. Just how much is now held in these forms is not known, but the best guesses do not exceed 20 per cent of national income, even though the sums involved may seem large in absolute terms. Neither is there any simple means of getting hold of these sums. Several countries (e.g. the United Kingdom) have made it an offence to hold gold or foreign exchange without declaring it to the Treasury, but the effectiveness of such laws depends partly upon how law-abiding the people are, and partly upon how vigorously and how drastically they are administered. The hoarding of gold is stimulated by inflation, so presumably one condition for voluntary dishoarding is confidence in the stability of the domestic currency Some hoards can also be brought out by a policy of offering an attractive price temporarily. Ruthless governments succeed in mobilizing private hoards almost as soon as they come into office but in less ruthless countries dishoarding contributes only slowly and in small degree to the foreign exchange required for development.

Some governments are themselves hoarding on a large scale, in so far as they continue to back their domestic currency fully with foreign exchange. This is the case, for example, with all the British colonial governments, since the colonial currency system requires that all colonial currencies be backed 100 per cent by sterling. It is obviously unnecessary to back a currency with foreign exchange to this extent, since there are no conceivable circumstances in which the whole of the domestic currency will disappear from domestic circulation. It is sometimes argued that this practice does not matter in the case of the British colonies. The surplus currency backing is invested in gilt edged securities, which yield the long term rate of interest, and if these colonies needed money they would have no difficulty in borrowing in London at similar rates. In so far as this is

true, the 100 per cent backing does not handicap development; it will become important only if a colony has difficulty in borrowing at rates corresponding to those at which it is lending.

Reference must also be made to the sterling balances which a number of countries accumulated during the second world war, and immediately after the war. Most of these countries have now run down their balances to levels where they are not much more than is needed for currency reserves, but one or two others are still increasing their balances, because their foreign earnings are increasing more rapidly than their imports. The existence of these balances has made it possible for such countries as India or Egypt to carry out development programmes without foreign exchange stringency, and is one of the main reasons (the U.S. foreign aid programme being the other) why the development of world production went ahead at full pace after the war in spite of the low recovery of international investment.

It may be thought that before passing from the mobilization of hoards to the possibilities of foreign assistance we should consider also the possibility of making more foreign exchange available for development by reducing the ratio of imports for home consumption relatively to exports. But this cannot be done without increasing savings; it belongs therefore to our previous discussion of domestic savings rather than to this section on external finance. More foreign exchange can become available by producing substitutes for imports, by expanding exports, or by rationing foreign exchange. To get hold of it for development purposes is not itself very difficult, given fairly efficient administration; what is more awkward is the consequences. For if the general public is not allowed to spend as much upon imports as it wishes to do, it will spend more upon domestic goods. This may reduce exports, if exports are of the same kind as goods consumed at home, and may in this way frustrate the purpose of import controls. If this problem does not arise, or is overcome, the additional domestic expenditure will create inflation at home, which is a form of saving. Or, if inflation is to be avoided, the reduction in imports must be matched by a fall in expenditure on domestic goods, resulting either from taxation or from an increase in voluntary saving. Control of foreign exchange earnings must therefore be seen as a part of a policy for increasing domestic savings, rather than as an additional source of finance for investment.

We come then to foreign assistance, whether by way of grant or by way of loan, as a source of finance for investment. Until the outbreak of the second world war foreign assistance depended almost entirely upon private initiative, which in turn depended mainly upon comparing the investment opportunities at home with those abroad. In general, the lending countries were the developed countries and the

borrowing countries the less developed, taking as the measure of development capital per person employed; but there is no simple law that it is more profitable to invest in less than in more developed countries, or that as a country develops it passes automatically from debtor to creditor status.

One reason for expecting developed countries to export capital is the belief that the rate of profit must otherwise fall in a developed economy as capital accumulation takes place. The doctrine of the falling rate of profit dates at least from the eighteenth century, and has been accepted by practically every school of economists, even though the reasoning with which they have supported it has not always been the same. The most notable exception to this agreement was the economist, Alfred Marshall. In *Official Papers* (page 49) he expressed the usual view, but in his *Principles* (page 681) he argued that whereas the increase in capital per head tends to reduce the return on capital, technical progress, on the other hand, provides new opportunities for using capital, and so tends to raise the rate of return. Thus, he said, the yield of capital in England fell from 10 per cent in the Middle Ages to 3 per cent in the middle of the eighteenth century—a long period of slow technical progress—after which the decline was arrested by the great increase in opportunities for using capital. If this is the right way to look at the matter—and it seems to be—there is no law that the yield of capital must fall in developed economies; it may, or it may not.

We get a different answer, however, if we turn from the rate of profit on capital in general to the rate in particular lines of invest-ment. In any particular line the possibilities of further expansion are soon exhausted, or at any rate greatly reduced. All industries develop on a logistic pattern, growing fairly slowly at first, then rapidly, and later on growing again quite slowly. Hence the investors in any particular line sooner or later come to a point where there is not much more scope for investment in that line at home. It is open to them to put their accumulating profits into quite different industries. But there is also the temptation to stick to the field in which they have specialized knowledge, and to use their profits to take the industry into new countries. Thus the British railway interests, having built railways at home, turned to the promotion and building of railways in foreign countries. The British tin companies sent their capital to open tin mines in Malaya and Nigeria; just as the American oil interests and the copper interests invested in the same lines overseas. Not infrequently the movement is helped by overseas restrictions on imports from the developed country, such as have stimulated U.S. manufacturing concerns to invest in opening subsidiaries in Latin America, or else by competition from newly developing industries in

low-wage countries, such as sent British capital to open jute factories and cotton factories in India.

This migration of capital is checked however, not only by the fact that new opportunities for investment are opening up all the time in the developed country, but also by the deficiencies of the less developed countries for investment. For it must not be taken for granted that it is profitable to invest in less developed countries just because they are less developed. The fact is that these countries have certain marked disadvantages for investment. For one thing, the social framework is not always suitable. Even though the genetic composition of peoples may be much the same, as far as potential productivity is concerned, their cultural inheritance is very different. Illiteracy, shortage of modern skills, and lack of adjustment to the wage relationship keep productivity low; while differences in forms of government and in social attitudes increase the uncertainties of investment. Hence new techniques which might yield handsome returns in developed countries are not necessarily an attractive investment in the less developed. There is also the vicious circle of capital shortage. If a new undertaking is to be started, the productivity of this undertaking depends not only upon itself, but also upon the efficiency of all other industries whose services the new undertaking would need to use—especially general engineering services, suppliers of components, transport, and other public utilities. This in turn depends partly upon how highly capitalized these other services are. Hence the productivity of one investment depends upon other investments having been made before in many directions. At least up to a point, there are increasing rather than decreasing returns to capital investment. It may well be more profitable to invest capital in countries which already have a lot of capital than to invest it in a new country. If this were always so, no capital would be exported; the gap between the standards of living of more and less developed countries would widen continuously; and we might even venture to compose a law that there is a natural tendency for capital to flow from less to more developed countries. In practice the international flow of capital is small, and the gap between standards of living does widen, so this is at least a warning against accepting generalizations based simply upon levels of development.

If any generalization is justified, it is probably more securely based upon available natural resources than upon the level of capital per head. The most productive investments are those which are made to open up rich, easily accessible natural resources, such as fertile soil, oil, coal or ores. It is also profitable to invest capital in introducing new techniques, even when there are no new resources, but this is not

as profitable as is using capital to make available both new techniques and new resources. This is the principal reason why most of the capital exported in the last hundred years went to the Americas and to Australasia, where there were abundant new resources, rather than to India or China, where the opportunity was to a greater extent one of using known resources better. This also explains why the United Kingdom and Western Europe rapidly became capital exporters (the limits of their natural resources were soon reached) whereas Canada, the United States and Australia are very late in reaching the capital exporting stage, despite their very high wealth per head when compared with the rest of the world.

The nearest generalization we can make, therefore, is that capital tends to flow towards those places where new rich natural resources can be fairly easily opened up, and away from places whose resources are already highly capitalized, and where new resources are much less abundant. This is not the same as saying that a country becomes a capital exporter when it needs to import raw materials or food. Britain invested in the nineteenth century wherever she thought there was money to be made, irrespective of her imports. In the earlier part of the century she was investing in Latin America; in the middle part in building railways in Europe; and later she was lending to finance miscellaneous activities in Egypt. Similarly, the foreign investments of the United States have not been shaped principally by shortage of supplies in the United States. American investment flowed into copper and oil long before the U.S. became an importer of these commodities; neither does the United States invest in Latin American manufactures as a potential source of supplies.

It is often asserted also, that Britain could not have adjusted to creditor status if she had not needed to buy ever increasing quantities of primary products, but the facts do not support this assertion. In the first place, Britain used her earnings on foreign investments, and repayments of the principal, not to pay for imports, but to add to her overseas capital; she merely reinvested overseas what was due to her. British retained imports were the same proportion of the national income (28 per cent) in 1913 as they had been in 1873, despite the enormous growth of her invisible earnings during these forty years. (It is possible that Mr. A. R. Prest's estimate of the national income for 1873, on which this calculation is based, is rather low; but raising the estimate by a reasonable amount would still leave our conclusion that the interest on foreign loans was used not mainly to increase the ratio of imports to national income, but mainly to increase the ratio of foreign investment.) This method of dealing with the situation, however, involves a rapid growth in the rate of foreign investment, which will presumably be at the expense

of home investment unless domestic savings are growing relatively to national income. If profits, savings, domestic investment, and foreign investment are to be held as constant proportions of national income, a prolonged bout of foreign investment must result in due course either in a rise in visible imports, or in a fall in visible exports, relatively to national income.

These embarrassments are due to the speed with which the inflow of interest and amortization payments catches up with the outflow of capital. For example, if national income were constant, and foreign loans constant, and repayments made after twenty years, then after twenty years repayments would be equal to outgoings, and in addition there would be coming in the interest on the past twenty years' investments, which could be accommodated only if the propensity to import were increased, or if alternatively visible exports were cut. If we assume instead that national income is rising, and that foreign lending is a constant proportion, then, as Professor Domar has recently shown (see Bibliographical Note), after twenty years the outflow will just equal the inflow if the rate of interest on the loans coincides with the rate of growth of the national income; but if, as is more likely, the interest rate exceeds the income growth rate, then the inflow will be stabilized proportionally at a level higher than the outflow. The result is even more embarrassing if, as in the British case, visible imports and exports are held constant relatively to the national income, and the inflow of interest and repayments is all reinvested. For in this case the ratio of foreign investment to national income rises all the time, in arithmetical progression if the interest rate and the income growth rate are the same, and even faster than this if the interest rate exceeds the income growth rate. For example, suppose that a country invests abroad 2 per cent of national income every year, that it receives 5 per cent interest which it also reinvests, and that national income grows by 3 per cent per annum. Then even if the loans are non-repayable, the annual investment will rise from 2 per cent of national income in the first year to 6 per cent in the thirtieth year, and will continue to rise at an increasing rate. Something very much like this is what happened to British foreign investment between 1870 and 1913. If it is to be avoided, and the propensity to import is also to be held constant, then visible exports must fall relatively to national income. As it happened, Britain's visible exports, allowing for cyclical and secular swings, remained a constant proportion of her national income, but her share of world exports of manufactures was falling rapidly in this period, and could have fallen even faster if she had not been willing to reinvest her invisible earnings abroad.

Erroneous beliefs about what happened in the British case have

caused some observers to fear that it is not feasible for the U.S.A. to take Britain's place as the world's leading creditor, but these fears are groundless. In the first place, it is not necessary to develop an import surplus if earnings are reinvested; in the second place, there is no reason to expect the U.S. imports of food and raw materials to grow less rapidly than U.S. income (many expect imports to grow faster); and in the third place, U.S. exports of manufactures are now so large, relatively to the world total, that there is plenty of scope for maintaining world equilibrium by checking the rate of growth of her exports of manufactures. So long as world demand for primary products continues to grow, it will pay investors to open up new natural resources, and there is no reason why the countries which make the investments must also be the countries which import the goods.

If the most profitable investments are those which open up new natural resources, it is plausible to argue that there is less scope for international investment in these days than there was in the nineteenth century, because there are no unfilled lands as rich as were those of the United States, of Canada, and of Australasia. If this is so, international investment must depend to a greater extent on the profitability of transferring new techniques, to start, in the less developed countries, industries and processes which have proved profitable in the more developed countries, and which are now showing slower expansion at home. (This kind of investment is not necessarily tied to food and raw materials and does not therefore necessarily raise the problems erroneously alleged to arise with primary products.) It is indeed arguable that, as the gap between the more and the less developed countries widens, the advantage to be derived from introducing new techniques becomes greater and greater, so that by now there is scope for a tremendous movement of capital from the more developed (in the sense of technique) to the more backward—for example in agriculture. Transference of technique, however, is not simply a matter of investment; it depends upon institutional changes in general, and upon an intensification of educational and extension facilities in particular, which require action at many different levels. Much of this action has to be taken by governments; in the field of agriculture, for instance, action creating extension services, extending irrigation facilities, building up a network of rural credit societies, and so on. The scope for direct private foreign investment is probably much more limited when it is a question of transferring new techniques than when it is a question of opening up new natural resources. There may be just as much need for foreign capital, and the effect on output may be just as great but the old channels are no longer so relevant. We shall be returning to this point in a moment.

The current breakdown of international investment is not, at least in the first instance, directly due to any of the matters which we have so far discussed. It stems rather from the Great Depression of the 1930's, and from subsequent events.

International investment revived fully after the first world war. Immediately before that war it was running at a level of about 1,600 million dollars, and by the end of the 1920's, it was running at about 2,000 million dollars, worth about the same in real terms, when account is taken of the change of prices. There were notable changes in the sources and direction of the flow. The United States had ceased to be a net borrower, and was now putting up half of what was lent, the United Kingdom's contribution having already shrunk very considerably. And Germany, which was lending substantially before the first world war, was now taking nearly half of what was lent. Correspondingly, the position of primary producing countries overseas had worsened; in real terms they were getting in the nineteen-twenties only about a half as much as they were borrowing before the first world war. Some people have attached much significance to this change in the direction of flow, arguing that investment in German reconstruction was necessarily more insecure than investment in primary producing countries overseas, since the overseas countries could pay acceptably in primary products, while Germany could pay only unacceptably in manufactures. We have already, however, expressed doubt as to the validity of this line of reasoning. And, in fact, when the collapse came in the 1930's, the primary producing countries were just as badly hit as Germany, and had just as much difficulty in meeting their commitments.

The emergence of the United States as the chief source of lending seems to have had special significance in the collapse which came, because of the absence of traditions and institutions for foreign lending in that country. The lack of institutions is thought to have increased the cost of lending, as well as to have caused lending to take place with insufficient discrimination, so that a smaller proportion of American lending than of British lending could weather a storm. The absence of a tradition of foreign lending also made the lenders more nervous. An experienced lender knows that slumps are succeeded by booms, and does not lose his nerve when the slump comes. Whereas many American lenders allowed themselves to be deceived by over-optimistic propaganda in the 1920's, and correspondingly became over-pessimistic in the 1930's. Whether this weakness of traditions and institutions was the real reason or not, the fact is that when the Great Depression arrived, and many borrowers were unable to meet their commitments, American lenders reacted violently against the whole conception of foreign lending. Particular

resentment was roused by failures in respect of war debts. A Federal Act of 1934 made it an offence to sell in the United States the bonds of any government which had defaulted on its obligations to the United States government: this Act applied to nearly every important government in the world except that of Finland. At the same time, the legislatures of several states passed Acts prohibiting institutional borrowers from holding foreign government bonds. Since governments are the largest borrowers, this was a major blow at international investment. Even in 1954 it remains impossible to float a foreign government loan successfully in the United States. When the United Nations International Bank for Reconstruction and Development was formed at the end of the second world war, its President had to spend nearly two years touring the state legislatures and persuading them to pass Acts permitting institutional investors to hold bonds issued by this Bank.

The defaults on war loan payments were a political decision, springing out of an agreement reached by the debtor nations at Lausanne in 1932, to the effect that they were willing to forgive the debts owing to them if the United States in return would forgive what she was owed. The United States refused to give up her claims, but everyone else (except Finland) decided to regard war debts as cancelled. The defaults on other loans, however, were to a greater extent due to circumstances beyond the debtors' control. The Great Depression was excessively severe. The dollar value of world trade fell in three years by 60 per cent. World production of manufactures fell by 30 per cent, and though the production of primary products was better maintained, the incomes of the primary producing countries were adversely affected by a sharp movement of the terms of trade against them. In the event, most of the countries of the world, except the United States of America, ran into very serious balance of payments difficulties. Foreign exchange had to be strictly rationed, and in some cases it was quite true that no foreign exchange could be made available for debt service if essential imports of food and raw materials were to be maintained. It was equally true that countries caught in such a whirlpool were in no position to borrow money, either on private or on government account. International investment dwindled away to nothing in the 1930's. On the average, repayments to the creditors in this decade exceeded new lending.

Since the second world war, world production and trade have revived beyond the levels of the inter-war period, but international investment, excluding U.S. government grants, and excluding transfers from one communist country to another, is averaging only about 2,000 million dollars a year. This is certainly very low when compared either with the 1920's or with the years immediately before

the first world war. If allowance were made for the increase of prices, the investment of the 1920's would now be worth about 3,000 million dollars; and if investment were also presumed to increase with world production, the appropriate figure would be somewhere nearer 4,500 million dollars. If we enquire why the present level is so low, the answer is to be found in deficiencies both of supply and of demand.

On the side of supply we may list the deficiencies as follows: (*a*) the relative decline of Western Europe, (*b*) the reduction of disposable savings, and (*c*) the demand for guarantees. And on the side of demand we may note a reduction in the spheres open to private investment.

The decline of Western Europe is a decline not of production but of balance of payment surpluses available for foreign investment. This is not to be explained by adverse terms of trade, since Europe's terms of trade are not now very different from what they were in 1913. Neither is there evidence that Western Europe is saving less now than it was saving in 1913; the evidence is rather merely that it is investing a much larger part of its savings at home. Western Germany is engaged in an enormous programme of reconstruction. France, awakening out of a 25-year period of near industrial stagnation, has embarked upon domestic investment at a level not attained since the early days of reconstruction after the first world war. And Britain is now investing at home at a rate, relatively to her national income, which was last reached in the 1870's. These countries cannot spare the goods for foreign investment, because they are using them up at home. Even when the United Kingdom permits foreign governments to borrow, or to run down sterling balances, the required movement is not always achieved in the balance of payments because the required capital goods are not exported. Hence, whatever promises may be made on paper, it is useless to expect Western Europe to be once more a large exporter of capital until such time as the domestic use of resources is reduced. When this will be cannot be foreseen. At present investment is in full spate—in houses, in electric power, in agricultural machinery, in coal mining and in every other sphere. There may come a time when the desired level is attained in one or other of these spheres, e.g. in housing or in agriculture. If domestic investment falls without an increase in other domestic demand, foreign investment will become possible. There may also be a fall in the government's use of resources, which has expanded considerably, especially for purposes of rearmament; the U.K. now uses (1953) about 13 per cent of gross national product for military purposes, as compared with 6 per cent in 1938. Some part of a cut in government use of resources would flow into direct consumption, but it would almost certainly also be matched by some tax reliefs of

the kind which increase savings rather than consumption.

Given that Western Europe is using up its own savings, it is hard to decide how much importance to attribute to the relative decline of disposable personal savings. If foreign bonds were offered in Europe's markets, who could buy them? For example, in Britain before the war dividends net of income tax were 55 per cent of the net income of companies (before tax), the government taking 32 per cent, and the companies keeping 13 per cent as undistributed profits. Whereas in 1952 dividends had fallen to 18 per cent (equal to 4 per cent of national income) out of which surtax had also to be paid. In these circumstances foreign investment is feasible on a significant scale only if companies or governments are willing to put up the money. Companies can and do finance direct investment, in subsidiary or associate undertakings in foreign countries. But the largest item of foreign investment used to be the purchase of foreign government bonds, and this is hardly likely to attract company finance. The financing of foreign governments must therefore now almost exclusively depend upon inter-governmental transfers. The United States of America shows the same trend as Western Europe— a fall in personal disposable savings associated with increased company and government savings. The shift is not as pronounced as in Europe, but in any case, for reasons already explained, U.S. private investors are either unwilling or unable to buy foreign government bonds. Foreign investment must in future therefore be mainly a matter of direct investment by companies, and of inter-governmental transfers.

Direct investment is further restricted by fear of arbitrary action by foreign governments; in particular, fear of refusal of foreign exchange for transferring profits or repatriating capital, and fear of nationalization. Refusal of foreign exchange occurred frequently in the 1930's, often for no worse reason than that no foreign exchange was available. The governments of capital importing countries are now asked to declare that they will not restrict transfers of profits or of capital, and several have done so. The declaration is important evidence of goodwill, but in a severe exchange crisis even the best goodwill may have to give way to shortage of foreign exchange. It has therefore been suggested to the governments of capital exporting countries that they may have a part to play in extending temporary foreign exchange loans for this purpose during a severe slump. Suppose, for example, that a foreign firm in country A applies for permission to transfer profits or capital to country B at a time when foreign exchange is not available; then country B may lend the Central Bank of A the sum required for this purpose, on the understanding that this sum is to be repaid in three years (by which time

the crisis is supposed to be over). Such a plan has been considered favourably in Washington and is now operating for certain classes of investment.

Nationalization is a more difficult problem. Foreign firms want to be assured that they will not be nationalized, and some governments are giving assurances that there will be no nationalization during a specified period, say the first 25 years of the undertaking's existence. It is doubtful how useful such assurances are, since no government can bind its successor. A better assurance is that if firms are nationalized, their owners will receive fair compensation determined by independent arbitrators. This kind of assurance can be written into a country's constitution, and is then not so dependent on the whims of changing governments. It is frequently argued that the time has come to have some sort of international code or convention outlawing arbitrary acts against foreign investors, such as discriminatory taxation, nationalization without compensation, restrictions on transferring profits, and the like. Such a convention would help to improve the atmosphere of international investment, and therefore to stimulate its flow. But since rules are most effective when they can be enforced, it is even more useful to have internal legislation within the capital-importing countries, which can be enforced in their own courts against their governments, than to have international declarations which carry only moral sanctions.

Apart from the protection of such direct investments as are made, there is also the wider question which direct investments shall be allowed. If the supply of foreign capital has been reduced, for the reasons we have just noted, the demand has also been reduced in the sense that direct investment is no longer allowed in several spheres where it was most important. In 1913 British overseas investment was distributed as follows: railways and other public utilities 46 per cent, government stocks 30 per cent, mines 9 per cent, all other 15 per cent. Nowadays most governments have nationalized or intend to nationalize railways and other public utilities, and many others object to foreign operation of mines and of plantations. The result is to leave very little scope for direct private foreign investment. Foreign capital is allowed into commerce, but there is usually adequate domestic capital for commerce, and the tendency to establish statutory agencies for marketing agricultural products further restricts the scope for private foreign capital in commerce. Foreign capital is usually quite welcome in manufacturing industry, but the demand for manufactures is small in most undeveloped countries, so Latin America is the only part of the world which is attracting much foreign capital for manufacturing. In view of the limited spheres now open to direct private investment, it is not surprising that in

R

recent years 70 per cent of American foreign investment has gone into oil.

The role of direct foreign investment in economic development is usually misconceived, both by those who dislike it, and by those who support it. The case for foreign investment is that it provides foreign exchange, raises domestic income, and increases domestic skills. Domestic income increases because the undertaking pays wages and salaries to local people, buys local supplies, and pays local taxes; and these payments not only increase consumption, thereby stimulating local production, but also make it possible to have larger local savings, and also to spend on schools, medical services, and other permanent improvements. If the choice is between local capital and foreign capital, the advantage may lie with the former, but if, as is more often the case, the choice lies between foreign capital or leaving resources undeveloped, then there is little doubt that foreign investment plays a most useful role in providing income to pay for higher standards of consumption, of education, and of domestic investment. Potentially more important than the foreigner's contribution of capital is his contribution of skill. In most countries at a low level of development it is the foreigner who brings new techniques, and it is the spread of these new techniques among the people which carries development along. For this reason many countries have gone out of their way in the past to invite foreigners to come in and establish new industries. The country does not get the greatest benefit if the foreigners keep the secrets of their craft to themselves, and therefore admission of foreigners may be accompanied by a requirement that the newcomers must train local people. In these days the most important craft which foreigners possess is the technique of managing large undertakings. Most other crafts can be learnt in technical colleges or universities, but business management can be learnt only in the practice of managing businesses, so if the foreigners refuse to employ the indigenous people in managerial positions, where they may acquire experience, the foreigners may acquire and retain a stranglehold over the economy. This is why so many countries in these days pass legislation requiring foreign businesses to employ at least a certain percentage of indigenous persons in supervisory jobs. One can think of no country, including Britain, Russia and Japan, where foreign business did not play a major role in the initial stages of development, both by providing extra income, and also by imparting new techniques.

Foreign investment is feared in under-developed countries both for political and for economic reasons. On the political side there is great fear that it may lead to loss of independence. Creditor countries may indeed be tempted into imperialist acts when the institutions and

habits of the debtor countries differ from their own. If money is lent to Canada the creditors know that they will have as good protection in Canadian courts as they would have in their own, but many other countries do not offer such assurance. The creditor may fear discrimination in the courts, or administrative discrimination, and is therefore tempted into imperialism simply as a way of protecting his investment. Apart from this desire for protection, there is also the urge to gain special favours—to get forced labour, or freedom from taxation, or contracts on favourable terms, or transport facilities put into the appropriate places—and this urge also may cause a powerful country to deprive its weaker neighbours of their independence. The loss of independence may be partial or complete; partial if the capitalists confine themselves to bribing politicians or backing one political group against another; or complete if the debtor country is reduced to colonial status. These fears are widespread, but their reality obviously to some extent depends upon the borrowing country itself—as to whether its institutions afford proper protection to foreign countries, and as to whether its political life is sound enough to resist foreign bribery. There was also much more substance in these fears in the nineteenth century than there is in the twentieth century, since openly imperialistic behaviour has now become less fashionable. Nevertheless the fears remain, and are one of the strongest reasons why the less developed countries are anxious that the United Nations should create adequate institutions for transferring capital, so that they should not become dependent upon receiving capital from any one of the great powers.

Politics apart, some people also dislike foreign investment for fear that it may give rise to excessive profits. There is a great tendency to exaggerate the profitability of foreign investment. The evidence suggests that foreign investment is not significantly more profitable than home investment, especially when allowance is made for investments lost through expropriation. For example, some 40 per cent of British investment in 1913 was in railways; much of this has proved unprofitable, because of the swift rise of road transport after the first world war, or because of price controls, or because of nationalization at pre-war prices. Similarly there were heavy losses during the inter-war period on direct investments in primary products (rubber, tin, tea, sugar, etc.). The only outstandingly profitable investments have been those few cases where rich mineral bearing lands have been leased for totally inadequate royalties, either through ignorance, or through political chicanery. It is also very important to distinguish those foreign investments which involve a monopoly position from those which do not. If foreigners are given monopolies of mineral bearing lands, or of the best soils, the local people cannot

displace them however competent they may become. But foreigners in commerce or in manufacturing industry are much less dangerous, since there is no element of natural monopoly to prevent local people from displacing them as they acquire finance and technical competence.

If a country can raise the capital and technical knowledge itself, its development can proceed without further foreign assistance. Sometimes it can raise the capital, but not the knowledge; then the best solution may be collaboration. A number of governments of less developed countries are entering into partnership with private foreign firms to start new industries, the firm supplying the management and more or less of the capital (ranging from none to 90 per cent). These partnerships are welcome to both sides: to the government, because it can exercise some control over policy, or can keep most of the profits at home, if it supplies most of the capital; and to the foreign firm because partnership with the government earns it goodwill, and provides some protection against discrimination or pressure. Governments are also favourable to partnerships between foreign and domestic capitalists, again partly to keep profits in the country, and partly to gain wider knowledge and experience for domestic capitalists. It is quite possible that direct foreign investment will develop mainly on these lines of partnership, especially where the capital involved in a single project runs into hundreds of thousands of pounds.

On the other hand, however strong the case one can make for direct foreign investment, this form of investment must clearly be insignificant when put into its proper perspective. It is entirely erroneous to think that direct investment ever has been or could be the most important form of foreign investment. As we have already seen, in the heyday of foreign investment in 1913, three-quarters of British foreign investment was in government bonds or public utility stocks. When we take account also of the need to develop small scale agriculture, by making capital available through government agencies, it is no exaggeration to say that 80 per cent of the foreign capital required today is required by governments. Direct investment is only the fringe of the foreign investment problem, hardly relevant outside the spheres of mining and of manufacturing. If foreign investment is to be revived, the major problems are not those associated with reviving direct investment, however desirable such investment may be, but are rather problems of making capital available to foreign governments.

One reason why direct foreign investment has always been small is the private lender's difficulty in assessing the merits of the private borrower, some thousands of miles away, and in keeping an eye on

what he does. The small plantation, or factory, or trading company, or mining concern, situated in Perak, or Kumasi, or Fiji, can hardly hope to issue shares which will be bought and sold on the London Stock Exchange. It is impossible for investors to know what such enterprises are worth, or to have confidence in their managements. Hence a good deal of foreign investment has had to be done through intermediaries. The gold mining companies in British Africa have come to be grouped under the sponsorship of a relatively small number of finance houses. These houses perform certain secretarial, marketing, and other functions for the companies under their wing, usually in return for a fee. They may also invest relatively small amounts. One of their main functions, however, from the point of view of the private investor, is to serve as guarantors of the bona fides of the companies under their wing. When one of these companies issues shares they will be more acceptable in London because it is known that the company is well sponsored. The same sort of development has occurred with tea and rubber plantations in the East. Many of these are managed and sponsored by a few well known houses, whose name serves similarly as a guarantee of bona fides. In the absence of such sponsorship the small or medium sized concern cannot have direct access to foreign capital markets. This has its further consequences. One is the great extent of the movement towards amalgamation, holding companies and monopoly among foreign owned concerns, e.g. in tin or copper mining: if the medium sized concern cannot get direct access to the market, one way out is to create a giant concern out of many small or medium concerns. This movement towards monopoly is not regarded with favour in the countries where it occurs, but it results inevitably from the fact that foreign capital markets cannot cope with small independent concerns. Another consequence is the extent to which foreign capital flows through companies already established in advanced countries opening up branches or subsidiaries in the less developed countries. This has been a feature of mining for tin, for copper and for oil. It is also practically the only way in which foreign capital has flowed into manufacturing; practically all the foreign-financed factories in the less developed countries are branches or subsidiaries of companies operating in the advanced industrial countires, or of the great overseas trading companies.

We have here the main reason why private foreign capital has gone so largely into government bonds and public utilities, and only to a very small extent directly into industry, agriculture or trade. The thing cannot be done effectively without intermediaries. In the past these intermediaries have been finance houses, secretarial companies, or firms established in the industrial countries; or alternatively there

has had to be a movement towards monopoly and concentrated ownership in order to gain a footing in the capital market. More recently a new intermediary has appeared in the shape of government sponsored financial institutions such as Agricultural Banks, Development Banks, or Industrial Finance Corporations, which borrow in foreign capital markets, under government guarantee, and reinvest in small firms at home. But this serves only to emphasize the importance of government borrowing in the perspective of international investment, and the minor role which direct investment by private shareholders necessarily plays. The main problem in the revival of foreign investment is how to make more capital available to foreign governments.

Before 1929 foreign governments could borrow in the capital markets from private lenders. This is no longer possible on any significant scale, whether because of American legislation, or because of exchange controls in Europe, or because of the reduction in disposable private savings, or merely because of unfavourable popular reactions to such loans. Hence, if governments are to borrow, they have mainly to borrow from other governments. The great era of private international lending ended in 1929; if international investment revives, it will be into an era of inter-governmental financing.

The first substantial provision made for inter-governmental lending was the establishment of the United States Export-Import Bank in 1933, which lends mainly, but not exclusively, to governments. Then at the end of the war the United Nations established the International Bank for Reconstruction and Development with contributions from the majority of the members of the United Nations. This Bank has also borrowing powers, which it has exercised in the United States and in Europe. Both these Banks make loans at low rates of interest (3 to 5 per cent), and with relatively long periods of repayment. In addition, the metropolitan countries have established facilities for investment in their colonies. The U.K. has established the Colonial Development Corporation, with government funds, which is primarily intended to invest directly, but which also lends money to private undertakings, to public utilities, and to public corporations. Other metropolitan governments in Europe have agencies for similar purposes.

Although these opportunities exist for inter-governmental loans, the total of loans is small, and the existing facilities are by no means fully utilized. The chief reason for this is that these loans are in practice limited to 'self-liquidating' projects, that is to say to projects which themselves yield revenue directly—e.g. electric power or a steel mill—so that out of this revenue provision can be made for interest and for repayment of capital. Now a good deal of the

development needed in these countries at present is non-self-liqui-
dating-expenditure on education, roads, public health, research,
agricultural extension, or community development; and many other
projects are only partly self-liquidating, such as rural water supplies,
soil conservation or reclamation. These happen to be the most
urgent priorities in most of the less developed countries. Prior to 1929
a solvent government could borrow in the capital markets for any
purpose it liked, or even without stipulating a purpose. These new
agencies do not substitute for this facility, which has disappeared.
They substitute for public utility borrowing, but not for the miscellaneous borrowing of governments, which used to absorb one-third
of foreign lending.

Moreover, the inability of governments to borrow merely to
expand the framework of public services, itself restricts their ability
to borrow for public utility and other self-liquidating projects.
Generally speaking, all investment depends upon an adequate public
framework. More particularly, if investment is to be accelerated a
strain is at once put upon all educational and training facilities. There
must be engineers, scientists and administrators to make plans, and
to carry them out, as well as skilled persons at all other levels, such as
masons, carpenters, welders, electricians and the like. The shortage
of trained persons is somewhat alleviated by the provision of technical assistance by the United Nations, by the United States, by the
Commonwealth countries participating in the Colombo Plan, and by
the metropolitan governments to their colonies; but, in addition to
the fact that there is a world shortage of experts, the fundamental
need of these countries is to train their own people. They need to
make great expenditures on education in all its forms, and until they
can find the money for this, their capacity to use self-liquidating
loans is held down.

Accordingly there has been much discussion of facilities for inter-
governmental transfers to finance non-self-liquidating expenditure.
Theoretically these could just as well be loan facilities, since any
expenditure which increases national productivity can afford to bear
interest and repayment charges. However, since the increased productivity does not accrue directly to the treasury, a government
which finances non-self-liquidating expenditure out of loans is liable
to be embarrassed financially when the time comes to make interest
and capital payments, unless it has a first class fiscal system. This
problem has therefore been discussed in terms of inter-governmental
grants-in-aid, rather than in terms of loans.

Here the lead was taken by the metropolitan powers, which during
or after the second world war created colonial development funds
with which to subsidize public expenditure in their colonies. The

British Colonial Development Act, under which expenditure has been running at between £15 million and £20 million a year, has its counterpart in other metropolitan countries. A further step was taken when the United States established its economic aid programmes in 1948. Much the largest share of this aid has gone to Europe, but in recent years the less developed countries have also been receiving aid (excluding military aid) at a rate of between 300 million and 400 million dollars a year. The United Nations also has resolved in favour of creating a United Nations agency, to make grants-in-aid, or low cost loans, for economic development, but it has still to decide how soon this agency should begin operations.

If one surveys the field of external finance, it is hard to escape the conclusion that a revival of international transfers to pre-war levels (in real terms) waits more on the establishment of an adequate system of grants-in-aid than upon anything else. Direct foreign investment is relevant only to a small part of the undeveloped countries' need for capital. Foreign investment in its heyday consisted largely of lending to governments or investing in public utilities, and now as then the problem is mainly to find finance for what is now the government sector of the economy. The facilities which exist for government borrowing are tied to self-liquidating projects, and seem to be adequate for this sphere. What is missing is money to finance the expansion of productive but non-self-liquidating government expenditures. Before 1929 governments could borrow money for these purposes, and borrowed almost as much as went directly into public utilities. Until this gap is filled, whether by removing the limitations on current lending facilities, or by establishing grants-in-aid, all other foreign investment is likely to be retarded, since all investment depends to some extent on the provision of an adequate framework of public services.

3. INVESTMENT

(a) The Institutional Framework

We have already in Chapter III considered in general terms the framework needed for the encouragement of initiative and risk-taking. Here we consider only certain special points connected with the links between saving and investment.

The first point to be noted results from the fact that a good deal of investment has to be done on a pretty large scale. Some writers on this subject present an idyllic picture of capital formation, in which the 'little man', adjusting himself to his environment, saves or borrows small sums, and gradually improves his situation. Some investment is of this kind. The little man can improve his own house,

or his small farm, or invest in a shop or a lorry, but this is less than half of the investment required for economic growth. The biggest lump of investment has to be in public works and public utilities, and while the little man can contribute usefully to public works through schemes of community development, there is need for vast expenditures by public and public utility agencies on roads, railways, harbours, electric power, and other big projects which are far beyond the capacity of the little man adjusting himself to his environment. The pessimist remarks that there have been many cases where these vast expenditures have led to nothing, because they have been misplaced, but to conclude from this that economic growth is possible without such expenditures is an absurd *non sequitur*; for his observations will not reveal to him any community where economic growth is taking place without tremendous expenditures of this kind. Other lumps of large-scale investment are found in mining, in manufacturing, in import and export wholesaling, in banking and insurance, in irrigation works, in processing some agricultural commodities, and in some forms of agriculture; and even urban housing, which expands rapidly with economic growth, absorbs large lumps of capital, because it is unusual for the working classes in the towns to own the houses in which they live. The distinctive feature of economic growth is not that the little man is saving and improving his productive capacity. This is a necessary and a desirable feature; but the distinctive feature of growth is that a few persons, private individuals, corporate bodies, or government agencies, are disposing of large sums on costly projects.

It follows that the distinctive feature of growth is entrepreneurship, that is to say, the emergence of a small group of persons, private investors or public officials, who are disposing of large sums of capital, which employ large numbers of other people. We have already considered, in various places, the problems to which this gives rise; we have speculated as to the origins of this group, its motivations, and the training it requires. We have noted also that the consequence is proletarianization of a large part of the community, which is required to work for wages or salaries in these large establishments without rights of ownership or of control. The further problems to which this gives rise, in terms of discipline, collaboration, and industrial peace, are among the most difficult of our century, and we have already referred to them in Chapter III without, alas, finding any easy solutions.

To the extent that investors do not use their own savings, it is necessary to have institutions which offer savers enough protection to encourage them to lend to investors. In the advanced industrial communities the investors are to a very large extent using savings directly

under their control. For example, manufacturing business is extending mainly out of undistributed profits whereas at an earlier stage it relied to a greater extent on raising capital externally. Similarly, governments are raising the funds they require for investment to a greater extent out of taxation, and to a smaller extent out of borrowing than they did thirty years ago. In theory undistributed profits belong to the shareholders, and taxes belong to the taxpayers, and there are of course considerable practical problems in maintaining adequate control of directors by shareholders, or of governments by the general public. But in a narrower sense undistributed profits and government savings are savings made by investors, in the sense that the amount and the use of these savings is determined in the first instance neither by shareholders nor by the public at large. This is more like the situation in the earliest days of capitalist development than it is like the situation of fifty years ago. In the earliest days of development there is very little free saving finding its way into investment. There is no properly organized capital market, and there are only rudimentary facilities for lending and borrowing money for productive purposes (there are of course always moneylenders and pawnbrokers). In this stage most of the productive capital is invested out of undistributed profits. It is only when economic growth is well under way that the saving function and the investing function are very substantially disintegrated.

The chief institutional requirements for an easy flow of savings from lenders to borrowers are limited liability and easy marketability of assets.

The principle of limited liability arises out of the distinction between a creditor and a partner. In the origin of these concepts a creditor is a person who commits his capital on fixed terms: he receives a stipulated interest, is entitled to repayment of capital at a particular time, and has no control over the undertaking. A partner, on the other hand, invests indefinitely, for a share of the profits, and has managerial rights; the law also takes the view that the whole of his personal fortune is liable for the debts of any undertaking in which he participates, and not merely that part of his fortune which he has invested in the undertaking. Limited liability created a cross between these two conceptions: an investor who invests indefinitely for a share of the profits, and has managerial rights exercisable in agreement with his fellow investors (usually delegated to directors under control), but who is liable to creditors of the undertaking only to the extent of his investment. The need for limited liability was created by the emergence of undertakings requiring more capital than two or three partners acting together could command—especially canals, railways, and such large scale investments. Limited liability

makes it possible for thousands of persons to participate in a venture on risk-bearing terms, and with managerial rights, without at the same time committing the whole of their private fortunes.

Eighteenth century economists did not attach much importance to the principle; they thought that it was necessary for very large undertakings, of the public utility type, but they also thought that the association of management with the ownership of capital was so important that in those cases where the amount of capital involved was relatively small, partnerships would prove much more efficient than joint stock companies, and would hold the field. What they did not foresee was that the habit of buying limited liability shares would become very popular in the nineteenth century, among very large numbers of persons who wished to spread their investments widely, and that this would eventually make limited liability investment the typical form. Indeed it is probably the easy availability of this facility which has spread the capitalist attitude towards saving amongst the rest of the community. We remarked, when we were discussing saving, that in pre-capitalist societies farmers, landowners, aristocrats, professional people, the middle classes and others either have no surpluses, or use their surpluses for charity, for maintaining retinues, for building temples and monuments, or in other non-productive ways; but that in the later stages of capitalist development all these classes take over the capitalist idea that surpluses should be invested productively. In the later stages limited liability shares are bought by landlords and even by clergymen, and the existence of this facility probably does as much as anything else to popularize the idea of saving and productive investment.

The second requirement for stimulating lending is that the lender should be able easily to restore his liquidity by selling either his right to payment, or if the borrower defaults, the borrower's assets. The former is mainly a matter of the adequacy of market facilities—for bonds, for shares, for mortgages, and for bills of exchange. The existence of such a market requires, of course, that there should be people or institutions willing to deal in 'finance', so that lenders who wish to restore themselves to liquidity can do so at a price without embarrassing the borrowers by demanding immediate payment. These dealers in finance are more often than not regarded with hostility by their fellow men, but they obviously perform an important function, since if they did not exist, savers would be more reluctant to lend, since lending would make them illiquid, and productive investment would therefore be reduced. It is not an accident that if one studies the economic history of any rapidly expanding community, the growth of markets for financial 'paper' is always a prominent feature of the early stages, and almost a pre-requisite for

further growth. Such markets are not required in communities where all land is publicly owned, and all operations are publicly financed, but they are essential where there is private investment, and if the usual run of bankers, traders, stock jobbers, and financiers did not emerge to fulfil this function, it would be necessary to create government agencies for the purpose. There is of course no technical difficulty in creating a government agency which stands ready always to buy mortgages, shares, commercial bills, or other financial paper of which lenders wish to divest themselves, but it seems very doubtful whether a government monopoly could perform these risky operations more efficiently or more cheaply than they can be done in a competitive market.

Behind the marketability of financial paper lies the marketability of the physical assets by which the paper is secured—the land, houses, jewellery, stocks of commodities, machinery, factories, and so on. This is partly again a matter of markets, and partly a matter of law. Markets are quickly formed where the volume of business merits a market. Once again, those who specialize in creating such facilities— the real estate men, the lawyers, the jewellers, and the wholesale dealers in commodities—are not always the most loved of our fellow citizens, because the riskiness of their trade, in doubtful and sometimes wildly fluctuating capital values, compels them to be sharp-eyed, unsentimental, and hard bargainers, if they are to be successful in the business. But the function they perform, of widening the market for assets, increases the opportunities for acquiring liquidity, and, therefore, makes it less risky for savers to lend their money to productive investors.

Apart from this question of markets, the law relating to ownership and sale of land is very important. In societies at an early stage of development land is the most important asset which borrowers possess, and which they can use as security for loans. In some countries steps are taken to restrict mortgages, so as to prevent small farmers from falling excessively into the hands of moneylenders. This issue apart, if it is desired to encourage lending and borrowing, it is very necessary that land should be mortgageable and saleable without a great deal of confusion as to legal titles. Systems of land registration, based if possible upon a cadastral survey, reduce the legal disputes arising out of the uncertainty of boundaries. Some communities also have difficulty in establishing ownership, where complicated laws of inheritance, an extended family system, or a complicated division of rights between owners, occupiers and communal authorities, combine to cast doubt on the right of any person or persons to pass a valid title. The rights of various classes of mortgagees may also be a nuisance at a sale, unless the law provides

for the buyer to acquire a title free of all encumbrances. Since the land laws of the less developed communities are usually extremely complicated, as well as obscure and uncertain, there is always plenty of work to be done by the legislature in the early stages of economic growth, in trying to introduce at least certainty, if not also order, into the legal framework of transactions in land.

The legislature in less developed communities is also involved in creating institutions for lending, to supplement the lending done by private individuals; either because the state has additional savings at its disposal, or because there are classes of investment which it wishes particularly to foster.

We have already considered the reasons why governments may in future have a great deal of saving under their control. It may be simply that they are taxing away savings which private persons would otherwise control; this is the effect of high taxation upon profits. Or it may be that they are forcing the community to save more than it otherwise would, by levying high taxes upon farmers, or landlords, or other classes who respond to taxes by reducing their consumption; or by resorting to credit creation and inflation. Or it may be that there are sources of external finance beyond those open to private borrowers, especially in these days of inter-governmental transfers, whether by way of loan or by way of grant-in-aid. Many governments have assumed in these days a responsibility for ensuring a high level of capital formation relatively to national income, which their predecessors did not accept. Its corollary is that they need to create institutions to dispose of the savings which thereby come under their control.

The other urge to create public financial institutions springs from the desire to make finance available to groups who have special difficulty in raising money from private lenders. Five classes have been receiving special attention—the farmers, the handicraft workers, the small consumers, owners of houses, and industrialists.

Small farmers are unable to borrow cheaply from private lenders because of the risks of this kind of lending, and because of the cost of administering it. Both the risk and the cost are greatly reduced when the lending is done through co-operative village credit societies, small enough for the members to know thoroughly the affairs and the credit-worthiness of each other. These societies are then sometimes able to borrow from ordinary private lenders, such as the commercial banks, or even to accept deposits from the general public. It is, however, usually necessary for the government to step in to supervise their affairs, and to ensure efficient management, and it is usually also necessary for the government to lend the societies additional sums, beyond what they can raise from their own mem-

bers' savings, or from private lenders. The amount of money which governments need to set aside for agricultural lending depends partly upon their attitude towards other lenders, and partly on how vigorous a programme of agricultural development they are pursuing. If they are trying to keep the farmer out of the hands of the private moneylender—and especially if for this purpose they are preventing the farmers from mortgaging their land, or are failing to recognize crop liens in the courts—then they need all the more to put up money for financing the farmers. Similarly, in those countries where the farmer depends to some extent upon his landlord for finance, if the government is taxing the landlords heavily, or is transferring land to peasant ownership, it has to step into the landlord's shoes as a financier. If at the same time it has a vigorous agricultural extension service, and is successfully persuading the farmers to use fertilizers, to improve their livestock, or to have better equipment, barns, buildings, or water storage facilities, it will have to meet a substantial demand for capital from the farmers—even though it may only be taking the money from the farmers with one hand (through land taxes or export taxes), in order to lend it to them with the other. The capital requirements of agriculture are usually underestimated. In less developed economies agricultural output is around fifty per cent of the national income. The working capital required is large, because the crop is seasonal, and it is this which borrowing mostly finances at present. If in addition 10 per cent of output were re-invested (the more developed countries reinvest much nearer 20 per cent of agricultural output), this alone would absorb 5 per cent of gross national income.

Handicraft workers are an important sector of the economy in Asia, though much less important in Africa or in Latin America. We have already discussed in Chapter III (section 4(e)) the conditions of their survival, and have seen what an important part they have to play in overpopulated countries which are also short of capital. We have also seen that the efficiency of these workers can be greatly increased by training in new techniques, by improving the organization of marketing, and by the provision of better raw materials and better equipment. All these matters require the creation of government agencies with considerable sums at their disposal to finance research, new equipment, and the holding of stocks of raw materials, of work-in-progress, and of finished goods. Since the inadequacy of facilities for holding stocks is one of the great weaknesses of these industries at present, this alone might be expected to absorb considerable sums.

The state pawnbroking service has proved in Indonesia, as in the Netherlands, to be popular, useful, cheap, and most profitable.

The service is widely available in the countryside, as well as in the towns. It is a 'social service', designed to free the people from exploitation by moneylenders, rather than a facility for productive investment, but cannot be omitted from the list of financial institutions created by some governments.

Facilities for financing new housing are also being created by some governments, in the less developed as well as in the more developed countries, and for rural as well as for urban housing. In some cases governments are building the houses themselves, e.g. on new land settlements, or in slum clearance; in some cases housing is provided by undertakings for their employees, e.g. on plantations, or mines, or railways, and the government is lending the employers money for the purpose; in other cases it is the occupier of the house who is being financed, either to build it himself, as on the farm, or to buy it from a speculative builder. Governments are drawn into housing finance either by their desire to control rents, or also by their desire to raise housing standards, at the cost of some subsidization of rents. (The U.S. and U.K. governments are now also in housing finance to encourage home ownership.) If rents are neither controlled nor subsidized there is usually plenty of private finance for housing, since this is a pretty safe investment; but the standards of housing are then also pretty low in those countries where people prefer to spend extra income on pleasures other than better housing.

Then there is the supply of funds for industrial development. Small factory owners have the same sort of difficulty in raising money as have small farmers. Besides, governments are specially anxious to encourage small local enterprise, as distinct from the large foreign firms which might otherwise monopolize manufacturing industry, and they therefore frequently create special financial institutions for this purpose. We discussed this problem in Chapter IV (section 3(d)), and saw that the difficulties of small enterprise are due as often to lack of managerial skill as to lack of funds; nevertheless, we agreed that it is desirable to have an agency which combines supervision and managerial advice with financing small industrialists. It is not, however, only small, or local industrialists who seek capital from the government. Big capitalists also find difficulty in raising capital for manufacturing, because of the imperfections of capital markets. The big domestic capitalists have difficulty because local capital, in the less developed countries, fights shy of new types of activity such as manufacturing. Local capital flows easily into large scale agriculture, into trade, or into mortgage business, but does not become available for manufacturing until manufacturing has become a familiar activity. The foreign capital markets also are not open to manufacturing activity on any significant scale. They have created special

institutions for financing overseas mining, or plantation, or public utility companies, but not for manufacturing. Hence foreign capital for manufacturing must filter either through industrial firms established in the industrial countries, which decide to open branch plants in less developed countries, or else through the great overseas trading companies, which occasionally branch out into running factories. Hence it is often the case that a foreigner who is willing to open a factory in a less developed country cannot raise all the finance he needs in his own country. And apart from those who cannot, there are those who do not wish to, because they prefer to be in partnership with locally owned capital, if only as a form of political protection. Some governments like this; they wish to participate in industrial undertakings, and even more particularly in those industrial undertakings which are under foreign management, and this adds to the amount of capital which they must find for industrial development.

The techniques of making capital available for industry vary. Some undertakings are exclusively financed by government, and managed by government agencies, or by private firms operating for a fee. Then there are the Industrial Development Corporations or Banks, which may be wholly owned by governments, or which may also have some private finance, and which in turn finance private capitalists, either by lending them money, or by taking up shares. Alternatively, some governments put up the money to build industrial estates, or isolated factories, which are then rented to industrialists, often at subsidized rents. Subsidy apart, some industrialists like this form of co-operation, since it reduces perhaps by £50,000 or more the capital which they must find if they build for themselves; and governments like this form of co-operation for its small risk since, if the firm fails, the factory can be leased to someone else.

In all the fields we have mentioned—agriculture, handicraft industry, pawnbroking, housing and manufacture—government lending is acting usually as a supplement to rather than in replacement of private lending; trying to fill gaps which the private capital market has left. The market itself creates special institutions to meet some of these needs, e.g. building societies for housing finance, and the 'Credit Mobilier' type of banking for financing manufacturing industry. Where there is no ideological objection, government finance can work in co-operation with private finance. For example, in some places the commercial banks and the government divide between themselves the financing of the agricultural credit co-operatives. In industrial finance also, some of the new Finance Corporations have both government and private funds. It is noteworthy that the United Nations International Bank, which favours these Corpora-

tions, and is willing to lend them money, likes to suggest that most of
the domestic funds should be put up by banks or by private financiers,
and that the management should be in private hands, or at least as
far as possible removed from political control.

There is often misconception, especially among small borrowers,
as to what these institutions can do to help them financially. Some
expect to get 100 per cent of their capital, or nearly that, from these
sources. No lender, private or public, can afford to lend more than
the value of the security he is offered. These borrowers consider that
the goods on which they will spend the money should constitute the
security, but no good is worth as security as much as it costs. If a
machine is bought for £1,000, its marketable value begins to fall as
soon as it is installed, hence a lender will seldom lend on the security
of a machine more than about a half of what the machine is going to
cost. It follows that would-be borrowers must always have some
private finance of their own, or some marketable asset which they
can pledge as collateral in addition to the things on which the money
will be spent. In the less developed countries this role is played most
often by land and by jewellery, since these are the only two marketable assets widely possessed (outside the large towns the houses are
often very poor and of very small market value). It is particularly
difficult to lend money to people who do not own land, and so in
countries where the farmers mostly do not own the land, but work
as tenants or share-croppers, the amount which the co-operatives
lend per head is usually very small when compared with what is
possible when the farmers have their own land to pledge. One solution
of this problem is the co-operative society with unlimited liability.
This seems to have worked quite well in its original home (Germany)
but some attempts to transplant it to the less developed countries
have failed, because the famers have been unwilling to bear unlimited
responsibility for each other's debts. In the long run, the best
solution would seem to be to promote ownership of the land by the
farmers who work it.

One limitation of government finance worth noting is that it
usually supplies not capital but credit, because scarcity of funds
forces the government to use its money on a revolving basis, unless
it has facilities for re-financing its lending in private capital markets.
The distinction we are making between credit and capital turns upon
repayment. If a business is financed by issuing shares, the shares do
not have to be repaid; hence profits beyond what is needed for
personal consumption can be used to extend the business. If on the
other hand the business is financed by borrowing on debenture or
mortgage, surplus profits have first to be set aside for repaying the
loan. Government financial institutions usually expect repayment,

S

so that they can get the money back to finance a second concern, after the first has been put on to its feet; but the need to repay may well handicap the growth of a firm, just at a time when it should be nestling firmly into its market. Of course, not all private business wishes to have a government institution as a permanent partner, especially since such an institution has to be pretty strict in keeping an eye on what the business does. But some would prefer greater flexibility in repayment, and others may actually like the protection or prestige afforded by association with the institution. If in future a large share of the public's savings flows into the government's coffers (as well as external finance) the funds available to its financial institutions can be increased every year, and the institutions can supply relatively more capital and less credit.

The importance of private financial institutions relatively to government financial institutions is changing all the time. A century ago it was taken for granted that finance was a private matter, and governments appeared in the market only as borrowers. Then governments began to finance classes for whom the home market did not seem to cater adequately, and nowadays even the wealthiest country in the world, the United States, has a great network of government financial institutions catering for special classes of borrowers, domestic and foreign. Add to this the effects of taxation on savings—either in transferring savings from private to public control, or in forcing the community to save more than it would otherwise do, and we can see why at all levels of development, the government is now an important channel of finance for investment. When we add to this the further fact, that personal savings out of disposable income are everywhere small, and that most personal savings flow through the insurance companies, building societies, and other institutional investors, we can see why investment is much more institutionalized than it was a century ago, when the individual saver to a greater extent met the individual lender and negotiated directly with him. It is as important as ever that savers should save and investors invest, but where these two are different people, the link between them is now increasingly likely to be some financial institution, private or public.

(b) Point of Departure

Once a country has grown used to investing net 12 per cent of national income, with all that this implies in attitudes and institutions, it is easy enough to see why it continues to do so. The baffling problems in economic growth are the beginning and the end: how a country makes its departure from the five per cent or less class, or, at a later stage of development, why investment shows a secular

decline. Something must be said on each of these problems in this chapter. Here we begin with the phase of acceleration.

We have already dwelt at some length on the changes in attitudes and in social institutions which are involved at this turning point, and will have more to say on the subject in our final chapter. In this section we confine ourselves to a more limited aspect of the matter, namely the difficulty involved in starting in one sector of the economy only.

This may be represented, first of all, as resulting from the fact that the flow of money is not circular unless those who receive money spend it all. Consider the position of a new entrepreneur coming upon the scene to provide employment which raises the country's level of employment beyond what it previously was. The act of employing people and buying goods and services from other producers puts money into circulation, and when our entrepreneur does this he expects to get his money back. But will he? It is most unlikely that the people one pays money to will turn round immediately and use it to buy one's goods. They use part of it to buy goods from other people, and these in turn may use a part to buy the goods of the original employer. If all income is spent he must get his money back in due course, when the multiplier process has worked itself out. But not all income returns to circulation; some part is used by the recipients to buy imports, some part goes in taxes to the government, and some part is saved. Hence a new employer cannot rely only on the demand which his employment directly generates; he must also expect to be able to capture some of the demand now enjoyed by other people. If this is home demand, he must believe that he is in a position to take other people's customers away, by offering a new good, or a more convenient or attractive service, or a lower price based on some new technique of production; he must be an innovator. Alternatively, he must be able to export, and so to capture foreign demand.

Accordingly, at low levels of economic activity, production for the foreign market is usually the turning point which sets a country on the road of economic growth. To make an upward movement by producing for the home market is at this stage extremely difficult. Unless some innovation is involved, merely to produce more for the home market is unprofitable, since extra receipts will not equal extra outgoings unless some demand is captured from some other producer, and this requires innovation. At low levels innovation for the home market is unusual. Not only does innovation require new techniques, which at these levels usually come from abroad, but more important is the fact that the social atmosphere is usually at these levels not very favourable towards some people trying to grow rich

by 'stealing' some part of the markets of their fellow producers. Innovation comes therefore usually first of all in foreign trade, partly because it is foreigners who bring the new ideas, and partly because the community would not be well disposed towards a struggle for markets at home.

The deficiency of spending out of marginal income, on which this argument partly relies, belongs to a stagnant, rather than to a progressive economy. For the assumption is that that part of marginal income which leaks away into saving, into taxes, and into imports, will not be compensated by additional investment, government spending, or exports to the same extent, or at least will not be so compensated without a substantial time lag. Now once the economy has started upon the progressive road, investment, government expenditure and exports tend to grow with a sort of momentum of their own, and it is saving, taxes and imports which lag behind. A progressive economy has a pronounced tendency towards inflation, even if it be only mild inflation, or inflation punctuated regularly by short crises of deflation; and since inflation stimulates investment, both by providing capitalists with profits to reinvest, and also by dangling large profits before them as an incentive, an economy which has started upon the progressive road tends to stay there. Correspondingly, a stagnant economy tends to remain stagnant. Investment, exports and government expenditure are by definition not growing on their own momentum. Hence, when part of new expenditure leaks into saving, into imports or into government revenues, even though the effect at some later stage may be to cause investment, exports, and government expenditure to increase, the immediate deficiency of demand depresses business activity. Business thrives better in an atmosphere where it is savings that try to keep up with investment, or imports with exports, or revenue with government expenditure, than it does in an economy where it is investment that follows savings, and exports that lag behind imports, or expenditure that follows revenue.

But even an economy which has no chronic tendency towards deficiency of marginal demand, and which is well disposed towards innovation and competitive struggles in the home market, has yet another hurdle to jump, namely, that the various sectors of the economy must grow in the right relationship to each other, or they cannot grow at all. For example, suppose that there is considerable innovation in the agricultural sector producing food for the home market. The result is either a surplus of food to sell to the towns, or a surplus of labour in agriculture seeking non-agricultural employment, or some combination of both. If manufacturing industry is growing simultaneously and at the right rate, it can absorb both the

surplus goods and the surplus labour. If it is not, the terms of trade will move against agriculture, and as there will be a surplus of farm labour as well as farm products, agricultural incomes will be depressed, and further investment and innovation in this sector may be discouraged. If the process nevertheless leaves the farmers not poorer but richer, they will buy more imports, and this factor will be deflationary, unless there is now either an appropriate growth of the production of home substitutes for imports, or an appropriate growth of exports. Innovation in one sector of the economy is checked unless other sectors expand appropriately.

Exactly the same difficulties arise if economic development is concentrated upon industrialization, to the neglect of agriculture, as happened in the U.S.S.R. There is then an acute shortage of agricultural products, and an inflation of their prices, which drives up all other prices in a spiral movement. There is also difficulty in disposing of the manufactures at a profit. If the farmers' real incomes rise, real wages of factory workers must rise in sympathy, while the prices of factory products are being kept relatively low. Alternatively, if farmers' real incomes are kept low, they cannot afford to buy the manufactures, which cannot then be sold profitably unless foreign markets are developed, or unless the government takes the surplus manufactures over, as the U.S.S.R. government did, for capital formation and for defence—but there is then the problem of financing these purchases in an economy where farmers' incomes are not rising. This links also with the analysis of saving we made in Section 2(b). If agriculture stagnates, the capitalist sector cannot grow; capitalist profits remain a small part of the national income, and saving and investment are correspondingly small. Smooth economic development requires that industry and agriculture should grow together.

The relationship can be expressed more formally if we consider the economy as divided into three sectors, A for agricultural production for the home market, M for manufacturing production for the home market, and X for production for export. If M expands, the demand for the products of A will increase. If the increased output of M substitutes for imports, the foreign exchange thus released may pay for the increased imports of A. If not, and if A is stagnant while M is expanding, either A's prices will rise, or imports will rise, creating a balance of payments deficit, and either of these events will check the expansion of M. The expanding demand, on the other hand, could be met by expansion of X, which would provide foreign exchange to pay for imports. So an expansion of M must be accompanied by an expansion of either A or X, or by import substitution if it is to continue. Similarly, an expansion of A must be

accompanied by an expansion of either M or X, or by import substitution. It is only X which can expand continuously by itself without being checked by a failure of either A or M to expand; for the demand generated by an expansion of exports can be met by imports, for which the exports provide the foreign exchange. This, as we shall see in a moment, is one reason why expansion usually starts with exports and not with production for the home market, whether of manufactures or of food; and this is also the reason why a country can have flourishing export industries while its production for home consumption still remains relatively backward.

If we confine ourselves for the moment to the closed economy, while it is necessary for manufactures and for agriculture to grow together, they do not have to grow at the same rate. The income elasticity of demand for manufactures exceeds unity, and the income elasticity of demand for food is less than unity. The income elasticity of demand for services is higher even than for manufactures. Hence economic growth is associated with services growing most rapidly, and with total manufacturing output growing more rapidly than the total output of agriculture. When we speak of manufacturing and agriculture growing "together", or "at appropriate rates', or 'in balance', in a closed economy, we refer to the rates which are determined by the community's marginal propensity to consume agricultural products as compared with manufactures. The open economy is more complicated, since the growth of manufactures for home consumption can be balanced by the growth of manufactures for export, instead of by the growth of agricultural production (or *vice-versa*, substituting 'agriculture' for 'manufactures'), so in the real world we have to keep a balance between imports, exports, manufactures and agriculture, and not just between any two of them.

The fact that an expansion of manufacturing production does not require an expansion of agricultural production if it is backed by a growing export of manufactures is particularly important to those over-populated countries which cannot hope to increase their agricultural output for food as rapidly as their demand for food however much they may try. In such countries industrialization in no sense waits upon agricultural expansion, even though it remains true that they should give great attention to agricultural production. Such countries have therefore to give urgent attention to increasing the export market for their manufactures since, in the last analysis, it is the rate of growth of their exports which sets the limit to their internal expansion. This is very obviously the case with the British economy. The Industrial Revolution was accompanied by an Agricultural Revolution, but home demand soon outstripped the

CAPITAL 279

possibilities of agricultural production, and from the end of the Napoleonic War to the outbreak of the American Civil War, what set the pace for the growth of the British economy was the fact that British exports of manufactures were growing by nearly 6 per cent per annum, cumulatively. Correspondingly, the much slower growth of the British economy in the past eighty years is probably best explained by failure, in the face of new foreign competition, to expand exports by more than 2 per cent per annum even in peace-time. In over-populated countries, such as Britain, Japan, or India, the rate of growth of exports of manufactures may be the most important limit of internal growth; but we return to this problem in our next chapter. In any case these countries must also strive to increase their agricultural output, since the more they can increase agricultural production the less they need to rely on pushing their exports of manufactures in the world market.

In practice in most backward economies the sector which usually responds least well to growth in other sectors, and which therefore acts as a brake on all economic growth, is the agricultural sector producing food for home consumption. This is because, when agriculture is in the hands of small farmers, the introduction of innovations depends more upon government initiative than upon the initiative of private entrepreneurs. If in other sectors, such as in manufacturing, there is an increase in demand, some private entrepreneurs will be stimulated to enter the field. To increase the output of peasants, however, requires a number of actions which are essentially in the government sphere; above all, considerable expenditure on agricultural research and agricultural extension, as well as expenditures on roads, rural water supplies, agricultural credit facilities, etc. The experience of Japan shows that appropriate expenditure by government in these spheres can have spectacular effects on the output of peasants (in their case productivity per head doubled in thirty years), and that agriculture, far from lagging behind other sectors, and acting as a brake on the rest of the economy, can be turned into a leader, generating demand for other sectors, and also providing them with capital. But most other governments in this situation have neglected peasant agriculture, with the result that its failure to expand has kept down the rate of growth in other sectors. Of all the explanations offered for the relative stagnation of France, compared with Great Britain, or of China compared with Japan, the relatively slow growth of agricultural productivity seems to this author to be the most fundamental. France still needs a quarter of her population in agriculture to feed herself, compared with 12 to 15 per cent in the most advanced countries.

These deficiencies of the home market, either in total demand, or

in the response of important sectors, or in the attitude towards a competitive struggle for markets, resulting from innovation, explain why it usually falls to foreign trade to give an economy that upward twist which sets it on the progressive road. Producing for export has not the same disadvantages as producing for the home market. It does not depend upon demand growing appropriately in other sectors; it gives rise to no competitive struggle at home, since in the early stages world demand is large relatively to the output of individual producers in a single country; and it is not dependent upon effective demand at home. Moreover, exports create new effective demand for other commodities, and so stimulate all the industries producing for the home market. Exports also stimulate home industries in other ways; some of the facilities created for the export industries, such as communications, training facilities, or engineering services, are also of use to the home industries; and export industries, by stealing labour from home industries at the same time as they create more demand for these industries, stimulate the home industries into innovations designed to increase their productivity. When nineteenth century economists such as Malthus and List emphasized the important role of foreign trade in initiating the earlier stages of economic expansion, they thought as often of the role of imports as of the role of exports. Imports create new tastes and so, they thought, stimulate new energies for work, and a new willingness to make the best use of available resources, so that extra income may become available to buy the new goods. Imports almost certainly have this effect in countries where the lack of variety in known consumer goods would otherwise keep the preference for leisure relatively high; but even where this effect is not important, foreign trade will alter the whole economic atmosphere of the economy through the effects of increasing production for export.

The importance of foreign trade in the early stages of development is also one of the reasons why in this stage leadership is usually in the hands of foreign entrepreneurs. It is conceivably possible that domestic entrepreneurs should develop an industry for export and go abroad in search of markets. But more usually it is the developed country, whose consumption is growing, that sends out emissaries to seek new sources of supply. Besides, the entrepreneurs in the more developed countries know a thing or two about techniques, whether of production, or marketing, or transportation, which give them an advantage over the entrepreneurs in less developed countries. After a time, the domestic entrepreneurs learn, and grow in number, and with the advantage of the lower cost of operating from one's home base, are able to drive the foreign entrepreneurs out. This story is much the same whether one is reading the economic history of

Britain in the fourteenth to the sixteenth centuries, in her relations with the Low Countries, or whether one is following Japanese history in the last quarter of the nineteenth century, or recent developments in Ceylon.

Though the expansion of exports has the advantage of being the easiest means of starting the economy on its growth, over-concentration upon exports is just as disadvantageous as over-concentration on any other sector. The disadvantage shows itself in adverse terms of trade. If nothing is being done to raise the productivity of peasants in producing food, they constitute a reservoir of cheap labour available for work in mines or plantations or other export enterprises. This is very much the case in the under-developed countries of the tropics, and it explains why tropical commercial produce—such as tea, cotton, oilseeds and various mineral products—can be had on terms so advantageous to the industrial countries. The labour required for producing these commodities can be had cheaply because its alternative is to stay on peasant farms growing food with very low productivity per man. So long as the peasant farms have low productivity, the temperate world can get the services of tropical labour for a very low price. Moreover when productivity rises in the crops produced for export there is no need to share the increase with labour, and practically the whole benefit goes in reducing the price to industrial consumers. Sugar is an excellent case in point. Cane sugar production is an industry in which productivity is extremely high by any biological standard. It is also an industry in which output per acre has about trebled over the past seventy years, a rate of growth unparallelled by any other major agricultural industry in the world—certainly not by the wheat industry. Nevertheless, workers in the cane sugar industry continue to walk barefooted, and to live in shacks, while workers in wheat enjoy among the highest living standards in the world. However vastly productive the sugar industry may become, the benefit accrues chiefly to consumers. This is one of the disadvantages to tropical countries (advantages to industrial countries) of the fact that their economic development has concentrated upon the export sector of the economy, and that foreign entrepreneurs and foreign capital have been devoted in the first place primarily to expanding exports. The result is that their exports are available on terms favourable to the industrial countries.

The moral is not that it is wrong to expand exports, but that it is wrong to concentrate exclusively upon this sector of the economy. It is just as important to take steps to increase productivity in the sectors working for the home market, above all in the agricultural sector, and if this is done the real wages of workers in the export sector will rise *pari passu*. It is just as much an error to neglect exports

as to concentrate excessively on exports, for it is quite possible for exports to be the laggard which holds up development. For example, there may be great willingness to invest for home consumption, which is held up only by lack of foreign exchange. Private entrepreneurs may have considerable plans for investing in manufacturing industry, or in agriculture, for home consumption, and the government may also have quite a programme for expenditure on education, public utilities, and the like. All such expenditures, however, would generate an additional demand for imports, either of machinery or materials required for home investment, or of consumer goods. All development programmes increase the demand for foreign exchange, so if the capacity to earn foreign exchange is not expanding, all development may be held up. There are quite a few countries currently in this position. Any development programme for a country as a whole must therefore make adequate provision for expanding exports, or for producing substitutes for imports. But this is only another way of emphasizing the role which foreign trade plays in the early stages of economic growth.

In the later stages of economic growth the dynamic role ceases to be monopolized by foreign trade, and may even pass from it altogether to the home market. This transition was effected in the United States somewhere about the end of the nineteenth century. With the passage of time the growth of home demand, first stimulated by exports, encourages domestic entrepreneurship, and after a while investment for home consumption may become the chief pillar of economic growth. This transition may be long delayed, as in France, if the agricultural sector fails to be revolutionized on capitalistic lines, and therefore continues to be a drag on demand and on the labour supply. Or a complete transition may not be possible at all, if, as in Britain, the size of the population relatively to natural resources forces the country to be greatly dependent upon imports, and so reduces the rate of all-over growth to the rate at which foreign earnings can be expanded, or substitutes for imports produced.

One corollary of this analysis is that it explains the conditions in which economic development can take place without pressure on the foreign exchanges. If the main reason why the economy is growing is that the demand for its exports is increasing rapidly, the economy will be in the happy state where imports for purposes of consumption are tending to lag behind exports. In contrast, if an economy is developing mainly at the home market end, imports will be tending to grow (unless it is developing substitutes for imports) without corresponding growth of exports, and unless it receives substantial foreign assistance (loans or grants), the development

programme may have to be pursued behind a barrier of foreign exchange controls. To have a growing demand for one's exports is always a blessing.

The conclusion of this analysis is not very startling; it is that in development programmes all sectors of the economy should grow simultaneously, so as to keep a proper balance between industry and agriculture, and between production for home consumption and production for export. Though this is rather an obvious conclusion, it conforms neither to current practice nor to current recommendation. There is, for example, a whole school of 'liberal' economists in the industrial countries who urge upon the agricultural countries, usually in lofty moral tones, that they should concentrate upon agriculture, and do nothing to advance their industry. The same school also extols the virtues of exporting, and is horrified by programmes which might have the effect of reducing dependence on foreign trade. The follies of this school have their match in Marxist and nationalist dogmas, according to which the road to economic progress lies through concentrating upon industrialization. In the heat of the passions aroused by these controversies it seems almost cowardly to take the line that the truth is that all sectors should be expanded simultaneously, but the logic of this proposition is as unassailable as its simplicity.

(c) Stability

An important characteristic of private investment is its irregularity, which in turn produces wide fluctuations in income and employment. This problem has been the subject of an enormous literature over the past hundred and fifty years, and it is both unnecessary and impossible to treat it fully in this book. On the other hand, a book on economic development which made no reference to fluctuations in investment would seem very odd, so something must be said here briefly on the main features of the problem.

Every country has its own domestic sources of instability, but in addition every country is subjected to fluctuations reaching it from outside through its foreign trade. The domestic sources of instability are associated with new mineral discoveries, with the exhaustion of some resources, with the opening up of new lands, with the application of new inventions, with the inflationary or deflationary policies of governments, with migration, civil strife, epidemic, earthquake, fire, drought, and much else. Even if world trade grew at a constant rate without fluctuations, every country would have fluctuations of its own. In practice, however, in most of the less developed countries these domestic irregularities are swamped by the fluctuations of foreign trade which result from the fluctuations of the more advanced

countries. These fluctuations in world trade are associated with large changes in volume and in prices, which result from the alternate expansion and contraction of demand in the advanced countries. In this sense, all the private enterprise economies in the world are in these days 'less developed' when compared with the United States of America, the country in which about two-fifths of the world's income is produced. In the nineteenth century Britain and Germany were also independent sources of fluctuation, and to some extent they still are, but their influence in originating fluctuations in world income is now very small, when compared with that of the United States, and they themselves are much more affected by the level of business activity in the United States than they are by their own independent movements (except in time of war or of inflation). Hence the problem of the trade cycle is now to explain what causes fluctuations of activity in the United States of America, or in the widest sense, in highly developed industrial communities.

Fluctuations in activity have not one cause but several, and an explanation which may feature prominently in one cycle may be of minor importance in another. One of the difficulties of trade cycle analysis, also, is to know how much importance to attribute to each of several potential causes, when they are acting together and possibly affecting each other. Trade cycle theory concentrates on creating simplified models to test each of several possible causes in isolation, but the step from this to explaining any particular fluctuation in detail, with the right weight given to each of its causes, has not yet been taken to anyone's satisfaction. Even the potential causes are not fully agreed, even at the level of the abstract model. In what follows there is no attempt to present a model of the trade cycle, or to follow the system through the usual analysis of upper and lower turning points and intervening self-reinforcing processes. To do this properly would demand more space than the subject merits in the context of this book, since the interest of this book is in the factors which influence growth over the long period, rather than in short period change. What follows is therefore only the briefest indication, for readers who are quite new to this subject, of some of the principal reasons which have been suggested to explain why investment does not grow steadily. The reasons selected for treatment here are: the irregularity of innovation, the flexibility of bank credit, the unstable relationship between investment and the growth of income, and changes in the distribution of income.

The irregularity of innovation is easy to understand. We have often remarked on the tendency of an innovation to show a logistic pattern of growth. When the motor car is invented, there is a long period in which it establishes itself before it achieves popularity.

Then follows a period during which it advances very rapidly, displacing alternative forms of transport, especially the horse. This is a period of very heavy investment, not only in factories for producing cars, but also in roads, and in a host of ancillary industries supplying raw materials and components—rubber, tin, steel, glass, etc. Ultimately there is reached, as in the United States, a stage where there are hardly any more horses to be displaced, and where nearly every family owns a car. Thereafter the industry cannot possibly grow at the same rate as it did in its middle period, and the rate of investment is correspondingly reduced. Actually, 'logistic' is too smooth a description of what happens to each innovation. Investment proceeds rather by fits and starts. When the car has proved to be popular, a lot of firms come into the business full of enthusiasm, and extend capacity beyond the current demand. Some go bankrupt, and the industry is depressed. Demand, however, continues to grow, and after a while catches up with capacity. There is another burst of enthusiasm, and another race to expand capacity, followed by another temporary check. It is of the very nature of economic growth that nobody knows what is going to happen, and that people therefore make mistakes, and it is too much to hope that these mistakes will always exactly cancel out to give us a smooth growth of investment. We notice the same tendency even in well established lines of investment, which do not involve much innovation. Population grows more or less at a smooth rate, but the number of houses does not. Instead, in every industrial community house-building goes in spurts. There is a period of great activity, lasting about ten years, during which so many houses are built that there are everywhere some houses standing empty—perhaps as many as one in ten. Then follow ten years or so of inactivity in building, during which population catches up with houses, and then the cycle starts again.

Given that there is this irregular behaviour in each line of investment, it would be the merest accident if the different patterns so fitted into each other as to keep total investment rising at a constant rate. This would require each new innovation to be starting off just as some other innovation was tailing off, and the fluctuations in one to be exactly offset by contrary fluctuations in others. Though there are always some investment opportunities waiting for a sponsor, there is no reason why the jigsaw should fit as perfectly as this. On the contrary, these fluctuations tend to reinforce, rather than to offset each other, because of another tendency of investments, which is to bunch together. When one big line of investment is going up— say motor cars or housing—all other business is prosperous, because of the incomes and demand generated thereby. This is the time when investors in other lines feel confident, and accelerate their investments

too. On the other hand, when some major line is reduced, all other business is depressed, confidence is lost, and there is a general decline of investment.

Now different lines of investment are of different importance, in the sense of the amount of investment involved, and of the time they take to reach their peak. The level of activity is therefore determined more by the big lines than by the small. For example, if house-building is on the average 5 per cent of gross national incomes, it makes a great difference to the general level of activity whether house-building is booming (say around 7 per cent) or depressed (say around 3 per cent), while fluctuations in the rate of opening up new milk bars are of much smaller importance. Again, if a community launches out on supplying itself with a railway system, this activity not only absorbs much capital, but also continues at a high level for a long time, say for two or three decades. During that time there will be some fluctuations in other investment, but there cannot be a major depression so long as the investment in railways is well maintained. This explains why slumps are not all of the same intensity. A slump which occurs at a time when house-building or some major innovation is in full spate does not become serious, and does not last long. Whereas a slump which occurs during the off-period of the building cycle, or just after a major innovation has reached one of its peaks (e.g. motor cars in the U.S.A. in 1929) may be of serious magnitude and long duration. Since building averages 25 per cent of gross invest-ment, and has a cycle of eighteen to twenty years, it is not surprising that decades of prosperity tend to alternate with decades of slower growth.

We have mentioned that investments tend to bunch together. This would not be possible to the same extent but for the flexibility of bank credit, which is the second major explanation of these fluctua-tions. In the nineteenth century, before the bank amalgamation movement got far, there were in the industrial countries thousands of independent banks, each pursuing its own policy in the matter of creating credit. Just as investments tend to bunch together, so also the banks tended to be greatly influenced by the general atmosphere of business activity; to advance credit rather easily when business was booming (thus contributing to the boom), and to be very stringent when conditions were depressed (thus aggravating the depression). One of the principal functions which Central Banks have developed in the last fifty years has been the control of credit creation by the commercial banks. Central Banks have nowhere succeeded in 'stabilizing' the level of credit, or in preventing the flexibility of bank credit from contributing both to the buoyancy of the boom as well as to the severity of the slump, but their work has nevertheless been very effective in preventing the worst excesses.

One can see this most clearly by comparing accounts of any nineteenth century crisis with any crisis in twentieth century Britain or in the United States since the 'New Deal'. In the nineteenth century every crisis was accompanied by the failure of some banks which had made rash and excessive loans during the boom, and by a run on banking institutions by depositors fearful that the banks would have to close their doors. This does not happen in the middle of the twentieth century. Some economists hold that efforts should be made to 'neutralize' money, that is to say to prevent the quantity of money in active circulation from expanding and contracting cyclically. If this could be done, both booms and slumps would be milder. It is, however, very doubtful whether it could be done altogether. Besides, some other economists are conscious of the fact that credit creation during the boom raises the level of investment beyond what it would otherwise be. They regard these recurrent bursts of mild inflation as an unavoidable feature of the process of economic growth.

Next we turn to consider the relationship between investment and the growth of income. If there were fixed ratios between capital, income and consumption, equilibrium could be maintained only if these three all grew in the right proportions. For example, if investment is a function of the rate of growth of consumption, any check to the rate of growth of consumption will reduce investment, even though consumption is still expanding; the fall in investment will then reduce incomes, and so reduce employment and consumption. So far, trade cycle theory has not got beyond the stage of elaborating possible abstract relationships which show how disaster may occur if rates of growth diverge from equilibrium rates. We have not yet got to the stage of establishing what the actual relationships are, or how inflexible they are, or what the quantitative significance is of divergence from equilibrium rates of growth. There are however some fairly obvious applications of the 'acceleration principle' (as the relationship between the growth of income and investment activity is called), one of which is the behaviour of stocks of commodities. Let us suppose that stocks of commodities, are normally required at a level equal to 40 per cent of national income. Suppose now also that, starting from a fair level of unemployment, national income rises by 10 per cent over two years, reaches full employment, and then grows only by 2 per cent per annum. In the first two years stocks are required to increase by 10 per cent, representing an investment rate of 2 per cent of national income per annum (the actual increase may be more or less than this). Next year the required increase in stocks is equal only to 0.8 per cent of national incomes; required investment in stocks therefore falls by 1.2 per cent of national income, equivalent to a fall of say 6 per cent of gross investment.

This itself may start a downward spiral. In practice, the fluctuation is increased by mistakes. Having increased their sales by 10 per cent in two years, many business men expect their sales in the third year to increase at the same sort of rate. When sales in fact increase only by 2 per cent, because full employment has been reached, they find that they have over-ordered, and are left with larger stocks than they expected. Instead of stock building then falling from 2 to 0·8 per cent of national income, the business community may cut its orders still more, in an attempt to reduce stocks absolutely, and this of course causes unemployment. Fluctuations in stock building are a prominent feature of the trade cycle. Nearly every boom is associated with wild speculation in stocks, especially of raw materials, and with a sharp rise in the prices of raw materials, followed by a sharp fall. In fact, it is pretty hopeless to expect investment, whether in buildings, in machinery, or in stocks, to proceed at some smooth continuous rate, exactly corresponding to smooth increases in income or in consumption. Investment proceeds rather in a hit or miss fashion, fluctuating alternatively above or below the rate which would just be right for steady growth.

The fourth cause of fluctuations which has been debated from time to time is the effect of economic growth on the distribution of income. For example, Karl Marx's picture of the trade cycle was somewhat as follows. During a boom capital accumulates, and the demand for labour increases. Eventually, the competition for labour raises wages faster than prices, and so reduces profits. As profits fall, investment is checked, and so a slump is started. Wages then fall faster than prices, until a time comes when new investment is profitable again. In this version there would be a 'right' level of wages in relation to prices which would just maintain stability, but this is not kept because wages always overshoot the mark, upwards or downwards. Non-Marxian socialists have put forward a similar but exactly opposite model (which some Marxists have erroneously believed to be what Marx himself taught). In this model what happens in the boom is not that wages rise faster than profits, but the opposite. Prices rise faster than wages, to the advantage of profits. Profits, however, are mainly saved rather than spent on consumption. So consumption grows less rapidly than income, and less rapidly than capital accumulates. This, they think, is an unstable position. After a while this disproportionate growth of capital and of the capacity to produce is embarrassed by the failure of consumption to grow in step. The rate of profit falls, investment is reduced, and income and employment contract. This model is related to what we have discussed in the previous paragraph, since it also depends on the maintenance of fairly closely defined ratios between various

magnitudes. In so far as the conflict with the Marxian version turns on a question of fact, it certainly is the case that profits rise relatively to wages during a boom and fall during a slump. But just how closely investment depends upon consumption is a more debatable point, considering that in industrial countries only about 30 per cent of gross investment goes directly into agriculture and manufacturing, that even in manufacturing much investment is geared not to current demand but to the creation of new demand by innovation (new commodities or cost-reducing processes), and that some choice is possible between more and less capitalistic processes. (The other 70 per cent of gross investment also depends on consumption indirectly, but depends much more upon expected levels of consumption in the future than upon what is happening to consumption at any particular time.)

It will now be apparent why fluctuations cannot be omitted from any treatise on economic growth, since all the principal causes of fluctuations which have been mentioned here derive from economic growth itself. The logistic pattern of innovations results from the displacement of old commodities, or old processes, by new ones. Then there is the tendency to overshoot the mark, exemplified in bursts of activity, followed by pauses, which is inevitable once static conditions are left behind, and men begin to thrust upwards to higher levels of demand. Or there are the difficulties in maintaining right proportions, between capital and consumption, between stocks and demand, or between wages and profits. This is not to say that there would be no fluctuations if there were no growth; but the reaching out into the dark, which is the process of growth, increases the uncertainties of investment and the possibilities of error. This is why many economists have taken the position that fluctuation is the price of economic growth; that if there were no slump there would be no boom; and if there were no boom capital formation would not proceed on the average as rapidly as it does.

It is hardly necessary to treat in this volume the various proposals which have been made for stabilizing the economy of the United States; this has its own enormous literature. Neither need we do more than refer to proposals which the United Nations Organization has debated from time to time for stabilizing the level of world trade irrespective of fluctuations in the United States or other major countries. We confine ourselves to a few remarks on what the less developed countries can do to help themselves, in face of fluctuations in world trade, and then we shall leave this subject.

The trade cycle usually affects the less developed countries more violently than it affects the industrial countries, because of greater dependence on the prices of food and raw materials, which fluctuate

T

more violently in the cycle than do the prices of manufactured goods. In the boom prices rise sharply. There is a sharp rise in wages in the less developed economies (especially if there are strong trade unions). This rise is not confined to workers in export industries. Because of increased domestic expenditure all domestic prices rise—food, rents, services, etc.—and the resulting rise in the cost of living sends all wages, salaries and profits spiralling upwards. Government revenues rise, but so also do government expenditures, on salaries of civil servants, as well as on providing extra services. Then comes the sharp break, as a result of which the prices of export commodities may fall by 30 to 50 per cent within twelve months. There is then a scramble to bring down the level of internal prices, wages, rents, salaries and so on. This is extremely difficult, and provokes grave dissension and civil strife, which is particularly acute if the agricultural sector is based on plantation wage labour rather than peasant production, and particularly bitter if employers and employees differ in race or religion. If these countries could insulate themselves to some extent from these violent fluctuations in world prices, their prospects of internal harmony would be enormously increased. In addition, their output might fluctuate less violently, because of less violent fluctuation in profits (output contracts sharply in the slump because of the difficulty in getting wages down). And they would get better value for their foreign exchange earnings if they saved up some to spend in the slump, when prices are low, instead of squandering so much during the boom.

None of these countries can insulate its balance of payments from the effects of fluctuations in world trade. If there is a world slump, the value of its exports falls. The best it can hope to do is to prevent this fall from transmitting itself to the home economy. If it is to do this, it must obviously interpose some barrier between the incomes of domestic producers and the proceeds received for exports. One way of doing this is to channel exports through a government agency, as has been done with the major exports of British West Africa, or Uganda, or Burma or Siam. This agency fixes a price which is paid to domestic producers, and which does not fluctuate with the price received for exports; or if it does fluctuate, fluctuates much less. If the purpose were simply to stabilize the domestic price, one would choose a price which was the average of expected future prices. Then, if this price were rightly chosen, the agency would make great profits during a boom, which would be held in a reserve, and would make equal losses during a slump. In practice no one knows what future prices will be, so it would be a most improbable co-incidence if a price chosen with the expectation of equating profits and losses were actually to have this effect. In all the successful cases

price stabilization has been combined with taxation. Mistakes have then resulted chiefly in increasing or in reducing the taxes received by the government, rather than in the agency running completely out of funds. It should also be noted that the withholding of domestic purchasing power during the boom has to be matched by equal reserves of foreign exchange. For the maintenance of domestic income during the slump results in the maintenance of imports at a time when exports are low, and this is not possible unless the reserves kept by the agency are backed by foreign exchange.

This channelling of exports through a government agency involves the government in assuming risks and responsibilities which many prefer to avoid. Much the same stabilizing effect can be had without affecting marketing channels if the government merely varies taxation inversely with the prices of exports. This is most directly done by taxing exports directly, but it can also be done less effectively by varying the taxes on imports, or by varying any other taxes. The direct technique is simply to levy export taxes which rise steeply as prices rise, such as an export tax which is zero at say £100 a ton, and which rises by ten shillings a ton for every one pound increase in the price between £100 and £150, and by fifteen shillings a ton for every one pound a ton increase thereafter. Or, if one desires even more precise stability than this, the tax on prices exceeding £100 can be matched by corresponding subsidies if the price falls below £100.

In practice absolute stability is neither attainable nor desirable. It is impossible to forecast accurately the future trend of prices, and it is desirable that changes in world prices should be allowed to have some effect on the volume of production of those commodities which feature in international trade. There are also problems of administration which make it difficult for the less well organized governments to run stabilization schemes without getting into trouble. All the same, some limited degree of insulation from world fluctuations is within the reach of most countries. What stops more countries from trying to reduce internal fluctuations is not so much the technical difficulty of the means available, as it is their unwillingness, for political reasons, to restrain themselves during booms. Consumption can be kept up in a slump only if it has been correspondingly kept down during a boom; for the foreign exchange which is to maintain imports during the slump must have been saved up during the boom. Now most of these countries, when the boom comes, engage in a spending spree. Proposals that there should be heavy taxation at this time are strongly resisted. And if, indeed, there is heavy taxation, governments are prone to use it to expand their own expenditures, instead of putting the proceeds to reserve, and backing the reserves by foreign exchange. To do this would pay handsomely, since any

given amount of foreign exchange buys more imports during a slump than it does during the preceding boom (because prices fall). It would be quite wrong to suggest that the less developed countries can insulate their domestic economies completely from external fluctuations if they want to; but it is certainly true that they could do much more to avoid the worst excesses of boom and slump if they had the will.

These remarks apply only to insulating the less developed economy against changes in the *price* of exports, and not to changes in the *quantity* of exports. Some countries do not reduce the volume of their exports during the slump; they sell for whatever price they can get, and it is the consuming countries which accumulate the surplus stocks. In others, output falls only because the price falls, so if the domestic price were stabilized the volume of exports would be maintained during the slump. Not all countries are in this position however. In some other countries the output of exportable goods could be maintained during a slump only if the government undertook to purchase and hold stocks until the export market for the commodity revived. Failing this, output would be cut, and if the commodity was produced by wage labour, unemployment would increase. Some of the governments of the less developed countries have indeed been so bold as to hold stocks when export demand declined. This offers equal prospects of great profit—if the market revives fairly quickly and the stocks can be sold off during a boom— or of great loss—if revival is delayed so long that the government is forced to dispose of its stocks when prices are still very low. It proved a dangerous policy to pursue during those decades when the secular movement of prices was downwards. It would be correspondingly profitable in decades when prices are moving upwards. But when a slump begins who can tell whether it is a passing phenomenon, or whether it will prove to be the beginning of a prolonged decline of prices?

The best hope that the less developed countries have of relative stability in their economies lies in the attempts which the more advanced nations are now making to control their own fluctuations, and to bring greater stability to international trade. In these spheres policy is still hesitant and experimental; yet there seems to be good ground for the present state of confidence that economic growth will be less irregular in the immediate future than it has been in the immediate past.

(d) Secular Stagnation

In the history of many countries there have been long decades or centuries of fairly vigorous growth, succeeded by long decades or

centuries of relative stagnation. In some cases actually the decline has been so complete that the country has even ceased to be populated altogether, rich plains and cities giving way to ruin and desert. Sometimes one can account for these changes in terms of natural phenomena. There has been an earthquake, or a volcanic eruption, or a flood. Sometimes the reason is political: revolutions, wars or just bad government—we refer to this class of reasons in the next two chapters. In the final paragraphs of this chapter we examine briefly those reasons which depend on the proposition that investment inevitably declines in a country after it has experienced one or more centuries of fairly rapid economic growth.

Apart from natural phenomena and politics, the arguments supporting the inevitability of secular stagnation rest upon technology, upon psychology, upon monopolization, upon income distribution, upon population, and upon international competition.

The argument from technology postulates a fall in the rate of improvement of technical knowledge. There is no reason to doubt that there have been wide variations in the rate of technological improvement over the centuries, though it is admitted that precise measurement of this concept is impossible. The use of annual patent registrations as a measure for recent decades has been discredited. Some industrial countries do show a tendency for the annual number of patent registrations per head of the population to grow more slowly, but it cannot be deduced from this that technical knowledge is growing more slowly. It may be that the increasing cost of patent litigation is reducing the use of the patent system; or that the higher educational standards of inventors reduces the number of trivialities now patented; or that the increased standardization of specifications, as well as the dominance of mass produced articles, reduces the urge to invent mere variations; or that the greater importance of physics and chemistry in technology, relatively to mechanical contrivance, and of research teams, relatively to lone inventors, reduces the number of patents even though invention continues on the same scale as before. Certainly, number of patents apart, there seems to be no ground for thinking that the rate of growth of technical knowledge is any smaller today than it was sixty or seventy years ago. However, even in those historical epochs where the rate of growth of knowledge has clearly declined, this cannot be regarded as an independent cause of secular stagnation, since it has itself to be explained in terms external to technological science itself. The scope for scientific invention does not diminish, since what remains to be discovered is for all practical purposes infinite. Neither is there reason to believe that the capacity of the human mind to learn deteriorates from one generation to another, in the biological sense (but see Chapter VI, section 1(*a*)).

Hence, if knowledge is not growing as rapidly as before, we must seek reasons why human beings are giving less thought to increasing knowledge. The answer may lie in political insecurity, which has reduced the interest of capitalists in productive investment; or in changes in class structure; or in natural disaster; or in increased secrecy, due to political factors or to monopoly; or in one or other of the factors listed in the preceding paragraph. Hence we must treat technological stagnation essentially not as a cause but as a symptom of more general social malaise.

The argument from psychology supposes changes in attitudes which are a natural reaction to the process of growth itself. There is that school of thought which believes that human society swings on a pendulum between materialistic and spiritualistic phases, so that after long decades of feverish preoccupation with materialistic improvement, men tire of economic growth and its conditions, and return to more contemplative attitudes. Some members of this school believe that there is actual biological change, if only in the sense that the small dominating groups in society are of one biological type in one phase, and are replaced by a different biological type in the other phase. Alternatively, one may assume other reasons why the urge to inventiveness may dry up, so that society enters into a long period when the best minds do not give themselves to science or invention, or alternatively when their effort is sterile. All this is pure speculation, since we have no means of assessing these psychological phenomena. We have already discussed these matters in Chapter III section 5(*b*), and have nothing to add to the subject here.

The argument from monopolization rests upon the two propositions that monopolization reduces investment, and that the degree of monopoly increases with economic growth. We have already discussed the first of these propositions in Chapter III, and have seen reasons for accepting its validity. The second proposition is more debatable. Two arguments are used to support it. First, there is the argument that technical progress makes for a secular increase in the size of the average firm. This is certainly true, in the sense that there are technical reasons why the average firm is larger in each successive century. But it is not sufficient. To establish increasing monopolization one must say that the size of the firm increases faster than the size of the market, and this is by no means clear. There is a secular tendency for the size of the potential market to increase because of the secular tendency for the real costs of transportation to fall, and for population to increase. The market grows in size from the village to the world. This tendency is hampered by tariff and currency restrictions, but we cannot claim any secular tendency here; sometimes the restrictions increase, and sometimes they diminish; this is

about all we can say if we look at economic history in centuries.

The second argument is the inevitable rise to dominance of the financial type. 'In the beginning', according to this argument, the typical capitalist is the industrialist, devoted to his factory and to the tasks of producing and selling its output; whereas 'in the end' the dominant type among capitalists is the financier, who may never enter a factory, but devotes himself to creating holding companies, mergers, amalgamations, subsidiaries and other financial empires. So, even where no technical development justifies it, monopoly emerges from the juggling of financiers. The rise of these financial types may be thought to be inevitable because they and only they love money for its own sake, and put money making before all else. The farmer loves his land, and is liable to ruin himself by over-investing in it. The industrialist similarly is distracted by loving the hum of his machines, or the men who work for him, his product, or his bricks and mortar, and lets sentiment to some extent affect his financial acumen. Only the professional financier, who deals in money, loves it for his own sake, and by this love is protected from the pits into which other men fall. So, runs the argument, the control of industry passes inevitably to financiers. And, as the market becomes world wide, so do the monopolistic arrangements between financiers. Actually, this line of argument was invented by people who had studied particularly the rise of factory industry in Germany, where the banks had played a much larger part in launching industrialism than they did in other countries. The argument can be turned on its head. 'In the beginning,' one can say, industry depends on the capital market for finance, and industrialists are liable to fall into the hands of financiers. 'In the later stages' of capitalism, however, industry is generating great amounts of saving in the form of undistributed profits; the capital market is relatively less important, and industrialists do not so much depend on outside support. Far from it being the case that industry falls into the hands of financial jugglers as it grows older, it seems rather to be the case that those who manage industrial concerns have become increasingly independent of outside financial control.

These speculations aside, we cannot escape the fact that *some* industries do become monopolized with age. This may indeed be a natural tendency for all industries, to which some succumb more fully than others. An obvious factor is the principle of logistic growth to which we have already referred; every new industry grows through a phase of rapid expansion, followed by slow growth when it has displaced its predecessor. As it enters its phase of slow growth it is easier for the large firms to expand relatively to the market, and if they do not drive the small ones out altogether, at least they pursue a

policy of live and let live, knowing that in a market which grows relatively slowly any fight for position is certain to be costly. This is the stage in which the industry may pass from the innovators to the bureaucrats; the stage when the managerial mind takes over, and when fundamental technical change ceases. What is true for each industry, however, is not necessarily true of the economy as a whole. For new industries challenge each other in continual succession. If an industry, as it ages, comes to be monopolized and to lose interest in innovation, this may be the very reason why it is superseded by some new industry, producing a rival product. Provided that there is a constant succession of new products, under new auspices, the economy as a whole does not become more monopolistic even if each industry does.

It may, however, also happen that the economy becomes more monopolistic not because of the behaviour of entrepreneurs, in the first instance, but rather because of the reactions of the community to this behaviour. Competition creates its own enemies, and, by a dialectical process, may therefore strangle itself. Competition hurts the weak, the inefficient, the unprogressive, and the unlucky, and since these are much more numerous than their opposite numbers, it is relatively easy to organize considerable hostility to the idea of competition. Farmers, small traders, handicraft workers and small industrialists are among the first to resent the effects of economic growth. A formidable hostility is also stimulated amongst skilled employees, whose skills are constantly menaced by technical change. Economic growth therefore stimulates the creation of trade associations and trade unions designed to resist various types of change, by exercising monopolistic pressures. These also call into their support the aid of the politicians, who are not slow to pass legislation protecting what seems to them to be majority interests against what they think to be merely the interest of a pushful minority. The philosophers of the day also adapt their philosophy to what seems to be the need of the times; the priests call for a return to the 'balanced' society of mediaeval times; the economists discover and pounce upon flaws in the arguments for competition; and the lawyers find loopholes in the law through which monopolistic agreements pass. It is not inevitable that competition should lose this battle, for the very fact that people have experienced the fruits of economic growth creates awareness that the general interest and the sectional interest are not the same. All the same, the resistances which growth creates to itself are so great that it is equally possible in some cases that they may have the effect of slowing down the rate of innovation and of new investment.

This brings us next to consider propositions based upon changes in the distribution of income as economic growth proceeds. We shall

consider first the theory and then the facts. If, at a time of full employment, distribution changed in such a way as to increase the desire to consume relatively to national income, we would expect the result to be a relative decline in the proportion of resources used for investment, and therefore relative stagnation of national income. However, it is also arguable that the increase of the propensity to consume would stimulate investment, the deficiency of savings being met by the creation of credit. Investment would therefore be kept up against a persistent background of inflation (punctuated no doubt from time to time by slumps, which would help to maintain confidence in the value of money). Conversely, it has been argued that if the effect of economic growth is to increase savings relatively to consumption, a country will find increasing difficulty in disposing of its savings as income grows, and will be peculiarly liable to bouts of prolonged depression. We referred to these arguments in earlier sections of this chapter (2(a) and 3(c)) and saw that they cannot be accepted at face value, since they depend on assuming a fairly rigid relationship between consumption and investment. However, it is right to note that, just as a majority of economists in Victorian times regarded a deficiency of savings as the main menace to growth in their day, so in our day probably a majority of economists would consider a superfluity of savings to be more likely to hinder growth in the United States of America.

If we turn to the facts, the relevant question to ask is what happens to profits as national income grows, since high profits and high saving go together. We have already seen in an earlier section of this chapter that profits grow relatively to national income in all that phase of economic growth where labour can be drafted into the capitalist sector of the economy from other sectors at a constant real wage. Once the accumulation of capital has caught up with the 'surplus' labour previously available from agriculture, or domestic service, or petty trading, or the female household, or casual trades or population growth, wages grow with capital accumulation, and there is no evidence supporting an inevitable secular change in one direction or the other. In the early stage the growth of profits does not inhibit investment; on the contrary it encourages investment. Since there is labour available, capital accumulation does not alter the ratio of capital to labour in employment, and so there is no tendency for the rate of profit to fall. In the later stage, when labour becomes scarce, the rate of profit would fall if innovation did not constantly provide new opportunities for investing capital. There have been more economists who have expected the rate of profit to fall rather than to rise at this stage (Smith, Ricardo, Marx, Keynes, and most others); and most of them, contrary to present fashions,

expected this to check rather than to stimulate investment. Profits may have fallen for some such reason in earlier phases of economic history, but there seems to have been no secular decline of the rate of profit over the past hundred years. Here again account must be taken of the behaviour of governments. If they have a secular tendency it is to tax profits and to stimulate consumption, but whether this checks or stimulates investment in 'mature' economies we must leave to the debate.

Events have also failed to fulfil another of Karl Marx's predictions, namely the increasing misery of the proletariat. In Marx's system real wages remained constant at the subsistence level (apart from cyclical fluctuations) despite the growth of productivity through increased knowledge and capital. All the benefits of technical progress went to the capitalists, whose profits correspondingly increased relatively to wages. This analysis, we have seen is good for the earlier, but not for the later stages of capitalism, when capital accumulation has caught up with the labour supply. At the same time Marx expected the increased monopolization of industry to diminish the ranks of capitalists, and to swell the ranks of the proletariat by destroying and displacing the smaller capitalists. This would both menace the wage level, by increasing the reserve of unemployed, and also widen the gulf between the classes. As for this gulf, the opposite has happened; economic growth has created an enormous and diverse middle class; in fact it has blurred social distinctions so much that nearly every one in the advanced industrial communities now considers himself to belong to some branch or other of the middle classes. On top of this, according to Marx, the growing use of machinery was to displace labour, and to create ever-increasing technological unemployment. All these circumstances were to combine in increasing the misery of the working class, who goaded by constant pressure on subsistence wages, and by ever-increasing unemployment, as well as united by their ever-sharpening sense of class differences, would one day rise up and make a successful revolution. It is always possible for a system to be brought to an end by revolution, whatever the causes of the revolution may be. The capitalist system in its later stage has made workers more comfortable, and not more miserable as Marx predicted; but he may have been equally wrong in believing that misery is the cause of revolution. In all capitalist economies the working classes have now much greater economic and political power than they had a hundred years ago, and no one knows what use they will make of it. They may accept the system, and confine themselves to improving it (e.g. by introducing greater stability, or by providing social insurance for the weak or the unlucky). Or they may destroy the system by restrictionism, by excessive taxation, or

by hostile words and deeds which undermine confidence. No one can predict of any economy that it will not be brought to a standstill by internal dissension; this outcome is always possible, and has often happened. On the other hand, there is no clear link between the distribution of income and civil strife, so even if we could predict what is going to happen to profits relatively to wages (which we cannot), we could not deduce from this whether the result would be increasing social harmony, or increasing dissension.

We come now to arguments based on predictions of what happens to population as economic development proceeds. Here too there are opposing schools. According to one school, economic growth inevitably causes population growth. This in turn exhausts natural resources; forests are cut down, soil is eroded, and minerals are worked out. Output may actually decline, and people may die off in famines. Or else the pressure of population has to be met by increasing imports of food, at unfavourable terms of trade. Then people and capital emigrate to more favourable localities, and the country stagnates. There are plenty of cases of this in history, such as for example the migration of people and of capital from the British Isles in the second half of the nineteenth century. It cannot, however, be taken for granted that the population will always grow up to the limits of natural resources. As we shall see in the next chapter, a prolonged fall in the death rate sets in motion after a while social forces which bring down the birth rate. It is not therefore impossible for equilibrium to be attained with low birth and death rates before the country becomes overpopulated in any sense.

It is precisely this possibility that worries the opposite school. According to this school economic growth inevitably after a while causes the population to grow more slowly, or even to decline absolutely. This has then awkward consequences which they fear may lead to secular stagnation, whether because the economy becomes more inflexible, or because risk-taking is diminished, or because the economy becomes less competitive, or because the opportunities for investment are diminished.

The economy becomes less flexible because the annual supply of new entrants, to the labour market is diminished. In any economic system there are constant changes in demand or supply which make necessary a redistribution of labour between industries and occupations. It is harder to effect this redistribution if it involves getting some people to change the jobs they have already started than if it involves merely getting newcomers to industry to go into the occupations where they are most needed. Hence an economy which has a high annual inflow of newcomers to industry is expected to be more flexible than one with a relatively lower annual inflow. It is probable

that the importance of this factor is exaggerated. There is in any case in any economy which offers fairly full employment an enormous turnover of labour. The industries which are said to be short of labour are frequently short not because they do not get enough recruits, but because they are unable to hold the labour they get. Any economy will of course find it difficult to effect sudden large transfers of labour between occupations such as are occasioned by wars, or by the aftermath of wars; but as far as the ordinary marginal transfers required in peacetime are concerned, it is doubtful whether the presence or absence of a large annual inflow makes much difference to the situation.

There is more to be said of the greater riskiness of investment in a stable economy. In a country where population is growing by 2 per cent per annum, and real income by this or more, it is hard to make great errors in investment. If entrepreneurs put 10 per cent too much into any particular line, the industry will be depressed temporarily, but within five years or less demand will have caught up with supply, and there will be some scarcity profits to enjoy. Mistakes in investment are rectified both by the natural depreciation of capital, which reduces supply, and also by the growth of income and population which increases demand. If population is not growing, mistakes are rectified only by depreciation, and by the growth of income per head, and this may be a long drawn out and painful process. All investment is therefore more risky. This brings us directly to the third point. For if risk-taking is discouraged, the economy becomes less competitive. Entrepreneurs are more anxious to enter into market-sharing arrangements than they would be in an economy where demand was growing rapidly. Both these factors, the decline of risk-taking, and the growth of monopoly, discourage investment, and so promote secular stagnation. But one could equally easily argue the other way: that the fight for markets is intensified as the markets cease to expand. Reliance on *a priori* argument leads to no definite conclusion, and neither is their adequate evidence on which to base a firm judgement.

Investment is also expected to decline because the slowing down of population growth reduces investment opportunities. Some part of investment is needed to provide for an increase of population: new houses, new agricultural areas, new roads, more transport facilities, more factories, and so on. Hence, as the rate of population growth falls, the opportunities for investment contract correspondingly. The question whether the rate of growth of income per head will slow down must not, however, be confused with the problem of maintaining full employment. If the difficulty is simply that people are saving more than is needed to keep capital per head rising at a

constant rate, this difficulty can be met by measures which increase consumption and discourage saving. The government can increase the types of taxes which fall upon saving, and reduce the types which fall upon consumption; or it can use the surplus savings to expand its own expenditures on housing, roads, medical facilities, and the like. Given appropriate measures, one would expect a slowing down of the rate of growth of population to increase the rate of growth of income per head, since some of the capital which was no longer required to provide for population increase could now be used instead to increase capital per head. On the other hand, if capital per head were increased, the rate of profit on capital would fall, unless there were an adequate stream of innovations, and this might decrease the willingness to invest (increase it if you think investment depends on high consumption rather than on high profits, and if the fall in the rate of profit raised the propensity to consume by increasing other incomes relatively to profits). Most arguments about secular growth come back in the end to the stream of innovations, and to whether there is any reason to expect this stream to dry up.

The population argument is therefore inconclusive. We cannot be confident that population will outgrow resources in the later stages of development. On the contrary, the menace may rather be that the later stages bring population stability or decline. Neither do we know how dangerous this menace would be if realized. On the face of the matter we expect a declining rate of population growth to make it possible to increase capital per head more rapidly, but the possibility of growing inflexibility and monopoly cannot be brushed aside altogether.

Finally we come to international competition. According to this line of argument, an 'old' country inevitably loses its place in world trade after a while; whereupon the rate of investment in the country declines, either because profits fall, or because it is more profitable to invest in the new countries which are coming up. The 'old' country may lose its place because of shifts in the pattern of international trade. New trade routes may deprive it of its geographical advantages, as with the discovery of America. Technical progress may destroy the demand for its minerals, or for other natural resources in which it is peculiarly favoured, as happened to the demand for Chilean nitrates. Apart from these shifts in the pattern of world trade, the 'old' country may lose its leadership in established trade to rising rivals, if this leadership is based simply upon priority in innovation. For other countries sooner or later learn the new techniques, and as they do so, the old country loses its monopoly, its superior productivity, and its superior earning power. Leadership based on innovation can therefore be maintained only if the country remains in the fore-

front of introducing new ideas, and this kind of leadership is hard to hold. When we take account both of changes of demand relatively to natural resources, and also of the difficulty of maintaining technical superiority for more than a few decades, it is not surprising that no one country maintains leadership in international trade for more than a few decades. Losing leadership does not necessarily lead to stagnation, in the sense of a fall in the ratio of investment to national income, but it may well have this effect if it is accompanied by adverse terms of trade, or if it results in investment being attracted overseas to the new countries. It seems that the rate of growth of production per head in Britain has been smaller since 1870 than it was in the first three-quarters of the nineteenth century, and some people explain the phenomenon in these terms. We shall have more to say about international competition in Chapter VI.

There are thus many pits into which a country may fall, as a result of prolonged growth: it may weary of material things, its entrepreneurs may behave less competitively, its public may create barriers to change, the distribution of income may alter unfavourably, it may exhaust its natural resources, it may lose its place in international trade, or it may run out of innovations. In addition, it may be a victim of natural disaster, or it may be ruined by war, by civil strife, or by misgovernment. None of these is inevitable. On the other hand, when there are so many pits into which a country may fall, it is not in the least surprising that countries have fallen into one or more of these pits in the past. One cannot predict when the rate of investment in any particular country will begin to slow down—whether it will be after decades or after centuries. But the expectation that a long period of growth is in due course succeeded by slower growth, by stagnation, or even by decline seems fairly well supported by the little we know of the economic history of the past four thousand years.

BIBLIOGRAPHICAL NOTE

Two books which cover several of the problems discussed in this chapter are Colin Clark, *The Conditions of Economic Progress*, 2nd edn., London, 1952, and R. Nurkse, *Capital Formation in Under-developed Countries*, Oxford, 1953. On capital requirements consult Clark; also S. Kuznets ed., *Income and Wealth, Series II: Income and Wealth of the United States*, Cambridge, 1952. On the effects of inflation on economic growth, C. Bresciani-Turroni, *The Economics of Inflation*, London, 1937, which analyses the German inflation; and Earl J. Hamilton, 'Profit Inflation and the Industrial Revolution, 1751-1800', *Quarterly Journal of Economics*, 1942. On sources of savings, B. F. Johnston, 'Agricultural

Productivity and Economic Development in Japan', *Journal of Political Economy*, December 1951; I. I. Kramer, 'Land Reform and Industrial Development in Meiji, Japan,' *Land Economics*, November 1953; E. A. Radice, *Savings in Great Britain 1922-1935*, Oxford, 1939; C. T. Saunders, 'The Pattern of Savings and Investment', *Manchester Statistical Society*, November 1954; United Nations Economic Commission for Asia and the Far East, *The Mobilization of Domestic Capital: Report and Documents of the Second Working Party of Experts*, Bangkok, 1953. The growth of profits and of savings relatively to income is further analysed in my article 'Economic Development with Unlimited Supplies of Labour'. *Manchester School*, May 1954. See also A. K. Cairncross, *Home and Foreign Investment, 1870-1913*, Cambridge, 1953.

On international investment see G. C. Allen and A. G. Donnithorne, *Western Enterprise in Far Eastern Economic Development: China and Japan*, London, 1954; N. S. Buchanan, *International Investment and Domestic Welfare*, New York, 1945; W. Cunningham, *Alien Immigrants* (to England), London, 1885; E. D. Domar, 'The Effect of Foreign Investment on the Balance of Payments', *American Economic Review*, December 1950; D. Finch, 'Investment Service of Under-developed Countries', *International Monetary Fund Staff Papers*, September 1951; H. Feis, *Europe, The World's Banker*, New Haven, 1930; V. I. Lenin, *Imperialism*, London, n.d.; W. A. Lewis, *Aspects of Industrialization*, Cairo, 1953; R. Luxemburg, *The Accumulation of Capital*, London, 1951; United Nations, *Report on a Special United Nations Fund for Economic Development*, New York, 1953, and *The International Flow of Private Capital, 1946-1952*, New York, 1954.

On the trade cycle see R. A. Gordon, *Business Fluctuations*, New York, 1952; G. Haberler, *Prosperity and Depression*, 3rd Edn., Geneva, 1941; W. A. Lewis and P. J. O'Leary, 'Secular Swings in Production and Trade, 1870-1913', *The Manchester School*, May 1955; United Nations, *Measures for International Economic Stability*, New York, 1951. For two views of secular stagnation, A. H. Hansen, 'Economic Progress and Declining Population Growth', *American Economic Review*, 1939; and J. Steindl, *Maturity and Stagnation in American Capitalism*, Oxford, 1952.

CHAPTER VI

POPULATION AND RESOURCES

IN this chapter we consider first the relationship between resources, population and output, and secondly the relationship between resources, population and the movement of men and goods across international frontiers.

1. POPULATION AND OUTPUT

(a) Population Growth

What effect has economic growth upon population growth? Malthus's answers to this question have excited controversy ever since his day. First, he said, a rising standard of living will cause population to grow. Secondly, population growth will exceed the rate at which food production will grow. So, thirdly, the growth of population is always checked by the limitation of the means of subsistence. From which it follows, fourthly, and in summary of his position, that any increase in the capacity to increase food will cause population to rise to the limits of this capacity. These, at any rate, were Malthus's original answers to the question. In later versions he laid more stress on the possibility that deliberate human control of fertility might break the link between the growth of population and food supply. This concession rather destroys the beauty of his theory, and some of his disciples, then and since, have been reluctant to accept it. On the other hand, the original version never found complete acceptance either, since there were always people who doubted each of the pillars on which the argument rested.

Let us first consider the effects of a rising standard of living upon the natural increase of population. The question has to be tackled by considering separately the effects on the birth rate, and the effects on the death rate.

Throughout most of the world's history birth and death rates have both been very high, and nearly equal to each other. Exact statistics do not go very far back in time. In the most primitive countries of our own day, where neither economic nor medical progress has yet had much effect, death rates run as high as forty per thousand. Much of this is accounted for by child mortality; in primitive conditions nearly half the children die before reaching the age of ten, and this accounts for about half the death rate. We cannot generalize from this what death rates must have been in history. Some countries are

healthier than others (e.g. less liable to malaria), and the incidence of famines, wars and epidemics must also have made the death rate very variable from year to year. All the same, over the long centuries death rates must have averaged somewhere around thirty to forty per thousand. Birth rates must also have been at about the same level, since population increased so slowly. It is thought that the world's population increased in the first 1,500 years A.D. at a cumulative rate not exceeding one per thousand per annum, so the birth rate can only have been very slightly larger than the death rate, when allowance is made for considerable fluctuations in the death rate, occasioned by sudden disaster.

Birth rates also have varied from country to country. In Western European countries they have seldom exceeded thirty-five per thousand, since records have existed, whereas in Asia or Latin America birth rates exceeding forty per thousand are quite common. One possible explanation is an earlier age of marriage. In communities where it is fashionable to have only two or three children later marriage may not make much difference to the birth rate, but it must be important in communities where birth control is not practised, since fertility falls with age. Another explanation is the differences in the percentage of women remaining single, which are due partly to differences in the sex-ratio of the adult population, and partly to differences in marriage customs. India and Ireland present the current extremes; in India only one per cent of women are still unmarried at the age of forty-five, while the corresponding figure for Ireland is twenty-six per cent. In most countries of Western Europe between fifteen and twenty per cent of women never marry, partly because the number of adult women exceeds the number of adult men; and though the figure has not always been so high, it seems always to have been much higher than the corresponding figures for Asia or Africa. If the fertility of married women is the same in two countries, and if in one all women marry and the birth rate is forty per thousand, while in the other twenty per cent of women do not marry, the birth rate in the latter will be nearer thirty-two. One must allow for illegitimate births among single women, and for the possibility that the women who do not marry would, if they married, have lower fertility than those who actually marry; nevertheless more single women and later marriage together explain well enough why the European birth rates have not exceeded thirty-five per thousand.

There is no evidence of birth rates rising with economic growth; the evidence is rather that they fall. Some writers in Malthus's day inclined to the view that the birth rate rises with economic development, the mechanism in communities which do not practise birth

U

control being presumably that the age of marriage falls as economic conditions improve. Marriage rates do fluctuate with the trade cycle, but over the longer period there is no evidence that the age of marriage falls in the early stages of economic development. The argument has been applied to the situation in England and in Ireland in the eighteenth century, but there is no evidence to support it, and, as we shall see in a moment, what happened to population in Ireland is easily explained without invoking any change in the birth rate. In the present state of our knowledge the best conclusion seems to be that in the initial stages of development all the effects are concentrated upon the death rate.

The death rate seems to fall in three stages, or alternatively because of three sets of factors. First it falls because of improvements in the food supply, due either to greater production or to better distribution. In the case of Ireland, where population quadrupled between 1700 and 1840, the main factor was greater production of food, due to the adoption of the potato, which yields much more food per acre than was previously obtained from cereals. In some other countries the main factor has rather been improvements in distribution, due to the cessation of wars, the opening up of trade in foodstuffs and the building of better communications. In the absence of trade and communications, each district depends for its food upon its own supplies, and a local failure of the crop may mean famine and death even if food is plentiful in other regions of the same country. Hence, countries in which the rainfall varies widely from year to year in each district may suffer very much from famine, if communications are inadequate, and may have a sharp fall in the death rate simply by building communications, and even without any change in their output of food.

A country which passes through this stage may knock as many as ten points off its death rate. This means that if its birth rate remains unaltered, its population will start to rise by one per cent per annum, doubling in seventy years and quadrupling in 140 years. This seems to be what happened in Ireland. There is no need to explain the Irish case by invoking an unusually low age of marriage, or unusually high fertility rates. What happened there is quite consistent with a birth rate of around thirty-five per thousand, associated with a death rate dropping to twenty-five per thousand as the potato came into general use. Similarly the upturn of populations in India and in Africa is adequately explained by trade, communications, and the elimination of local famines. The populations of India, and of some African countries, have risen in the past fifty years at an annual rate of one per cent, which is consistent with birth rates of forty and death rates of thirty per thousand. Death rates are still high in these

countries because they have not yet progressed far into the stages of medical improvement.

There are two medical stages, which occurred successively in Europe, but which are tending to occur simultaneously in the rest of the world. One of these stages is the adoption of public health measures, which get rid of the epidemics. The other is the widespread extension of medical facilities to private persons. The extension of curative medicine takes longer to accomplish than the public health work because it requires much greater resources; hospitals have to be built, and medical practitioners trained and spread throughout the country. Very few of the less developed countries have entered into this final stage of bringing down their death rates. But very many have entered the second, or public health stage, in which the great epidemic diseases are wiped out—plague, smallpox, typhus, cholera, typhoid fever, malaria, yellow fever (and eventually tuberculosis). In this second stage the death rate comes down another ten points. If the birth rate remains at forty, the population will increase by two per cent per annum, doubling every thirty-five years. Ceylon, Egypt, Mauritius, the West Indies, and many countries in Africa and in Latin America have already passed this stage. India is only just entering it, and this is why her population is increasing at the moment only by about $1\frac{1}{4}$ per cent per annum; in a very short time the extension of her public health facilities may be expected to rid her of cholera and malaria, and the other epidemic diseases from which she now suffers, and if her birth rate does not drop her population will then be increasing by around two per cent per annum.

In the third state the death rate drops to around ten per thousand, more or less, depending upon the age structure of the population. This results from making medical attention available to everyone. If the birth rate is still forty, population increases by three per cent per annum, doubling in twenty-five years. Some communities have reached this state, e.g. Puerto Rico, and others are well advanced towards it, such as Ceylon.

We can see from this analysis that it is too crude to link population increase directly to food supply in the first instance. Food supply may set a limit to population growth, but improvement in food supply is not the only cause of a falling death rate. Improvement in food supply operates only at the lowest levels of subsistence, and at these levels it will increase population only by 1 per cent per annum. If this were all there were to cope with, food supply might keep up with it for a very long time. The truth is rather that that part of the fall in the death rate which is due to medical improvement is even more spectacular than that part which is due to improvements in the food supply.

But whether population increases because of food supplies or because of medical improvements, Malthus asserted that the increase must in due course be brought to an end by the failure of food supply to grow so rapidly. This part of his analysis was falsified by the events of the nineteenth century. The best estimates we have suggest that in the half century or more before the first world war, world food supply was growing at a rate not much below two per cent per annum, while world population was growing only by about 0·7 per cent per annum. There was, as we know, a tremendous improvement in the diet of the working classes in Europe, America and Australia, corresponding to a great increase in the consumption of livestock products. Malthus over-estimated the rate at which improvements in the food supply would cause population to gorw (he spoke of three per cent, which no European community ever approached). He allowed for the possibility that a growing population might feed itself merely by bringing new lands into cultivation, but he did not foresee how rapidly this would be done in the nineteenth century; and he also underestimated the possible annual growth of yields per acre. None of this, however, diminishes the importance of the problem to which he drew attention. If no community reached the three per cent rate of population growth in the nineteenth century, several have reached it in the twentieth century; and there is not an unlimited supply of fresh lands to bring under cultivation.

It needs no elaborate argument to establish the proposition that if death rates fall from forty to ten, the world will soon be in a mess unless birth rates fall to much the same extent. This proposition does not depend wholly upon arguments about the supply of food. The food supply argument is important now, but may not matter in coming centuries. What the present carrying capacity of the world is no one knows. Different calculations are made, corresponding to different assumptions about diet, and about fertility. The present population is about 2,500 million, and the lowest estimate is that this is the largest population for which an *adequate* diet could be provided with current agricultural techniques; that is to say that if all the cultivable land not now cultivated were opened up, the result would only be sufficient to raise feeding standards everywhere to the European level. Other estimates run to as high as a carrying capacity of 10,000 million, assuming current average levels of feeding. Part of the difficulty in making these estimates lies in uncertainty as to the ultimate carrying capacity of the less well watered lands in the tropical parts of the world, say between 30°N. and 30°S. In this zone there are millions of square miles of arable land, receiving twenty-five to forty inches of rain per annum, mostly concentrated in a few months of the year,

and suffering from a long dry season during which vegetation dries up and the soil may be baked. The revolution in agricultural techniques which occurred in nineteenth century Europe applied to lands where some rain falls throughout the year, and where the land is never baked by extreme heat. The techniques which have been so fruitful in Europe and North America are not all directly applicable in the tropics, and may indeed do harm when transplanted, e.g. if mechanization exposes the soil to leaching. One of the great problems which the human race may have to solve, as population increases, is how to make the best use of these millions of square miles, now very sparsely occupied; and we cannot now be certain whether they will soon prove very productive, or whether they will continue for long to make small contribution to the world's food supplies.

Even the largest estimate of the present capacity of the world does not leave much leeway, since at its present rate of increase the world's population will reach 10,000 million in just over a century. However, the carrying capacity of the world grows all the time. Yields per acre in the most progressive agricultural countries have increased over long periods by figures ranging from 0·7 per cent to 1·5 per cent per annum (the greatest technical possibilities lying in the most backward countries). It is quite right to worry about the capacity of the world to feed itself during the next thirty years, during which it seems quite likely that population and food supply may be racing neck and neck. But what will happen to our techniques of producing food in a longer period than that is anybody's guess. If, for example, we learn to use the leaves of plants and not only their fruit, the world's feeding capacity will multiply enormously. Again, it was reported in 1954 that photosynthesis has been achieved in the laboratory, and if this becomes economically feasible on a large scale, food will be abundant for any conceivable population.

Accordingly the arguments about food are subsidiary to considerations of space. We may learn to make food out of hydrogen atoms, and to produce it in virtually unlimited quantities, but what are we to do about space? The total land area of the globe, including desert, ice and mountain, is only fifty-six million square miles. Suppose we allot each person only one square yard for standing room. Then if world population increases by as little as one per cent per annum, there will be standing room only in as little as 1,120 years from now. Perhaps in 1,120 years man will have taken again to the seas, or will have covered the earth with skyscrapers, or will be synthesizing more land out of hydrogen atoms, or will have colonized other planets. It is possible to shrug the problem away, either on the ground that something will turn up, or else on the ground that we need not worry about our descendants. But if one accepts neither of these evasions,

even those of us who most love the company of our fellow men would agree that it is undesirable that world population should grow by one per cent per annum for the next thousand years. Once the death rates are brought down, it is inescapable that the birth rates must fall to much the same extent if men are to live comfortably within the limits set by the land area of our present planet.

Apart from these global considerations, the individual country which goes through a phase of high birth and low death rates has to pay a substantial economic price for so doing. First, there is the cost of supporting the children. Whereas children under fifteen are only about twenty per cent of the population of Great Britain, they are about forty per cent of the population of Puerto Rico. The British proportion is a little too small to keep the population stable. On the other hand, the Puerto Rican proportion is a considerable burden upon the adult population, which has therefore to devote time and resources to bringing up children which could alternatively be used for raising the living standards of adults. The fact that this is regarded as a burden is, as we shall see, probably one of the most important reasons why falling death rates tend to be followed sooner or later by falling birth rates. Another cost of disequilibrium between birth and death rates is the effect of a rising population on output per head. There are a few countries still in the increasing returns stage, where a larger population would mean better use of public utilities and of facilities for manufacturing industry. These are located chiefly in Africa and in Latin America (see section 1(b) of this chapter). These, however, are very few in number. In most countries of the world an increase of population must tend to reduce output per head, unless capital is used up in providing additional resources for the new hands to work with. This is capital which could alternatively be used to raise capital and output per head of the existing population. We cannot be sure just how much capital is required for preventing the standard of living from falling in spite of population growth. If we use a capital-output ratio of four to one, then a country needs for this purpose net investment of four per cent of national income, if its population is growing by one per cent, of eight per cent if growing by two per cent, and of twelve per cent if growing by three per cent. When we remember that the least developed countries barely manage to invest five per cent of their national incomes per annum, it is clear that their standards of living must fall if they indulge in the luxury of increasing their populations by two or three per cent per annum.

Fortunately the available evidence suggests that falling death rates result in due course in falling birth rates. We cannot be absolutely certain of this because we do not really know why birth rates have

fallen, in the same sense as we know why death rates have fallen. In the past hundred years some European birth rates have fallen from around thirty-five to as low as fifteen per thousand. Some part of this fall was due to an increase in the number of women remaining unmarried, and some part may even have been due to the later age of marriage, but much the greatest part has been due to a decline in the willingness to bear children. We do not know what caused this decline. We assume, and argue, that it followed inevitably from the processes of economic growth, and that it will therefore be repeated in all countries as they undergo the same processes, but we have no certainty that things will turn out in this way.

It is pretty safe to assume that the fall in the birth rate is due to a change of attitude towards childbearing and not merely to new techniques of birth control. This can be safely assumed for two reasons. First, the decline of birth rates started before the new techniques were brought into use. The French birth rate had already started to fall at the beginning of the nineteenth century, and other European birth rates were falling from the middle of the century, whereas the new birth control appliances belong to the end of the century. Secondly, even today a very large proportion of the people who successfully practise birth control do not use the modern appliances. The method they use is that which is recorded in the Bible, and which has been known to human beings through long ages. If birth control was not practised two centuries ago, the reason was not that people did not know what to do, but rather that they did not wish to do it. Of course, once the changed attitude had occurred, the new availability of improved and more convenient techniques helped to spread willingness to control births, but these techniques would certainly not have spread so rapidly if there had not been a change of attitude towards childbearing.

What brought this change of attitude? Probably the most important reason is simply the fall in the death rate. In a community where sixty per cent of children born never become adults, if the average family wishes to have three adult children it must give birth to eight children, five of whom, on the average, die in childhood. Now an average of eight children per mother is just about the limit of human fertility, when childbearing takes place without restraint, so at these levels of mortality childbearing without restraint barely suffices to produce two to three adult children for the average family. Unrestrained childbearing gives a birth rate not much in excess of forty per thousand. Hence, if the death rate is around forty, the population will barely be maintained if women have as many children as they can. Childbearing then becomes a religious duty, in the interest of the preservation of the tribe, and the most fertile

women are held in high honour and respect, while barrenness is regarded as a curse. This attitude changes automatically when the death rate drops. As more children survive, it is not necessary to give birth to so many children. As far as population stability is concerned, if the expectation of life at birth rises to sixty-eight years, the population will be stable with birth and death rates of only about fifteen per thousand, which corresponds to the average family having only slightly more than two children. Sooner or later the disadvantages of a rapidly growing population become obvious to the leaders of the community, and the religious precepts urging maximum childbearing are dropped. Many primitive societies, fortunate enough to have death rates below forty, have adopted forms of population control, including taboos on sexual intercourse for two years after childbirth, abortion, and even infanticide. (Ireland took to very late marriage, and to a quarter of her women not marrying at all.) Parents also change their attitude; if one wishes to have three adult children it is no longer necessary to give birth to eight. At first it seems marvellous to be able to raise up so many fine sons and daughters, but as the number of people who can raise ten children increases rapidly the novelty and the distinction of the achievement wear off, especially if food is in short supply, or if jobs are hard to get, or if there is little land to bequeath to them. People begin to feel that having so many children has grave disadvantages, and interest in the techniques of birth control is aroused. If this analysis is right, it follows that a decline in the death rate is automatically followed, after a lapse of time, by a decline in the birth rate. Population grows by three per cent per annum only as a temporary phenomenon—temporary, however, only in a relative sense, since it may take two or three generations before the disadvantages of large families become so obvious as to change social attitudes.

Other factors work in the same direction. There is the improvement in the status of women, which results from women's education, and from widening opportunities for the employment of women outside the home; this causes some women to look upon childbearing as a temporary phase in their lives, which will soon leave them free to give their time to other things. Then there is the increase in other things to do with one's time. Economic growth means that there is a larger income to enjoy, and such enjoyment takes time. There is especially a growth of amusements outside the home, such as the cinema and visits to the seaside. Some nineteenth century women in the low income groups without domestic help hardly ever left their homes, except to go to church; where nowadays they demand much greater freedom of movement. It is sometimes said

that the secret of birth control is to introduce electric light into the homes, so that the family has plenty to do in the evenings, instead of going to bed at dusk, but it is hard to take this seriously. The point of the increase in the ways of using one's time is not that it diminishes the opportunities for childbearing, but rather that it makes child rearing rather more of a burden. Another change is that children have grown more costly; they can no longer be sent out to work at seven or eight, but must be kept at school until fifteen or later. In the western world the attitude towards children has also changed over the past two centuries or more, in that a cult of childhood has grown up. Children as such were not highly regarded in the seventeenth century or earlier, they grew up much as they could, without much attention. In these days, however, the development of personality in childhood has come to be regarded as of supreme importance. Parents feel a duty to do as much as they can for each child, and a corresponding duty not to have more children than they can attend to. Economic growth has also brought greater social mobility, and with it the desire of some parents to give their children as good an education and start in life as they can afford, so that they can move up the social ladder; this also increases the cost of children, and diminishes their number. It is particularly marked that people who are rising in the social scale have fewer children than those who are not; though it is hard to say whether this is because those who wish to rise find it easy to 'travel light', or because it is easier for those who have fewer children to rise. Behind all this also lies the greater application of reason to human conduct; people cease to regard children as 'coming from God'; they think they are entitled to plan their own lives for their own enjoyment, and to have no more children than fits into their plans. What was a subject for religion and morality becomes a subject for convenience and calculation. Many of these factors are associated with urbanization—greater education for women, greater employment outside the home, more opportunities for using leisure, restricted employment opportunities for children, greater social mobility and the more reasoning approach to life—so it is not surprising that the birth rate tends to be higher in rural areas than in towns.

All these factors are fruits of economic growth, so there seems to be justification for concluding that it is economic growth which brings down the birth rate and so restores the equilibrium which economic growth itself originally destroyed. The analysis is relevant to one of the controversies which divide the makers of population policy. According to one school of thought, if you wish to bring down the birth rate, concentrate on making propaganda for the new birth control techniques. According to the other school of thought, these

techniques will not be adopted unless there is first a change of attitude towards childbearing. This change is brought about by economic growth. Hence the way to bring down the birth rate is to concentrate on economic development. This is obviously a sham controversy. One needs to put all the ingredients into this pie: to convert social leaders into seeing the dangers of a high birth rate, so that the taboos and religious sanctions turn against it, instead of in its favour; to raise standards of living and of education rapidly, so that women find it convenient to have fewer children; and to make widespread propaganda about birth control techniques. Action is needed on all fronts simultaneously.

None of this is easy. Perhaps the easiest task is to persuade leaders to give guidance in the right direction. The fact that there will be standing room only in 1,000 years if populations increase by as little as one per cent per annum is easy to grasp, especially by the men who have been coming into power in the less developed countries in the last decade or two, who have for the most part the western rationalistic outlook. Priests are more difficult than politicians, but the only church which has taken a strong stand on these matters is the Roman Catholic Church, and even this approves of family limitation, provided that none of the modern birth control appliances is used. The great Eastern religions have no clear teaching on the subject, and in each of them some of the religious leaders have expressed their approval of birth control. There is not yet a sense of urgency in any of the countries which have the highest birth rates, but this may come. And, in any case, the birth control movement swept through Europe with neither religious nor official blessing.

To spread propaganda is not as easy in illiterate societies, in some of which women are kept in seclusion, as it was in Western Europe. In addition, the appliances used in Western Europe are both costly, in relation to the incomes of people in the poorer countries, and also inconvenient having regard to housing conditions and to their ways of life. Hence it is very desirable to invent some cheaper or more convenient form of birth control. This is why in birth control circles so much interest attaches currently to the possibility of manufacturing a pill which would induce temporary sterility, without other effects. Research is proceeding actively on this subject.

The hardest task of all is to raise the standard of living. If population is growing by 1½ per cent per annum, the minimum target we can set is to increase total output by 2 per cent per annum. This would double the standard of living only in 140 years, compared with the 40 to 80 year doubling achieved in Western Europe or the United States. But raising total output by 2 per cent per

annum is no mean feat. It requires considerable expenditures on education and other public services, a doubling of current capital formation, and many changes in beliefs and institutions. The 3 per cent increase in output which is required where populations are increasing by 2 to $2\frac{1}{2}$ per cent is even more difficult to achieve. A 4 per cent per annum increase in output is all that the United States achieved from 1870 to 1930, with all its vast expenditures on capital and on education, and its materialistic outlook and institutions. There is no sign of the less developed countries this side of the Iron Curtain beginning to adopt the sort of heroic measures which a 2 to 3 per cent per annum increase of output would demand Neither is there any sign of the more developed countries recognizing the magnitude of this problem to the extent of being willing to make an adequate contribution towards solving it. If raising the standard of living is a necessary condition for bringing the birth rate down, it looks as if the population problem will be with us for a good long time yet.

The population problem of the less developed countries is more acute than the European problem ever was, because European populations were never anywhere near a three per cent per annum rate of increase. (It is possible that the population of the U.S.A. was growing by three per cent per annum by natural increase in Malthus's day, as he said, corresponding to a birth rate of about fifty and a death rate of about twenty; but a birth rate of fifty requires the average mother to bear more than eight children, and this is the very limit of human fertility.) The lower rate of increase in the European countries was partly due to the fact that their birth rates at the inception of the change were around thirty-five instead of around forty to forty-five. And partly due to the fact that their death rates fell so gradually that birth rates had begun to fall before the death rates reached their lowest levels. Whereas it took Europe over a century to knock twenty points off the death rate, some other countries have recently achieved this feat in forty years or less. Since it takes some time before the birth rate responds to falling death rates—in Europe death rates were falling for half a century or more before birth rates started to fall—a rapid fall in the death rate may bring it down to ten while the birth rate is still at forty, and may thus produce a tremendous increase of population. The bigger the increase the harder it is to check, since the greater is the rate of growth of total output needed to achieve a rise in the standard of living. On the other hand it is not impossible that when the birth rates begin to fall in the under-developed countries they will, like the death rates, fall more rapidly than occurred in Western Europe. Whereas a fall in the birth rate of ten per thousand took seventy years to accomplish in France,

forty years in Sweden and Switzerland, and thirty years in England and Denmark, in the twelve years from 1924 to 1936 the birth rate fell from 40 to 26 in Bulgaria, from 35 to 26 in Poland, from 26 to 17 in Czechoslavakia, and from 35 to 27 in Japan. Everything tends to happen faster in these days than it did in the nineteenth century.

While it is true, for the reasons given above, that the population problem of some of the poorer countries is very serious, it is not true that population growth, actual or potential, is the principal reason why their levels of living are not rising. For example, the population of India is growing currently by $1\frac{1}{4}$ per cent per annum. This rate is lower than the current rate of population growth in the U.S.A., where nevertheless output per head doubles every forty years; and it is no greater than the rate at which European populations grew during the nineteenth century, when their levels of living were rising substantially. If Japan has been able to double output per head every twenty-five years since 1880, despite population growth, the rest of Asia, or Africa, could do the same. Japan is not particularly rich in natural resources; on the contrary, she is less well endowed than India is with coal and mineral ores. Population growth at the rates likely in the next two or three decades is not an insuperable obstacle to economic growth. Raising output per head is more difficult if population is growing by 2 per cent per annum than if it is growing by 1 per cent per annum, but the principal obstacle to raising output per head in these countries is not the rate of population growth but the fact that their rates of capital formation, at around 5 per cent, are much too low. If they were investing 10 to 12 per cent per annum their output per head would be rising, and this itself would be bringing down the birth rate, and reducing the rate of population growth.

When family limitation first catches on, it spreads in much the same way as other fashions; that is to say, it is first adopted by the highest social classes, and spreads downwards. Hence, a society in transition always shows fertility correlating inversely with income and with education. This is sometimes incorrectly interpreted as a sort of answer to Malthus, in the sense of arguing 'as people get higher incomes (or education) their fertility falls'. It is doubtful whether these correlations belong to other than a period of transition. There is no firm evidence that the rich have fewer children than the poor in stable societies, either when the birth rate is very high—e.g. in eighteenth century Europe or contemporary India—or when it is very low—e.g. in contemporary France; though it must be admitted that there is some evidence that it is the less fertile members of society who tend to rise into the highest social classes.

Another phenomenon which belongs to the transition, and which follows from the class difference in fertility, is a scare that intelligence

will decline. If the highest social classes have the highest intelligence, and produce fewer children relatively than the lower classes, it is argued that the average intelligence of the community must decline. This argument is disputed by those who deny that the higher social classes have higher intelligence; their greater wealth assures them better education, but their inheritable characteristics are not necessarily superior. This controversy has never got far for lack of acceptable evidence. Quite apart from class differences, there is evidence that in each social class the children of large families do not do as well in intelligence tests as the children of smaller families. This has been interpreted as meaning that it is the more intelligent members of the community who are most likely to limit their families, an interpretation which again leads to apprehension that the average intelligence of the community must fall. It may equally well be, however, that the children of smaller families show more intelligence only because their parents can give each of them more individual attention, and because they imitate and pit their wits against their parents to a greater extent, while children of large families move more in their own childish orbit.

Equally disquieting to some eugenists is what they expect from the decline of the death rate, irrespective of whether the population continues to increase, or declines. These eugenists argue that when the death rate is high, those who fail to survive to the age of reproduction, or who die without having had time to have large families, are to a greater extent the biologically inferior than is the case when the death rate is low; hence they conclude that the average biological quality of successive generations is not as high if the death rate is low as it would be if the death rate were high. Not everyone accepts the argument that the young people who survive a high death rate are on the average biologically superior to the young people who survive a lower death rate. As we have seen, high death rates are associated with nearly half the children born dying before they are ten; this accounts for about half of the death rate. Is there reason to believe that the half who die are on the average less physically fit or mentally alert than the half who live, or is their death due rather to a different exposure to the factors involved, such as bad living conditions, inadequate care, or the fortuitous incidence of epidemics? It is certainly true that a modern community deliberately keeps alive many adults who would otherwise perish in the competitive struggle, because they are temporarily ill or physically unfit, because they are insane or mentally distraught, or because their laziness, their fecklessness or their stupidity renders them incapable of earning a living. Some of these characteristics are transmitted biologically, while some are not. Firm conclusions on these matters await a clearer definition of

superior and inferior qualities, and a clearer understanding of the extent to which each quality depends upon a biological inheritance.

The decline in the death rate also gives rise to other, more transitional, problems. One of its effects is a very great increase in the proportion of people living beyond the age of sixty. If sixty is the normal age of retirement, this means an increase in the number of older people to share in the output of the younger people. This problem is only partly solved by raising the age of retirement, for even if the age of retirement is raised to seventy the number of people of that age and over is quite large in a stable population with an average expectation of life at birth of say sixty-eight years. On the other hand, the importance of this problem is usually exaggerated. For against the rise in the number of old people, which is due to the fall in the death rate, we must set the greater fall in the number of children, which is due to the fall in the birth rate. For example, the proportion of the population aged fifteen to sixty-four has risen in Britain during the past century from about sixty per cent to about seventy per cent; it is due to fall, but will still remain substantially higher than it was in the days when the birth rate was high. These changes are only transitional, in the sense that the proportions will be stabilized if both the population and the death rate become stable. If the population were stable, and everybody lived seventy-five years, the age-groups fifteen to sixty-four would contain sixty-seven per cent of the population. It is only if the birth rate increases sharply that the population aged fifteen to sixty-four may again fall below the level of sixty per cent.

There are also fears associated with stability in the numbers of the population, apart from the difficulties associated transitionally with a declining rate of growth. As we have already seen, the prophets of secular stagnation fear that in a stable population the economy may become less flexible, and that investment opportunities may be insufficient (Chapter V, section 3(d)). To these economic fears must be added the political fears of those who desire their country to have a large and growing population, whether for defence, or for aggressive purposes.

It is not inevitable that the birth rate, once it begins to fall, will fall to exactly the level which keeps the population stable. In several countries of western Europe it fell below this level during the nineteen-thirties, though it has since risen to the stability rate and beyond in most of them. Similarly we cannot be certain that it will ever fall in the less developed countries to the low levels to which it has fallen in Europe. If the population is to be stable at a low death rate, it must become fashionable to have not less than two children and not

more than three. In Europe during the twenties it was becoming fashionable to have only one child (at which level the population must decline), but this is now no longer fashionable. For all we know the fashion in Asia or Africa or in Europe may become three or four children (at which level population will double in about a century). At present these fashions seem to be determined mainly by ideas of personal convenience, featuring on the one hand love of children and family life, and on the other hand the cost and inconvenience of rearing children. One of the great advantages of current discussion of population problems is that it may result in parents taking into account the social problems which arise if it becomes fashionable to have less than two or more than three children. Probably we ought to be doing much more in the education of women and girls to bring the social issue into their consciousness.

We can see, in summary, how right Malthus was to revise the original version of his theory. It is simply not true that subsistence determines the rate of population growth. This is true enough in communities living in the high birth and high death rate stage of human history, but it ceases to be true as soon as men learn to control both birth and death rates. Human history then enters into a new era, in which our fate is in our own hands. The human race may die out because we fail to have enough children, or it may breed itself, subsistence permitting, into a stage where there would be standing room only if we were confined to living upon this planet. In which of these directions we shall travel no one knows.

(b) Size and Output

Our discussion of the effects of economic growth upon the size of the population leads straight to the next question which is sometimes asked, namely, what is the right size of population in relation to resources?

This is not primarily an economic question. One may ask, for example, what size of population would maximize output per head. There is not much hope of getting a precise answer to this question because of the great number of *cetera* upon which output depends; but the question is valid and meaningful. It cannot be assumed, however, that the right population is that which would maximize output per head. A country may prefer to have a smaller population than this; because of the alleged advantages of being a small nation, the compactness of the people, easier national unity, and freedom from external political responsibilities; or because it dislikes the processes by which population is enlarged—immigration, or the having of large numbers of children. Or alternatively it may be desired to have a population larger than that which maximizes output per head;

because of its value in defence or in aggression; or because of a desire to play a big part in world affairs; or because of a desire to accommodate immigrants, especially if they are refugees from religious or political persecution; or because of a liking for the company of other people in general, or of large numbers of children in particular. Thus the question what is the right size of population raises issues well beyond the scope of economic analysis.

Confining ourselves to economic aspects we observe four different senses in which the term 'over-population' is sometimes used. First, a country is said to be over-populated if it would have a larger output per head with a smaller population. Secondly, the term sometimes means no more than that the population is larger than can be fed without importing food. Thirdly, the term is used in an extreme sense, indicating that the country's population is so large relatively to its resources that a change in population would have no effect on total output. Finally, the term is used in a vague sense to indicate that a country is using up irreplaceable resources at an excessive rate. Let us dispose of this last sense first, since, as we shall see, it leads to no positive conclusions.

Other things being equal, the size of the population determines the rate at which mineral resources are used up. The more we consume of oil, or coal, or iron, or tin, or other minerals, the less there is left in the earth's surface for future use. Can we establish a 'right' rate at which these resources should be consumed?

Resource conservation raises three different issues. First, is it possible that in using up one resource we create another of equal value? Secondly, how much would it cost to use up the resource more slowly? And thirdly, how much do we weight the claim of future generations to consume when compared with our own claim? In addition, in answering these questions we must distinguish between the position of any one country and the position of the world as a whole, since it is open to one country, but not at present to the world as a whole, to exhaust its own minerals gaily, while trusting to be able to import from other places in future.

If we take first the using up of one resource in order to create another, we can see this most clearly if we consider the position of a single country. A country with a low standard of living, like Northern Rhodesia or Malaya or Trinidad, may find itself to be possessed of a mineral resource which the rest of the world values highly. If it refuses to exhaust this resource, its standard of living remains low. On the other hand, if it exploits the resource, funds become available for improving its capital equipment in other ways. More can be spent on education, on improving its agricultural land, on irrigation facilities, on public utilities, on research, and on surveying to find

new resources or new uses for other resources. As a result the exhaustion of its minerals may yet leave the country in a much better position to earn its living in the future than it would otherwise have been: one resource has been transformed into another. This is not, of course, always the case. Often the proceeds are used wastefully, or mainly on current consumption, so that when the resource is exhausted there is nothing left to show for it, and the economy lapses into stagnation: this is a common feature of former mining towns, and of some countries formerly rich in minerals. Often, too, the proceeds accrue to some other country; it may be foreign shareholders who reap the lion's share of the proceeds of mining, and use the funds to improve the capital equipment of their own countries, instead of the country out of whose soil the mineral is coming; or it may be that the mining is done by immigrants, who rush in, extract what they can, and emigrate when the mineral is exhausted, leaving nothing but an ugly mess behind. Mining can be made to create resources as valuable as those which are being exhausted, but this does not happen unless the country insists that a large part of the proceeds is to be invested in new resources (including education). All the same, the new resource is not always an adequate substitute for the old. Take the position of a primitive country which discovers that it possesses coal, or iron ore. These are resources on the basis of which great industries can be established. It may not be in a position to establish such industries, because its people lack the necessary education and capital. So it may decide temporarily to export its ore or its coal, as a means of earning funds with which to build up its productive capacity. Yet, if it is exporting the ore or the coal, when the time comes that it is in a position to establish industries on these bases, there may be no ore or coal left. With these two minerals in particular it is not always easy to decide whether they should be exported now, as a source of funds, or kept for some uncertain future as the basis of local industries.

Much the same difficulty arises when we move from the level of the individual country to that of the world as a whole. It is then only in a very limited sense true that in using up one resource one may create another of equal value. It is true that the rapid using up of minerals in the past two centuries has stood behind the enormous increase of our knowledge and of our productive capacity; future generations would not have been advantaged if we had bequeathed them the minerals in the ground without the knowledge of how to use them or all the other scientific knowledge which they will inherit. But what use will they find in a great deal of knowledge if they do not also get the resources to which to apply it? It is possible also that this knowledge may enable them to discover new resources, or new uses

x

for what was previously considered useless (bauxite and uranium were until recently just types of 'stone'). It may even enable them to synthesize all they need from the air, building it up from atoms of hydrogen. In other words, it is difficult to assess just how much of a bad turn, if any, we do to our descendants by using up resources now. They may be better off, because of the knowledge and other capital which we are thus enabled to bequeath them in exchange; or alternatively they may curse us for our improvidence, just as some Middle Eastern and North African peoples may now feel inclined to curse their ancestors for destroying the forests which were once there, and whose removal has so extended the area of the desert.

The rate at which we use up resources is also determined by the cost of using resources with greater care. For example, in mining there are ores of varying degrees of purity. It is always possible to get more mineral out of a given patch of ground by taking out also the inferior ores. Similarly, forests can be cut more or less destructively, and greater or less care can be taken in replanting. Exactly the same applies to agriculture. In most countries it is becoming a moral law (sometimes even with legal sanction) that soil fertility must be conserved. This has by no means been the universal attitude. On the contrary, in many countries shifting cultivation is still exceedingly common, with its implication that it does not matter if we exhaust the fertility of this bit of soil because we can pass on to another bit next year; the case differs slightly from that of minerals if the soil is able to regain its fertility when left fallow, but in fact many soils treated in this way have lost their mineral content, and even their capacity to rebuild their humus supplies. In all these cases the natural resource could be preserved, whether absolutely or merely to a greater extent, at some cost. The commercial user matches this cost against the gain; the cost of mining the inferior ores, against their price; the cost of replanting the forest, or of cutting more selectively; the cost of measures of soil conservation. If the community does not accept this judgement, it has ways of inducing or of enforcing more careful use of resources. Inducement takes essentially the form of subsidizing methods which give more intensive use; such is the effect of the method of levying royalties on gold mines which is now used by the government of South Africa; or of subsidies for planting trees; or subsidies for bringing inferior land into cultivation, or subsidies for soil conservation measures. Alternatively, the law is called upon to enforce more careful use, by laying down standards for replanting or for soil conservation, and by imposing penalties for breaches of these standards.

Behind all this lies the question, what does our generation owe to the future? Why should we not use what we want now, and leave

future generations to fend for themselves? Why should their happiness in the future be accounted of greater importance than our happiness now? For example, take the population problem. Suppose that a country has enough coal to supply 10,000 million man-years of consumption. Why is it better to have twenty million people consuming it over 500 years rather than fifty million people consuming it over 200 years? Or take the case of soil conservation; if we use up enough of our labour now for this purpose we can bequeath the soil to our descendants not only in as good but also in a much better condition than that in which we have found it. But why should we incur these costs on their behalf? Or why, for that matter, do we make any investments now whose fruit will not be fully enjoyed in our own lifetimes—investments in damming rivers for hydro-electric power, for instance? These questions are not answerable except in terms of our respect for the continuity of the human race. Most of us have a feeling—whether it is an innate instinct or something we are taught cannot be said—that the future of our community is important, and that each of us in particular, and our generation in general, ought to make some sacrifice of present comfort in the interest of generations to come. There is no means of measuring how large this sacrifice should be, and, correspondingly there is no objective answer to the question 'what is the right rate at which to use up resources?' Each community has to decide these matters for itself in each generation.

We are on firmer ground when we enquire into the relationship between current output and current population. The relationship between population and output per head is a matter of the advantages of specialization and the economies of large scale production on the one hand, and the diseconomies of more intensive and extensive use of natural resources on the other hand. The bigger the population the greater are the opportunities for specialization, not only of persons, but also of firms and of industries. 'The division of labour is limited by the extent of the market.' It is true that the existence of international trade makes specialization possible to some extent irrespective of the size of the country—indeed in another sense the smaller the country the more highly specialized it usually is. But since there are many activities which cannot be supplied by foreign trade— housing, personal services, internal transport, etc.—it remains true that there will be larger internal specialization the greater the internal market. Besides, foreign trade has its own handicaps and instability which diminish its attraction when compared with internal trade. All this line of reasoning applies equally to the economies of large scale production. These economies can sometimes be secured by producing for export, but in many cases (e.g. some public utilities)

the product is not exportable; and in any case, because of the greater risk of foreign trade, the economies of scale are more likely to be exploited for the domestic market than if the investor has to rely on disposing of the major part of his output in foreign markets.

The industries which benefit most from a large market are the public utilities, and some factory industries which work with metals, especially in the early stages of metal production. The public utilities—transport, electricity, gas, water—show very marked economies as population grows denser, since their roadways, pipes, and transmission lines are then more fully utilized. The factory industries making consumer goods and machinery on the whole reach their optimum size very soon, unless they are assembly industries. It is mainly the factory industries processing the metal ores, and those making basic chemicals, which enjoy the largest economies of scale. All the same, most industries gain advantage from operating in a country which is large enough to support a range of other industries, even if the average factory is small, because of the extent to which industries depend on each other either as sources of materials, components, and services, or else as purchasers of intermediate output or of by-products. On the other side, the diseconomies of scale show up most quickly in agriculture and in mining. As population increases it becomes necessary to cultivate the less fertile lands, or to work the fertile lands more intensively, and in either case the result is diminishing returns.

It follows that the population which a country can carry without diminishing returns depends upon whether its natural resources fit it to be a manufacturer of metal goods and heavy chemicals, or whether they fit it primarily to engage in agriculture. In the former case, it may continue to secure increasing returns over a considerable increase in population, whereas in the latter case diminishing returns set in much earlier. We have also the paradox that a country may be over-populated relatively to its agricultural resources, but underpopulated relatively to its capacities for industrial development. Some very small countries, like Jamaica or Mauritius, face the problem that their populations are much too large in relation to agriculture, and at the same time much too small to support a wide range of industrial development.

It follows also that a country is not to be described as overpopulated simply because it has more people than can be fed from its own lands. This is another sense in which the term is sometimes used. It would indeed be a useful sense if international trade in food were not possible, or were very costly, or if one were studying the problem mainly in the light of military strategy. In Western Europe it takes about one acre to feed one person, if we include children as

one unit each, and if we take three acres of grassland as roughly equivalent to one acre of arable land. In the United States of America the standard of feeding is about the same, but the productivity of land is much lower, so it takes more than two acres to feed each person. The position of other countries is determined on the one hand by their standard of feeding, and on the other by productivity. A great deal depends upon the amount of livestock products consumed (meat, milk, butter, etc.), since these are very costly in terms of land. For example, India consumes less than two-thirds of the calories per head consumed in Europe, and only a fraction of the protein, but this is offset by the lower productivity of land; her population therefore feeds at the rate of about four-fifths of an acre per person.

Given the possibility of importing food the carrying capacity of agricultural land ceases to be decisive in determining what the maximum population should be. A country may be in a position to increase its income by concentrating on developing other more valuable skills or resources, and may deliberately leave lands idle and import food, even though it could feed itself if it had to. A country which has not enough land to feed its population may yet be under-populated if it has other resources or skills such that a further increase in population would increase output per head. This is not to say that a country cannot be over-populated so long as it can engage in manufacturing, or in some other activity, for it is quite possible to be over-populated in manufacturing, as well as in agriculture, or in anything else, if a smaller population would show a larger output per head. The point of this paragraph is merely that one must take all activities into account when judging whether a country is over-populated, and not its agricultural resources only.

However, while it is true that the individual country is not necessarily over-populated merely because it cannot feed itself, the same argument does not apply to the world as a whole. As we have seen, estimates of the current carrying capacity of the world lie between 2,500 million and 10,000 million people, and at the present rate of increase ($1\frac{1}{4}$ per cent per annum) world population would reach the upper figure in just over a century. On the other hand our techniques of producing food are improving all the time. Yields per acre in the agriculturally advanced countries have in the past shown some substantial increases, and it is quite impossible to foresee what the rate of technical progress will be in the future. The fact that world population is growing faster than world yields per acre causes many people to give added weight to the argument that it is dangerous for any country to rely on being able to import food. They think, for example, that the British future would be much more secure if the population of Great Britain were not more than twenty-five million,

arguing that at that level the population would be large enough to exhaust practically all the large scale economies of the public utilities and manufacturing industry, while at the same time small enough to reduce dependence on outside food supplies to very small proportions. All these arguments, however, necessarily rest upon speculations about a most uncertain future.

It is also necessary to make the point that even if we could establish that output per head would be bigger if population were say twenty per cent smaller, it would not follow that output per head would rise if that number emigrated, or if the birth rate fell. These population comparisons are based on the assumption of an unchanged population structure in the sense that the proportions of old and young, male and female, skilled and unskilled remain the same. Whereas, as the population changes, its structure also changes, not always for the better. We have already discussed the problems of transition in section 1(a) of this chapter.

The remaining sense of the term over-population refers to the state of affairs where the population of a country is so large that if it were larger output would be no bigger. This is the extreme form of the first sense of the term. In the first sense output per person decreases as population increases, but total output increases; in this sense total output does not even increase. This extreme state of over-population is, alas, not unknown. It can usually be recognized from the excessive numbers attached to certain sectors of the economy, especially domestic service, petty trade, casual employments and agriculture. Domestic service swells because such economies adjust themselves to the need for each person to provide as much employment as he can; social prestige requires each person to have servants if he can, and the wealthier members of the community have to fill up their households with hordes of retainers who are little more than a drag on the purse. An extreme example of this is the island of Barbados, where sixteen per cent of the population is recorded by the census as engaged in domestic service. Petty trading shows similar extension; market places are crowded with stalls, in which each seller makes only a very few sales—selling and passing the time away in gossip being almost indistinguishable. Then there are the hordes of porters, jobbing gardeners, and others who get such casual employment as they can, averaging perhaps a day a week or less. In agriculture the phenomenon shows itself in the smallness of the farms; the plot cultivated by the average family is so small that it cannot fully occupy all the time of members of the family. Whether the excess of population shows itself mainly in agriculture, or mainly in domestic service, trading and casual jobs, depends on whether agriculture is operated with wage labour or by peasants. If it is operated with

wage labour (e.g. Barbados) it will not employ more people than are needed for cultivation, and the surplus must then find a living outside agriculture. But if it is operated by peasants, the surplus lives on the family farms, and there may be very little surplus in other occupations. The normal tendency in over-populated countries is for the great landowners to let their lands to peasants for rent, rather than to hire agricultural labourers. They get more this way, since the wage they would have to pay to labourers is more than is left to the peasants when rents have been extracted from them.

Various attempts have been made to measure over-population in this extreme sense. The measurement of the rural surplus depends upon estimating how many gainfully occupied persons are needed in agriculture per acre under cultivation, given the crops, the techniques, and the equipment in use. Some crops are much more labour intensive than others; rice much more so than wheat, and sugar or tea much more so than maize or cocoa or rubber. The equipment also makes a great difference, since whereas a family with hoes is fully stretched with three or four acres, a family with draft animals and ploughs can manage ten to fifteen acres, and a family with a tractor thirty acres or more. It has also to be remembered that labour requirements vary with different operations; in some crops the maximum labour requirement is for ploughing, while with others it is for harvesting. It follows that the degree of over-population cannot be estimated by some generalization, but must be calculated separately for each locality. When such calculations are made for the less developed economies the labour requirement in cereals (excluding rice) with plough and draft animals, ranges from about fourteen to about twenty persons per 100 acres under cultivation. Detailed calculations for India, where there are currently about twenty-seven persons gainfully employed in agriculture for each 100 acres under cultivation have led to the conclusion that at least a quarter of the agricultural population is surplus to requirements. This is equivalent to having some twenty million people permanently unemployed; hence the phenomenon is often referred to as 'disguised unemployment'. This phenomenon is rare in Africa and in Latin America, but it repeats itself in China, in Indonesia, in Egypt and in many countries of Eastern Europe.

This sort of over-population, in addition to wasting labour frequently also reduces the fertility of the soil. One reason may be that in extreme cases the people cannot afford to keep cattle, because cattle eat too much; so the land does not get manure. (The Indian peasants cannot afford to keep as many cattle as they do, but hold on to cattle for religious reasons; the land does not benefit as it might, however, since half the dung is burnt as fuel.) Another reason is the

pressure to use every inch of ground; land is put under the plough which ought to be left in forest, or which should be left for purposes of soil conservation. Then there is the temptation to over-crop the land; to take off too many crops in one year, or to cut down on fallow periods. The Law of Diminishing Returns states that if there are too many people on too little land the marginal product of labour will be negative, and this, alas, is only too familiar a feature of over-populated countries.

Given a population of this size the obvious policy is to develop as much employment as one can off the land. This is not only the obvious means of increasing non-agricultural output, but it may also be a necessary move in trying to increase soil fertility itself. If one could get some of the people off the land, return some land to forest, use some more for erosion control, and increase fallow periods, agricultural output would by definition increase, though not necessarily at once. It would also be possible to increase the size of the average farmer's holding, but this would not necessarily increase agricultural output, since yields per acre tend to be highest on the smallest farms; it might increase output, however, if the farmers, now better off, were able to save more and to invest in improving their land. It is not, however, by any means easy to expand non-agricultural employments rapidly enough to cope with the increase of population and as well to reduce some of the agricultural surplus. Suppose that the farm population is 70 per cent of the whole, and that population is increasing by $1\frac{1}{2}$ per cent per annum. Then, if the rural surplus is to be reduced, non-agricultural employments must expand by more than 5 per cent per annum. Not many of the less developed economies have succeeded in industrializing rapidly enough to reduce their agricultural populations absolutely. Japan and the U.S.S.R. have managed to do this, but their rates of industrial expansion have been phenomenal, compared with say the U.S.A. or Germany.

Employing more people off the land does not provide food; on the contrary, it increases the demand for food relatively to the supply. Any such policy must therefore be accompanied by a vigorous programme for increasing yields per acre, through an extensive network of agricultural instruction, through greater use of fertilizers, through multiplication and distribution of better types of seed, through greater conservation and distribution of water, and in all the other ways which Japanese experience has demonstrated to be capable of increasing agricultural output rapidly. But the policy also involves much more than this. When the standard of living is low the home demand for manufactured goods is small—less than fifteen per cent of national income, in terms of income generated in manufacture (i.e. excluding the value of the materials used), and even less than this in

terms of numbers employed. Hence if the people are to be employed producing manufactures there will soon come a point where more manufactures cannot be sold profitably on the home market, so that if full employment is to be attained surplus manufactures must be exported. This is the common fate of all countries which are over-populated relatively to their agricultural resources—Britain, Japan, Egypt, Germany, India or others—they can make a living for all their people only by exporting manufactures in return for food and raw materials. The development programmes of all such countries have to provide for making a bid for capturing foreign markets in manufactures (e.g. Germany, Japan), or else (like India's 'First Five Year Plan') they have to play down industrialization, and to leave the rural surplus where it is.

Capturing a larger share of the world market for manufactures is no easy task. The market for metal goods and engineering products generally increases steadily, but the market for other goods grows very slowly, or in some cases (e.g. textiles) contracts absolutely. Hence the countries which are well endowed with coal and ores can increase their shares of world trade in manufactures relatively easily if they try to. On the other hand, those over-populated countries which have very little coal or metallic ores can compete effectively only in the types of goods (textiles, leather goods, finished small wares) which are increasingly difficult to sell. To say this, however, is only to say that a country which allows its population to grow excessively in relation to its natural resources will have very great difficulty in providing full employment for its people, and in assuring them a reasonable standard of living.

Is it possible, in the light of this discussion, to arrive at conclusions on the present degrees of under- or over-population of the various countries of the world? This is an extremely hazardous exercise, since the resources of the various countries are not known, and since the potentialities of what is known change with new techniques and new demands. However, for what it is worth we may hazard the following guesses about the continental masses. Africa is under-populated, in the sense that that continent still has empty cultivable lands, and in the sense that its present sparse population makes the provision of public utilities very expensive; if Africa had a larger population the cost per head of roads, electric power, water supplies, railways, hospitals and other services would fall, while the quality could also be improved. There are some congested areas in Africa, in Eastern Nigeria, in parts of Kenya, and in parts of the Union of South Africa, but the continent as a whole, south of the Sahara, is under-populated. Latin America and Australia are probably both under-populated in the same sense, though the extent of the empty

cultivable lands is in both cases much more uncertain. At the other extreme, Asia is heavily over-populated, though there are parts of South-East Asia of which this is not true. Time may alter the value of the natural resources of Asia; new techniques may make her soils much more productive than we at present imagine possible, or great new mineral resources at present unsuspected may become available. On current knowledge, however, there is no doubt that the number of mouths there are to feed keeps down the standard of living of Asia. In between come the economies of Europe and of North America. These can be complementary, and should be considered together. Europe is not over-populated if she can get food and raw materials cheaply from North America, as was the case until 1939. Canada may be under-populated, having regard to her newly discovered resources. The United States is a very doubtful case, probably neither over- nor under-populated. The tentativeness of judgements relating to Europe and North America emphasizes how difficult it is to weigh in the balance the diseconomies of a large population with regard to food and raw materials on the one hand, and its economies in regard to manufacturing, public utilities, and other services on the other hand.

(c) Occupations

The occupational structure of the population is a function of its age structure, of the nature of its resources, of its size, and of real income per head.

The proportion of the population which is 'gainfully occupied' or 'economically active' in the census sense is determined partly by the age structure, and partly by the extent of women's employment. Counting the gainfully occupied on an internationally comparable basis is difficult because it is not easy to know just how to classify farmers' wives. What the census shows has therefore always to be taken with reserve. However, when the figures have been adjusted to a nearly comparable basis, it seems that the proportion gainfully occupied runs from about 33 per cent to about 45 per cent, with the poorer countries at the lower end and the richer countries at the upper end.

Age structure is important. It makes a great difference whether children under fifteen are twenty per cent or forty per cent of the population, and whether adults over sixty-five are five per cent or fifteen per cent. So also it matters whether the young and the old are at work or not. With economic growth the proportion of children in school grows, and the number of years of schooling. The age of retirement also tends to fall, because of greater use of insurance and pension schemes. Despite these factors however, the influence of the

declining proportion of children is such that, if we were to consider males only, the proportion of the population which is gainfully employed would in nearly all cases be much higher in rich than in poor countries.

The proportion of women gainfully occupied depends partly upon the proportion of women to men in the adult population, and partly on the extent of women's work within the household. These two factors together make an enormous difference. In the United Kingdom the number of women gainfully occupied is equal to 47 per cent of the number of men, whereas the comparable figure for the United States, where the numbers of adult men and of adult women are nearly equal, is only 33 per cent, and the figure for Egypt, where women's opportunities are very restricted, is only 17 per cent.

The difference between the number of men and the number of women in the population arises out of war, migration, the fact that more boys are born than girls, and the fact that women live longer than men. In the U.K. there are 11 per cent more women than men in the age groups 20-64, and this is the principal reason why the ratio of women to men gainfully occupied is much higher there than in the U.S.A. (The fall in child mortality, which affects boys more than girls, is reducing the surplus of women.) On the other hand if we compare the developed countries with the under-developed, the principal reason for the higher ratio of women in employment is the greater opportunity for women to work outside the household.

The extent of women's employment outside the household depends primarily on the stage of economic development which has been reached. Economic growth emancipates women from the household. Many of the jobs which they have been doing inefficiently and with drudgery in the home are transferred to external establishments, where they are done with greater specialization and greater capital— transporting water to the home, grinding cereals, cooking the mid-day meal, spinning, weaving and dressmaking, teaching children, minding the sick, and so on. Correspondingly women are released from working in the home, and transfer to working in these external establishments, where they do the same kind of work, or else to working in offices, in shops, in factories and in professions in a variety of jobs which were not open to them before. Hence most censuses which are taken on a comparable basis show the proportion of women gainfully occupied outside the household increasing from decade to decade with economic growth. (If population is increasing rapidly without economic expansion the reverse may happen; in the scramble for employment men displace women, and the proportion of women gainfully occupied falls. There is some evidence for this in British West Indian censuses, but these censuses are diffi-

cult to interpret confidently because of changes in definitions.) The increase in the proportion of women gainfully occupied is not all an addition to output, because there is a corresponding reduction in work done at home. But there is no reason to doubt that it represents a net increase, because of the superior productivity of the work done in the external establishments, with greater specialization, capital and mechanical power. The effect in raising the status of women, and of increasing the opportunities open to them is also tremendous.

The extent of women's employment also varies very much from one locality to another even inside the same country. For example, in 1939 whereas there were 52 women gainfully employed for every 100 men in the county of Lancashire, there were only 15 women gainfully employed for every 100 men in South Wales. This difference is due in the first place to the basic industry of each community; women find more employment in areas which specialize in the lighter industries than they find in areas which specialize in heavy industries, in mining, in agriculture, or in other occupations which do not traditionally employ women. This means that in every area of the latter kind there is a large reservoir of potentially employable female labour which would come into the labour market if some enterprising employers were to start new light industries there. In fact a good deal of the expansion of employment in Great Britain since 1939 has been due to the establishment of new factories in such areas, creating new opportunities for female labour. This is one of the surest ways of adding to the national income of the less developed countries. In many of these countries, especially in Africa and in Latin America, there is a shortage of male labour, which could be offset by making much better use of female labour. The question is not so important in those countries of Asia where there is in any case a surplus of male labour, but even there income could be increased by fostering some of the industries for which women are specially suitable. The experience of highly industrialized countries, such as the United Kingdom, shows that while there is naturally a tendency for private industry to move into the localities where women's labour is not fully utilized, private initiative works very slowly—or there would not be such a disparity between the figures quoted for Lancashire and for South Wales. This is one of the matters very much to be borne in mind by Departments of Labour and others whose concern it is to match demand and supply in the labour market.

So much for the factors which determine what fraction of the population is gainfully occupied. Next we come to the way in which the gainfully occupied are distributed between different activities. This depends partly upon the country's resources, and even more

upon the stage of economic development which it has reached. This branch of economic enquiry owes much to Dr. Colin Clark, whose famous book, *The Conditions of Economic Progress*, was the starting point of recent researches in this subject. The raw material for these researches is provided by population censuses, but there are difficulties in interpreting these censuses to which we must refer before proceeding further.

The first difficulty arises out of the increasing specialization which occurs with economic growth. For example, at a low level of development a man may build his own house, grow food, transport it to market, sell it there, buy textile fibres, and make them up into clothes for himself. He appears in the census as a farmer. At a much later stage of development each of these activities is done by specialists—by builders, by farmers, by transport workers, by commercial agents and by manufacturers—so the census shows a great expansion of these trades, and a fall in the proportion of farmers. The census shows the degree of specialization, rather than the sort of work which is done. There is a similar difficulty in interpreting the expansion of trades to which household activities are transferred; as the housewife ceases to fetch her own water, to grind her own grain, to nurse her own sick, and so on, the census shows a sharp expansion of the numbers specializing in these trades which greatly exceeds the net increase in the amount of such service which the community actually consumes. Then there is the further difficulty that some of the trades which contract in the census figures contract not because there is a fall in the amount of work done in these trades, but simply because their members are more fully occupied. In the over-populated countries the farmers, the petty traders, the domestic servants and many classes of casual labour are not fully occupied. As economic development occurs there is a shift to the new types of employment which open up, and the reduction of 'disguised unemployment' shows itself in a relative contraction of the trades which have been carrying the surplus. The moral is that the census figures only indirectly reflect the demand for services; hence when we compare the results of successive censuses we should strictly speak only of changes recorded in the numbers in different occupations, and only more gingerly refer to these changes as reflecting changes in demand.

The most striking feature which we observe when comparing censuses of rich with censuses of poor countries, whether it be different countries at the same date, or the same country at different dates, is the sharp fall in the proportions recorded in agriculture as we pass from poverty to riches. The poorest countries show seventy per cent or more engaged in agriculture, whereas the richest can feed themselves twice as well with only twelve to fifteen per cent in agriculture.

As we have just seen, this seventy per cent or more overestimates the amount of farm work done—farmers at this level do much more than farming, there may be some 'disguised' unemployment, and there are difficulties in classifying the farmers' wives. All the same there are real forces on the side of demand and of supply which also reduce the real labour done in farming. On the side of demand there is the fact that the income elasticity of demand for food is less than unity; that is to say, as real income per head increases, the demand for food does not increase so rapidly. And on the side of supply there is the increased use of capital in agriculture which makes it possible for each farm worker to cultivate an increasing number of acres, and the increased technical knowledge which makes each acre more productive. What happens to the proportion required in agriculture depends simply on whether the demand for food per head is increasing faster or more slowly than is productivity per person in agriculture. If these two rates are the same, the proportion required in agriculture will be constant; whereas if for instance demand per head increases by 0·8 per cent per annum whereas productivity per head increases by 1·3 per cent per annum, then in fifty years the proportion required in agriculture will fall by 22 per cent (say from 60 per cent to 47 per cent). The main reason why the proportion recorded in agriculture does fall as income per head rises is that agricultural productivity per person does increase faster than consumption per head.

Indeed one may reverse the relationship and say that in a closed economy it would be one of the conditions for economic growth that agricultural productivity should be rising rapidly. For if productivity were not increasing faster than demand, agriculture would not be releasing the labour which was needed for expanding other industries, and the expansion of these industries would also be held up by the steady movement of the terms of trade against them (i.e. food prices would be rising relatively to all others). Even in an open economy it is very convenient to have agricultural productivity increasing, for without this, economic growth raises food imports, and since this upsets the balance of payments unless other imports can be cut or unless exports are growing *pari passu*, economic growth then becomes dependent upon the rate at which exports can be expanded. In addition, if agricultural productivity is rising fast enough, the savings of the farmers, forced or voluntary, may become available to finance investment in other sectors of the economy. This is why the proportion of the population engaged in agriculture, and the rate of growth of agricultural productivity are two of the best indices of the extent and rate of economic growth.

Nearly as spectacular as the fall in agriculture is the rise of the

proportion recorded in manufacturing. Here again we have to discount the figures, remembering that some of the rise is merely a transfer from unrecorded work in households to recorded work in factories. All the same, there is without doubt a considerable increase in the proportion of manufacturing activity as income per head grows. Census figures show as little as from five to ten per cent of the population in manufacturing in the poorest countries, depending upon whether the domestic handicraft industries have been more or less preserved (as in India) or whether they were destroyed at an early date by cheap factory imports (Ceylon). The proportion rises to twenty-five per cent or so in the richest countries if they do relatively little trade in manufactures (U.S.A.), and to as much as thirty-five per cent or more if they earn their living in foreign trade by exporting say one-third of their manufactures (U.K., Belgium). The proportion in manufactures rises because the demand for manufactures increases much faster than productivity, as income grows, and also, in the over-populated countries, because exporting manufactures is the only way of providing full employment and food. The proportion engaged in manufacturing is therefore, like the proportion engaged in agriculture, one of the clearest indices of the degree of economic growth.

Within the sphere of manufacturing there is also considerable change as between the different manufacturing industries, as Dr. Hoffmann has shown (see Bibliographical Note to this Chapter). In the earliest days of economic development capital per head is small, and both the investment and the replacement demands for machinery are small. Hence consumer good production figures most in manufacturing employment—especially the production of clothes. In the later stages of development, however, gross investment is higher—it may have risen say from 6 to 20 per cent of gross national income, and there is a corresponding expansion of the industries producing steel, machinery, cement and other building materials relatively to the consumer good industries. This change can be speeded up. It is theoretically possible to embark upon economic growth by going through a period of enormous investment, while postponing increased consumption until considerable capital has been created; this was the basis of Soviet planning in the 1930's. If this happens, we get first an enormous expansion of capital good industries, and only subsequently an expansion of consumer good industries. The main obstacle to this procedure is of course to finance a programme of large capital investment at a time when real income is still very low. The expenditure on the capital good industries generates consumer demand, with the result that if the capital good industries are expanding more rapidly than consumer good production the country must

run into all the economic and political results of inflation, unless it has a growing propensity to save. Most countries find it easier to begin their industrialization by expanding their consumer good industries, because of the difficulty they have in saving enough or raising enough in taxes to finance a high level of investment.

The relative importance of consumer good and capital good industries depends also upon natural resources, and the possibility of foreign trade. The most important capital good industries are based upon cheap fuel and metallic ores, and countries which have not such fuel and ores cannot get far in building up such industries. We can check the importance of metals by various indices. For example, the Gold Coast imports most of its requirement of manufactures; roughly 40 per cent of its imports of manufactures (excluding mineral oil) consists of metallic manufactures. Or take the example of the United Kingdom, where 47 per cent of the people engaged in manufacturing are in metal making or metal using industries. Or the example of world trade in manufactures, of which 56 per cent is in metallic manufactures. Since fuel and metallic ores are not widely distributed, some countries must specialize in metallic industries to a greater extent than others. Metallic commodities will be imported by some and exported by others. Hence, as we have seen before, countries which are over-populated relatively to their agricultural resources are in a very bad way if they are also poor in fuel and minerals, since they are then compelled to specialize in producing for export just the kind of manufactures which each country could make for itself; for example Japan, where in 1936 only 28 per cent of the factory population was in the metal industries; and only 20 per cent of exports of manufactures was metallic.

The decline of the proportion recorded in agriculture is not exactly offset by the increased proportion recorded in manufacture. If we take the richest countries, while agriculture may have declined say fifty-five points (say from sixty-seven to twelve per cent) manufacture may have grown only twenty-five points (say from five to thirty per cent), the remaining thirty points representing the expansion of other types of employment. There is usually a rapid expansion of government activity, of teaching, of medical services, of entertainments of various kinds, and of commerce and finance. It is an open question how much of this activity is to be considered a net addition to the national income (e.g. that part of transportation which is used for travelling for pleasure) and how much rather as a cost of making the national output available (e.g. that part of transportation which carries freight, or carries people to work). Some people trying to measure the real increase in national output would exclude most of these service industries. They would take indices of the output of

farms, mines and factories, and would make limited allowances for residential building, for education, for health and for entertainment, thus leaving out most of the increase in public administration, in transportation, and in commerce. We need not enter into these questions here, since it is not part of the purpose of this book to discuss how the national income should be measured (see Chapter I). It suffices for our present purpose to observe that as economic growth proceeds the census records the proportion of the population engaged neither in agriculture nor in manufacturing as rising from around twenty-five per cent or less to fifty per cent or more of the gainfully occupied population. Some recent distributions are shown below.

	Egypt 1937	Japan 1947	Italy 1936	Great Britain 1931
Agriculture, Mining	71	56	49	12
Manufacturing	8	17	22	35
Commerce	8	7	9	16
Communications	2	5	4	7
Construction	2	4	5	5
Government	3	4	5	8
Other services	6	7	6	17
Total	100	100	100	100

One consequence of the growth of service occupations which is worth noting is that the proportion of the population working for wages declines—at any rate in urban areas—and the proportion of independent persons and of employers increases. This is because the proportion of wage earners in services is relatively low. This result is exactly the opposite of what Karl Marx predicted.

Because economic growth reduces the importance of agriculture in the economy, it is necessarily associated with urbanization. The proportion of people living in towns with less than 2,000 inhabitants falls from eighty per cent or more to thirty per cent or less. This is because of the economies of scale in doing the sort of things which are done in towns—manufacturing, wholesale distribution, public utilities, central government administration, theatrical entertainment, and so on. Dr. H. W. Singer has shown (see Bibliographical Note) that in any country the number of towns of each size follows a particular statistical distribution (a Pareto Law) such that there is a simple inverse logarithmic relation between the size of towns and their number. This does not mean, however, that all countries which reach a given level of real income per head are, or need to be, urbanized to the same extent.

It is quite useless to expect real income per head to grow without

Y

reducing the rural population below the eighty per cent level, for the simple reason that towns of 2,000 inhabitants or less do not permit the economies of scale to be enjoyed. If the proportion of the population required in agriculture drops to twelve per cent, even a vigorous policy of keeping in rural areas such manufacturing industries as do not require much concentration can hardly prevent the population in towns of 2,000 and less from falling below the thirty per cent level. Neither can it be taken for granted that urbanization is undesirable. As we have seen in Chapter III, many people consider that it is from the towns that come all that we value most—science, religion, art, etc. What can be done, without much loss of production or of cultural values, and perhaps with considerable gain in other directions, is to keep down the number of towns with populations exceeding 100,000. It will always be necessary to have some 'Ruhr' areas, where the presence of fuel and ores together is exploited in vast industrial areas with large populations. The danger is that such areas tend to attract other industries to themselves, which could be developed in other places without much loss. Hence it is necessary, if one wishes to prevent excessive urbanization, to have some control over the location of industry, such that building is strictly controlled in areas which are considered to have reached the desirable limit of size.

The speed with which urbanization occurs is a problem in all countries where economic growth is just beginning. In these countries population is usually growing fairly rapidly. There may also be severe under-employment in rural areas, with a tendency for people to drift into the towns in search of casual labour. The large towns are also specially attractive because they are the first to taste the fruits of economic growth—in the shape of cinemas, electric light, water supplies, transportation facilities, and so on; and they also get the greatest provision of social services, in the shape of health services, schools, subsidized housing, poor relief, and the like. It is not unusual, therefore, for cities to be doubling their populations in twenty years, even if not much economic development is occurring. In this situation those governments which are pursuing an active policy of industrialization have to decide whether they will encourage the establishment of factories in a few large towns, or whether the new factories should be dispersed as widely as possible, even in the countryside itself. This question raises very wide issues. There is the political issue; in some areas the industries must be put into the large towns in order to cope with the anger of the unemployed, whereas in other countries it is the possible disaffection of outlying provinces which gives more cause for concern. And there is the battle between those who like the way of life of large towns, and those others who

regard large towns as blots upon the surface of the earth. All that economic analysis can contribute to the dispute is the fact that there are some economies in concentrating factories together—up to a point. From which it may be concluded that from the economic standpoint it is better in the early stages of industrialization to concentrate on building up a small number of well integrated industrial centres. When these are well established, and industrialization has got over its growing pains, other centres can be started in much the same way.

The changes in the occupational structure which we have noted—from agriculture to manufacturing and other services—are effected by differences of remuneration. Since agriculture is declining and the urban occupations are increasing, there is usually a marked difference between incomes per head in agriculture and in industry. Some of the difference in money income is illusory; rural workers get some income in kind, pay less for many things they buy (especially food and living accommodation) and do not have to spend so much as the urban population on some other costs of living and enjoying (e.g. transportation). Nevertheless, when account is taken of this, it remains true that in countries where agriculture is declining relatively to other occupations, real income per head is lower in agriculture than it is in manufacturing. The qualification is important, for if economic growth occurs without an increase in agricultural productivity farm incomes will rise relatively to industrial incomes; the difference between the two usually means no more than that the demand for food is not rising as rapidly as is agricultural productivity.

If one lumps together all services other than agriculture and manufacturing, one finds that income per head in other services exceeds income per head in manufacturing, just as the latter exceeds income per head in agriculture. Income per head, however, is a misleading aggregate. It is not the case that wage earners earn more in these other services than they do in manufacturing. What seems rather to be true is that the proportion of independent workers, of salaried workers, and of skilled workers, taken together, is higher in these services than it is in manufacturing. This is the group that includes the shopkeepers, the hairdressers, the lorry owners, the professional classes, and others working on their own account. Its relatively high earnings are probably due mainly to its class structure.

Since income per head differs in agriculture, in manufacturing, and in other activities, it follows that the contribution of these sectors to national income is not exactly proportional to the distribution of the occupied population. Income per head in agriculture ranges between fifty per cent and seventy-five per cent of average income per head, with the result that even when eighty per cent of

the population is in agriculture, the income of agriculture very rarely exceeds sixty per cent of the national income. (The share of agriculture in the national income, as calculated by the statisticians, varies considerably, according to whether they calculate the food consumed on the farms at wholesale or at retail prices.) Income per head in manufacturing ranges from about average income per head to perhaps fifty per cent more than the average, and income per head in other activities ranges up to twice the average.

A very misleading conclusion has occasionally been deduced from these differences in average income per head. Income per head is lower in manufacturing than in 'other activities', but it does not follow that the way to increase real national income would be to bring about a swift transfer from manufacturing to retailing, to government service, or to the other services which show higher income per head. Neither would real income be raised merely by transferring people from agriculture to manufacturing. The transfer from agriculture to other occupations which occurs with economic growth is the result and not the cause of growth. For it to take place without embarrassment there must be either increasing productivity in agriculture, or else increasing exports of non-agricultural commodities. If the transfer were effected without first increasing agricultural productivity, the result would be a shortage of agricultural products; this would cause a deficit in the balance of payments, or alternatively an increase in the cost of living which, by raising wages, would make it hard for the new manufacturing enterprises to pay their way. If labour is to be transferred from agriculture without an increase in productivity, it must be to industries which earn foreign exchange with which to purchase food, either by saving imports, or by increasing exports, and the profitability of this depends simply upon comparative costs at home and abroad (see section 2(a) of this chapter).

2. INTERNATIONAL RELATIONS

(a) International Trade

The extent to which a country participates in international trade depends partly upon its resources, partly upon the barriers it places in the way of trade, and partly upon its stage of development.

A country which has a wide range of natural resources—fertile soil, a wide range of climates, and a wide range of minerals—can be virtually self-sufficient. The best example is the United States of America, whose imports are only about four per cent of her national income, compared with the United Kingdom, whose imports are about twenty-five per cent, and were around thirty per cent in the

days before they were stringently controlled. It follows that the extent of foreign trade is partly a matter of the size of the country, or to put it the other way round, is partly a matter of where the political boundaries are drawn.

In the second place the extent of foreign trade depends upon policy; all countries can make themselves relatively more or relatively less self-sufficient, as they wish. The case for and against government control of foreign trade has been debated continuously ever since political economy became a recognizable subject, four hundred years ago, and we need not say much on the subject here. The economic case for free trade rests on the advantages of international specialization, which are obvious to all. The economic case against free trade depends upon defects in the free enterprise system, which cause prices not to be a true index of social costs. These defects are particularly obvious in certain spheres. There is the tendency to over-specialization, which neglects the risks which the economy as a whole may bear: of shortage of supplies in war-time, of wide fluctuations in the terms of trade, or of the spread of epidemic diseases which results from monoculture. There are the economies of scale in manu-facturing, which take time to bear fruit, and which therefore justify special measures to protect manufacturing industry in the early days of industrialization. And there are the problems of unemployment, which give special difficulty in countries which are over-populated relatively to their agricultural resources, and which justify the development of new industries behind protective barriers. To these economic reasons for protection are also added political and emo-tional reasons, which cut across the economic interests of the nation as a whole. There is no secular trend to be observed in the extent of barriers to trade. If economic issues were the only ones that counted, nations would have fairly high tariffs in the early stages of their industrialization and very low tariffs as their industries were well established. Britain followed this pattern in the eighteenth and nine-teenth centuries, and the United States seems to be following it in the twentieth; whether the U.S.S.R. will also follow suit remains to be seen. But it is rash to make generalizations connecting tariff behaviour with economic growth, since tariff behaviour is as much determined by political interests and political fashions.

Imports may also be restricted because foreign exchange cannot be found to pay for all the imports which the public would like to buy. This is usually a sign of maladjustment between production for home consumption and production for exports. As we have already seen (Chapter V, section 3(b)), the less developed economies are par-ticularly liable to run into this difficulty if they develop home produc-tion without a proper balance between different sectors of the

economy. Currency difficulties may also arise as a result of inflation (Chapter V, section 2(*a*)), or as a result of the change in the propensity to import which occurs as the rate of investment is accelerated (Chapter V, section 2(*c*)). Again, the less developed economies have to cope with much wider cyclical fluctuations in their foreign earnings than the industrial countries face, because of the wider fluctuations in the prices of primary products (Chapter V, section 3(c)). They therefore need relatively larger reserves of foreign exchange if they are to ride the cycle without foreign exchange restrictions.

The ratio of foreign trade to national income is usually low in a primitive economy, before economic development begins, but it rises rapidly with development. We have already seen how important a role foreign trade plays in initiating economic development (Chapter V, section 3(*b*)). One consequence is that in the early stages of development foreign trade grows more rapidly than income. This is true whether we think of a single country, or of world trade as a whole. The individual country is self-sufficient in the early stages because such a large part of its production is by self-sufficient farmers, who handle very little money, and trade only a very small part of their output. This is the main reason why imports are only ten per cent of the national income of Nigeria, and seven per cent of the national income of India; we can be quite certain that these percentages will grow as income per head grows, and as the growth of internal communications links isolated regions up with the world economy. Much the same happens to world trade as a whole. Between 1870 and 1913 world production of food grew by a little under 2 per cent per annum, and world production of manufactures by a little under 4 per cent per annum. The world's real income probably grew by $2\frac{1}{2}$ to 3 per cent. During this period the volume of world trade grew by about $3\frac{1}{4}$ per cent per annum. It is clear that the early stages of economic growth are marked by increased international specialization, associated with the development of communications, and that as a result trade grows faster than national income.

The later stages are not so clear. The ratio of British imports to British national income increased sharply in the first three-quarters of the nineteenth century, but seems then not to have changed very much for the next sixty years, if we exclude re-exports, and allow for changes in the terms of trade. The United States shows rather the pattern of the economy with large unused resources. Her imports grew less rapidly than her national income, as she developed these resources, and are now only half as large in relation to national income as they were eighty years ago. Now she is reaching the limit of some of her mineral resources, and is becoming an ever larger

importer of raw materials. Some people expect her imports hereinafter to grow at least as rapidly as her income; but we must wait and
see. Two world wars have played such havoc with international trade
that we cannot speak with any confidence of what is likely to happen
in coming decades. Here, for what they are worth, are recent figures.
From 1948 to 1952 world production of manufactures increased by
27 per cent, world agricultural production by 9 per cent, and world
trade by 34 per cent (all figures excluding the U.S.S.R.). These
figures suggest that world trade continues to grow somewhat faster
than world production—though part of this high rate of growth is
due merely to recovery from low wartime levels.

Economic growth also affects the composition of world trade both
as to the relative importance of commodities, and as to the relative
importance of different countries.

It has sometimes been expected that economic development would
diminish the importance of manufactures in world trade, relatively
to raw materials and to foodstuffs, since it was thought that as each
country developed it would import relatively less manufactures and
more raw materials. This has not, however, been the case. The share
of manufactures in world trade, by value, has remained constant (at
thirty-five to forty per cent) for the eighty years for which we have
the figures. Raw materials have increased their share of world trade
continuously, but at the expense of food, the demand for which
grows more slowly than income. World trade has developed on the
basis that there are certain countries which import mainly food and
raw materials, and pay for them mainly by exporting manufactures
and invisible services (shipping, dividends, commissions, etc.). This
does not explain the whole of world trade. Manufacturing countries
specialize and buy a lot from each other, and the agricultural countries also specialize and buy from each other. The Law of Comparative Costs applies as much between one manufacturing industry and
another as it does between industry and agriculture. All the same the
industrial nations take two-thirds of the primary products and only
one-quarter of the manufactures entering into world trade, so the
exchange is mainly between them and primary producers. If the
industrial countries buy more primary commodities, the producers
of these commodities correspondingly import more manufactures.
Hence the trade in primary products and the trade in manufactures
grow in step. It is always possible that this relationship may be
altered; more manufactures may be exchanged against manufactures,
or more primary commodities against primary commodities, in which
case the proportion of manufactures in world trade will alter. All
we can say at present is that there has been no significant change
during the past eighty years.

Given that the proportionate *value* of manufactures is constant in world trade, the behaviour of the *volume* of trade in manufactures relatively to the *volume* of trade in primary products is determined by the relative prices of these two. If the relative price of manufactures rises, its relative volume falls, and vice versa. Thus the 1930's was a period when the volume of trade in manufactures was very low, and the 1950's has so far been a period when this volume has been very large, but in each case the relative volume is explainable in terms of relative prices. Hence changes in relative prices play a large part in determining whether world trade in manufactures seems to be depressed or prosperous.

Though the share of manufactures in world trade has been fairly constant, the composition of this trade has altered remarkably. Textiles have declined in importance, and metals and engineering products have increased in a steady trend. In 1899 textiles and clothing were 40 per cent of world trade in manufactures; in 1950 they were only 20 per cent, the proportion having declined steadily. Metallic products grew from 31 per cent to 56 per cent; while all other manufactures fell slightly from 29 to 24 per cent. These changes are easy to understand. As industrialization spreads, countries first make their own clothes. This kind of manufacture can be conducted almost anywhere, since the raw materials are light and easily transportable, and the skills required are easily learned. It is otherwise with metals. Their production is tied much more closely to the countries which have cheap fuel and ores. There is also continuous technical progress in engineering, so that the established countries have always some skills which give them an advantage over the newcomers. There is accordingly every reason to expect these trends to continue. Metallic manufactures will continue to grow relatively to all others, and the countries which are well endowed with fuel and ores will have the best prospects in international trade.

The distribution between countries of world trade in manufactures has also changed remarkably during the past fifty years. Comparing 1899 with 1937, the shares of the U.S.A., Canada, and Japan have risen markedly, at the expense of France and of the United Kingdom. The Canadian gain has been almost entirely in non-ferrous metals and in pulp and paper. Japan has gained mainly in textiles, but has also competed effectively all along the line. The U.S.A. also has gained all along the line, principally as the result of wars. For example, the U.S. share rose only from 11 per cent to 12½ per cent, from 1899 to 1913; jumped to 20½ per cent as a result of the war but was only 19½ per cent in 1937; and jumped to 29 per cent in 1950, again as a result of the war. Whether the U.S.A. can hold this large share of world trade in manufacturers must depend partly on how

many dollars she puts into circulation, through imports and foreign investment, and partly on whether the rest of the world has to depend on her to a greater extent for food. Foreign investment apart, the U.S.A. cannot be a net exporter both of primary products and of manufactures; which of these groups of exports will contract more remains to be seen.

The decline of the British share of world trade was not in itself a cause for concern. A change in one country's share means no more than that the exports of that country and world exports are increasing at different rates, and there is no reason why all countries should increase their exports at the same rate. The older industrial countries need not worry if their percentage share of world trade in manufactures falls, provided that their absolute share remains adequate to enable them to have full employment at home, and to pay for all the imports they need. What mattered in the case of Britain was not just that her relative share fell (from thirty-two per cent in 1899 to twenty-two per cent in 1937), but that it was not adequate after 1920 to provide full employment, and has not been adequate since 1930 to pay for all the imports desired.

These developments call to mind the theory of economic development which some economists held in the eighteenth century. This was a form of the secular stagnation thesis. They argued that a country which becomes prominent in international trade automatically behaves in ways which cause it to lose its leadership in due course. The great demand for its exports raises its prices relatively to those of other countries, and so stimulates competing production elsewhere. Capital flows into other countries partly to start there industries whose potential success the pioneer has demonstrated, partly to take advantage of lower wages and other prices, and partly because of the logistic principle: each industry in the old country grows up to the limit of its market there, and then its capitalists have to look elsewhere to invest their profits (on this see Chapter V, section 2(c)). Then there is the alleged disadvantage of the early start: the old country has committed itself to skills and capital equipment of the (say) 1850 vintage, and finds difficulty in competing with the new country decked out in the latest of (say) 1880. This alleged disadvantage seems most dubious; if two countries have the same amount of capital to invest in 1880, the one which has also been investing since 1850 can hardly be at a disadvantage in competing with the one which is only beginning in 1880, since any new equipment that it pays the new one to buy the old one can also afford to buy. The old country may find it more economical to keep its old equipment, but it has then the advantage of being able to use its savings to develop new lines, while the new country catches up in

the old lines. More plausible is the argument that the older country loses by its specialization; in 1850 and onwards it develops its facilities (banking, marketing, training, transport, engineering, etc.) to supply what is wanted in 1850; then it gets into a rut, or to use a finer phrase, it gets carried along by the momentum of its endeavours in the 1850's, and fails to adjust to the changing demands of the 1880's. So when new industries come along they go to newer countries not yet so heavily committed elsewhere. This rut may show itself also in loss of technological leadership; the best brains are engaged in solving the problems of the old industries. Meanwhile, the brains in the new countries not merely catch up with or copy the old country in the old industries, but also forge ahead in the new industries, and wrest technological leadership from the old country in the trades which are now expanding.

The British case fits this formula suspiciously well. Lower wages go a long way in accounting for the rise of the textile industry in Asia, and for the loss of world markets in textiles. The investment argument also fits well; from 1870 Britain invested an increasing part of her savings abroad, as much as one-half in the years just before 1913, and this of course helped to build up competing industries elsewhere, especially in North America, in India, and in Japan, while technological progress lagged in Britain. And there was also a marked failure to hold an adequate share of the rapidly expanding industries, such as chemicals, machine tools, or electrical equipment, or to achieve technological leadership in these fields; a failure which may have stemmed from preoccupation with the well-established textile trades, as well as from the contempt of her ancient universities and their products for scientific and technological studies. On the other hand, two factors make one suspicious of applying such formulae to Britain. First, up to 1913 the British balance of payments surplus was growing from decade to decade, despite the slow growth of commodity exports. This may partly have been because the slow growth of exports inhibited production and therefore the growth of imports. But it may also have been simply that the U.K. found it more profitable to develop shipping, insurance and other 'invisible' income, than to push commodity exports. Secondly the formulae imply that Britain could not do better if she tried. There is nothing in organizing an export trade drive which the Germans and the Japanese can do and which the British could not do equally well if they wanted to. These things were not done for so long as trade came easily to Britain, but they may have to be done in the near future, and if they have to be done it is very doubtful that the 'gentle-manliness' of the British character will be allowed to stand in their way. Besides, since it is the United States of America which has

captured the largest share of world trade in expanding markets, and not either Japan or Germany, there may be less inhibition against squaring up to a richer country than there was when conscience suggested that poorer rivals should not be treated too severely.

Leadership in world trade, apart from merely holding an adequate share, depends upon innovation. Britain led in innovation for over a century, but leadership in innovation (which is not the same thing as science or invention) has now passed elsewhere. These changes in leadership are inevitable, since no people has a permanent monopoly of intelligence or of vigour. Before the rivalry of Britain, Germany and the United States, based upon innovation in the production and use of metals and chemicals, there was the rivalry of France and Holland, for the carrying trade. Before that, leadership lay for a time with Spain, and so we can continue backwards, beyond the days of the rivalry between Rome and Carthage. It takes more than a simple economic model to explain why great nations cede their place to others. There are attitudes of mind, internal strains, political developments, changes in institutions, wars and much else in the picture. Probably the changes in international competitiveness merely reflect much deeper changes at home.

Just as interesting as the successive changes of leadership between the advanced industrial countries is the failure of the less developed countries, with the single exception of Japan, to force their way into the charmed circle. This also is sometimes explained in terms of the impact of one country upon another. According to this theory, the mechanism of international trade is such that the gap between developed and less developed countries must inevitably widen. When one country experiences technological innovation and becomes more productive, its exports fall in price. These exports reach into the less developed economies, where their effect is to destroy competing industries. So far, so good; we know for example, that this is what happened to India in the nineteenth century. Her quite highly developed handicraft industries were adversely affected by cheap imports from Lancashire and from Birmingham. This effect, the theory goes on to argue, is cumulative. There are large scale economies in manufacturing industry, so, as the industries in (say) England expand, and those in (say) India contract, the gap between the productivity of the two countries widens. India is driven to specialize more and more in agriculture where there are no economies of scale to be had, while England grows steadily richer, partly at her expense.

This theory is diametrically opposed to the theory we have just considered, according to which the cumulative forces work to narrow rather than to widen the gap. It is unsafe to make simple generalizations about the effects of increasing productivity in one

nation upon all other nations, for these effects are very numerous. If one country becomes more productive, it does not necessarily sell its goods more cheaply; its money incomes may rise, and its terms of trade remain unaltered. If it does sell its goods more cheaply to other nations, they do not necessarily lose by specializing in other lines, and the impact on their economies may prove to be just what is needed to shake them out of stagnation. We have often seen before that an expansion of foreign trade is frequently what starts a stagnant country upon the road to economic development. All the same, it is certainly true that the less developed countries have great difficulty in starting upon industrialization because of the competition of the advanced industrial countries, and we must consider this problem in more detail.

From the economic point of view it is not desirable for countries to produce manufactures for themselves if they can buy them more cheaply abroad. This is not, however, just a matter of comparing the *money* cost at home, with the *money* cost abroad, since money costs often bear no relationship to real costs. Neither is it a matter of comparing only current costs, since the whole point of development is that it brings down costs. One has therefore to think about the effects of industrialization on costs when deciding what is the right policy to follow. If the rate of industrialization were left exclusively to decisions made by private enterprise, it would nearly always be below the economic rate.

Take first the difficulties presented by making a start. There are always initial costs to overcome, and this is one of the reasons for sticking to a particular line once it has started. The economies of specialization are economies of scale. These economies are to be found in most lines of production, and they always inhibit moving from one line to another. Thus countries which specialize in agriculture equip themselves with appropriate transport facilities, training facilities, and the like, rather than with the type of services which are developed by countries which specialize in manufacturing. It may then be the case that while a shift of resources at the margin would be unprofitable, a major shift, involving heavy expenditure to develop new lines, might in due course prove to be much more economical than would continuing in the original specialization. In practice these major shifts cannot be made quickly. If they are to be made there must be an act of faith, taking the country through a period, long or short, during which productivity in the new lines is relatively low. Some private entrepreneurs are willing to make such acts of faith, but generally speaking, they have to be made by governments, and to be supported by protection or subsidization of the new lines. This argument applies with special force to industrialization: when the·

industrial sector first begins to grow its productivity is low; its labour force takes a generation or two to acquire the industrial aptitudes after changing over from rural life; the public utilities are not yet fully utilized, and make high charges for their services; the network of numerous firms supporting each other has not yet developed. It pays to see manufacturing industry through this phase if there is reason to expect that current high costs are only 'growing pains'. This is merely an elaboration of the 'infant industries' argument, which has been accepted by practically all economists for a century and a half, and adopted by all countries in the early stages of their industrialization. England, for example, was behind Europe in industrial techniques up to about the year 1700. Before that time her greatest periods of industrial growth were three periods when she was borrowing techniques from the continent, by encouraging immigration of artisans—especially in the reigns of Edward III, Elizabeth, and the later Stuarts. All this was done with careful protection; it was not until England was well ahead of other industrial countries that she adopted free trade. The same pattern of protection in the early stages of industrialization was followed by Germany, by France, by the United States, and by all the other industrialized nations. It must, however, be remembered that the argument applies only in the early stages of industrialization. Once a country has reached a stage where it is already enjoying the economies of scale, this argument for protection ceases to apply.

Besides initial cost there is also initial ignorance to be overcome, since this inhibits the starting of new industries even in cases where these industries would be successful without protection. In the advanced industrial countries there are plenty of experienced entrepreneurs seeking out new lines of endeavour, but this is not the case in the less developed countries. In the early stages of growth, entrepreneurs have specialized in agriculture and in trade; they are not familiar with new manufacturing industries, in the sense both that they do not know their techniques and also that they do not know how much risk to attach to new ventures. If a government believes that new industries which would prove profitable are being neglected through ignorance, it has then a pioneering function to fulfil. It can initiate research, into demand, and into production problems, and publicize the results for the enlightenment of potential entrepreneurs. If this is not enough, it can invite experienced entrepreneurs from abroad to establish the industry in the country, and lead the way. If risk is the obstacle, it can itself shoulder the risk of pioneering, whether by putting up the capital or some part of it, or by guaranteeing the interest on private capital, or by entering into a contract to buy the industry's product (for use in its own

hospitals, offices, prisons, etc., or for re-sale), or by subsidizing or protecting the industry in other ways. Japan more than any other country has shown how effective such leadership can be; nearly every industry started in that country between 1870 and 1900 was started on the initiative of the government, and mostly in factories opened and operated by the government and sold to private enterprise when the teething troubles were past. The pioneering function is particularly important because of the high incidence of failure even in industries which eventually prove very profitable. When an innovation is introduced, whether it be a new machine, or a new product, a railway, or a new foreign market, it frequently happens that the pioneering firm goes bankrupt, and that the undertaking passes through two or three other hands before it becomes a commercial success. This high cost of pioneering frightens off entrepreneurs, especially in the less developed countries, where entrepreneurs are not in any case either numerous or widely experienced. The role of the government as a pioneer is therefore very much greater in the less developed than it is in the more developed countries.

In some small countries industrialization needs not only the temporary protection of the home market but also the temporary protection of a customs union if it is to be established. Take two small countries A and B neither of which has a market large enough to enjoy the economies of scale. It is possible that if A specializes in certain industries and B in others, and they share markets, both will *in due course* become efficient and profitable without continued protection. If there is no customs union A may not be able to get its industries started, since it may not be able to compete right from the start in B's market. So neither A nor B may get its industries. Or, alternatively, both A and B may start industries, each protecting its own market, and none of these industries will be economic. The customs union benefits both parties if both industrialize, each specializing on different industries. If only A industrializes, B gets no benefit unless its people are allowed to emigrate to A, in order to share the new employment opportunities. And, of course, if the industries ought never to have been started, even with a customs union, because they cannot be economic, then both parties lose. The merits and demerits of a customs union, as a means of fostering economic growth, have therefore to be considered very carefully in each case. However, there is no doubt that there are cases where countries now divided from each other by tariff barriers would gain, not by reducing their barriers altogether to all the world (in which case their infant industries cannot be born), but by entering into limited arrangements with other adjacent countries under which each specializes in a limited range.

Marketing problems, the initial cost of new lines, and ignorance, inhibit the industrialization of the less developed countries to a much greater extent today than in the nineteenth century, since the most advanced industrial nations now have a greater technical superiority over all others than was the case when they were beginning their industrial careers. If special measures of protection were not adopted in the less developed countries, the gap between them and the industrial nations would continue to widen, for no better reason than the momentum of specialization. The case for temporary industrial protection, which the classical economists recognized, is now stronger than ever.

This case applies equally in the over-populated and in the under-populated countries. Over and above what has been said so far, those less-developed countries which are over-populated relatively to their agricultural resources have an additional reason for protecting their manufacturing industry, namely the fact that in these countries price relations fail lamentably to reflect real social costs. This is because their surplus labour, whose marginal productivity in agriculture is by definition zero, or negative, is paid more than its marginal productivity. It is profitable in the real social sense to use this labour in manufacturing so long as it produces any net output at all; whereas it is not profitable to use labour in the financial sense unless its net output exceeds its wage. Many of these countries, e.g. India, have suffered from permitting (or being forced to permit) free trade in manufacturing, the result of which has been to destroy their indigenous production, and to increase their unemployment problem, without any gain to set against this loss. In such countries the correct policy is rather to provide as much employment as possible in manufacturing, and to ignore the prices of competing imports so long as the net output of labour in manufacturing is positive. This argument must not be generalized to all under-developed countries; it applies to those which are over-populated, like India, Egypt or Jamaica, and not to those which are under-populated like the Gold Coast or Brazil.

Though these over-populated countries need more rapid industrialization than any others, their difficulties are also greater because of the problem they face in disposing of what they produce. Their low standard of living causes them to have relatively high demands for food, and relatively low demands for manufactures. Hence, in a sense, one of the major objects of their industrialization is to export manufactures in return for the food they want; that is to say, they have to capture an increasing share of world trade in manufactures. This can be done; it has been done in turn by Britain, by Germany, and by Japan, and will be done in due course by India and by others. But it is now much less easy than it was in Britain's day, because of

the superior competition which is met. Both Japan and Germany achieved their break into world trade only with the aid of government backed export drives. They pursued aggressive policies; flooding the world's markets with their salesmen, offering extensive credits, cutting prices, and paying great deference to the customer's wishes. Alternatively, a country may capture world trade not by competing in selling, but rather by inviting business men from other countries, who already have the marketing outlets, to come into the new country, to build factories, and to supply their existing markets from these sources. This is how England started her incursion into world markets, some six centuries ago. Many countries have followed her example, perhaps the most spectacular recent instance being Puerto Rico's successful invitation to American manufacturers. Gaining a market is so difficult that one wins half the battle if one starts with entrepreneurs who already have established outlets. Besides, the industrial nations seem to make less fuss if they lose markets through the emigration of their own business men and their capital than if they lose markets in other ways. It is the less developed countries which tend to resist the idea of building themselves up in this way (see Chapter V, section 2(c)).

One of the difficulties these less developed countries have is that of keeping their wages at a level which enables them to compete in world markets. If industry is producing only for the home market it can be kept alive by protection even though its prices exceed those of other countries, but an over-populated country seeking a share of world markets is not much helped by protection at home, since, if it cannot produce at prices which hold its own home markets its chance of capturing other markets is small. This difficulty arises from the difference between money costs and real costs, to which we have already referred. Given that there is surplus labour, the real cost of using labour in manufacturing industry is negligible, but the money cost is substantial. Wages in manufacturing have to be kept above the average level of peasant earnings, in order to attract and hold labour in the towns, where also the cost of living is higher. On top of this there are the trade unions, which tend to specialize in organizing industrial labour, and which tend constantly to be raising the level of money wages. Given the level of money wages, it is very often the case (is currently the case in Jamaica, for example), that a country which ought to industrialize cannot do so because its money costs of production are too high. The remedy for this is either to subsidize production, or to devalue the currency. Open subsidization is resented by industrial competitors; hence most industrial countries confine themselves to the less obvious kinds of assistance, such as the leasing of factories at less than commercial rents, exemption from

rates and taxes, low charges for electric power, or water or trans-portation, and the like. This is not always enough, so the start of an export drive may be marked, as in Japan, by a devaluation of the currency. The less-developed countries are better placed for devalua-tion than the more developed, since it has only a small effect on their terms of trade (because the prices in terms of foreign currency of what they import and of the primary products they export are not affected by devaluation), and since their external debts and assets are usually valued in any case in foreign currency. What makes devalua-tion of more doubtful utility is its effect on the cost of living, and therefore possibly on money wages. It is of no use devaluing the currency if money wages are then raised to the same extent. But to say this is merely to say that a country cannot solve its economic problems unless its people are willing to co-operate for the purpose.

There are so many obstacles to breaking into the world market that only bold and resolute nations succeed in doing it. Britain achieved it in the first half of the nineteenth century, by sending her salesmen to the four corners of the earth. It was easier then than now, since she did not then have to face rivals much bigger than herself. Germany came next, with an even more resolute effort, more deliber-ately backed by government help; it was more difficult for her, but she achieved the share she needed. Japan was unfortunate in coming in during the great depression, when world trade as a whole was contracting; but this did not prevent her from doubling her exports between 1929 and 1937. Some other countries, whose need is as great, have lacked the will, for example India and Italy, whose shares of world trade in manufactures moved from 2.3 and 3.7 per cent in 1899 to 2.1 and 3.6 per cent in 1937 respectively. These are both countries which cannot provide all their people with employment and good food unless they raise the proportions of their populations in manufacturing to around thirty-five per cent, and this they cannot do unless an export trade drive in manufactures is put in the forefront of their economic policies. The best placed are those, like India, which possess the fuel and ores needed for the metal trades. Others, like Egypt, are in a bad way since the lines in which they can compete are not likely to meet a rapidly expanding demand. These need to struggle all the harder if their populations are to be employed and fed. One effect will no doubt be to divide industrial countries into those which export metals and chemicals, and others which, being poor in minerals, specialize in exporting textiles and other non-metallic goods, or goods in which the cost of metals used is small in relation to final price.

Needless to say, the established industrial countries resent these trade drives. They attack their methods—the salesmen, the credits,

z

the subsidies, the attractions offered to incoming manufacturers, the devaluations, the low wages, the tax exemptions—and they make a great point of the fact that these trade drives have to have government backing behind them. But the newcomers have an unanswerable defence; since they buy as much as they sell, they need not be reducing anyone else's market. If their extra demand for primary products calls forth extra supplies, the ability of the older industrial countries to exchange their manufactures against primary products is unimpaired. The industrialization of new countries causes difficulty to the old ones only if world production of primary products is not expanding *pari passu*. This is a problem of the balance of the world economy as a whole. Clearly the responsibility for expanding the supply of primary products rests chiefly upon those countries which have the resources—above all on the sparsely populated continents of North and South America, Australia, and Africa. If these countries both exclude immigrants and fail to develop their primary resources, so as to be able to supply the rest of the world with the surpluses they need, the blame (if any) will rest chiefly upon them.

We are thus brought back to the point we made before—the maintenance of equilibrium in world trade depends upon a balanced growth of manufactures, of raw materials and of food in the world as a whole. In the half-century before 1929, when world production of manufactures was growing by about 4 per cent per annum, the terms of trade remained constant if world production of raw materials grew by about 3¾ per cent, and world production of food by 2 per cent per annum. We do not know whether this relationship still holds, but there is no reason why it should have changed drastically. There may be greater changes in the rates of growth. Actually, the industrialization of the less developed countries makes much less difference to these rates than is normally feared. Thus, no conceivable change in the rate of growth of industry in Asia can make as much difference to the growth of world manufacturing production as can be made by a comparatively small change in the rate of growth of industry in the United States of America. For example, if the United States learns to control her slumps, the resulting increase in her average rate of growth may put much greater pressure on world supplies of primary products than if Indian industry now grows by ten per cent per annum. Similarly, since Asia and Africa together consume much less than half of the world's food, it will take a long time before the development of these continents makes the sort of difference to world demand that is made by relatively small changes in the rate of growth of Europe and America. We get the effects of economic development in these continents quite out of perspective unless it is seen in relation to world demand and

supply as a whole. If a shortage of primary products occurs in the next two or three decades it will be primarily because of rapid expansion of the already large demand in Europe and the Americas, and not because of anything that can happen to the relatively small demands of Africa or Asia, whether in terms of population growth or of industrialization.

There is currently much fear that the balanced growth achieved before 1929 will not now be resumed. World industrial production, it is thought, may now grow faster than four per cent per annum, on the average, both because the industrial countries control their slumps, and also because other countries push their industrialization. This depends upon the growth of raw material production, without which it cannot occur. However, raw material production is mostly undertaken on a commercial basis, so apart from shortages of particular minerals, there is no reason why it should fail to respond to the growth of demand.

The prospect for food production is much more doubtful. The two per cent per annum increase which occurred up to 1929 resulted partly from settling new lands in the Americas and in Australasia. Since new settlement has slowed down, maintaining this rate of growth of output will depend to a greater extent upon increasing yields per acre. There is no reason to doubt that yields per acre could be increased at the appropriate rates in Asia and in Africa for two or three decades, just because current yields are so low; but there are great political and educational obstacles in the way of achieving in most of these countries the sort of results which were achieved in Japan, so we cannot be confident that world food production will increase during the next two or three decades at the desired rates. Not everyone shares these fears. Some believe, on the contrary, that we are on the threshold of a new agricultural revolution which threatens to embarrass the world with food. If they are wrong, there is only one part of the world which can be relied upon to make up any deficits elsewhere, and that is North America. Those who fear world shortages can point to the changes which have occurred in the past twenty years. Compared with 1934-38, the *net* agricultural exports of Latin America had fallen thirty-seven per cent in volume in 1952, and those of the Near East and the Far East had fallen by twenty-two per cent and sixty per cent respectively. These deficits were not completely made up by expansions elsewhere. Africa's net exports were up nineteen per cent, and Oceania's twenty-one per cent. The greatest expansion however, occurred in the United States, which doubled her (gross) agricultural exports. The danger of unbalance lies not so much in the possibility that world food production will not grow adequately in total, but rather in the possibility that the rest of the

world may become increasingly dependent upon the United States to make up its deficits. The United States may not always be in a position to export food, if her population continues to grow at its present high rate; but for the time being—i.e. for the next quarter of a century or more—she can make up the world's deficits if it pays her to do so.

There are two reasons why it would be embarrassing to be dependent upon the United States for food; first the effects on the terms of trade, and secondly the effects on the demand for dollars and their supply. Such dependence would move the terms of trade sharply against other industrial countries. The great superiority of the United States lies in her productivity in manufacturing rather than in agriculture. Hence if the United States is to export food, she requires to be paid a price which is very high in terms of manufactures. The other industrial countries then find that they have to export a tremendous amount in order to pay for the food they need. At the same time, the United States has only a small propensity to import manufactures. If she is to export more food, she will not import more manufactures, but must balance her accounts instead by exporting less manufactures. Hence the share of manufactures in world trade diminishes. Since U.S. manufactures are very competitive in world trade, it is a struggle to diminish their share, and this struggle reveals itself as a dollar gap. This gap is then a sign that other nations are trying to continue to buy both American food and American manufactures when they ought instead to buy relatively less manufactures from the United States and relatively more from other countries.

The post-war dollar gap is exactly of this nature. Because of the effect of the second world war in diminishing industrial production in Germany and Japan, and agricultural production in Europe and Asia, the world became much more dependent on the United States simultaneously for food, raw materials and manufactures. The dollar gap will disappear only as this dependence is reduced. Before 1939 the rest of the world had become independent of the United States for food. The United States was a net importer of food. This will happen again if food production grows fast enough in the rest of the world. But if food production does not grow fast enough, food will be expensive relatively to manufactures, and industrial countries will face a struggle to reduce the share of United States manufactures in the world's markets. How fierce this struggle is depends mainly on how rapidly prices adjust to the situation. The existence of a dollar 'gap' merely signifies that the United States is charging too little for her exports of manufactures or paying too little for her imports of primary products. The gap disappears automatically as prices are

adjusted, but it takes time for prices to adjust.

In sum, it is impossible to prophesy what will happen to world trade. Since some countries of the world cannot feed themselves, the division of the world into net importers of primary products and net exporters of primary products must continue, and must even intensify as some of the over-populated countries develop and come on to the market in a big way (India, Italy, China, Java, and perhaps the U.S.S.R.). These countries can be expected, as their industry grows, to generate an ever-increasing demand for food and raw materials. It will be largely a question of relative prices and supplies that will determine which other countries are net importers or net exporters of primary products. The United States has crossed the line twice (from net exporter to net importer and back again) and there can be no certainty on which side she will stay. We may take it for granted that world trade will continue to grow, while remaining agnostic as to which countries will be prominent in supplying the primary products, or as to what prices will have to be paid to call forth adequate supplies.

(b) Migration

The causes of international migration are numerous, and are not all associated with economic growth. Some peoples have migrated for religious, for political, or for racial reasons, either to escape persecution at home, or else to carry their message to other lands in missionary zeal. There are numerous examples in history; the migration of the Jews from Egypt, of the Puritans to America, of the Huguenots from France, and so on. Migrations for such reasons have, alas, been greater in the first half of the twentieth century than at any other recorded time, since freedom and tolerance have not grown with science or with wealth. These fifty years have seen the vast flights and massacres associated with the rise of Communism and of Fascism, and with the partition of Palestine, of India, and of Korea. The human animal has not lost any of its viciousness during its five thousand years of literacy.

If we confine ourselves to economic causes, some of the greatest migrations of history have been simply to avoid famine and hunger. The great outbursts from the central plains of Asia—the movement of the Huns and the Mongols for example—are usually attributed to the effects of climatic change, though, in truth, we do not know enough about such matters to be sure. Hunger apart, people migrate because they think they can find more security or better opportunities in the country to which they are going. The great migration movement which started in the middle of the nineteenth century, and which reached its peak just before the first world war, when over a million

Europeans, Chinese and Indians were leaving their countries permanently every year, was based primarily upon this hope that better things lay upon the other side of the water.

Emigration is linked to the theory of economic growth by the doctrine of inevitable over-population. According to this doctrine, any nation which has the good fortune to find some means of raising its standard of living—e.g. an opportunity for foreign trade, or some new agricultural technique, such as irrigation, or better seeds, or new rotations—or some means of lowering its death rate—such as improvements in water supply or in public sanitation—must inevitably be brought low again by the growth of its population. Hence any nation which experiences economic growth ultimately 'bursts at the seams', and has to find new lands for its people. This has happened often enough in history: the classical case is the foundation of the Greek colonies between 750 and 550 B.C.: while in the recent past much the same can be seen in the emigrations from Ireland, from Britain, from India, from Italy, from China and from Japan. Paradoxically, the same line of argument leads to the conclusion that emigration affords no real relief from over-population. For if population breeds to the limit of subsistence, the gap created temporarily by emigration is soon filled up again. There may have been cases where this was true. All the same, as we have already seen, explosive population growth is not inevitable—or if it used to be inevitable it is no longer so. Man has learnt to practise birth control as effectively as death control, and anything may happen in the future.

Besides, as we have also seen, emigration is not the only remedy for over-population, in the sense of carrying a larger population than the domestic soil can feed. An alternative remedy is to participate in foreign trade: developing manufacturing industries, or shipping, insurance, tourism, a film industry or other sources of foreign exchange with which to purchase food. This may not stop the country from being over-populated in the sense that its citizens could earn more elsewhere—it was profitable for British factory workers to migrate to do farm work in New Zealand—but it can stop over-population in the sense that the people cannot be fed adequately (e.g. the current situation in India and in China). Even here, however, we cannot escape the secular stagnation theorists. As we have seen, they argue that the development of an export trade in manufactures can be only a temporary relief from over-population, since the necessary share of trade cannot be held; forces come into play which cause the country to lose its place in the market (see section 2(a) above). Hence they argue that the inevitable end of economic success is over-population and migration. There is no denying that such things have happened; one resists only the word 'inevitable'.

Sometimes the over-populated country is anxious to facilitate emigration, but this is not always so. Some tribes have sold some of their members into slavery. In other places, such as China and India, governments have given facilities to recruiting agents from other countries who come to take labour away on contracts of indenture not always far removed from temporary slavery. The United Kingdom has encouraged its own emigration, its efforts ranging from the transplantation of convicts and of rebels in the seventeenth, eighteenth and nineteenth centuries, to the subsidization of passages to the Dominions in the twentieth century.

Emigration raises problems for the country which is losing people. There is not only the question of protecting the emigrants, from fraud by recruiting agents, from the dangers of overcrowded or unseaworthy shipping, from mistreatment by employers in the countries to which they emigrate, or from racial or religious persecution. These problems are formidable enough, and dissatisfaction has on several occasions caused the Indian government to ban further emigration to countries where it thought its people were unfairly treated. The problem of allegiance is one of the most difficult here. Some of the countries which receive immigrants are anxious to assimilate them, so as to have as few minority problems as possible. Thus they refuse to recognize the language of the immigrants in their schools, or in their courts; the children of the immigrants are to be as like other native children as possible. This is the basis of the immigration policy of the United States. Britain pursued the same policy towards her continental immigrants in the sixteenth and seventeenth centuries; the law required them to take native Englishmen as apprentices, and administrative practice discouraged them from congregating or from resisting assimilation in other ways. These policies are opposed by those immigrants who would like to keep their own separate culture and language alive in the new country, and by the unwillingness of the Chinese emigrants, for example, to give up their allegiance to China. The political difficulties raised by migration are indeed insoluble if the migrants refuse to be assimilated, or if the countries from which they have migrated seek to interfere in the domestic affairs of the sovereign countries to which their people have gone. On the other hand, if the immigrants are not allowed to assimilate, or are subjected to discrimination, their country of origin is certain to protest, as Britain protested to China in the nineteenth century, and as India has protested to the Union of South Africa in the twentieth.

Apart from these political difficulties, emigration creates also its economic difficulties. The largest proportion of emigrants consists of people in the twenties and thirties. The country has to bear the cost of

rearing and educating them, only to lose them when they reach working age. As the young leave, the proportion of older people and dependants in the population rises, and the burden on people of working age is correspondingly larger. On the other hand, there is no burden if the emigrants send back remittances to support those whom they have left behind, and such remittances are sometimes a large and welcome item in the balance of payments of countries which are losing people. The sexes are also unbalanced, since more men emigrate than women; in Barbados in the nineteen twenties there were nearly twice as many adult women as men in the population, as a result of heavy emigration. There is also frequently great reluctance to lose skilled people, especially if it is feared that they will start competing industries in new countries to the disadvantage of the old country; many countries, for example eighteenth century Britain, have tried to prevent emigration of skilled artisans for this sort of reason.

When we turn to the attitude of the receiving countries it is as varied as the attitude of the countries losing population, and is governed by the same mixture of economic, political, racial and religious motives.

On the economic side, nearly all countries welcome skilled immigrants, especially if they are able to start new industries. The welcome is the greater if the new immigrants desire complete assimilation, since most countries are suspicious of foreign groups within themselves. And also if the immigrants will undertake to teach their skills to native apprentices. Indeed, English legislation of 1484, repeated in 1523, forbade the immigrant to have foreign apprentices, other than his own children. There is greater difficulty if the skills are not new, especially if the immigrants are nearly all specialists in the same trade. Immigration of a large group of doctors or of miners is likely to arouse more resistance than immigration of a group with a wide range of skills. Immigration of foreign business men raises the same sort of problems. Many countries insist that they must employ natives. Some wish to confine them to new industries, and make rules to prevent them from competing with small traders at home. Business men who bring new industries, such as new factories, are almost certain of some sort of welcome, on terms, whereas business men who merely compete with native traders, like Syrians in West Africa, or Chinese grocers in the West Indies, are liable to meet with hostility.

The immigration of people with special qualifications is, however, a minor political issue compared with mass immigration of the unskilled. Mass immigration is welcome only in very restricted circumstances. A country may welcome it if there is much empty land, and if it is thought that a larger population would enjoy economies of

scale; thus the door was kept open into the United States for so long as the frontier was open; but as soon as there was no more vacant land the opposition to immigration grew until it could no longer be resisted. Or immigration may be welcomed for political reasons; Australia is taking immigrants not because of economic considerations, but primarily as a defensive measure against Asia. Israel continues to receive immigrants in spite of economic considerations, because she feels it her duty to accept all Jews who live under the shadow of persecution. Desire to offer a home to people fleeing from persecution has played quite a large part in the immigration policies of several nations, such as Britain and the United States.

As far as economic considerations go, there may well be a clash between wage earners on the one hand, and capitalists and landlords on the other. If there are economies of scale, all classes of the population stand to gain from immigration, but even in this case the gain may accrue chiefly to capitalists and landlords. Mass immigration keeps wages down, near to the wages of the countries from which people are coming, and pushes up rents and profits. Landlords and capitalists may be willing to push their interest to the point of importing slaves (see Chapter III, section 4(b)), or of bringing in labour on indenture from India or China. This in due course produces the social problems of a mixed society, but capitalists and landlords are seldom deterred by this. The native peasants or wage earners may tolerate the newcomers so long as there is plenty of land, or so long as new industries are being created as fast as the immigrants arrive. But they sooner or later organize resistance to mass immigration, and, given the vote, they sooner or later succeed in cutting it off.

There is also sometimes quite a fuss about immigrants' remittances, which may indeed be an awkward problem if exports are tending to lag behind internal growth. Usually, however, immigrants' remittances are a minor item in the balance of payments, and are made into a political issue only as a part of a general campaign against further immigration.

How soon the country is filled up by immigrants depends, among other things, on the sex distribution of the immigrants. If only men immigrate, there is no second generation, and a native population is not established. In this sense, the migration of males by themselves is wasteful. For example, millions of Africans were transported as slaves to the West Indies, with very small result. Since not enough women were transported, the immigrants could not replace themselves by reproduction, and a large slave trade was needed year by year merely to keep the slave population stable. All immigrant communities tend to have an excess of males, and a considerable wastage from one generation to the next, unless care is taken to secure

a balance of the sexes. This is why countries which assist immigration are usually careful nowadays to assist immigration of women as well as of men. In any case, in these days when the range of women's occupations is much wider than it used to be, women are welcome in their own right as gainfully occupied workers, as well as for their services as wives and mothers.

Given a favourable attitude towards mass immigration, the rate at which the immigrants can be absorbed depends on many factors. Race, religion and culture determine the rate at which they can be assimilated, and some countries (e.g. the United States, Australia) give great weight to these factors in deciding whom to admit, and in what numbers. On the economic side, the immigrants need houses, land or jobs, and cannot be absorbed faster than these can be provided. Their provision requires capital. Some of the immigrants bring their own capital, or it may be possible for the country to borrow abroad. If no capital is available from abroad, the rate of immigration is limited by the rate of domestic saving, and by the acute balance of payments deficit which would emerge if domestic investment exceeded domestic saving. Even if finance is available, physical factors may limit the rate of capital formation. As we have already seen (Chapter V, section 1) fifty to sixty per cent of capital investment consists of work in building and construction, hence investment is limited by the capacity of the building industry. It is of course always possible to expand this industry, if care and thought are given to the matter, but it is surprising how frequently investment plans are frustrated merely by failure to ensure that the building industry can cope with the work which will be required of it. Bearing in mind these financial and physical limitations, it is not strange that even the biggest immigrations of the past century have seldom exceeded one or two per cent per annum of the population in the countries receiving the inflow.

Immigrants have usually a hard time when first they arrive, and some proportion always return home. The willingness of immigrants to come and to remain depends to some extent upon the preparations made to receive them. Will they find houses waiting for them, or be lodged in barracks or tents, or be left to fend for themselves? Will jobs be found for them on arrival, or will they have to tramp the streets, exhausting their meagre savings? If they are expected to work on the land, will the land be ready, or will they have to cut the forest for themselves? Will it be accessible, and have water near at hand, or must they cut their own roads and dig their own wells? And how are they to live until the first crop comes, or to find money for fertilizers, livestock, or other capital? Settling people on the land has proved particularly difficult. Some governments have taken to spending large

sums to make the land ready, and to lending the settlers the very large sums required for housing and for working capital. Alternatively, it has proved convenient, for example in Sumatra, for immigrant settlers to spend their first season living with other farmers, and working for wages, so as to acquire some knowledge of the country, some savings, and also friends. Since only a small proportion of emigrants are skilled farmers it is probably very desirable, as Gibbon Wakefield suggested, that they should go first of all into jobs, whether in towns or on farms, before they take on the responsibility of running farms of their own.

International migration produces its greatest problems when it brings together two peoples of different race, religion, or culture. In the past the effect of migration has often been to wipe out the aboriginal inhabitants of the country, wholly or in part. Often enough they are decimated simply by the strange diseases which the newcomers bring with them, to which their bodies have not built up resistance—though there are also cases where this works in reverse, just as the coastal peoples of West Africa were protected against invasion from the north by the tsetse fly, which killed off the Muslims' horses, and protected from immigration from the sea by the mosquito which made the Europeans die of malaria and of yellow fever. Disease apart, the indigenous people may be wiped out by being enslaved, by being driven from their lands, or by other treatment they receive—just as the Celts withered before the Anglo-Saxons, the Hottentots before the Zulus, the Red Indians before the Americans, or the Maoris before the New Zealanders. Much depends on how strong is the culture of the invaded, compared with that of the invaders. Sometimes it is the conquered who assimilate their conquerors, as Islam assimilated the Turks, or the Chinese the Mongols.

If two cultures are sharing the same country, it is seldom that they have equal competitive power. Jews and Arabs, Malays and Chinese, Indians and Africans, Boers and English, Indians and Burmans, English and French Canadians, Ibos and Muslims—the pattern is repeated over and over again. These differences are sometimes attributed to race, not with much plausibility, if race is taken in a biological sense, considering how little we know about the biology of race. They are also frequently attributed to religion, but we have already seen how implausible this is as well (Chapter III, section 4(a)). (After all, the Boers are Calvinists, and there used to be a theory that Calvinism is the religion most likely to inspire dynamic business behaviour.) The principal explanation is much more probably to be found in the psychology of immigration. Immigrants are a selective group to begin with: they have moved in order to better themselves, and they are that sort of person. The migration itself sharpens their

wits, bringing them into contact with a new environment, and sharpening their critical faculties (criticizing everything for being different is the first reaction of nearly every immigrant). They naturally tend to look down upon the natives, and to wish to show that they can do as well or better. In some cases, also, the members of immigrant communities go out of their way to help each other; to find each other jobs or to lend each other money; with the result that the community as a whole prospers relatively to the native community, which is not so particular to reserve its opportunities for itself. These attitudes change after the migration has faded into memory; third or fourth generation immigrants may be hardly distinguishable from earlier stocks (e.g. Indians in Ceylon), and if members of another race begin to arrive, they in their turn may look down upon their predecessors as an idle lot.

If members of two races are to share the same country without friction, race must not be a factor of economic significance. That is to say, members of the two races must be found in all social classes, at all levels of income, in all occupations; and their competitive power must be equal. This is first of all a matter of education; the same amount per head must be spent on educating their children, if possible in the same schools. Then there are such questions as the ownership of land; the tendency for some immigrant communities to specialize in and 'monopolize' retail trade; the relative degrees of urbanization; and so on. If the races start unequal in these matters—for example, if the immigrants are much better educated than the natives, or have much more experience of business—equality can be achieved only by taxing them severely in order to pay for education and other equalizing policies. In fact, living together on equal terms requires a degree of toleration which is seldom found except when it is imposed. The great virtue of the best imperial regimes—the Roman Empire, the Austro-Hungarian Empire, the Ottoman Empire and the British Empire—was their ability to have members of different races living side by side with minimum friction. Their secret was, as often as not, an impartiality born of the contempt of the imperial race for the minorities, tempered with a liberal willingness to let each go about his own business, and to keep the peace between them.

On the other hand, imperial regimes are seen at their worst where the government is in the hands of a few members of the imperial race, who are themselves trying to earn a living in competition with the much larger body of native peoples. There is then a strong temptation to drive the natives off their lands, in order to make way for imperial settlers; to force them to work in mines or plantations or in domestic service, either in slavery, or under the compulsion of taxa-

tion or other economic force; and to establish racial barriers in employment so as to ensure that the most profitable jobs and trades are reserved to members of the imperial race. No race is fit to govern another, where its own economic interest precludes impartiality.

The great migration of European peoples in the nineteenth century to the Americas and to Australasia did not raise these problems acutely, because the native races in those continents were not numerous, in relation to the empty spaces, and were too weak to offer much resistance. It was otherwise with the migration of Europeans to Asia and to Africa, or the migration of Japanese, Indians and Chinese to other Asian countries, or to Africa, Australia, or America. If one were to take a world viewpoint today, the migrations most obviously necessary are of Indians, Javanese, Chinese and Japanese into the Outer Indonesian islands, into Africa, into Australia, and into the Americas. There is, however, no such thing as a world viewpoint. None of these receiving countries would welcome such migration, because of the racial problems it entails. In addition, in the Americas and in Australia it would entail a considerable lowering of the standard of living of those who are already there, if it were done on a really significant scale. One defence which the European peoples sometimes offer is that the Indians and the Chinese have no business to be multiplying so rapidly, and have no business to expect other countries to take the consequences of their improvident fertility. But, in truth, the rate of natural increase is higher in the Americas and in Australia than it is in India or in China, and even if Indians and Chinese had birth rates of ten per thousand there would still be the same resistance to admitting them in mass immigration, on racial and on economic grounds.

The future of this problem cannot now be foreseen. Peoples who have felt themselves cramped for space have always moved, seeking to conquer those whose lands they coveted. Japan has already launched two aggressive wars for this purpose, and there is no obvious reason why India and China will not one day do the same. It would be pleasant to be able to think that economic growth is necessarily a harmonizing process, which makes it easier for men to live together without friction, but this is not at all the case. On the contrary, it has been argued by many different schools that economic development issues inevitably in imperialism and in war, and to this problem we now turn.

(c) Imperialism

The causes of imperialism are not entirely economic, but even the political causes are not entirely unrelated to the stage of economic growth. We first examine the alleged economic causes, then glance

at the political causes, and then turn to the effects of imperialism, both upon the subject and upon the imperial nations. This is an enormous problem, only marginally related to economic analysis, and we can touch it only very briefly.

First of all, some nations are driven to imperialism and war because they want more or better lands upon which to settle their peoples. We have seen that this may be one of the consequences of economic growth. The first result of economic growth is that population begins to grow, and it is quite possible that it will grow beyond the country's capacity to feed itself. The alternative remedies are then migration, or developing an export trade in manufactures, or levying tribute upon some other country, and any of these three may lead to war.

Migration may lead to war because other countries refuse to accept immigrants, or because they treat them badly, or because the immigrants want to dispossess the natives, driving them off their lands, or depriving them of political power, or even wiping them out altogether. Dispossessing weaker peoples of their lands is the favourite method by which the economically stronger nations solve their population problems. Levying tribute is a related method, and this also takes many forms. It does not always pay to wipe out the conquered peoples. They may be enslaved, and made to work for their conquerors in mines or plantations, as serfs or as slaves. They may be converted into tenants of their own lands, and made to pay rents and taxes equivalent to fifty per cent of their production or more. Man's propensity to exploit his fellow man is virtually unlimited.

Given this propensity to exploit, it is obvious that imperialism need not derive from economic necessity, It may be population growth and fear of famine which is driving one nation to conquer another, but it may not. The attacker may equally well be the less populous nation, looking out for human cattle to milk. Similarly, it is not always the more developed nations who fall upon the less developed. It may equally well be the barbarians who are brought by envy to pillage a rich and peaceful civilization. The history of the Eurasian continent from about 4,000 B.C. when the great city civilizations began, shows frequent eruptions of the nomadic equestrian peoples from their grasslands to plunder the richer agrarian settlers. These periodic onslaughts of the nomads did not end until modern times, when technological development gave the decisive military advantage to the city civilizations. Similar tension continued in Africa, in the Western Sudan, right up to the end of the nineteenth century. If economic growth tempts a nation to exercise its strength at others' expense, it has as often exposed peaceful nations to the temptation which others feel to soak the rich.

The third remedy for over-population, apart from migration and levying tribute, is to develop an export trade in manufactures, to specialize in the carrying trade, or to export service in other forms. In a liberal world this could be done without war, but this is not a liberal world. Other nations may not want to buy manufactures, or may insist on protecting their own shipping services, so war may be made to force illiberal nations to trade. This was one of the excuses which other European nations made in the sixteenth and seventeenth centuries for fighting Spain in Latin America; it underlay relations between Europe, China and Japan in the nineteenth century, and was one reason why every European nation wanted to have its own piece of Africa. A 'liberal' war may be made to open up trade, or an 'illiberal' war to ensure some special favours in trade. One of the uses of empire is to force the subject peoples to buy imperial produce at high prices, and to sell their produce to the metropolitan country for lower prices than they could get elsewhere. The British Empire abandoned this practice between 1846 and 1919, but in doing so it was acting very exceptionally. Any country which has to live by shipping or by exporting manufactures is almost certain to be driven to war, whether 'liberal' or 'illiberal' war. Germany and Japan are only the most recent examples; no doubt there are more to follow, unless the world can create new political institutions which eliminate war.

The search for markets, the drive for foreign currency, and the search for sources of food and raw materials are all aspects of the same phenomenon. This must not be confused with the argument that a manufacturing nation must seek for external outlets because it cannot consume its own production. We must distinguish between exporting in order to bring in imports, and exporting in order to sustain a gap between consumption and production. A manufacturing nation may seek outlets for manufactures in order to be able to import food. This is virtually inevitable if it has a larger population than the nation's soil can feed. Or it may seek exports because it is a small country and cannot enjoy the economies of large scale production unless it specializes in a few lines, produces more of each of these than it needs at home, and exports the difference. These exports also are matched by imports, which may equally be of manufactures or of primary products. All the smaller manufacturing nations (e.g. Holland and Sweden) export for this reason. This is also the reason why manufacturing nations are themselves large importers of manufactures; e.g. Holland and Sweden, which are self-sufficient in food, export manufactures in exchange for other manufactures and for raw materials. All this is quite different from exporting manufactures because there is a net deficiency of consumer demand in the home

market. If there were such a net deficiency, the imports which match the exports could not be absorbed.

The argument that an advanced industrial nation has to export capital because of a net deficiency of home demand takes us back to the secular stagnation thesis which we examined in Chapter V, section 3(*d*). If saving is rising faster than consumption, and if investment is governed mainly by consumption, the investment opportunities available at home may not be enough to absorb all the savings available, or at any rate to absorb these savings at what is considered to be a reasonable rate of return. As we have seen, most economists have expected the profitability of capital to fall in the 'later' stages of economic development, as a result of the accumulation of capital. We have also seen that there is nothing inevitable in this process, if an adequate flow of new inventions is being maintained, since this keeps up the demand for capital. The rate of investment does not inevitably tend to fall as economic development proceeds. On the other hand, we have also seen very many reasons why some foreign investment may prove profitable (Chapter V, section 2(*c*)), including also many reasons why leadership in international trade may pass from one nation to another (this chapter, section 2(*a*)). Consequently, though it is not inevitable that the more developed economies find it profitable to make some investments in the less developed, it is not surprising that they do.

It does not follow that a nation must embark upon imperialism and war because it wishes to embark upon foreign investment. The greater part of foreign investment is not, in fact, done in colonies; among the greatest borrowers have been the United States, Canada, Australia and Argentina—in all cases when their governments were fully sovereign. Foreign investment need not provoke war, but it may do so if the country in which the foreigners wish to invest is reluctant to grant concessions for the purpose, or discriminates between lenders, or tries to repudiate its obligations. Any such action may lead to a 'liberal' war, designed to maintain the open door, equality of treatment, and respect for contracts. The less developed countries are quite prone to find themselves engaged in such wars, since they are often suspicious of foreigners, or reluctant to grant concessions, or lax in meeting their obligations; Egypt is perhaps the classical case. Whereas lending between two countries similar in outlook, in culture and in legal institutions need not lead to war, it is almost inevitable that the capitalists of the advanced industrial nations should lose patience with the customs and institutions of under-developed countries to the point either of not investing in such countries, or of wishing to bring them under imperial rule. Equally there may be 'illiberal' wars, in which one country tries to gain special advantages

for its own investors, either to the exclusion of other foreigners, or at the expense of the native peoples. One of the advantages of empire is that steps can be taken to ensure that adequate labour is made available for mines and plantations, that roads and harbours are built where foreign capital most needs them, and so on. There is a strong temptation to take advantage of weaker peoples which many strong nations have not been able to resist.

There are thus plenty of economic reasons for imperialism and war, ranging from 'necessity'—famine, the need for land, markets and primary products—to 'greed'—envy, the desire to exploit or the search for more profitable outlets. Corresponding to these causes are the remedies advocated by those who believe that the economic causes are the principal causes of war. Thus there is the 'liberal' view that if all countries adopted free trade and the open door the danger of war would be diminished; certainly it would then be less profitable to hold empires, since one could not then benefit by excluding other foreigners from the opportunities of migration, of trading, or of investing, and it would not be necessary to acquire colonies in order to prevent oneself from being excluded by others; but could one be sure that everyone else would stick to the open door? Then there are the relations between the governed and the governing; so long as forms of exploitation are possible, some countries will wish to have countries to govern. Hence there is the school which hopes to reduce the risk of war by subjecting all imperial powers to international supervision, or even by transferring all colonies to international trusteeship. Again it is clear that if all imperial powers were required to spend heavily on developing their colonies, without return, imperialism would be less popular. Then there is the school which believes that the only way to abolish war is to develop the less developed countries rapidly, so that they cease to be weak and exploitable. Again there is no doubt that the strong would be less tempted to attack the weak if the weaker were stronger. Then there is Hobson's view, now adopted by the Leninists, that war results from foreign investment, which results from the falling rate of profit at home, which in turn results from inadequate consumption. This can be remedied by raising consumption via the tax structure, or by expanding government expenditure, if one keeps within the capitalist framework; or it can be remedied within the socialist framework either in the same ways, or in addition by disconnecting the rate of investment from the level of consumption. Socialism is neither a necessary nor a sufficient condition for the prevention of war. If war is due to over-population, to the need for food and raw materials or to the desire to exploit other races, all these causes are as likely to operate in a socialist as in a capitalist society; Sparta was a near-

AA

communist society, as far as relations between the original Spartans were concerned.

There is no doubt that some of the causes of war are economic, and that action directed to these causes would diminish war. But war cannot be eliminated by economic policy only, since war is not exclusively or even primarily economic in its origin. Alexander did not subdue the East, nor Caesar the West, because these gentlemen were thinking primarily in terms of trade, or investment, or land. It is difficult to assess what part economic factors have played in making war. If we were to list all the wars in history, the great majority would be seen to have little relevance to markets or to population pressure; they were primarily dynastic, or religious or ideological in their origins, or else they were inspired by military adventure or by the desire for empire for its own sake. Even these wars have had an economic aspect, but it was seldom the dominant one. Economic growth may come into the picture in so far as the desire for imperial greatness follows upon economic success. If a country is successful economically, and grows rich relatively to others, its economic superiority may give it ideas of political grandeur which launch it upon a military career. But this is not always so. Often in history the richer nations have been peaceful traders, and their luxurious living has been despised by poorer but more militaristic nations which have fallen upon them.

What causes a nation to believe in militaristic glory is one of the unsolved puzzles of the universe. Class structure throws a little light on the problem, for such nations are usually dominated by an aristocratic military caste, which keeps all other classes in relative subjection—including the commercial classes, who, on the whole, fear war, and resist the militarists. There are always some business men who favour war—manufacturers of armaments or of other supplies for the troops, and others who hope to gain concessions after the conquest or to make profits during the war—but these are usually a minority compared with other business men, who know that war brings taxes, interrupts their relations with commercial friends abroad, and gives over-riding power to the military aristocracy which the business community, on the whole, distrusts. A community ruled by business men goes to war much more reluctantly than a community ruled by a military caste. It is not however always the military caste which drives a nation to war. There are also occasionally the great military adventurers, dreaming of power and glory and empire—the princes, such as the Alexanders and the Suleimans, or the upstarts, such as the Mussolinis and the Napoleons. But if we go on to ask why some nations keep themselves free from military obsessions, while others deliver themselves to military castes and military

adventures, we have to admit that we can find no wholly satisfactory answers to this question.

If there is any connection between dreams of glory and the stage of economic development, it is found in the 'middle' stages of economic growth. The richest countries tend to be peaceful, enjoying what they have, and envying none; and the poorest countries are too lethargic and disorganized for war. It is the up and coming country, which has risen a cut above its neighbours, which often develops aggressive aspirations, wishing to make for itself a place in the sun. Growing competition with the older and richer countries for markets and for raw materials may urge in the same direction. The countries which are dangerous to world peace are more often those which think they have a great future ahead of them than those which are able to glorify their great past. And so the military leadership of the world tends to pass from one country to another in much the same way as leadership in international trade passes, and possibly for reasons of the same sort (see section 2(a) of this chapter).

To analyse all the causes of war is beyond the scope of this book. Our purpose has been the more limited one of noting the connection between economic growth and war. Since war is not exclusively or even primarily economic in origin, economic analysis sheds little light on the fundamental causes of war. The explanation of war is a subject rather for students of psychology, of diplomacy, of law, of religion and of anthropology than for economists.

We turn from the causes of imperialism to its economic effects. Its effect upon the subject peoples varies from one extreme to the other, according to the treatment they receive. At one extreme they may be wiped out altogether. At the other extreme they may make more rapid economic and cultural progress than ever before in their history. Even the same imperial power may treat different people in different ways; contrast the rigid colour bar in employment which the British operate in Central Africa with their policy of almost complete social equality with Africans in West Africa. The best empires have added greatly to human happiness; they have established peace over wide areas, have built roads, have improved public health, have stimulated trade, have brought improved systems of law, have introduced new technical knowledge, and so on. Whereas the worst empires have brought pillage, and slaughter and slavery in their train.

The effect on the imperial power also depends upon how it behaves. All imperial powers have to bear the costs of empire. Some gain more than they lose, but others are in due course ruined by their own imperialism.

Empire has many costs. There is the direct cost of the wars which it entails. Armies have to be recruited and supplied, and even if there

are considerable levies of colonial troops, war is still a heavy drain on the resources of the metropolis. It is also necessary to maintain large armies in peace time, garrisoning the empire, and the larger the empire the greater the metropolitan manpower which this uses up. The empire has also to be governed, and this may use up some of its best brains. There is always a temptation to send the second class brains out to rule the empire, but if this is done the empire may collapse. On the other hand, if the best brains are sent out, metropolitan affairs may suffer in consequence. It is not unusual in empires to find the second class metropolitan brains lording it in the empire, while the first class colonial brains make their way in the metropolis. Empire also helps to maintain the caste system; soldiers are very important in an empire, and the military caste carries a prestige which it would not hold but for its responsibilities. It is no accident that so many of the greatest empires (e.g. the Roman and the Ottoman) have ended their days at the mercy of their soldiers.

Economic growth makes possible ever larger and more costly wars. In primitive communities where seventy per cent or more of the population is needed in agriculture just to provide food, the numbers who can be put into an army are very small. Campaigns are confined to the period between harvest and sowing. Or alternatively the army has very largely to rely on such food as it can pillage in its campaigns. It is different when twenty per cent of the population is enough to provide food; armies can then grow to enormous size, and can be fed from the home base. Simultaneously more people are available to manufacture the implements of war, and the growth of science makes these instruments all the more terrible. War is thus marginal to the lives of primitive peoples, whereas in highly developed economies it may use up fifty per cent of resources or more.

It is sometimes thought that war stimulates economic growth. It may do so to a limited extent. It may produce some useful inventions, but the number of useful inventions resulting from war turns out to be surprisingly small, according to the researches of Professor Nef. War may give a fillip to industries whose expansion is in any case desirable—e.g. taking British examples, to the iron industry during the Napoleonic wars, or the chemical industry after the first world war, or to electronics and jet propulsion in the second world war; but it as often produces over-expansion and unemployment for some years in the industries which catered for the war. War also enables some business men to make inflationary profits, some of which result in fixed capital formation, but the net effect of war on capital formation is usually to reduce it during the war. There is also a loss of foreign investments and of gold, which have to be used in purchasing supplies from neutrals. The destruction of property is not

always as great a loss as might be expected; since property depreciates anyway, and has to be replaced sooner or later, the main cost is that which is involved in accelerating depreciation. War is also not as costly as it seems if one can use idle resources either during the war, or to make good depreciation afterwards. The United States is an outstanding example of this; the second world war brought to an end a decade of stagnation, and output increased so rapidly that the war could be fought without reducing the civilian standard of living. On the other hand, the American economy would probably have revived sooner or later even without a war, as the depreciation of its houses and other capital must sooner or later have initiated a new investment boom. A war may be fought to gain markets, but it may equally result in their loss. The principal gainer of markets from the two world wars has been the United States, which gained an extra eight per cent of world trade in manufactures during the first war, and an extra nine per cent during the second war, keeping its gains permanently. And finally the economy may also suffer through losing some of the finest brains of its young generation on the battlefield. The French gave this explanation of their lack of political and economic vigour between the two world wars, and it may have some validity.

The economic costs of war are without doubt very high. Against these costs may be set any benefits derived from conquest. Contemporary anti-war propaganda maintains that these are negligible, but this is not always so. The conquerors may acquire rich lands, or slaves, or valuable trading concessions. Even if they do no more than impose peace where before disorder ruled, they and everyone else may benefit from the resulting expansion of trade to an extent much greater than the cost of the war. Modern wars fought between two nearly equal parties on a totalitarian basis certainly cost more than either party gains, but not all wars have been so costly or so fruitless. The up and coming country, fighting a short swift war (Germany 1870, U.S.A. 1898, Japan 1894) may make what seem to it to be substantial gains for relatively small expenditure.

In the end, those who take the sword perish by it. Imperialism may pay handsome dividends for two or three centuries or more, in slaves or tribute or trade, but it brings its own nemesis. Inside the empire the subject peoples tend to revolt sooner or later—all the sooner if they are well treated, for then they benefit enormously both economically and culturally, and come all the quicker to resent their inferior status. In the best empires inferior status disappears more or less, and men from distant subject peoples are found holding some of the highest posts in the metropolis, but even this has never sufficed to to hold the peoples of an empire together; the centrifugal forces of local nationalism tend always to break it up. And then the metro-

politan peoples, long grown accustomed to making their living in administration, in commerce, in tourism, and in the other occupations of metropolitan life, find it very hard to adapt themselves to a new world of agriculture and industry. Or, even before the subject peoples break away, the empire may be destroyed by its external enemies. The larger and richer the empire, the more it is envied by the have-not nations. Coalitions are made against it, hemming it in on all sides. Its defence becomes increasingly costly. Its wars, increasingly numerous, yield no gain at all, since they are purely defensive wars, which, even if successful, bring no new lands or concessions to set off against their cost. Its people tend to lose heart, and even to question their own right to be ruling over so large an area. Then it is merely a matter of time before the empire disintegrates, yielding to both internal and external pressures.

Those who doubt whether an empire is a net gain economically also sometimes suggest that the happiest and most prosperous states are those whose empire lies behind them. They are happy because they have their past glories on which to reflect, and know better than to fall for the frustrations of looking towards a glorious future. But they are not necessarily more prosperous. Sweden is prosperous but not Spain. Turkey gained a new lease of life when she lost her empire and took to looking after her own affairs. Who can say whether Holland, the latest country to join the ranks of the ex-imperial nations, will wilt away, or will find new vigour in the experience?

BIBLIOGRAPHICAL NOTE

Population theories and statistics are excellently surveyed, with extensive references to the literature, in United Nations, *The Determinants and Consequences of Population Trends*, New York, 1953. See also H. Brown, *The Challenge of Man's Future*, New York, 1953; Sir Charles Darwin, *The Next Million Years*, London, 1952; G. F. McCleary, *The Malthusian Population Theory*, London, 1953; Sir John Russell, *World Population and Food Supplies*, London, 1954; L. D. Stamp, *Our Underdeveloped World*, London, 1953.

On the effects of economic growth on occupational structure and urbanization see Colin Clark, *The Conditions of Economic Progress*, 2nd edn., London, 1952; S. Kuznets, ed., *Income and Wealth, Series II: Income and Wealth of the United States*, Cambridge, 1952; H. W. Singer, 'The *courbe des populations:* a Parallel to Pareto's Law', *Economic Journal*, June 1936. On industrialization, W. Hoffmann, *Stadien und Typen der Industrialisierung*, Jena, 1931, (of which a revised version will be published in English in 1955); W. A. Lewis, *Industrial Development in the Caribbean*, Port-of-Spain, 1950; K. Mandelbaum (now Martin), *The Industrialization of Backward Countries*, Oxford, 1945; J. U. Nef, *Industry and Government in France and England, 1540-1640*, New York, 1940; P. N. Rosenstein-Rodan,

'Problems of Industrialization of Eastern and South-Eastern Europe', *Economic Journal*, June-September 1943; H. W. Singer, 'The Mechanics of Economic Development', *Indian Economic Review*, August 1952.

On the structure and growth of world trade, A. J. Brown, *Industrialization and Trade*, London, 1943; A. O. Hirschman, *National Power and the Structure of Foreign Trade*, Berkeley, 1945; W. A. Lewis, 'World Production, Prices and Trade, 1870-1960', *Manchester School*, May 1952; W. A. Lewis, 'Trade Drives', *District Bank Review*, December 1954; E. Staley, *World Economic Development*, Montreal, 1944; H. Tyszynski, 'World Trade in Manufactured Commodities, 1899-1950', *Manchester School*, September 1951; United Nations, *Industrialization and Foreign Trade*, Geneva, 1945.

On migration, W. J. Cator, *The Economic Position of the Chinese in the Netherlands Indies*, Chicago, 1936; I. Ferenczi and W. F. Wilcox, *International Migrations*, New York, Vol. I, 1929, Vol. II, 1931; J. Isaac, *Economics of Migration*, London, 1947; C. Kondapi, *Indians Overseas, 1838-1949*, New Delhi, 1951; W. A. Lewis, 'Thoughts on Land Settlement', *Journal of Agricultural Economies*, June 1954; Brinley Thomas, *Migration and Economic Growth*, Cambridge, 1954. On war, Grover Clark, *A Place in the Sun*, New York, 1937; J. A. Hobson, *Imperialism*, 3rd edn., London, 1938; J. U. Nef, *War and Human Progress*, London, 1950; L. C. Robbins, *The Economic Causes of War*, London, 1940; E. Staley, *War and the Private Investor*, New York, 1935; Quincy Wright, *A Study of War*, Chicago, 1942.

CHAPTER VII

GOVERNMENT

THE behaviour of governments plays as important a role in stimulating or discouraging economic activity as does the behaviour of entrepreneurs, or parents, or scientists, or priests. It is, however, harder to get into perspective because of political prejudice. On the one side are those who distrust individual initiative, and are anxious to magnify the role of government. On the other side are those who distrust governments, and are anxious to magnify the role of individual initiative. Both sides can appeal to history. No country has made economic progress without positive stimulus from intelligent governments, least of all England, the foundations of whose greatness as an industrial power were laid by a series of intelligent rulers, from Edward III onwards; or the United States, whose governments, state and federal, have always played a large part in shaping economic activity. On the other hand, there are so many examples of the mischief done to economic life by governments that it is easy to fill one's pages with warnings against government participation in economic life. Sensible people do not get involved in arguments about whether economic progress is due to government activity or to individual initiative; they know that it is due to both, and they concern themselves only with asking what is the proper contribution of each.

Governments may fail either because they do too little, or because they do too much. The first two sections of this chapter will consider what governments can do usefully to promote economic development. The final section will examine the ways in which mischievous government holds back growth, or brings stagnation and decline.

1. THE FRAMEWORK OF ENTERPRISE

In this section we are concerned with the relation between the government and the economy as a whole. The next section considers specifically the public sector of the economy; hence in this section greater emphasis is given to relations with the private sector.

(a) The Functions of Government

Governments are found operating in many ways which are relevant to economic growth. We distinguish nine categories of function as follows: maintaining public services, influencing attitudes, shaping economic institutions, influencing the use of resources, influencing

the distribution of income, controlling the quantity of money, controlling fluctuations, ensuring full employment, and influencing the level of investment. We have already met each of these problems in preceding chapters, when we were concerned with it in a much wider context than that of government activity, so we need not do more in the paragraphs which follow than summarize the issues involved.

First the public services. The primary function of a government is to maintain law and order. To this time has added other services—roads, schools, public health, surveys, research, and on and on in a constantly growing list. Side by side with these internal functions are the external functions of government, in its relations with other governments—the protection of citizens, the making of treaties, war, and so on. There is not much to be said about the public services; such as there is we leave for the next section of this chapter, confining ourselves in this section to the relations between government and the private sector of the economy.

Secondly attitudes—to work, to thrift, to the size of the family, to foreign business men, to inequality of income, to caste, to social mobility, to profit making, to the sacredness of cattle, to new techniques—we have seen over and over again to what a great extent economic growth depends upon the community having attitudes which are favourable to growth rather than attitudes which are inimical to growth. Governments play a considerable part in determining these attitudes. It is true that they are circumscribed by public opinion; they cannot go too far in advance of public opinion, or lag too far behind it. But it is also true that they help to determine public opinion. The speeches and writings of well known public figures, plus the decision of the legislature to take certain action, or equally its refusal to take action, are part of the process by which public opinion is made. Some governments have more latitude than others in moulding or in transgressing public opinion, either because their people trust them more, or because their people fear them more.

In this context, government is exercising the function of leadership. It shares this function with many others in the community—with the priests, with newspaper editors, with trades union leaders, with teachers, and with all others whose opinions carry some weight. In stable communities government interferes in very few matters: it is content to leave it to the priests to pronounce on the birth rate, or to the scientists to pronounce on artificial fertilizers, but in communities which are undergoing a rapid transition there is hardly anything that the government can afford to ignore. Societies making the transition from stagnation to economic growth undergo stresses in every part of their life—religion, class relations, ethics, family life

and so on—and government leaders have frequently to make speeches, if not also to legislate, on matters which in more stable societies politicians would be content to leave to other institutions. This is also one reason why after a revolution—whether violent or peaceful—the new government usually proceeds to get rid of the old leaders in most spheres of life—the church, the newspapers, the law, the professions, the army, the banks, the universities, industry, etc.— and to have new men of its own persuasion installed, for then the politicians can safely confine themselves again to their 'normal' spheres, knowing that in other spheres public opinion is being moulded in the directions they favour. Revolutionaries who fail to take their revolution into every major social institution can hardly hope to effect their purpose, or to hold on to power.

Next we come to economic institutions. Every government has to take an attitude on such questions as whether it favours large or small scale enterprise, competition or monopoly, private entrepreneurship, co-operatives or public operation, and whether its attitude is to be backed by legislation and by administrative action. It has also to satisfy itself that the legal framework combines fairness with incentive. Thus the statute book carries elaborate laws relating to contract, to land tenure, to companies, to partnerships, to co-operatives, to trade unions, to monopoly, to family property. There is also a framework of administrative agencies, either regulating or assisting (with money or advice) private institutions: anti-trust agencies, co-operative departments, agricultural extension, government credit agencies, and the like. In all these matters the laws and customs of countries which have not been experiencing economic growth tend to be unsuitable for economic growth. Hence, in the early stages of economic development much time can profitably be spent on creating a new legislative and administrative framework more suitable for economic growth.

Governments need to influence the use of resources because the price mechanism, which mainly determines the use of resources, gives results which are not always socially acceptable. We have already met several examples of this. There is, for example, the problem of the conservation of resources (Chapter III section 3(c) and Chapter VI section 1(b)); individuals may use soil, or water, or forests, or mineral bearing strata in ways which are considered too wasteful; or the government may wish to develop some basic resource—e.g. a river basin—in ways which require it to control land use throughout an entire region. Related to this is the general problem of controlling land use by zoning activities; this is specially important in towns, if towns are to grow with shape, and with a proper segregation of space for work, for homes, and for recreation;

but there is also some need for zoning in the countryside, to prevent
an undue loss of fertile land to non-agricultural activities; and some
need to control the location of industry to prevent excessive concentration, excessive dispersals, and the emergence of depressed areas
(Chapter II, section 2(b), and Chapter VI, section 1(c)). There is also
the general problem of over-specialization, which may make it seem
desirable to curtail some activities—e.g. to tax export crops which
are in danger of becoming monocultures, or to license road transport—or to encourage other activities—e.g. industrialization—by
protection, by subsidy, or in other ways. Some governments also
control resources directly in order to alter the pattern of consumption—e.g. they restrict the production or importation of luxuries, or
they subsidize the production of milk—while others prefer to influence consumption indirectly by influencing the distribution of income.

The distribution of income raises peculiarly difficult problems for
the less developed countries, in so far as they wish to combine
equality with incentives and with a high level of saving. Economic
growth demands that there shall be adequate differentials for skill,
for hard work, for education, for risk bearing and for willingness to
take responsibility. It also demands that an adequate share of increases in the national income shall go into savings, rather than
into the pockets of those who will spend the proceeds on consumption. The lowest income classes—the unskilled wage earners and even
perhaps the peasants—fit into neither of the categories whose advancement favours growth; if differentials and savings alone were
taken into account, their incomes would have to be depressed
relatively to those of other classes, rather than raised. (See Chapters
IV, section 2(b) and V, section 2(b).) At the other end of the scale,
penalizing landlords does not make much difference to growth, in
those countries where landlords do little productive investment.
Penalizing profits, however, may sharply inhibit growth, both by
removing the incentive to invest, and also by depriving firms of the
finance for new investment. The decision to take a large part of
profits in taxes has therefore momentous consequences. If the state
spends the proceeds on expanding the consumption of the poor, the
result is to keep the rate of saving low; the proceeds of taxes on
profits should be spent productively, on education, and on capital
formation. Secondly, some part of the proceeds should be set aside
for financing productive enterprises through government financial
institutions, such as Development Banks. And thirdly, if incentives
are to be diminished, the government itself must pioneer in establishing new industries, and must be more willing to guarantee a
reasonable return in cases where the incentive to bear great risk
would be too small. The less developed countries have awakened into

a century where everybody wishes to ride two horses simultaneously, the horse of economic equality, and the horse of economic development. The U.S.S.R. has found that these two horses will not go in the same direction, and has therefore abandoned one of them. Other less developed countries will have to make their own compromises.

If money consists entirely of precious metals, government need not regulate its quantity, though it may control the manufacture of coins for the purpose of ensuring their fineness. In these days, however, money is more usually made of materials whose intrinsic value is less than their face value; if the quantity of money were not regulated by government, private persons would produce so much of it that prices would rise very sharply, until the nominal and the intrinsic value of each coin or note were equal. When money is made of paper or of base metals its quantity must be strictly controlled. It may be controlled by an automatic system. For example, under the Gold Standard the quantity of money which a Central Bank may issue is determined by the amount of gold it possesses. Or, in the British colonial currency system, the notes issued by banks, or by currency authorities, have to be backed by an equivalent amount of sterling securities. Alternatively, the quantity of money may be controlled not automatically but deliberately; that is to say the government may retain to itself the right to issue or recall money at its own discretion, irrespective of any backing by gold or by securities. Similarly, the volume of bank deposits, which is the most important kind of money in industrial countries, may be left to the discretion of the banks, or it may be controlled by the Central Bank working on some automatic rules, or it may be controlled by the government acting through the Central Bank virtually according to its own discretion. Discretionary control of the quantity of money is very difficult to exercise wisely. Many countries have suffered over and over again in recorded history from unwise use of this discretionary power by governments, and it was considered to be one of the triumphs of the nineteenth century when automatic systems of control came into widespread use. The automatic systems have not, however, survived the wars, the great slump, and the increase in the power of governments, which the twentieth century has brought, and discretionary control of the quantity of money by governments is the contemporary fashion. In the hands of intelligent governments, discretionary control has considerable advantages; equally it can be most devastating in the hands of weak, corrupt, or unintelligent administrations.

One of the principal reasons for the current popularity of discretionary control in industrial countries is that fluctuations in the quantity of money can be used to offset other economic fluctuations, and so to bring greater stability to the economic system. Most

governments have accepted the proposition that one of their functions is to bring about greater stability. We have already referred to this subject in Chapter V, section 3(c) and it is not necessary to say anything here about the control of fluctuations in industrial countries. We also saw, in our previous discussion, that the less developed countries derive their major fluctuations from fluctuations in world trade which they are powerless to control. The most they can do is to reduce the effect of such fluctuations upon their internal economies, by preventing their home prices from fluctuating as much as their foreign trade prices, and by building up during the boom reserves of foreign exchange which will see them through the slump. This is a difficult sphere in which to operate, since no one can foresee the future behaviour of prices. Nevertheless, most of the less developed countries could do more to protect themselves than they do.

Industrial countries also practise discretionary control of the monetary supply because they have accepted the obligation to ensure full employment in their economies. However, in their case this is mainly a matter of evening out fluctuations. In the less developed countries, on the other hand, the primary cause of unemployment is the absence of resources for people to work with. This can be remedied only by capital formation, which adds new resources, or makes existing resources (e.g. land) more usable. The employment problem is thus coincident with all the problems of economic development. Discretionary control of the supply of money is relevant only in so far as it helps capital formation. As we have seen (Chapter V, section 2(a)) credit creation can be used to promote capital formation in certain circumstances; in others, or in the wrong hands, it produces the evils rather than the advantages of inflation.

We come then to the last of the functions which some governments have assumed, namely that of stepping up the rate of development by forcing up the level of investment. We have seen in Chapter V, (section 2(b)), that, in the absence of government intervention, the rate of domestic saving is determined principally by the ratio of profits to national income. It is small where profits are small, and grows as the capitalist sector extends. There is no very obvious reason why the rate so determined should be regarded as the most desirable rate. Besides, countries which have surplus labour can do some forms of capital formation at virtually zero real cost; to refrain from proceeding with useful measures in these circumstances doesn't make sense. On the other hand, a higher rate of domestic saving can be achieved only by force—by taxing farmers and landlords, or by inflation. Whether such force should be exercised is a political problem which every country must solve for itself in the light of its own circumstances. The Japanese government 'got away with it' in one

set of circumstances, and the Gold Coast government seems to be getting away with it in another; but the Russian government's force in the nineteen-thirties was violently resisted by its peasants, to the extent of some millions of deaths. The greatest political question which such a country as India now has to face is whether it can force a doubling or trebling of domestic saving without involving its people in hatred and violence on a large scale.

As the above list of governmental functions shows, the range of activities which the government can usefully undertake is very wide. Moreover, it is even wider in the less developed than in the more developed economies. For example, in the less developed economies research depends to a greater extent upon public than upon private funds; the government has to concern itself to a greater extent with attitudes; the price mechanism functions less adequately; more pioneering by government is necessary; saving is more of a problem; there is greater poverty to be alleviated; and so on. On the other hand, the governments of the less developed countries are at the same time less capable of taking on a wide range of functions than are the governments of the more developed. Their administrations tend to be more corrupt and less efficient, and a smaller part of the national income can be spared for government activity. This is another of the paradoxes of economic growth. Just as poor countries need to save more than rich countries, but cannot afford as much, so also poor countries need more and better government activity than rich ones, but are apt to get less and worse. In fact, one cannot usefully consider in an abstract way what functions a government ought to exercise without taking into account the capabilities of the government in question. It is very easy to overload the governments of less developed economies, and it is quite clear that it is better for them to confine themselves to what they can manage than for them to take on an excessive range.

This is the peculiar relevance of international technical assistance programmes. Just as domestic saving is supplemented by external finance, so domestic government can be supplemented by external help. Thus the imperial governments are well placed to help their subject peoples, if they so desire, by subsidizing the cost of administration, by making available qualified staff, and by giving these countries more efficient and less corrupt administrations than they would otherwise have. However, what the colonial governments gain in efficiency they frequently lack in will, for not all colonial governments put into the forefront of their programmes measures for raising the standard of living of their peoples. The failure of imperial governments to convince their subjects that this is their intention has everywhere played into the hands of nationalist leaders, who protest

that they would have the interest of the people more at heart. However, not all the governments of independent countries are specially concerned about raising standards of living; several fall far behind the imperial governments in this respect. And what others gain in will, they often lack in competence. International technical assistance, freely offered and freely accepted, helps to make good deficiencies of funds or of technical skill, and it is proving very useful to those governments who know how to use it. But technical assistance is no substitute for the will to develop, or for honesty in administration.

(b) Production Programmes

It is possible to draw up a complete programme for an economy, showing the uses to which the government would like the country's resources to be put. The statistical part of such a programme takes the form of various tables, each representing a different aspect of the economy. One table shows the various types of labour (of varying skills), and the industries and services in which the population will be employed. Similar tables can show the uses of raw materials, of land, of buildings or of machinery. Another table can show the outputs expected from each industry, in accordance with the proposed dispositions of resources. Another table can show incomes generated, and the uses to which they will be put; this table will show how the national income is to be divided between consumption, capital formation and government service. Yet another table can show the expected receipts from exports, and the expected payments for imports, visible and invisible. Clearly a comprehensive programme for an economy can run into many scores of pages of statistics.

Several issues arise in making production programmes. The first is, what is the point of the exercise? The second is, how to know what use should be made of resources—the problem of balanced growth. The third is the problem of consistency. And the fourth is how to translate the aspirations of the programme into reality.

What is the point of the exercise? The answer depends on whether the economy is in the main governed by prices, or in the main governed by licensing. If the government has constantly to be making decisions about the use of labour, or buildings, or raw materials, or about the level of imports or consumption or capital formation, then it needs to have pretty comprehensive figures about the economy as a whole, if only to ensure consistency in its decisions. On the other hand, the fewer the decisions to be made, the less the information it is necessary to compile. Those economies which are governed by prices get along without production programmes; each person carries out his own programme, and the market mechanism co-ordinates the activities of all with only limited central control.

The case for a comprehensive production programme therefore stands or falls by the case for planning the economy in detail from a central office. It would take us too far to discuss this case in all its detail here; the present writer has already published a whole book devoted exclusively to this topic. Broadly speaking, the case against detailed central planning is that it is undemocratic, bureaucratic, inflexible, and subject to great error and confusion. It is also unnecessary. There is a much better case for piece-meal planning; that is to say, for concentrating on a few matters which it is particularly desired to influence, such as the level of exports, or of capital formation, or of industrial production, or of food production; and for leaving all the rest of the economy to adjust itself to demand and supply. Some planning is necessary, since the results of demand and supply are not socially acceptable in their entirety; but planning can be confined to those spheres where it is considered most important to modify the results that market forces acting alone would yield.

Piece-meal planning is most required in those sectors of the economy where demand and supply are out of equilibrium at the ruling prices. This will be practically the whole economy, if inflation is taking place, especially if the government is trying to cope with the inflation by controlling prices. Inflation creates shortages, and therefore makes necessary some rationing or licensing of essential resources, especially of food, of some raw materials, of foreign exchange, and of building capacity; and such rationing cannot be done effectively unless there is a budget for each rationed commodity, showing expected demands and supplies. Inflation apart, a developing economy frequently experiences pressure in some sectors, even while other sectors may be depressed. There is almost certain to be pressure on skilled labour in general, and on the building industry in particular, so that it is very desirable to have as much statistical knowledge as possible about the supply of skilled labour, and about the demands likely to be made on such labour. There may also be pressure on the foreign exchanges, if the expansion of home production is exceeding the expansion of exports, without sufficiently substituting for imports. There may also be pressure on food supplies if agricultural productivity is lagging behind development in other sectors of the economy. Since it is too much to hope that all sectors of the economy will proceed in perfect balance with each other, economic development is bound to give rise to some surpluses and some shortages, and it is at those points of the economy where the disequilibrium between demand and supply is most obvious and most vital that it is necessary to collect as much information as possible, and to try to ensure that limited resources are put to the best uses.

The three over-riding shortages which determine the shape of most

production programmes are the shortage of capital, the shortage of skilled labour, and the shortage of foreign exchange. Each of these in turn imposes three restraints, namely that the size of the total programme must be kept within total availabilities, that the methods used in carrying out projects must be those which economize the scarce resources, and that priority be given to projects which will most quickly increase the supply of what is scarce. This last is fundamental, though often neglected; the true test of planning is not how effectively scarce resources are licensed and rationed, but how quickly shortages are eliminated by increasing supplies.

Not all economies suffer from capital shortage. There were even, immediately after the Second World War, quite a few countries which had ample capital and ample foreign exchange to finance large investment programmes, which found their difficulties instead to be lack of suitable labour, or physical shortage of such commodities as steel and cement. This, however, was only a temporary phase, due to war-time accumulations of financial reserves. Most of the under-developed countries are now back in their chronic condition of having very little capital to spare. It is then necessary both to keep the total size of investment programmes within the limits of available finance, and also to make more finance available by curbing consumption. It is necessary to have a proper balance between investment and savings, because a positive difference between these two results in inflation. We have seen that a little inflation is helpful to capital formation, but that it is more helpful in industrial than in agricultural economies, and that it needs very careful control if it is not to damage the economy (Chapter V, section 2(a)). Hence the total investment programme must not be allowed to exceed the savings available plus what is considered to be the permissible extent of inflation, if any. And at the same time, measures to curb consumption must be an integral part of any programme which proposes to step up the rate of capital formation, whether the curb takes the form of voluntary saving, of the rationing of luxury consumption, or of taxation. We shall be returning to this subject later in this chapter (section 2(b).)

Capital shortage affects both the choice of projects for the programme, and also the methods chosen for carrying them out. In choosing projects the rule is to make only those investments where the yield per unit of capital is marginally highest. This is not to be calculated solely in terms of what the product can be sold for, since some projects confer benefits greatly in excess of their monetary returns; this is particularly true of the public utilities—the improvement of transport, water, or electricity supplies may increase the output of other industries far beyond any return shown in the utility's receipts. Neither does this rule correspond to using capital

BB

chiefly in projects with a low ratio of capital to labour, since some of the industries where capital adds most to output happen also to be rather capital-intensive—such as some public utilities, mines or steel factories.

Next, almost any project can be carried out by methods which use capital sparingly, or in more capitalistic ways. If capital is scarce, one should choose the less capitalistic methods, where the ratio of initial cost to running cost is low, and where the gestation period is short. This will follow automatically if a high rate of interest (higher than the rate on government bonds, which is usually below the true value of capital to the community) is used in calculating the comparative cost of different methods.

Special care has to be taken in those countries which have a large surplus of unskilled labour, for in such circumstances money wages will not reflect the real social cost of using labour. In these circumstances capital is not productive if it is used to do what labour could do equally well; given the level of wages such investments may be highly profitable to capitalists, but they are unprofitable to the community as a whole since they add to unemployment but not to output. This wasteful use of capital is most liable to occur in the mechanization of agriculture, and in competing with cottage industries (Chapter III, section 4(d) and (e)), and it may be desirable to discourage these types of investment. Sometimes, even though the investment adds nothing to output, it seems particularly attractive because it is so economical of labour (e.g. earth-moving machinery) or so much cheaper in money terms than hand methods, and Finance Ministers who have difficulty in finding money for public investment will certainly be reluctant to use more expensive labour-intensive methods; but the fact remains that it is a waste, from the social point of view, to use machines in these countries to do what surplus labour could do equally well. Their capital is most productive where it is used to increase employment opportunities, by bringing into existence projects where the work could not be done by hand, or where the cost of doing it by hand would be prohibitive (this is the Finance Minister's escape clause). Their capital is equally productive when applied to work which is already done by hand, if the extra output can be absorbed without reducing employment, thanks to the elasticity of demand, or to the improvement which the use of capital effects in the product itself. There are also lines where capital will increase the national output, but will also reduce employment; e.g. if the food available for human consumption increases when machines are substituted for horses-and-men. The decisive economic test is what happens to total national output, and not what happens to employment or to money cost, but in practice it is not politically easy to prevent wasteful use

of capital in place of labour when the money cost is substantially lower, or wasteful use of labour in place of capital where considerable unemployment would otherwise result.

Shortage of skilled labour creates the same sort of problems as shortage of capital. If skill is short, it must be economized, by choosing methods which make smaller demands on skill. One of the shortages is almost certain to be the skill of administering large enterprises, so the programmes of under-developed countries should be conceived in terms of small-scale rather than of large-scale organization (Chapter III, section 2(c)). It is necessary also to keep the total programme within the limits of available skills, if there is not to be confusion and waste. This applies particularly to the building programme. We have seen (Chapter V, section 1) that fifty to sixty per cent of investment consists of construction, and that scarcity of building capacity is often the principal obstacle to stepping up the rate of capital formation. It is not a formidable obstacle, since it is no more difficult to expand the building industry swiftly than to expand an army swiftly, if one takes the problem seriously and adopts measures for recruiting and training the necessary labour. But it is surprising how often production programmes fail to make this provision.

Whether a country is short of foreign exchange depends on whether development is being generated mainly in its export sectors (Chapter V, section 3(b)), and on how much foreign capital it is importing. If development is primarily in the domestic sectors (India, Australia) foreign exchange is almost certain to be a difficulty. In this case methods of production which economize the use of imported machinery or raw materials will be specially attractive, and it will also be desirable to support industries which earn or save foreign exchange, a little beyond what is justified by their monetary cost or their money receipts. Every development programme should seek to maintain a proper balance between home and foreign trade. In less developed economies imports rise at least as rapidly as income, and usually more rapidly. Countries which have a wide range of natural resources and climates, like the U.S.S.R. or China or the U.S.A., can substitute home production for imports as they develop, and it is possible for their incomes to expand without a proportionately equal expansion of their imports. Most other countries are too small for this. As their incomes rise they need a wider range of commodities and raw materials, and if their populations are growing rapidly they may also need to import more food. Hence in any development programme the highest priority needs to be given to the expansion of products capable of being exported, and to the development of new markets. The possibility of getting foreign investments or grants to pay for

part of imports complicates the situation; it reduces temporarily the need for exports, but, when capital and interest payments have to be made, the ultimate effect is that exports must rise even more than imports. This problem is particularly difficult in two cases. The first is where exports consist of foodstuffs. If food production is not rapidly expanded, the expansion of home demand may cause home consumers to eat what would otherwise be exported; this has happened in Argentina. The other case is that of the over-populated country which has to industrialize and break into the world market for manufactures (Chapter VI, section 2(a)). Discovering what to export and where to sell it is not always easy, but the problem cannot for that reason merely be pushed aside.

The shortage of foreign exchange often merely reflects failure to maintain a proper balance between the growth of manufacturing industry and of agriculture. If either of these sectors expands its output, the effect is to increase the demand for the products of the other sector, and any deficiency throws its strain on the balance of payments. A rapid growth of industry calls for a rapid growth of agriculture. The industrial workers will want more food; the factories will want labour from the countryside; the expanding market of the farmers will be needed to take up the output of consumer goods; or alternatively the savings or taxes of the farmers will be needed to finance industrial construction. Similarly, if agriculture is expanding, it will need a growing industry, to absorb its product and its labour, and to provide the farmers with more consumer and capital goods. Stagnant agricultural productivity per man holds up the expansion of industry, and puts a strain on the balance of payments, since the growing industry will require more imports and may have to dispose of its surplus as exports. Or alternatively, if agricultural productivity is rising, industrial production must grow even faster, since the demand for food rises less rapidly and the demand for manufactures more rapidly than income per head. Balanced growth means not equal growth, but growth in the proportions dictated by the different rates of growth of demand. If the balance between industry and agriculture is neglected, as in Australia or Argentina, or bungled, as in the U.S.S.R., further progress is held up; the superiority of the development planning of Japan over that of the other countries mentioned stands out clearly in this respect.

It is possible to show up lack of balance in a production programme by testing the various parts of the programme for internal consistency. First of all, one can apply tests of over-all balance, to see whether the programme as a whole matches up with available resources. For example, a manpower budget, distinguishing the various categories of skilled labour, will show whether the programme

does not call for more labour of various kinds than actually exists. Similar budgets can be made for raw materials, for capital, for foreign exchange, for transport facilities, for buildings, or for any other resource which may prove to be scarce. These over-all tests consider the demands of the economy as a whole upon inputs. Next, one may test the demand for the outputs. Budget studies give some indication of how consumption increases with income. This is the test which shows up whether the projected supply of food is equal to the projected demand, given the projected level of income. The same test shows how large the market for consumer manufactures will be, as compared with projected supplies. And how large projected savings may be, compared with the savings required from consumers. One can then test individual industries using the Leontief input-output technique. Projected inputs can be compared with the plans made for expanding the outputs of the industries which are expected to supply components, transport, water, engineering service, and the like; and projected outputs can be compared with the projected expansion of exports, of consumer demand, and of industries which are to absorb by-products or other intermediate output. Since building is often the bottleneck, special attention must be paid to the projected output of building materials and components —especially of cement, bricks, steel and timber—to ensure that adequate supplies will be available, either from production or from imports. In the countryside one of the chief bottlenecks is water, so the rate at which the programme seeks to conserve and expand rural water supplies is one of the chief points to be examined.

Given the necessary information, there are plenty of statistical tests which can show up lack of balance in a production programme. The main difficulty, of course, is that the information is not given. The statistical data required—the budget studies, the consumption functions, the manpower censuses, the output censuses, the input-output tables, the national income tables and so on—do not always exist, or are subject to wide margins of error. Even if the figures are accurate, demand and output relations are apt to alter in unforeseeable ways. And all the projections of output and of exports depend upon the effectiveness of the measures which will be taken to give effect to the programme, and which certainly cannot be foreseen. A production programme is to a great extent an exercise in hope; it cannot be taken in precise quantitative terms; it shows no more than the general orders of magnitude which it is hoped to reach in various sectors. All the same, however tentative the programme, it ought to be tested for its internal consistency, however tentative the tests, since sectors may otherwise be hopelessly out of balance with each other. In such matters it is better to rely on figures and hunch rather than upon

hunch alone, even when the figures are themselves partly based on hunch.

The discussion so far has related only to paper work: the setting of the targets for various sectors of the economy. But of course what really matters in the last analysis is not the paper targets, but the measures which are taken to move resources in the right directions— to train the labour, to stimulate food productivity, to hold consumption in check, to stimulate investment, or whatever it may be. This is the hardest and most neglected part of planning. To the extent that the programme relates to the public sector of the economy it is relatively easy to carry out; the difficulty is to get the private sector of the economy to do what is required of it—to get labour to go into the right sectors, or to take the training courses; to get entrepreneurs to invest, or the public to save; to get the farmers to adopt the new techniques; or foreigners to play the parts assigned to them, as lenders, buyers, or technicians. The crucial test of a production programme is how effective it is with private individuals.

To secure the collaboration of private persons, governments rely on persuasion, on force, and on reward. Persuasion is only the sauce to the dish; people will not for long act against their own private interest merely because politicians tell them that it is in the public interest to do so. It is useful to have speeches and propaganda setting out the main objectives of the programme, and it is very desirable to win the people's enthusiastic support, but this is more likely if each sees what he will gain from it than if the programme requires people to do what it does not pay them to do. Force, also, is of limited use. It can be used negatively to prevent people from doing what you do not want them to do, but is of much more limited use for making people do what you want them to do, especially in a democracy. Thus goods can be rationed, or raw materials or building can be licensed, to prevent some people from having as much as they otherwise would; but entrepreneurs cannot be forced to invest in industries, and farmers cannot be forced to have a food surplus, as the U.S.S.R. has discovered. Some licensing may be required, and in so far as it limits the undesirable it makes the desirable more likely. But the main instrument for effecting a development programme must be reward. If labour is to do what is required of it, there must be adequate wage differentials. If the farmers are to collaborate, the framework within which they operate must make this worth their while. And if the entrepreneurs are to invest, there must be a fair likelihood of adequate profits. Much the best way of ensuring the success of a production programme is to tax the activities one wishes to discourage, and to subsidize (in one way or another) the activities one wishes to encourage.

A further moral is that, in so far as production programmes require the collaboration of the private sector, they ought to be made in consultation with the private sector. This is not always politically easy. Some governments in the less developed countries are hostile to private enterprise in general, and to foreign enterprise in particular, and will not allow these classes to participate in production planning. They make programmes which could be effective only if business men found it profitable to collaborate, but the governments at the same time do their best to avoid both profit and collaboration, and are rather surprised when their programmes come to nothing. Farmers can be just as difficult to handle. Some governments are dominated by landlords, who are unwilling to pursue the measures of land reform without which the farmers have little incentive to produce more. Others have an eye to getting hold of part of the farmers' surplus to finance capital formation. If a government can secure the support of both its capitalists and its farmers it is well on the way to getting something done, but governments which can hold political confidence whilst putting through painful measures are rather rare—at least in the democratic world.

Very close collaboration may be required to carry out the programme. Entrepreneurs will certainly be reluctant to make some of the investments which the government wants. Its agencies will have to do research and to supply information, and it may have to put up some of the capital, and to guarantee markets or dividends. In an economy where the government is trying to inspire, guide and stimulate private entrepreneurs, business and government get pretty mixed up with each other, e.g. Japan. Similar close collaboration is needed with the farmers. The government's agencies are doing research, trying to persuade the farmers to change their methods, lending them money, taking a hand in marketing, bringing more water to the villages, and so on. Unless the confidence of the farmers is won, much of this work comes to nothing.

Because it is difficult to get the required response from individuals, at any rate on the government's terms, some governments prefer to try to launch upon development without the collaboration of individual producers. If the farmers are slow, or suspicious, or insistent on high prices for food, then they establish state farms, and concentrate on increasing the output within their own control. This was the policy of the U.S.S.R. in the nineteen-twenties (before collectivization) and it is also the attitude which led the British government to launch upon great schemes of mechanized agriculture in Africa, instead of spending the money on stimulating production by African peasant farmers. When this policy failed in the U.S.S.R., the government resorted to forcing the peasants into its collective farms, where

they had to do as they were told, rather than let up on its policy of high taxation and low prices. Much the same attitude may be taken towards industrialists. Some governments consider that the profits which private business requires, both as an incentive and as a source of finance for further development, are too high a price to pay for prosperity. They fix low prices and low profits, and when this discourages investment, they start public undertakings to do the job instead. This puts all the greater burden upon them to find the capital, the technical knowledge, the managerial skill and the enterprise required to initiate industrialization, factors which are all scarce in the less developed economies. Economic development is so difficult that one would think it desirable to mobilize all available knowledge and initiative, at least in the stage of getting off the ground, but this opinion is clearly not shared by all the governments of countries with low output per head.

2. THE PUBLIC SECTOR

(a) Public Expenditure Programmes

Whether a production programme is made for the whole economy or not, it is necessary to have a programme for public expenditure, if only to exercise control over public officials. Practically every government in the world makes an annual expenditure programme, incorporated in the budget. Most of the less developed countries are also making such programmes for a longer period than a year, some for five or six or even as many as ten years. Indeed, some are required to do so, as a condition of international assistance. When in 1945 the United Kingdom government set aside a sum of £120 millions for making grants to British colonial governments, it called upon each of them to submit a ten year programme of development expenditure; similarly the countries included in the Colombo Plan in 1950 were asked to submit six year plans. The United Nations International Bank also likes to see such plans, and willingly sends missions to less developed countries to help in formulating such plans. The United States government went even further when it offered Marshall aid to Europe; each of the countries aided was required to produce a four year plan covering every sector of its economy, public and private—and this for the country where the word 'plan' is most suspect!

The advantages of multi-year planning are fairly obvious. In the process of drawing up the first of these programmes the several departments and agencies of the government have, perhaps for the first time, to formulate clearly for themselves their detailed objectives. Looking ahead gives their work a purpose and a series of

stages which it might otherwise lack. Then, when the programmes of the various agencies are put together, there is an opportunity for ensuring both consistency and the due observance of priorities. The left hand of the government does not always know what the right hand is doing, and the need to make a programme for all government activities provides an opportunity for co-ordination. Also, the heads of some departments have more initiative than others, and succeed in getting more money for their departments than a true system of priorities would justify. This may happen even if there is a comprehensive programme, but it is less likely to happen if all departments are asked to submit their programmes at the same time, and if the agency which does the final selection is conscious of the importance of consistency and of priority, and has the necessary authority for securing reasonable balance. Much depends on the efficiency and the authority of this central planning authority. Since the programmes put forward are certain greatly to exceed the resources available, difficult choices have to be made and enforced, and the planning authority needs to have the full backing and interest of the chief minister of the government. Then, once the programme is made, it has great value for those who have to execute it. The financial officers of the government can look ahead and make their plans in good time. The engineers can get their blueprints ready. The purchasing departments can order their materials in time; and so on. And finally, the existence of the plan enables progress to be tested. Everyone knows what is expected of each agency, and its performance can be measured against what is laid down in the programme.

The dangers of multi-year planning are equally obvious. Since no one can foresee the future, even for so short a period as five years, it would be a disadvantage to be bound strictly by the provisions of such a plan. These programmes get quickly out of date. Prices may rise sharply or the funds available may be more or less (usually less!) than was expected. A few projects are executed ahead of schedule; most are held up by unforeseen shortages of materials, of skilled labour, of scientists, or of money. Hence any such plan must be subject to constant revision. To meet this difficulty the government of Puerto Rico revises its six-year plan every year, making in each year a plan for the next six years. No device can ensure that the plan will always take account of changed circumstances. On the other hand a plan is needed because, though we cannot foretell the future, we also cannot act rationally without making plans for the future, in the light of whatever information is available at the time.

Some of these programmes are confined to listing proposed capital expenditures, of government departments, public corporations, government finance corporations and other government agencies.

CC

Others list all expenditure which normally appears in the budget, whether on capital or on current account. It is better to programme all expenditure than capital expenditure only. For one thing, capital expenditure often gives rise to subsequent current expenditure; the building of schools is followed by the payment of teachers, or the purchase of tractors by the hire of their drivers. If capital expenditure is stated without recurrent expenditure it is difficult to see just how much any project is going to cost, and financial planning may go sadly awry. In the second place, the planners themselves may be deceived if they are asked to submit programmes confined to capital expenditure. Development does not depend upon capital expenditure only; it requires for example heavy current expenditure upon various education programmes, such as agricultural extension. If the emphasis is on capital expenditure these programmes tend to be overlooked.

It is very desirable that the right priorities be accorded in drawing up public expenditure programmes, but it is impossible to lay down rules for determining what the right priorities are. The best that we can do here is to indicate the points where some of these programmes have been found to be weak.

First, it is important that the programme for the public sector should be properly related to what is happening in the private sector. The whole programme for public utilities, for example—for railways, docks, water supplies, electricity, etc.—has to be shaped in accordance with the intentions of private investors, so that facilities are made available when and where they are required. Similarly the programme for training skilled labour depends upon the kinds of skill which will be required. Public expenditure programming and production programming have therefore to be done side by side. The public authorities need to know what private enterprise is proposing to do, and private business should have a hand in shaping the public programme.

Secondly, some programmes bear too much the mark of having been made in the capital city, and too little the influence of the countryside. Many programmes do too much to beautify the cities, or to provide them with better houses, schools, water supplies or medical services, in comparison with what they do for the rural areas where most of the people live. Plans made for the country from the town also tend to be of the spectacular kind, which can be shown off to visitors. Too much is spent on constructing a few elegant highways, and too little on a multitude of small farm-to-market roads, which might add more to output. Or vast resources will be poured into controlling a single river, where the same money would yield much more if spent on a great number of wells, tanks, and small streams. The spectacular is sometimes also the right policy; one big

project may do more for development than a large number of small ones costing just as much. The remedy is not to eschew the spectacular, but to take care that the planning process is adequately decentralized. The rural areas should be encouraged to make their own plans, and their representation in the planning process should be adequate to ensure that their wants are not overlooked. The best way to ensure this is of course to follow the 'Community development' method (Chapter III, section 1(a) and Chapter V, section 2(a)). Since this relies on voluntary labour, only schemes which the people really want can be executed. Community development is the best development of all, and every programme should set aside for this work sums amounting to one or two per cent of the national output.

Community development has also the advantage of cutting extravagance in capital expenditures, which is the third defect of several programmes. Capital is so scarce in under-developed countries that it should be used most sparingly. What is needed is often the cheapest structure that will do the job. It is wrong to build schools or hospitals or thermal power stations capable of lasting fifty years, when a structure lasting thirty years would cost much less—many such structures are pulled down in thirty years anyway, because of changing standards and rising income. Similarly, second-hand machinery is often more appropriate than new, and it may even pay to buy equipment which more advanced countries consider obsolete, if it can be had very cheaply. A good government likes to do properly whatever it is doing, and to leave behind it structures which are permanent and outstanding, but most poor countries cannot afford to do things properly in this sense. Over-lavish use of cement and steel is one of the commoner faults of development programmes.

Indeed, it is also a common fault of such programmes that they conceive of development too largely in terms of investment in concrete things, and too little in terms of investment in persons. This shows itself especially in deficiency in public health programmes, and in education programmes. As for public health, we have seen before (Chapter II, section 2(a) and Chapter IV, section 3(c)) that measures for the improvement of diets and for the elimination of debilitating diseases can considerably increase productivity. And as for education, we have suggested that in addition to the usual expenditures on primary, secondary, technical and university education, the governments of agricultural countries should set aside up to one per cent of national output for expenditure on agricultural research and agricultural extension. (Chapter IV, section 3(b).)

Finally, the role of the government as a provider of capital for use outside the public sector has also to be borne in mind. We have seen

reasons (Chapter V, section 3(*a*)) why the low level of domestic saving may make the government a major channel of capital for small scale agriculture, for industrial development, for public utilities, and for housing; whether the capital is provided from its own savings, or comes from abroad, or is forced by inflation. One of the dangers of drawing up programmes for public expenditure is that excessive attention may be given to the requests of public service agencies, and that too much of the community's resources may go in this direction at the expense of other sectors of the economy. This is another reason why public expenditure programming should go hand in hand with surveying the economy as a whole. In the last analysis the public services have to be paid for by the 'productive' sectors of the economy, and it is important to ensure that social and welfare services do not run away with resources beyond the productive capacity of the economy.

(b) The Fiscal Problem

The needs of governments for finance grow all the time, because the public sector grows faster than the economy as a whole. We can measure this in various ways; in terms of the number of people in government employment, in terms of resources used by the government, or in terms of the share of taxation in the national income. Take first numbers employed. Civilian employment, excluding defence, is seldom less that 2 per cent of the gainfully occupied, and ranges up to about 10 per cent in the U.S.A. and 11 per cent in the U.K. (including central and local administrations). To this must be added the armed forces, ranging from nearly nil in Denmark, through the U.K's record peace time (1954) figure of 4 per cent to even higher figures in Greece, Turkey, and elsewhere. If we add again public utilities and nationalized industries, the figure of government employment in the U.K. becomes 25 per cent, viz., 11 per cent civilian public services, plus 4 per cent armed forces, plus 10 per cent nationalized industries. Next we turn to consider resources used, excluding nationalized industries. The proportion of resources used exceeds the proportion of employment, since government also buys supplies from the private sector of the economy (ranging from ink to aeroplanes). The governments of the U.S.A. and the U.K. were using about the same proportion of the national output in 1938, namely about 14 per cent; now, with expanded defence programmes, they use more like 22 to 24 per cent. But even this is not all; for on top of the resources they use, they also need funds to finance transfer payments which do not involve them in buying goods or services for their own use—pensions, interest on the national debt, unemployment benefits, and such. In consequence taxation in the United King-

dom runs currently at around 35 per cent of the national income, compared with around 8 per cent in India, and around 5 per cent in Nigeria.

These differences in the share of the national income used by government are of course associated with considerable differences in the quality of government. Visitors to the less developed countries frequently complain about the inefficiency of the public services— bad roads, impure water, poor sanitation, mosquitoes, inefficient administration and so on. The answer is that good public services cannot be provided for 5 per cent of the national income. Defence and transfers apart, the countries of Western Europe and North America use up about 12 per cent of their national incomes in their public services, and the less developed countries would need even more to pay for the same standard, since incomes per head are lower.

The less developed countries need not carry the same military burden as the great industrial countries. On the other hand, where they determine to contribute towards capital formation in the private sector, they may need quite large sums for the purpose. If for example they would like net capital formation in the economy as a whole to be twelve per cent of national income per annum, and if their economies are saving only five per cent, there is a difference of seven per cent to be found from somewhere. Twelve per cent is not an extraordinary target; it is the sort of rate achieved by European economies in the first stages of their industrial revolutions, and is lower than the U.S.S.R. and Japanese rates. If we guess a capital-income ratio of 4 to 1, real income would increase by 3 per cent per annum if investment were 12 per cent; real income per head would increase by $1\frac{1}{2}$ per cent per annum, if population was increasing by $1\frac{1}{2}$ per cent and would double in about fifty years. At this pace the standard of living in the less developed countries would rise at the same rate as in Western Europe; no progress would be made towards closing the gap between the richer and the poorer countries. If this gap is to be closed even greater investment than this will be needed.

The reason why the governments of the less developed economies raise less revenue than those of more developed economies is not that they need less revenue, but that revenue is harder to raise. It is easiest to consider the matter in terms of real resources. If an economy needs seventy per cent of its population in agriculture to provide food, the amount of labour which can be set aside for government purposes out of the remaining thirty per cent is clearly very much smaller than can be set aside by an economy which needs only twelve per cent of its people in agriculture. The less developed econo-mies cannot afford to pay as large a percentage of their incomes in

taxes as the more developed can. All the same, most of them could pay more than they do, if they wished to. Raising more revenue in these countries is hard, but it is not as hard as it is sometimes made out to be. It would be out of place to put into this chapter a potted treatise on public finance; this section confines itself to a few remarks on some of the special problems of the poorer countries.

First of all, there are problems of technique. One of the canons of taxation is that one should avoid taxes which are costly to collect because they have to be collected from a large number of persons, each of whom pays only a small sum. This applies equally to direct and to indirect taxation. It is one of the reasons why one confines income taxation to persons with relatively large incomes. For example, in most countries it is not thought to be worth while to collect income tax from people earning less than £150 a year. But the proportion of the population earning more than £150 a year is very small in poor countries. Correspondingly, the income tax yields a proportionately smaller revenue in poor than in rich countries. In fact, the poor countries have to rely to a greater extent upon indirect taxation not because they wish to distribute the tax burden differently —this does not necessarily result—but because the proportion of the national income over the practicable exemption limit is so much smaller. The problem of evasion is related, for when a large part of the income subject to taxation is received by petty traders who do not keep proper accounts, it is extremely costly to enforce the income tax provisions. Most of the less developed countries would profit substantially by enforcing their tax laws more rigorously, but even the most rigorous enforcement cannot make the income tax the major source of revenue, unless there are a few large mining or other corporations that can be milked.

Some countries have also great technical difficulties in raising indirect taxation. Such taxes are most easily levied at points where a large part of the national income is passing through a small number of hands. Imports and exports are usually handled by a small number of wholesalers from whom import and export duties can be collected cheaply. In industrial countries a large part of output is produced by a few very large firms, and excise taxes and purchase taxes are therefore cheap to collect. Not all the less developed countries are so favourably placed. Exports are around forty to fifty per cent of the national income of Ceylon, so it is easy in that island to raise a large part of the national income in import or export taxes, at small administrative cost. But next door in India exports are less than ten per cent of national income, so the yield of taxes on foreign trade is correspondingly low. Countries like India have to rely to a greater extent on taxing domestic trade, but this is costly because their out-

put is not concentrated in a few firms; it is produced by millions of small producers, and sold through millions of outlets. It is then impossible to prevent considerable tax evasion, and the cost of collection is necessarily high.

A further difficulty in some less developed economies is that a large part of output is not traded at all. The farmer produces his own food, and some of his own manufactures, and disposes of only a small surplus in the market. If the farmers were taxed only on their money incomes (presumably by means of import or excise taxes on what they buy), they would largely escape taxation. It is different where the farmers are growing commercial crops for export (cocoa, rubber, cotton, etc.), for they are then easily reached by export taxes. Self-sufficient farmers have to be taxed directly. African tribes have used the poll tax for this purpose, whereas Indian princes relied mainly on a land tax. Some land taxes have been made to yield very large revenues, e.g. in Japan and in the U.S.S.R. In fact, it is not unusual in over-populated countries for rents and taxes together to be absorbing fifty per cent or more of the peasant's output. On the other hand, land taxes are direct taxes, and as such they arouse much more hostility than indirect taxes, whose existence is not always so obvious or so well known. The U.S.S.R. government met extreme resistance in its attempts to levy upon the peasants enough to support the forty to fifty per cent of the national income which it required for capital formation, for defence, and for its other expenditures. Land taxes tend therefore to give way to export or import taxes as soon as this becomes convenient.

This brings us to consider the distribution of the burden of taxation in less developed economies. Whether the distribution of income is more uneven or less uneven than in the developed economies depends first on the relationship between population and land, and secondly upon the extent of the capitalized sector of the economy. In the over-populated countries rents are high, perhaps as much as forty to fifty per cent of the output of agriculture, and the distribution of income tends to be even more uneven than in developed industrial economies. In the capitalized sectors the ratio of profits to wages tends to be higher than it is in the industrial economies—indeed in some cases, such as copper mining in Central Africa, profits may be a half of net output or more. One cannot therefore generalize about the less developed economies; in some the distribution of income is more uneven than it is in the United States, while in others, such as the Gold Coast or Nigeria it is much less uneven.

How far down in the income scale taxation has to be taken depends partly on how uneven the distribution of income is, but it also depends partly upon the effects of taxation upon incentives and

savings. This latter question is more important in the less than in the more developed economies. It is important in the more developed economies too, but these economies have a certain development momentum which carries them along even when incentives and savings are diminished. The class which it is easiest to tax in the less developed economies is the landlord class—easiest both because neither incentives nor savings are involved, and also in the political sense because landlords are nearly everywhere (but not quite everywhere) now in political disfavour. Peasants have always had to carry a high tax burden, but in some countries where they have recently acquired the vote (e.g. India) their political restlessness has given them a degree of immunity from high taxation which has been embarrassing to the government. The salaried middle classes are also difficult to tax in most of the less developed countries, partly because they wield political power in the new nationalist governments, and partly because incentives are required for the expansion of this class; one of the chief effects of economic development is enormously to increase the number of semi-skilled, skilled and professional people in the community, and this may be adversely affected by high taxation on the people in these categories. Profits are also a difficult category. They are easy to tax politically, especially when the capital belongs to foreigners, but the taxation of profits may damage both incentives and savings. The savings point is not so important, since an intelligent government can substitute public saving for private saving, but the incentive point may be important in countries where entrepreneurship is scarce. Some countries which are anxious to encourage development are actually going in the opposite direction: they are offering temporary exemption from income tax to capitalists who start new industries.

What to do about the rich is certainly a serious problem for governments whose support comes mainly from the poor, but who are at the same time very anxious to promote development. Non-cultivating landlords are not much of a problem. They can be bought out, and may then, as in Japan, finding themselves with money and no duties, convert themselves into capitalists and supply much needed entrepreneurship (Chapter V, section 2(b)). Even if they are expropriated the consequences for economic growth are not likely to be adverse, unless they have been cultivating the soil themselves on large-scale estates with modern methods. It is quite different with commercial and industrial capitalists, who are the major source of saving and of enterprise. Economic growth causes the share of profits in the national income to rise, in the initial stages (Chapter V, section 2(b)), and this has meant in the past the creation of large private fortunes in the hands of a very few people. It is easy to under-

stand why democratic governments are most suspicious of this process, and are very reluctant to let the capitalists make substantial profits out of economic development; on the other hand, if profits are kept low, or taxed heavily, private saving will be small, and there will be little incentive for private enterprise. The Liberal way through this dilemma is to encourage private capitalists to make all the profits they can while alive, and to tax them severely when they die. If this were done ruthlessly, as it has never been so far, it would mean that each generation could start with more or less equal opportunity; the incentive to make a fortune would be reduced somewhat, but this might well be more than offset by the increase in opportunities (Chapter III, section 3(*b*)). The Socialist solution is to do away with private capitalists, and to have the state supply the enterprise, earn the profits, and make the savings. The feasibility of this solution depends on how enterprising the state can be, and how willing it will be to engage in productive investment. There is no doubt that this solution can be made to work, especially by countries which need only to imitate and not to pioneer (Chapter III, section 3(*a*)). What will not work is if the state taxes private enterprise to the point where incentives and private savings are inadequate, without itself stepping into the breach with initiatives and savings of its own.

This analysis brings out as well the importance of political considerations in taxation. Most governments find it easiest to tax those who oppose them and to exempt those on whose support they rely, and this fact plays as large a part in determining the distribution of the tax burden, as considerations of equity, of incentive, or of savings. Yet the fact remains that in most of these economies it is impossible for the government to play the roles it needs to play in economic development unless it taxes *all* classes more heavily than they are taxed at present. The major political problem in most of these countries is to persuade the people that this is so, and to gain their consent to the necessary measures. The authoritarian governments are in this respect at an advantage in comparison with the democratic governments. They can push the government's share up to twenty or thirty per cent of the national income, and use half the proceeds for capital formation, without bothering about what will happen in the ballot box, if there is a ballot box. The democratic governments are in greater difficulty. Here and there a great democratic leader is able to carry his people through a phase of relative privation for the sake of building up the nation, and holds their confidence and enthusiasm. But such leaders are rare. In many other countries democracy is an obstacle to speeding up the rate of economic growth. Perhaps this is as it should be; we are not con-

cerned in this chapter with the desirability or otherwise of economic growth (see Appendix).

While it is difficult to increase the government's share of a given national income, it is not so difficult politically to ensure that a greater share of increases in the national income should accrue to the government. This is the main hope of increasing the share of government in the national income. In less developed economies the marginal rate of taxation should always be considerably greater than the average rate. This principle is indeed adopted by the more developed countries as well. It is one of the chief ways in which they combat fluctuations in the national income, since its effect is that government revenues fall sharply in a slump and rise sharply in a boom. It is also the way they combat inflation; for example it is one of the reasons why the United Kingdom and the United States were able to go through the second world war with an increase in their price levels of fifty per cent or less, whereas many other countries whose war effort was much smaller had price increases of 200 or 300 per cent or more; and it is also the reason why British prices have not risen faster since the war despite the great pressure of monetary demand upon resources. In these countries some forty to fifty per cent of marginal income is taken in taxation. If this results in raising revenue too rapidly, it is possible to reduce the average burden of taxation without reducing the marginal rate.

In the less developed countries, in contrast, it is frequently the case that the marginal rate of taxation is below the average rate—that government receipts increase less rapidly than national income. This is due to reluctance to raise government-controlled prices as other prices rise. Railway rates, postal charges, telephone charges, and other government prices are slow to rise; land taxes lag, if fixed in money; import and export duties may be fixed on a specific rather than an *ad valorem* basis; and so on. Inflation ought to make a government rich, because of its high marginal share of income; instead in many less developed economies a rise of prices produces a budget deficit. In these days, when the secular trend of prices seems to be upward, taxes should always be on the *ad valorem* rather than the specific basis, and the arrangements for altering the prices of public utilities and public services should permit rapid adjustment to changing costs.

The way to ensure a high rate of marginal taxation is to have an income tax with a high marginal rate, high taxes upon those consumer goods for which the demand increases most rapidly, and export duties with high marginal rates.

There is not much to be said about the income tax. The average burden of the tax depends upon the exemptions and allowances,

given the marginal rates of tax. Hence the marginal rate can be forty per cent or more while the average rate is only five per cent or less. The problem posed by a high marginal rate is its effect on incentives. This is often exaggerated, but it is nevertheless real. Indirect taxes do not have the same effect on incentives because people are not so conscious of them. Hence opinion is veering towards indirect away from direct taxes. The idea that indirect taxes are necessarily less progressive than direct taxes is fallacious. The poor, the rich and the middle classes consume different goods in different proportions. If one puts low indirect taxes upon what the poor consume and high indirect taxes upon what the rich consume indirect taxes can be just as progressive as an income tax, in so far as people spend their incomes. The difference is that indirect taxes reach only that part of income which is spent, whereas an income tax falls also upon savings, but this difference also can be exaggerated since both taxes can be so adjusted that they have the same effect on total savings—though the effects on individuals will vary according to their expenditure patterns.

In levying indirect taxes, the principle is to put high rates upon luxury articles, and other articles for which the demand is increasing rapidly, whether they are strictly luxury articles or not. The latter category is quite wide in some countries, because the spread of westernization is increasing fairly rapidly the demand for such things as electrical appliances, radios, bicycles, motor transport, beer, cigarettes, gramophones or furniture. An import duty or excise tax of 100 per cent of the wholesale value may be only thirty to forty per cent of the retail price. Some governments are reluctant to levy 100 per cent duties, but quite a few duties at this level may be needed if the marginal rate of taxation is to be brought up to forty to fifty per cent. Most countries levy import duties but this is not enough in countries where imports are low relatively to national income, or where inflation is raising domestic prices without raising the prices of imports. In either of these cases it may be necessary to have a fair battery of excise taxes and sales taxes if the government is to get a large share of increases in money income.

We have already discussed export duties in relation to forced saving (Chapter V, section 2(b)), and in relation to economic stability. The principle is to levy a tax which rises sharply as the price of the commodity rises, in accordance with a sliding scale fixed in advance. Government marketing agencies have much the same effect when they keep the domestic price of the commodity from rising as fast as its export price. We have seen that some countries, notably Burma and the Gold Coast, have generated enormous savings in this way. The best time to initiate such schemes is when there is a reces-

sion in the United States. Prices are then low, and the effective tax is also low. Sliding scales are more acceptable if they are introduced during a slump than if they are started when prices are high, and impose high taxation right from their inception.

It should be noted that this discussion of a high marginal rate of taxation is meant to apply to rising money income, and not just to rising real income. In the countries which most need to make this effort real income per head is not rising at all (e.g. India), so if the government confined itself to getting a larger share of increases in real income per head the operation might never get off the ground. If real income per head is rising, so much the better, but it is just as important to get hold of an increasing share of a constant real income. Whatever may happen to real income, money income is likely to rise. The tendency of prices in the industrial countries is upward, partly because of inflationary pressures, and partly because trade union action keeps raising money wages faster than productivity. This increasing monetary demand in the industrial countries tends to keep agricultural prices rising, subject to some fluctuation, and the fact that the agricultural surpluses available for export have not risen *pari passu* with industrial demand may continue to have the same effect for the next few years. Given a tendency for prices to rise, a government can get a constantly increasing share of the national income if it has the right fiscal structure, whether real income is rising or not.

If it is politically too difficult for the government to get a larger share of the national income through taxation, it can arrive at the same result through inflation, if this is not equally difficult politically. In the less developed countries inflation and taxation have much the same effect (Chapter V, section 2(a)). They transfer consumer goods towards those who are employed on capital formation, away from the rest of the community. In an industrial economy with unemployment, credit creation is superior to taxation for financing capital formation, because it creates simultaneously more consumer goods, but this is not possible to any considerable extent in the less developed economies, even when they have surplus labour. Inflation differs from taxation also in that it tends to raise profits, and may therefore stimulate capital formation by private entrepreneurs. Some inflation is helpful to economic development, provided it is kept within bounds. If prices are rising at a rate less than the rate of interest, there is no profit in speculation. Hence, if prices rise on the average by three or four per cent per annum, we can have all the advantages of inflation for capital formation without much danger that this will give rise to a speculative boom and to a flight from money—especially if the movement is punctuated every three or four years by a little

deflation of prices. Moreover, as we have already seen, inflation for the purpose of capital formation is in due course self-destructive. The inflation has three stages. Prices rise sharply in the first stage while the capital is being created. In the second stage the inflation may peter out of its own accord because the rise in prices has redistributed income in such a way that voluntary saving is rapidly catching up with investment. Then in the third stage prices fall, as the additional output of consumer goods made possible by the capital formation begins to reach the market. It is only the first stage that is dangerous and painful.

The effect of inflation on capital formation depends on the purpose of the inflation. If the inflation is due to the government spending money on paying high salaries to civil servants, or on making war, there is no reason to expect the inflation to increase capital formation, unless the economy has a fair proportion of the kind of industrial capitalists who invest inflationary profits in fixed capital—and this is more likely in advanced than in under-developed countries. On the other hand, whether the country is under-developed or not, if the inflation is due to the government spending money on creating useful assets, such as an irrigation system, the immediate effect will be an increase in these useful assets, quite apart from what happens to the inflationary profits. In recent literature some naïve investigators have professed to show that inflation does not increase capital formation by showing that in a number of places where inflation has occurred (notably in Latin America), capital formation has not increased. It is not sensible to generalize about the effects of inflation in this way. Inflation used for destructive purposes has destructive effects whereas, as in the U.S.S.R. or Japan, or in the upward phase of every trade cycle, inflation which is due to the creation of money for the purpose of accelerating capital formation results in accelerated capital formation.

Some countries can stand more credit creation than others, both economically and politically. On the economic side the relevant issues are such matters as: Who will get the inflationary profits, and what will they do with them; spend them on consumption, speculate in commodities, create new fixed capital, hoard them, or buy government bonds? Can the output of consumer goods be expanded rapidly, or will the first stage of the inflation be long? Is it the kind of economy where prices of essential goods can be controlled fairly easily, without a great growth of black markets? Is there a strong trade union movement, which will turn a demand inflation into a cost inflation? Can the foreign exchange situation be safeguarded? Is there a high marginal rate of taxation mopping up fifty per cent of money income as fast as it is generated by inflation? Countries differ

very widely in the answers to these questions, with the result that an amount of credit creation which would raise prices by ten per cent in one, might double prices in another. There are also wide differences in the political response to inflation. In some countries it is politically imperative that the government should take measures to raise real income substantially, even if this involves some inflation, and inflation may thus be the condition for political existence. In other countries the public has been through quite enough inflation in recent years, for destructive purposes, and it expects its governments to keep a tight rein on money. Since inflation is primarily a substitute for taxation, the decision whether to resort to it is primarily political, and has to be made in terms of the political alternatives.

One of the strongest political arguments against inflation is that once the possibility of resorting to it is admitted, governments cannot be trusted to know where to draw the line. The great advantage of the principle that budgets must be balanced is that it allows the Minister of Finance to discipline his colleagues in the Cabinet. They may plead most eloquently for the expansion of this service or that, but his position is impregnable so long as his budget has to be balanced. Once this principle is abandoned, what control remains over government expenditure? One way of getting round this difficulty is to have two budgets, one which must be financed out of revenue, and another, consisting exclusively of services which rapidly increase output (especially expenditures on land reclamation, rural water, training facilities and agricultural extension) which may be financed by creating credit. This, however, does not evade the problem altogether, since it then becomes possible to argue about what should be transferred to the second budget. No administrative device can relieve a government of the need to exercise courage and restraint.

Another source of revenue, apart from taxation and credit creation, is small savings lodged in government institutions, of which the most important are the Post Office Savings Banks. Small savings of all kinds, including savings in the co-operative movement and in friendly societies, vary from nil to about two per cent of national income, in those less developed countries which have put effort into this movement. It need hardly be said how important it is to stimulate such savings. For the saver they signify independence, self-respect and security against a rainy day, and this is even more important than the contribution such savings make to the nation's financial problem. The country which has had the greatest success in this sphere is Japan, where small savings are estimated to be as much as eight per cent of the national income. This is certainly a model to be emulated (Chapter V, section 2(*b*)).

Finally, there is the possibility of raising funds externally, whether by grant or by loan. Some countries are better placed for this than others. Taking the less developed countries as a whole, however, the prospect does not seem to be very great. The national incomes of Africa and Asia (excluding China, Japan and the U.S.S.R.) add up to about 75,000 million U.S. dollars annually. One per cent of this is 750 million dollars, a sum which greatly exceeds all the foreign investment and foreign aid now going into those two continents. If capital formation in these continents is to be brought up to twelve per cent of national income net, the sums involved are far beyond any likely foreign investment or foreign aid. Hence, whatever these countries may get from overseas, they have to pull themselves up by their own bootstraps if they are to make substantial progress.

There is no reason to doubt that most of the less developed countries can increase their capital formation substantially if they wish to. Before them all lies the challenge of the U.S.S.R. and of Japan, two countries where real output per head has risen faster than elsewhere, namely by about three per cent per annum—in the U.S.S.R. since 1929, and in Japan continuously since the 1870's—compared with under two per cent in the U.S.A., which ranks next. (An increase in output is not the same as an increase in consumption; consumption per head was no higher in the U.S.S.R. in 1939 than in 1929, because of the enormous increase in the use of output for defence and for capital formation.) These high rates of growth have been associated with changes in every sphere of human life, including net capital formation at an annual rate of fifteen per cent per annum or more. In both cases inflation and high taxation have played major roles. The U.S.S.R. concentrated its attention upon industrialization, and fought its peasants instead of teaching them how to increase output per acre. In ten years its large-scale industrial output trebled, while its agricultural output increased only a little faster than its population. This unbalance contributed to a tremendous price inflation, of something like a 700 per cent increase in price in ten years. The Japanese were more sensible. Over-all their output increased just as rapidly as that of the U.S.S.R., but they gave equal attention to industry and to agriculture. In the thirty years before the first world war they doubled agricultural output per person. Yet even with this, and with enormous taxation, their price level doubled in this period. It seems likely that these high rates of capital formation and of growth cannot be achieved without some inflation, since the levels of taxation and of savings required for fifteen per cent net capital formation or more are not otherwise attainable. But ten to twelve per cent capital formation is not outside the possibilities of taxation and voluntary savings without inflation, if government and people share

the objective of economic growth, and should be all the easier to achieve in those economies where the existence of surplus labour makes it possible to create some forms of useful capital without reducing consumption while doing so.

What is in doubt is not whether it is economically possible to step up the rate of capital formation, but whether it is politically possible to do so within the democratic framework. The main problem is whether it is politically feasible to levy adequate taxation upon the peasants. As we have already seen (Chapter V, section 2(b)) it is impossible greatly to accelerate capital formation in under-developed countries without substantial taxation of agriculture for purposes of capital formation. Authoritarian regimes can do this, and this is essentially what they do; but they do not have to bother about the ballot box. Democratic regimes can do the same—it is currently being done both in the Gold Coast and in Burma—but they can do it only if they are led by statesmen who enjoy wide popular confidence and support. In many countries of the world new nationalist regimes have swept into power on a tide of national feeling; it remains to be seen whether they will command the courage and the will to lead their countries out of poverty.

3. POWER AND POLITICS

Governments can have a notable effect on economic growth. If they do the right things growth is advanced. If they do too little, or the wrong things, or too much, growth is retarded. In this section we shall begin by examining the ways in which growth may be retarded, and conclude by asking what are the social conditions which produce good government.

(a) Roads to Stagnation

We distinguish nine ways in which governments may bring about economic stagnation or decline: by failing to maintain order, by plundering the citizens, by promoting the exploitation of one class by another, by placing obstacles in the way of foreign intercourse, by neglecting the public services, by excessive *laissez-faire*, by excessive control, by excessive spending, and by embarking upon costly wars. A word may be said on each of these.

Weak governments fail to maintain order within their borders. Burglary and arson render property unsafe. Bandits, footpads and highway robbers prey upon the traveller, and diminish internal commerce. Petty chiefs rebel, levying tolls upon trade, and plunging the country into civil war. Every time the ruler dies, there is a struggle for the succession. Most of the history of the world can be written in

these terms, except at times when one strong empire or another has thrown a mantle of peace over wide regions. Essentially this is a matter of maintaining an efficient police, effective courts, and a loyal administration stretching over the whole country. The secret of so doing is not, however, widely shared amongst the world's peoples. Government relies on obedience, and it is extremely difficult and costly to maintain order once the will to obey breaks down. Hence the problem is not simply one of establishing the right machinery, but is also one of acting in such a way that the people recognize the right to obedience and freely obey. It is possible that economic development makes it possible to enforce obedience more easily, by concentrating greater power in the hands of the government and by forging new weapons—the press, the radio—with which to influence men's minds. Nevertheless, there was less disorder in the world in 1900 than there is in 1954.

Very few governments are free from corruption, which is the second obstacle to economic growth. In most countries either the civil service, or the politicians, or both, consider themselves entitled to make fortunes out of bribery, embezzlement, nepotism, or awarding themselves favourable contracts. Indeed it is somewhat of a puzzle how these practices came to be put down in the course of the nineteenth century. In 1800 British public life was as corrupt as public life in most other countries, but by 1900 there had been a considerable change in public opinion, which greatly reduced the extent of corruption. No doubt one of the causes of corruption in some countries is failure to pay adequate salaries to civil servants; it is much easier to stamp out corruption when civil servants are reasonably well paid than it is when their salaries are well below those of their colleagues in comparable occupations. In any case, the harmful effects of corruption on economic growth can be gravely exaggerated. From the business man's point of view, corruption is just a form of payment for service. Provided that the required bribes are reasonably small, having regard to the profit involved in the transaction to which they relate, and provided also that they can be foreseen when entering into contracts, they are just a form of cost like any other, and they are passed on to the consumer in prices. What handicaps business is unexpected behaviour by officials; not knowing who may suddenly pounce, and how much it will take to buy him off. In pre-capitalist societies the commercial classes are usually at the mercy of lords and princes, who demand loans which they have no intention of repaying, and whose arbitrary levies drive the capitalists into keeping their wealth in forms which are easy to hide and easy to transport. The resulting discouragement of productive investment is one of the principal reasons why the capitalist

sector grows so slowly in such economies (Chapter V, section 2(b)).

We come thirdly to the exploitation of class by class. History abounds in examples: in fact Marxists hold the view that history can be understood only in these terms. There are many forms of exploitation. The most common is the exploitation of peasants by landlords, who in conditions of over-population, may be taking half their produce. Slavery and serfdom have also been common in history. These divisions may be based solely on the ownership of property by a small minority. There are also other barriers designed to maintain special privileges for a particular racial, religious or cultural group— such as the industrial colour bar; these barriers may be maintained by a minority, but they may equally well be maintained by a majority against a minority. And of course there is the 'class war', which employers and employed are now expected to maintain against each other.

Practically all governments are engaged in promoting one or other of these divisions, since governments usually get their support from one or other of these groups. There are peasant governments, against the landlords and the towns; landlord governments against the peasants and the industrialists; white supremacy governments, anti-white governments, slave-owner governments, Catholic governments, Protestant governments, capitalist governments, Labour governments, in fact governments based upon almost every conceivable division among mankind. 'Neutral' governments hardly ever exist. Some of the best authoritarian regimes have tried to maintain impartiality between various classes, but even to be impartial is to support the *status quo*. Democratic governments cannot so easily be impartial as authoritarian governments, since there is always a tendency for the most votes to go to those who can stir the greatest passions, unless the electorate has already a tradition of toleration and good sense.

Our interest in class exploitation is in its effects on economic growth. The relevant points are its effects on social mobility, and on incentives. Slavery, serfdom, the concentration of property in a few hands, and all divisions based upon caste, upon birth, upon race, or upon religion, reduce mobility, vertically and between occupations, thereby depriving society of the use of some superior talents in superior positions, and correspondingly compelling it to depend upon some inferior talents in positions for which superior talents could be had (Chapter III, section 3(b)). How important this is depends upon how large and tolerant the privileged class is. If it is large enough it can supply all the talent needed for superior positions. If it is tolerant, it will make exceptions for the best talents in the excluded classes, and may even strengthen itself by using exception-

ally the talents of clever slaves, or Jews, or other outcasts, while keeping the rest firmly in subjection. Prosperity demands only a relatively small amount of vertical mobility—only for the best individuals in the submerged groups. It demands, however, rather wider incentives than this, since it is desirable that each individual should have some incentive to make good use of the opportunities open to him.

There is now general agreement about the effect of lack of incentives on serfs, slaves, peasants and most of the other submerged classes of the past. Current interest in incentives centres on the currently fashionable class war, namely that between employers and employed. At present all capitalist governments are being propelled in the direction of taxing capitalists heavily and using the proceeds to supply employees with a whole range of social services. Both parts of this policy are assailed; the taxes on capitalists on the ground that they discourage investment, and the social services on the ground that they remove the worker's incentive to work and provide directly for his children's education, or for insurance against unemployment, sickness, etc. There is no doubt whatever of the theoretical possibility that the pillaging of the rich by the poor can bring prosperity to an end; the practical question is only within what limits it can safely be done. There are historical instances—very doubtful speculations as to the causes of the eclipse of Egyptian prosperity between 2500 B.C. and 2000 B.C., equally doubtful speculations about the part played by arbitrary taxation in damaging the prosperity of the Roman Empire in the third century A.D., and the doubtfully relevant example of the aftermath of revolution in Haiti. If the Roman case can be established, probably what is to be deduced from it is the destructive effect of arbitrary rather than of high taxation. The business community can probably adjust itself to almost any level of taxation, provided that it knows what to expect. As with corruption, probably what is destructive is what cannot be anticipated: sudden levies such as the Romans were subjected to. We may accept the proposition that stagnation may be brought about as much by the pillaging of the enterprising minority as by the exploitation of the majority, while remaining agnostic as to which cases fit into these categories.

Fourthly, governments may retard economic growth by placing obstacles in the way of intercourse with foreigners. We have seen reasons why foreign trade is most usually the starting point of accelerated economic development (Chapter V, section 3(b)). Foreigners bring new skills, new tastes, capital, and expanding markets. They may also bring exploitation, but if in one's zeal to prevent the exploitation one keeps them out altogether, the country is

deprived equally of their stimulus. Most governments have difficulty in resisting the temptation to hinder foreign intercourse, since baiting the foreigner is one of the surest roads to popularity. On the other hand, there have equally been weak governments which have signed away valuable concessions to foreigners for small recompense, or have lost their sovereignty through placing themselves too easily at the mercy of foreign financiers (Chapter V, section 2(c) and Chapter VI, section 2(c)). Only the best governments can use foreign monies and skills to best advantage. At present most of the less developed countries are in a state of reaction against nineteenth century imperialism. They have acquired a distaste for foreign capital and foreign administration, and they are more anxious to protect themselves from further exploitation than to take advantage of current opportunities.

Fifthly, governments may retard economic growth by failing to spend adequately on the public services. Development requires roads, water supplies, education, public health, and the like. This defection is not serious if there are adequate opportunities for private entrepreneurship to supply the deficiencies. Nearly everything that governments do private companies have done at some time or other, not excluding providing roads, police, fire services, or arbitration. Indeed in most of the spheres of public service the pioneering has been done by private entrepreneurs, and governments have come in only at a relatively late stage. They have, however, everywhere come in to take these services over from private entrepreneurs, since it has everywhere seemed preferable to have the 'public' services operated by 'public' authorities. In any case, whether governments are needed for these services or not, one of the ways in which they can advance economic growth is by developing adequate public services, since these are a necessary framework for other enterprise.

Governments have also an important pioneering job to do, in which many fail. How much they need to do depends on the quantity, the quality and the risk-bearing propensities of their private entrepreneurs. The more backward the country, the greater the scope for a pioneering government. Excellent examples have been the economic activities of Burleigh in the reign of Elizabeth I, and of the Japanese governments at the end of the nineteenth century. Governments are needed to support research, to invite immigrants to set up new industries, to protect infant industries, to support foreign trade drives, to establish agricultural extension services, to make credit available cheaply, and so on. It is therefore a misfortune for a backward country to have a government which is committed to *laissez-faire*, whether from indolence or from philosophical conviction. This has been the misfortune of the British colonial empire in the nineteenth and twentieth centuries. The British colonial empire has

been exploited less than any other empire in history; for close on a
century there were no preferential restrictions on trade, no tribute
levied, and very little by way of a caste system in economic life.
Peace was established, corruption diminished, justice administered
fairly, foreign trade advanced, and public services created and
extended. Where this Empire failed, economically, was in its devo-
tion to *laissez-faire.* In agriculture the peasants were not taught new
methods or provided with new seeds or fertilizers; and in industry
nothing was done to foster new manufactures and to see them through
their growing pains. Hence the rate of growth of total output was
always slow, and hardly greater than the rate of growth of population,
which other beneficial measures stimulated. Not all modern Empires
have pursued this *laissez-faire* policy. The Dutch abandoned
laissez-faire in Indonesia in the 1930's, and launched a most interesting series of measures, but they were too late to win the allegiance
of their subjects. The Belgians in the Congo are pursuing a vigorous
economic policy, whose results it will be interesting to see.

At the opposite pole from *laissez-faire*, governments may retard
economic growth by showing excessive zeal for regulating the
economy. Colbert thought it necessary to prescribe the widths of
cloths, and the government of the U.S.S.R. thinks it necessary to
repress private retail trade. Since no government can substitute for
the initiative and common sense of its people, a government which
prevents its people from exercising initiative and common sense must
restrict economic growth. The U.S.S.R., for example, attributes its
economic success to central planning, but this is mistaken. Its success
is due to a high level of capital formation, such as was achieved in
Japan without the Russian type of planning and without so much
inflation. If more initiative had been allowed in the U.S.S.R. the
quality of the services received by consumers would have been much
better, for the same resources, and agricultural output would have
been much larger. The problem for governments in economic life is
to find the right road between too much planning and too little, and
between too much and too little nationalization. This is not the place
to elaborate lengthily on this issue, which the present writer has
already treated in a previous book.

Next, governments may retard economic growth by using up too
much of the community's resources for their own purposes—for
building monuments, town halls, pyramids, public gardens, roads,
schools, or other public services. Nearly all government activity
contributes indirectly towards increasing other output, but some of
it is more productive in this sense than other activities. If government
spends lavishly on its own services, it may be using up resources
which could be invested more productively in the private sector.

This kind of lavish expenditure is sometimes defended in countries where there is surplus labour on the ground that if the labour were not used for these purposes it would remain unemployed. It is true that the cost of using surplus labour is negligible if other scarce resources—materials, machines, etc.—do not have to be used with it, but this proviso is not always fulfilled. Besides, even if using surplus labour wastefully does not subtract from other output, using it productively would have added to output. If there is surplus labour it is better to use it to extend the irrigation system than to build pyramids with it.

Apart from the actual waste of resources, lavish government expenditure may also retard economic growth if the taxes from which it is financed are levied in such a way as to blunt incentives. This is largely a question of technique. People may be discouraged from making extra effort if they know that they will have to pay a large part of the proceeds to someone else; this is not absolutely certain, since the effect may equally be to make it necessary to work harder in order to attain the desired standard of living, but it is a possible reaction. If people react in this way, income taxes and land taxes proportional to output discourage incentive, all the more so, presumably, when they are marginally above say one-third. This effect can however largely be avoided by levying indirect taxes instead of direct taxes. The taxpayer usually does not know how much tax is included in the prices of the articles he buys, so in so far as the disincentive effect of taxation is psychological it can be avoided by using indirect rather than direct taxes. (We have already seen in section 2(b) above that indirect taxes can be as progressive as direct taxes.)

Apart from this, it is probable that changes in taxation are more important than the absolute level of taxation. People resent increases in taxation, and may react unfavourably to any increase until it has faded from their minds. If it is an increase in indirect taxation, the effect is more probably to increase effort than to reduce it. As we saw in Chapter II, section 2(a), people work less as the return to their effort rises, because they buy more leisure with increasing income. From this it follows that the effect of raising the tax rate must be to increase effort, provided that the tax in question is an indirect tax. People also particularly resent uncertain taxes, which the taxing authority may change at his will. Given stable taxes, levied not on income but on commodities, people will adjust themselves to any level of taxation which leaves them a 'reasonable' standard of living. The effect of high taxation upon effort is then the same as the effect of infertile soil or other poverty of natural resources upon effort; low productivity may stimulate or discourage effort, or may be

irrelevant to it; we cannot say (see Chapter II, section 3). (It is possible to feel certain as to the effect of raising the tax rate, while remaining agnostic as to the effect of a high tax rate, since the immediate and the ultimate reactions to a tax are not necessarily the same.) Correspondingly, there is no simple limit, such as twenty-five per cent or fifty per cent, to the proportion which taxation can reach over a long period, if it is levied indirectly, and if changes are avoided. Thus, if real income per head is increasing, and indirect taxation is higher at the margin than it is on the average, the government's share will be increasing all the time, but the people's standard of living will also be rising, and since taxes are not changed most of the public will be indifferent to them. Hence, though high taxation may discourage incentive if taxation is badly handled, it may have no effect on incentive if appropriate techniques are used. The real burden of high taxation upon economic growth is that it may use up resources which could be invested more productively.

The extreme example of waste of resources is the use of resources for making unsuccessful aggressive wars, or successful wars which do not result in concessions adequate to cover their cost. War keeps down capital formation, kills off many intelligent and enterprising young men, strengthens the power of the military-minded *vis-a-vis* the economically-minded, and, contrary to popular belief, does very little to stimulate useful invention (see Chapter VI, section 3(*c*)). The most recent example of its cost is provided by Germany; who can doubt that the prosperity of the German people would now be much greater if they had succeeded in avoiding the wars of 1914 and of 1939?

This completes our list of the ways in which governments may retard economic growth. Clearly, good government is very difficult, so it is not in the least surprising that most countries have failed to show economic growth during the greater part of their history, or that some of the most prosperous have been brought to decay by public mischief. The government must not spend too much or too little, not control too much or too little, not initiate too much or too little; it must not discourage foreigners, and not fall into their hands; must not permit class exploitation and not promote class war; and so on. Some countries seem to be much better at picking their way through these opposing dangers than others. Can this be explained?

(b) Background to Statesmanship

What has to be explained is not occasional periods of good or of bad government, lasting one or two decades, but long-run propensities lasting one or two centuries or more. All countries get good or bad governments from time to time, irrespective of whether the

general run of their governments is good, bad, or mediocre. Good government, extending over a century or more, tends to perpetuate itself, since high standards of public behaviour are set which then enter into the country's traditions and restrain the behaviour of subsequent generations. Similarly a long period of bad government diminishes the chances of establishing better government, since the new generations are born to low standards and have no good traditions to uphold. It follows that at any period in a country's history, one can explain the quality of its public life largely in terms of its previous history, and of the traditions which that history has bequeathed. The problem is why the country has had a history of relatively good or relatively bad government.

Once more we have to look at physical resources and their possible connection with human quality. Some people believe that some races have a better capacity for government than other races. If 'race' is used in a cultural sense, this merely re-states the problem we are seeking to solve; if it is used in a biological sense, this hypothesis cannot be taken any further until we know more about the genetic composition of different peoples. The little we know so far discounts the idea that the genes which make for good government have a peculiar geographical distribution. The climatic hypothesis also does not take us far. There seem to have been good and bad governments in all the climates of the world, among all races, and in all conditions of poverty or richness of natural resources. The human response to resources is not to be explained by the resources themselves.

The political philosophers, since Plato, have sought to explain good government in terms of constitutional forms, arguing that it is more likely to survive in conditions of democracy, or dictatorship, or benevolent autocracy, or monarchy, or whatever the particular philosopher or the fashion of the times supports. This approach does not survive much acquaintance with history. Italy, for example, has a recorded history which stretches back 2,500 years, and which includes experience of every constitutional form. It is not possible to pick out any one of the forms—say the democratic periods, or the periods of monarchy, or the periods of dictatorship—and say that Italy was always better governed under this form than under any other. The same applies to Greece, to Egypt, to India, or to China, whose recorded histories are even longer. Good government demands a combination of wisdom in the rulers with the consent of the ruled, and this combination is not monopolized by monarchs, by democrats or by dictators. This is not meant to belittle the importance of institutional checks or of constitutional forms. The democratic forms of government do away with the worst excesses of government if they adequately restrain the power of the executive. But not all

democratic forms include adequate restraints, and even the best constitution will not guarantee that a good government will be elected. The quality of the government depends rather upon the quality of the governed than it does upon the forms of government.

The twentieth century version of the institutional thesis sometimes puts forward the claims of self-government as against imperialism. We cannot, however, with any respect for history assert that countries are necessarily better governed when they govern themselves than when they are governed by others. On the contrary, some of the happiest periods of history have been the periods when great empires in their heyday have kept the peace over vast regions, and provided a reasonable framework of public services. The new nationalist governments which have come to birth in the twentieth century have some advantages over the imperial governments which they have displaced. They are not so disposed to *laissez-faire*, in backward conditions where *laissez-faire* is inappropriate. They are more concerned with the well-being of the peasantry, and are more anxious to protect them against exploitation by landlords and by moneylenders. Most of them are opposed to colour bars, and other restrictions on the enterprise of native peoples. And they are sometimes able to awaken an enthusiasm for development, founded on self-respect, which their imperial predecessors could not command. On the other hand, they have substantial disadvantages. They are much less stable, and cannot even in some cases maintain order within their borders. They are as a class (with individual exceptions) more corrupt than their predecessors. They tend to be too wedded to urban interests, and too willing to advantage the towns at the expense of taxes on the peasants. They fall very easily into xenophobia. Their imperial predecessors could maintain a lofty neutrality between religions, classes and races, which they tend to abandon for internecine strife. And so on. The more cynical supporters of self-government support it on the basis that 'self-government is better than good government'. Certainly it cannot be supported on the basis that self-government always gives better government than the alternatives.

Another approach to our problem sees the solution in cultural homogeneity. If the members of a nation are all of the same race, religion and language, they have less to quarrel about, and may develop a habit of tolerance. If also property is widely distributed, without extremes of riches and of poverty, political life is relatively simple. Cultural homogeneity, on the other hand, while it removes some of the causes of strife, does not ensure that government will act positively or with wisdom. Besides, some of the best governments have been imperial governments ruling over many races,

religions and tongues, with relative impartiality. Tolerance is a plant that grows in many soils.

For believers in original sin, good government is always a temporary phase in the history of a nation, since it is beyond the wit of man to prevent governments from moving in one or other of the directions which lead to economic stagnation. Thus, the up and coming nation has great difficulty in resisting the temptation to launch upon a succession of aggressive wars, which may bring gain over some decades, but which eventually ruin the country (Chapter VI, section 3(c)). Or else, if peace is maintained for some decades, the bureaucrats come to the fore, with their excessive ambitions for public expenditure, and the nation is ruined by heavy taxation. Or else the itch to control the economy and to set wrongs right becomes too strong to be resisted, and individual initiative is throttled by a mass of controls. Or the government inevitably gets involved in class disputes, harassing the entrepreneurs, or binding the peasants into serfdom, or otherwise supporting exploitation or restricting incentives. If we follow this line of approach, what is surprising is not how little good government there has been in human history, but, on the contrary how much good government there has been, having regard to the limitations of human wisdom, and to the innumerable temptations which lie in wait for unwary statesmen.

Whenever we have sought the clue to human history in this volume we have failed to find it. Perhaps there is no clue. Every explanation we give of human behaviour is itself only another question. If we ask why a people has made a certain choice, the answer lies usually in its history; but if we ask why it has had that particular history, we are back among the mysteries of the universe. Fortunately, not all the answers depend upon history. It is possible for a nation to take a new turn if it is fortunate enough to have the right leadership at the right time. In the last analysis history is only the record of how individuals respond to the challenge of their times. All nations have opportunities which they may grasp if only they can summon up the courage and the will.

BIBLIOGRAPHICAL NOTE

On the role of the state see H. G. Aubrey, 'Deliberate Industrialization', *Social Research*, June 1949; E. F. Heckscher, *Mercantilism*, London, 1934; W. A. Lewis, *Principles of Economic Planning*, London, 1949. British industrialization lagged behind that of the European continent up to about 1700, and it is instructive to see the measures adopted to catch up; W. Cunningham, *The Growth of English Industry and Commerce*, first published in 1882, and also in many subsequent editions, is still the best introduction to this subject; see also J. U. Nef, *Industry and Government*

in France and England, 1540-1640, New York, 1940. For Japan see references at the end of Chapters I and V. The International Bank for Reconstruction and Development has published a whole series of reports on various countries, which amount to a basis for production programmes and public expenditure programmes; see also H. S. Perloff, *Puerto Rico's Economic Future*, Chicago, 1950. For the use of input-output tables see W. W. Leontief, *The Structure of the American Economy*, 2nd Edn., New York, 1951. There is regrettably very little theoretical discussion of the fiscal problems of under-developed countries.

APPENDIX

IS ECONOMIC GROWTH DESIRABLE?

LIKE everything else, economic growth has its costs. If economic growth could be achieved without any disadvantages, everybody would be wholly in its favour. But since growth has real disadvantages, people differ in their attitude to growth according to the different assessment which they give to its advantages and disadvantages. They may dislike the kind of society which is associated with economic growth, preferring the attitudes and institutions which prevail in stable societies. Or, even if they are reconciled to the institutions of growing societies, they may dislike the transitional processes in the course of which stable societies are converted into growing societies; they may therefore conclude either that the benefits of growth are not worth the cost of the disturbance it involves, or also that growth should be introduced slowly, so that the society may have as long as possible to adjust itself to the changes which economic growth requires. We shall begin with the advantages of growth, and then consider the costs of growth in terms of the attitudes it requires, and in terms of the disturbances involved in the process of transition.

(a) The Benefits of Economic Growth

The advantage of economic growth is not that wealth increases happiness, but that it increases the range of human choice. It is very hard to correlate wealth and happiness. Happiness results from the way one looks at life, taking it as it comes, dwelling on the pleasant rather than the unpleasant, and living without fear of what the future may bring. Wealth would increase happiness if it increased resources more than it increased wants, but it does not necessarily do this, and there is no evidence that the rich are happier than the poor, or that individuals grow happier as their incomes increase. Wealth decreases happiness if in the acquisition of wealth one ceases to take life as it comes, and worries more about resources and the future. There is, indeed some evidence that this is the case; in so far as economic growth results from alertness in seeking out and seizing economic opportunities, it is only to be expected that it should be associated with less happiness than we find in societies where people are not so concerned with growth. There is evidence of much greater mental disturbance in the United States of America than there is in other countries, and, even when allowance is made for differences in

statistical reporting, it is at least plausible that the higher suicide rate is causally connected with the drive for greater success in an already rich community. We certainly cannot say that an increase in wealth makes people happier. We cannot say, either, that an increase in wealth makes people less happy, and even if we could say this, it would not be a decisive argument against economic growth, since happiness is not the only good thing in life. We do not know what the purpose of life is, but if it were happiness, then evolution could just as well have stopped a long time ago, since there is no reason to believe that men are happier than pigs, or than fishes. What distinguishes men from pigs is that men have greater control over their environment; not that they are more happy. And on this test, economic growth is greatly to be desired.

The case for economic growth is that it gives man greater control over his environment, and thereby increases his freedom.

We can see this first in man's relations with nature. At primitive levels, man has to struggle for subsistence. With great drudgery he succeeds in wresting from the soil barely enough to keep himself alive. Every year he passes through a starvation period for several months, because the year's crop barely lasts out until the next harvest. Regularly he is visited by famine, plague or pestilence. Half his children die before reaching the age of ten, and at forty his wife is wrinkled and old. Economic growth enables him to escape from this servitude. Improved techniques yield more abundant and more varied food for less labour. Famine is banished, the infant mortality rate falls from 300 to 30 per thousand; the death rate from 40 to 10 per thousand. Cholera, smallpox, malaria, hookworm, yellow fever, plague, leprosy and tuberculosis disappear altogether. Thus life itself is freed from some of nature's menaces. Not everybody considers this a gain. If you think that it is better to die than to live, and best not to be born, you are not impressed by the fact that economic growth permits a reduction of death rates. But most of us are still primitive enough to take it as axiomatic that life is better than death.

Economic growth also gives us freedom to choose greater leisure. In the primitive state we have to work extremely hard merely to keep alive. With economic growth we can choose to have more leisure or more goods, and we do indeed choose to have more of both. The opposite impression is created if a comparison is made between impoverished agricultural countries and rich industrial countries, since in the former labour is idle through much of the year, when the weather is unfavourable to agriculture, whereas in the latter men work regularly throughout the year; but this is a false comparison. If we compare not industry with agriculture, but the industrial sector

in rich with the industrial sector in poor countries, and similarly
the agricultural sector in both countries, we shall find almost invari-
ably shorter hours of work in each sector, as income grows; and
also less drudgery, with increased use of mechanical power.

Also, it is economic growth which permits us to have more services,
as well as more goods or leisure. In the poorest communities sixty or
seventy per cent of the people are needed in agriculture to procure
food; whereas in the richest countries twelve to fifteen per cent
suffice to give a standard of nutrition twice as good. The richer
countries can therefore spare more people for other activities—to be
doctors, nurses and dentists; to be teachers; to be actors and enter-
tainers; to be artists or musicians. Many of the 'higher' activities
which philosophers value—art, music, the study of philosophy
itself—are in a sense a luxury which society can afford to develop
only as economic growth permits it to spare increasing numbers
from the basic task of growing food. It is true that only a relatively
small surplus is needed to support the arts, and that some of the
highest artistic achievements date back to societies where the masses
of the people were very poor. The raising of living standards over the
past century has widened the opportunity to appreciate and practise
the arts, without necessarily affecting the quality or quantity of the
best art one way or the other. However, leaving aside the highest art,
there has without doubt been an enormous increase in popular
leisure and the popular opportunities for enjoying what were previously the luxuries open to very few. Relatively far more people
hear the work of the best composers today than heard the work of
Mozart or of Bach in their own times, or saw the work of Rembrandt
or of El Greco.

Women benefit from these changes even more than men. In most
under-developed countries woman is a drudge, doing in the household tasks which in more advanced societies are done by mechanical
power—grinding grain for hours, walking miles to fetch pails of
water, and so on. Economic growth transfers these and many other
tasks—spinning and weaving, teaching children, minding the sick—
to external establishments, where they are done with greater specialization and greater capital, and with all the advantages of large scale
production. In the process woman gains freedom from drudgery, is
emancipated from the seclusion of the household, and gains at last
the chance to be a full human being, exercising her mind and her
talents in the same way as men. It is open to men to debate whether
economic progress is good for men or not, but for women to debate
the desirability of economic growth is to debate whether women
should have the chance to cease to be beasts of burden, and to join
the human race.

Economic growth also permits mankind to indulge in the luxury of
greater humanitarianism. For instance, at the lowest levels of subsistence there is little to spare for those who cannot help themselves,
and the weakest must go to the wall. It is only as the surplus increases that men take increasing care of the leper, the mentally de-
ranged, the crippled, the blind, and other victims of chance. The
desire to care for the sick, the incompetent, the unlucky, the widow
and the orphan is not necessarily greater in civilized than in primitive
societies, but the former have more means to spare for the purpose,
and therefore do in fact display greater humanitarianism. Some
people are disturbed by this; they think that it is against the eugenic
interest of society to maintain persons who are not able to keep up
in a competitive struggle, and they consider that the long run effect
will be to reduce biological vigour unless such persons are sterilized.
But these are as yet in a minority.

Economic growth may be particularly important to societies where
political aspirations are currently in excess of resources, since growth
may forestall what might otherwise prove to be unbearable social
tension. For example, in some countries, such as Great Britain, the
working classes or their spokesmen are demanding ever larger wage-
packets, and ever increasing expenditure on housing, education,
health and other amenities. If in such societies income per head is
stable, the desires of one group can be met only at the expense of other
groups, and this is bound to lead to civil strife. In these democratic
days, most countries of the world are passing through a phase where
bitter civil strife is inevitable unless there is a rapid increase in production per head, so that resources are brought nearer to aspirations.
This is the aspect of economic growth which impresses itself most
upon statesmen, so it is not surprising that democratic statesmen are
everywhere very much convinced of the urgency of stimulating rapid
economic growth. At the same time it must be admitted that economic growth does not always diminish strife. It may on the contrary
have the effect of disturbing relatively stable social relationships, of
stimulating envy and desire, and of precipitating class, racial or
religious conflict. This is related to the proposition that economic
growth does not necessarily increase happiness. Neither does it
necessarily increase political freedom. It increases the opportunity
for dictators to control men's minds, through mass communication,
and men's bodies, through highly organized police services. So it is
not possible to argue that economic growth necessarily improves
political relations.

Another aspect of the disproportion between aspirations and
resources is to be seen in the political attitudes of countries of low
international status. Peoples now in colonial status are anxious to

become independent. Independent nations, numerous in population but poor in income, are anxious to have a higher status in the counsels of the nations. Rightly or wrongly such peoples think that if they were richer, and especially if they were rich enough to have powerful armed forces, they would count for more in international affairs, and there would be more respect for their nationals and for their way of life. There are some nationalists whose reaction to the modern world is to turn away from it, and to urge their people to return to the old ways of life. But most of the nationalists who have acquired power believe that it is necessary to have rapid economic growth. Many people believe that great differences between countries in wealth or economic development provoke war, and that the world would be nearer to peace if there were not wide disparities in standards of living. This is a very doubtful proposition, since societies which are undergoing rapid economic growth are often tempted to fall upon their neighbours. In any case, the causes of war are so numerous, and so indirectly related to economic considerations that it hardly helps to discuss the case for economic growth in terms of possible effects on peace or war.

It is sometimes argued that any expectation that all the nations of the world can raise their standards of living continuously must be illusory, since the effect would be only to exhaust rapidly the world's accumulated stocks of minerals and of fuel. This argument rests upon two uncertain assumptions. First it presumes that human ingenuity must in due course fail to find new substitutes for what is used up, an assumption which is rendered increasingly doubtful by what we are learning about the nature of the atom, and about the transformation of one element into another. And secondly it assumes that future generations have an equal claim to the world's resources. Why should we stay poor so that the life of the human race may in some centuries to come be extended for a further century or so? Is there not as good a case for the present generations to make the best of the resources they find, and to leave the distant centuries to look after themselves? Even if these questions are answered negatively, there remains the further point that it is not the poorest nations of the world who are using up the minerals and fuel rapidly, but the richest. If the argument has validity it may be taken as a counsel to Europe and to North America to stop raising their standards of living any further, but it is much less forceful as counsel to Asians and Africans, whose current draft on accumulated reserves is so small, to continue in their present poverty.

(b) The Acquisitive Society

If the benefits listed above were available without cost, nearly

everyone would favour them. Many people, however, consider that the attitudes and institutions which are necessary for economic growth are undesirable in themselves; they prefer the attitudes and institutions which belong to stable societies.

In the first place, they dislike the economizing spirit, which is one of the conditions of economic growth. If other things are equal, growth is most rapid in those societies where people give their minds to seeking out and seizing opportunities of economic gain, whether by means of increasing earnings, or by means of reducing costs. And this propensity to economize, though it might equally well spring solely from a desire to reduce drudgery and increase the leisure available for enjoyment or for spiritual pursuits, seems in practice not to be well developed except when it is associated with a desire for wealth, either for its own sake, or for the social prestige or the power over people which it brings. It is arguable that economy is a virtue, in the sense that there is the same sacred duty imposed upon man to abhor waste and to make the best use of his resources as there is to abhor murder and to look after the widows and orphans—in fact the parable of the talents says that this is so. Not everyone agrees that we have a sacred duty to fuss and bother about resources, or about fleeting time; these would say that economy costs too much in nervous energy and human happiness, and is rather a vice than a virtue. They might admit a duty to economize or work enough to reach some minimum standard of living, necessary for health and comfort (a dubious concept) but would argue that economy beyond this level is not worth the effort. Moreover, even those who accept economy to be a virtue may nevertheless deplore the fact (if it is a fact) that this virtue is found only in association with the vice (if it is a vice) of materialism. It is possible to desire that children should be taught to make the best use of the resources and opportunities available to them (the virtue of economy), and at the same time not to want more than they already have (to avoid the vice of cupidity). If this were done, and if the teaching were effective, there would still be economic growth; only, instead of its showing itself in ever rising material standards of living, it would show itself in ever increasing leisure at constant material standards; and if this leisure were not to result also in the ever-increasing vice of idleness (if this is a vice), children would have also to be taught to use their leisure in ways which resulted neither in idleness, nor in the production of economic goods and services. We cannot, in practice, get very far by pursuing lines of enquiry which depend on assuming human nature to be other than it is. Man likes to have more wealth, likes to economize, and likes to be idle. None of these desires seems to be intrinsically either virtuous or vicious, but any one of them pursued to its extremes, in dis-

EE

regard of other duties, obligations or rights results in unbalanced personalities and also in harm to other persons. It is just as much possible for a society to be 'not materialistic enough', as it is for it to be 'too materialistic'. Or, to put the matter the other way round, economic growth is desirable, but we can certainly have too much of it (more than is good for spiritual or social health) just as well as we may have too little of it.

Exactly the same comment can be made in relation to individualism, which is the second score on which economic growth is attacked. It seems to be the case that economic growth is more likely if individuals attend primarily to their own interests and those of their more immediate relations than if they are bound by a much wider net of social obligations. This is why economic growth is associated, both as cause and as effect, with the disappearance of extended family and joint family systems; with the erosion of social systems based on status (slavery, serfdom, caste, age, family, race) and their substitution by systems based upon contract and upon equality of opportunity; with a high level of vertical social mobility; and with the decline of tribal bonds, and the reduced recognition generally of the claims of social groups. This is another problem which cannot be solved by making a virtue of one side of the argument and a vice of the other. There are some rights which all individuals ought to have, and which should be protected against all social claims; and at the same time every individual belongs to a group, or whole series of groups, whose existence is necessary to his own social health, and whose continuance depends upon his recognizing the claims of the group and loyally accepting its authority. The growth of individualism in the past five hundred years has had its evil side, but it has also been a valuable and liberating influence. Economic growth cannot therefore be attacked for being associated with individualism as if the only good things in human relations were tribalism, social status, extended family relations, and political authoritarianism.

A third line of attack upon economic growth derives from its association with reliance on reason. Economic growth depends upon improving technology, and this in turn is greatest where men have a reasoning attitude both towards nature and also towards social relations. Now the reasoning mind is suspect, either because it is believed to result in religious agnosticism or in atheism, or also because it is considered incompatible with the acceptance of authority. As for religious belief, it is an open question whether decline of belief in God or gods is to be blamed for the evils of our time, or even whether the evils of our time are greater than those of previous ages in which religious belief was commoner. But, in any case, it is not true that belief in the importance of reason is inconsistent with belief in God.

The existence of God cannot be proved or disproved by rational means, so there is no reason whatsoever why the most rational of men should not also believe in the existence of God. Reason erodes not religion but authority, and it is only in so far as religion is based upon authority that the reasoning mind is hostile to religion. But in this sense the reasoning mind is just as hostile to science as it is to religion; for it is hostile to any attempt to claim that current doctrine is not open to re-examination from the roots upward, or that only the initiated have the right to question its validity. Here again, however, as with materialism and with individualism, so also with reason; truth is not to be found by identifying virtue with one only of two opposites. For, just as materialism and spirituality are both desirable, so also society needs to have both reason and authority. The good life is founded in weaving a pattern of opposite principles, not in rejecting some and using only the others.

A fourth line of attack is pursued by those who do not like the growth of scale which is associated with economic growth. The economies of scale show themselves, in the first instance, in the division of labour, and in the use of machinery. This is disliked by some who dislike machine made goods, and who prefer the products of the skilled handicraftsman. Economic growth destroys old handicraft skills, and though it creates even more new skills, machine skills and others (for specialization greatly increases the range of skills) there are many people who regret the passing of the old skills and the old craft products, and who find no consolation either in the growth of the new skills or in the multiplication and cheapening of output which mass-production makes possible. The principle of specialization is itself attacked, for specialization results in people having to do the same thing over and over again and this, whether it be turning nuts on bolts, or packing chocolates into boxes, or repeating the same university lecture, or practising musical scales, or taking out appendixes, is necessarily boring, until one gets so used to one's job that one can do it without giving the whole of one's mind to it.

The economies of scale show themselves also in the growth of the size of the administrative unit. Thus businesses, units of governments, and other organizations grow in scale. In the process, men are separated from the ownership of their tools, and are proletarianized. Large scale organization brings with it also peculiar social tensions; such organizations have to be run on hierarchical lines, which means that a few command while the majority obey, however much one may seek to democratize the process; these organizations have also to find some means of distributing work and reward which is at the same time efficient and accepted as just. We have not yet succeeded in learning how to run large scale organizations without creating unrest,

and many people therefore think that we would be better off without
them.

Large scale organizations are also disliked because of the discipline they impose; day after day men must rise at the same hour,
arrive at their place of work at the same hour, do much the same
things, and return home at the same time. Some think that this makes
life drab and monotonous, and reduces human beings to the mechanical role of cogs in some vast wheel. They would prefer that men
should not be tied to the clock, and should have greater freedom of
choice from day to day, though it is by no means clear either that
the man who works in the one-man business is less a slave of the
clock, or that having regular habits is something to be deplored.

The economies of large scale organization also result in the growth
of towns, especially when this is associated with growing real income
per head, which increases the demand for manufactured products
and for services relatively to the demand for agricultural products.
In so far as the revolt against large towns is associated with a preference for agricultural occupations, it is really a revolt against
technological progress. For it is technological progress which
enables a country to produce with fifteen per cent of its population
enough food to feed the whole, and if we are to return to the days
when seventy per cent of the people were needed upon the land
either we must abandon all that agricultural science has taught us,
or else we must reduce hours of work to about ten a week. It is technological progress in agriculture which results in the growth of urban
occupations, but it is the economies of large scale organization which
result in these urban occupations being concentrated in ever larger
towns. That this is undesirable is by no means clear. The majority of
people, when given the chance of working in the town or in the
village, choose the town—this is why towns grow at the expense of
villages; only a minority prefer the village to the town, and many of
those who denounce the town are in fact careful to avoid living in
villages. If towns are thrown up in a great hurry, without proper
planning or control, they can indeed be slummy, drab, ugly and unhealthy; but in these days there is no reason why new towns (or even
old ones for that matter) should not be as beautiful, gracious,
healthy and inspiring as any village, as well as providing far wider
opportunities for exercising body, mind and soul than any village
could ever hope to offer.

Finally, economic growth may be deplored in so far as it is dependent upon inequality of income. That this dependence exists cannot
be denied since growth would be small or negative if differential
awards were not available for hard work, for conscientious work,
for skill, for responsibility and for initiative. It is arguable in any

given situation whether the existing differentials are too great or too small, in the restricted sense of being greater or less than is required to achieve the desired rate of economic growth. But it is not arguable, as the rulers of the U.S.S.R. soon discovered, that significant economic growth could be achieved even if there were no differentials at all. Now, part of the revolt against economic growth on this score is no more than an argument that in some particular place or time the differentials existing are greater than are necessary for the achieved level of growth, and are due to faulty social organization. To this extent the argument simply becomes one of altering social institutions (inheritance of property, ownership of land, taxation, educational opportunities, etc.) in ways which alter the distribution of income or of property without reducing the rate of economic growth. But there are also situations where the degree of differentiation which economic growth demands is not acceptable even when it is fully admitted that smaller differentiation would reduce growth— for example, situations where foreign teachers or technicians cannot be had except at salaries which are high by local standards, or where pioneering foreign or domestic entrepreneurs are unwilling to initiate developments unless they are allowed the chance to make and keep profits at a rate far in excess of what is locally thought to be 'reasonable'. The economic test in such matters is that of supply and demand: 'reasonable' differentials are those salaries or profits which are objectively necessary in the situation to secure the required supply of skill or initiative. But what is 'reasonable' on this test may well be 'unreasonable' by some other standard of merit or social justice.

Three conclusions follow from this analysis. First, some of the alleged costs of economic growth are not necessary consequences of growth at all—the ugliness of towns or the impoverishment of the working classes, for instance. Secondly, some of the alleged evils are not in fact intrinsically evil—the growth of individualism, or of reasoning, or of towns, for example. As in all human life, such things can be taken to excess, but they are not intrinsically any less desirable than their opposites. From this it follows, however, thirdly, that the rate of economic growth can be too high for the health of society. Economic growth is only one good thing among many, and we can take it to excess. Excessive growth may result in, or be the result of, excessive materialism, excessive individualism, excessive mobility of population, excessive inequality of income, or the like. Societies are not necessarily wise to choose to speed up their rate of growth above its current level; if they do, they will enjoy substantial benefits, but they may also incur substantial costs, in social or in spiritual terms, and whether the potential gains exceed the potential losses must be

assessed separately in each situation as best we may. It is because economic growth has both its gains and its losses that we are all almost without exception ambivalent in our attitudes towards economic growth. We demand the abolition of poverty, illiteracy and disease, but we cling desperately to the beliefs, habits and social arrangements which we like, even when these are the very cause of the poverty which we deplore.

(c) Problems of Transition

Special problems arise when it is a matter of introducing economic growth into societies which have existed for some centuries at low levels more or less of economic stagnation. For it is then necessary to transform beliefs, habits and institutions, and though in due course when the new beliefs, habits and institutions have been going for some time, and have become firmly rooted, a new dynamic equilibrium may be reached which is in every sense superior to the old static social equilibrium, nevertheless the transition may produce temporary but very painful situations.

One of the more obvious of these is changing peoples' habits of work. For example, suppose that copper is discovered in a very primitive country where all the people have land of their own which enables them to live to their own satisfaction, though at very low levels of health, of material standards, or of culture. These people do not want to work in copper mines, and it may be that they will not voluntarily accept employment at any wage which would make it remunerative to work the mines. On the other hand, it is also possible that if they were forced to work in the mines the wealth they could thereby produce would make it possible to give them very much higher standards of material well-being, of health, of education and of culture. Suppose also that if initially forced they would after a while acquire such a taste for the new kind of work, such an appreciation of their high standards, and such contempt for their previous ways of life that in due course they would be glad to work in the mines after the force was removed. Is the temporary use of force justified in these circumstances? This abstract example is by no means a mere academic exercise, since it is not at all dissimilar to what has happened in some parts of Africa, where the people have been forced to work in mines or on plantations, whether by orders issued through their chiefs, or because this was the only way of earning money to pay the taxes imposed on them for this purpose, or because they were driven off their lands. What actually happened in these cases is more complicated than the facts given in our abstract example, because of the additional fact that those who exercised force in these circumstances did it primarily to enrich themselves,

and not because they wished to benefit the Africans. In some of these cases there is also the further fact that the Africans have not even benefited materially; on the contrary, their former villages are ruined economically, their way of life has been destroyed, while they themselves live in barracks, slums and shanty towns in material no less than in spiritual impoverishment. We have always emphasized in this enquiry that it is possible to have economic growth, in the sense of increasing output per head, without the majority of the people being any better off, because the increased output enriches only a powerful few. Most people in the world would agree that such developments are immoral, and would condemn economic policies which benefit the few at the cost of the many no matter how great the increased output that would result. This, however, is quite different from the abstract case we are examining, since it is one of the pre-suppositions of this case that the effect will be greatly to increase both the material and the cultural standards of the people involved, and that they themselves will in due course prefer the new way of life to the old. Faced with this example people react in different ways. Some rest their case on opposition to compulsion: however good the ultimate effects, they say, no man should be coerced for his own good, or for the good of his descendants. Others rest their case on happiness; even if the people come to prefer the new way of life to the old, they say, they are not really any better off because they are not any happier; hence they have had a painful transition to no purpose, since they have gained nothing that matters—a questionable argument, as we have already seen, since it is doubtful whether happiness is an appropriate test of change. Still others react differently, and would justify coercion if it greatly benefited the coerced. Thus, Negroes in the New World condemn the act of slavery which took them there, but in truth not all of them regret that their forefathers were not left in the jungle villages of West Africa. So also there will always be politicians and statesmen, while the world lasts, who will not hesitate to coerce their subjects for the ultimate good of the coerced.

The question of the limits of permissible force is currently very acute since it has been demonstrated by the U.S.S.R. that a ruthless government can raise real output very rapidly if it is willing to deal severely with those who oppose its plans. All under-developed countries are being invited, by communist or other propaganda, to yield up their liberties in return for a promise of rapid economic growth. The invitation is somewhat misleading. They are told that the loss of liberty would be temporary; that the 'dictatorship of the proletariat'—or the caudillo, or the army leader, or whoever it may be—is only a transitional phase, to be followed by the 'withering

away' of the state; but we may well doubt whether liberties once surrendered are ever so easily regained. Neither does the invitation guarantee a rising standard of living; output may rise rapidly, but the dictator may decide to use it for purposes other than raising the standard of living of ordinary people. In any case, it is quite clear that it is not necessary to have a dictatorship in order to have economic growth. One or two democratic governments of under-developed countries—Burma, the Gold Coast—have shown that they have the will and the courage to find the resources which are necessary for growth, and that this can be done within the democratic framework by leaders who enjoy widespread confidence and support. It is up to other democracies to show that they can do the same.

Another painful transition is that which has to be made in social relations. The opposition of reason to authority, the movement from status to contract, and the change from social stability to vertical social mobility all upset existing relationships, whether in the matter of class, religion, political obedience, or family ties. This is clearly enough the case if the transition comes to a head in violent revolution, but even without this the transition is painful because it frustrates existing expectations and rights in every sphere. Many people are opposed to economic growth on this account. Some take the view that the old relationships are as good as the new or even better—they dislike the new freedom of family relations, the alleged 'rights' of the 'common man', and the destruction of the old social harmonies. Others, who do not believe that the old relationships were particularly harmonious, and who prefer the new, nevertheless question whether the difference is worth the cost. This, clearly, is an issue which can be decided only in terms of the valuation which one sets upon such matters as increased knowledge, equality of opportunity, better health standards, longer life, and the other fruits of economic growth.

Then there is the transition which has to be made in moral values. In the old society children are brought up into a code of behaviour, of duties, and of loyalties. The new society has a different code. Good behaviour in one society may be bad behaviour in the other. The duties and loyalties shift from one set of persons and institutions to another set—from the age-group to the trade union, or from the chief to an employer, or from the family to impersonal customers. In due course the new code may be established, and may work as smoothly as its predecessor, but meanwhile the community may pass through a trying time, during which the old morality has been cast off before the new has taken hold. Such transitions have been particularly painful in the past because we have not understood what was taking place. The transition is made much easier if the morality of

the old society and the morality of the new society are both well known, and if those who are responsible for setting or guarding the moral standards of the community (especially the priests, the teachers and the legislators) deliberately set out to preach the new morality, right from the beginning of the change. But, in the first place, it is only recently that we have come to understand these matters, and to appreciate in particular the extent to which moral codes are bound up with and appropriate to particular social and economic patterns. In the second place, those who guard the moral standards of the community usually consider it to be their duty to guard the old code; they are hostile to the change, and regard the new code as immoral. And thirdly, even if they were won over to the new code, much of their authority disappears in the transitional phase, because of the growth of reliance on reason, and because of the public's loss of confidence in the institutions and practices with which these guardians have hitherto been identified. Thus the new code is not introduced systematically, or authoritatively. It is picked up only gradually, and in parts. New beliefs and old beliefs mix inconsistently. And there is much frustration and bewilderment when people do what they know to be the right thing to do, and find themselves ridiculed, scolded or punished for behaving in that way.

Painful transitions are inherent in the transformation of a society from one way of life to another; they cannot be altogether avoided except by avoiding change itself. This no one can do. The propensity to change is inherent in the nature of man. For man is essentially curious, and therefore forever accumulates knowledge, which alters his way of life. He is also prone to dissatisfaction, wanting more than he has, or moving about, or coveting his neighbour's status or possessions. He has also a sense of adventure, which makes him take chances, and a sense of rebellion, which is a constant challenge to hierarchical relations. It is therefore a waste of time to think in terms of stopping social change, and a waste of sentiment to regret that all established institutions must pass away. For social change arises just out of those parts of our nature which distinguish us from the rest of the animal kingdom.

All the same, though we cannot prevent change we can accelerate it or retard it. We have already emphasized that the rate of change can be too high, as well as too low. In the present context our problem is not the appropriate rate of growth of output, but rather the appropriate length of the period of transition from one pattern of social attitudes and institutions to another. Here there is no easy generalization; there is as good a case for getting transitions over quickly as there is for allowing plenty of time for adjustment.

In practice, we have no opportunity to choose retardation. The

leaven of economic change is already working in every society—even in Tibet—thanks to the linkage of the world which has been achieved in the past eighty years by steamships, by imperialism, by aeroplanes, by wireless, by migration, by Hollywood and by the printed word. There have, in particular, been two developments which make it imperative not to retard but to accelerate further growth. One of these is the fact that aspirations have grown faster than production. And the other is the fact that death rates are falling faster than birth rates.

In all the under-developed world aspirations now greatly exceed production, and the gap is growing. The masses of the people are beginning to believe that their poverty is unnecessary, and that it could be ended by changing their allegiances. Some few believe that it could be changed by their own individual endeavour, but many more believe that the solution lies in repudiating their landlords, or their employers, their priests or their present political rulers. Some politicians also have great aspirations, whether it be to raise the material and cultural standards of their people, or also to raise the standing of their country in international affairs. Now a large gap between aspirations and production can be very dangerous, since it produces frustrations from which almost anything may emerge. Many people fear that the result will be 'communism' (a word which no longer has any precise meaning). Some fear the spread of native breeds of 'fascism' (a word which has to be interpreted to include the traditional warlordism of many eastern countries, as well as the Latin American 'caudillo'). Others again see a strong likelihood that power will pass to religious fanatics (to mullahs, Mahasabas, rabbis and the like). It is not therefore surprising that the leaders of many under-developed countries give a very high priority to measures for rapidly increasing production. Whether they will have the courage, and the necessary internal and external support, to raise the necessary resources may be doubted. And it is also doubtful whether in any case aspirations will not continue to outdistance production. But those who believe that it would be wrong to speed up production because of the effects on social relations, or on moral codes, usually forget both that these are already changing rapidly, and also that the results of frustrated aspirations may be even more dangerous to existing patterns than speeding up production would be.

The population dilemma is even less escapable. Under-developed countries untouched by external influences seem to have stable populations, with birth and death rates both very high by current standards. Once these countries are drawn into the modern world, with the consequent eradication of local famines and introduction of public health and medical care, the death rate begins to drop rapidly,

and may fall from forty to ten per thousand in less than two generations. It then becomes necessary to begin to increase total production
by rates of one or two or three per cent per annum, to keep up with
rising population. Also, unless there is plenty of land available, it
also becomes necessary to take steps to reduce birth rates to the same
spectacular degree as death rates. This seems, however, almost
certainly to require that production should grow even faster than
population, since most of the explanations of the reasons why people
adopt family limitation ultimately turn upon rising standards of
living. In such a situation we cannot really choose to retard the
growth of production; on the contrary in practically every one of the
countries usually called under-developed the situation is that the
current rate of growth of production is not adequate to permit the
population problem to be tackled seriously. Again those who argue
for retardation have usually overlooked what is happening to population, and have forgotten that the consequences of a population
explosion may be much more damaging to existing social structures
and moral codes than the consequences of any likely increase in production would be.

INDEX

Absentee ownership, 37, 63, 115, 125
Acceleration principle, 287–8
Accessibility, 53, 147, 151–4, 156, 166, 434
Africa: Arabs in, 198; attitude to cattle, 43, 227; colour bar, 371; communal tenures, 121; contractual relations, 46; cottage industries, 140, 270; cultural change, 114, 146, 149, 152–3, 179; debt burden, 128; family relations, 114; Indians in, 198; international aid, 407; international investment, 261; international migration, 198, 361, 363, 365; labour mobility, 39, 50, 92–3, 193, 430–1; mechanization, 130, 391; natural resources, 204, 329; population, 305, 306–7, 310, 316, 319, 327, 329; religion, 24, 104; soil erosion, 125; taxation, 399; unemployment, 218; war, 366–7; women at work, 116, 332; world demand and supply, 354–5, 424. *See also* Africa, Central; Africa, French; Africa, North; Africa, West; Bechuanaland; Belgian Congo; Egypt; Gold Coast; Kenya; Morocco; Nigeria; Northern Rhodesia; Union of South Africa; Sudan; Tanganyika; Uganda
Africa, Central, 33, 399
Africa, French, 85–6
Africa, North, 322
Africa, South. *See* Union of South Africa
Africa, West: emigration, 431; immigration, 198, 363; innovation, 179; mechanization, 130; price stabilization, 290
Agricultural marketing. *See* Co-operatives; Marketing
Agricultural Research Council, 170
Agricultural Revolution, 278
Agriculture: balanced growth, 141, 191, 238, 276–83, 334, 340, 342, 343, 354–7, 383, 384, 388–90, 393–4; basis of earliest civilizations, 52, 366; capital requirements, 20, 51, 205–7, 210, 212, 215–6, 255, 279, 334; co-operative farming, 62, 64–7, 121, 131, 135, 391–2; education and extension,

127, 132–3, 136, 138, 184, 185, 187–91, 225, 252, 263, 270, 279, 328, 378, 394, 395, 406, 413; economies of scale, 77–8, 126–7, 129–36, 137, 328, 347, 400; finance for, 127–9, 136, 181, 191, 222–3, 226–8, 230, 241–2, 260, 261–2, 268, 269–70, 272–4, 396; financing other sectors, 229–31, 235, 236, 243–4, 279, 334, 381–2, 391; innovation, 48, 150, 166–7; land tenure, 7, 12, 20, 62, 80, 90–2, 120–8, 135, 136, 166–7, 268–9, 273, 378, 413, 434; mechanization, 129–31, 135–6, 206, 309, 386, 391; monoculture, 71, 341, 379; opportunities for women, 137, 330, 332; over-population, 218, 234, 324–30; proportion of population required, 18, 92, 191, 206, 212, 230, 333–4, 336, 338–40, 372, 397, 422, 428; research, 97, 133, 138, 170, 175–6, 188, 279; soil conservation, 91, 121, 125–6, 134, 135, 208, 227, 299, 320-3, 327–8, 378; tropical agriculture, 308–9; way of life contrasted with industry, 40, 54, 191–2. *See also* Co-operatives; Farmers; Finance; Land; Landlords; Land settlement; Livestock; Marketing; Research; Water.
Alexander the Great, 370
Allen, G. C., 22, 303
America, Latin: agricultural exports, 355; cottage industries, 140, 270; foreign investment in, 248, 257; government, 150, 434; imperialism in, 367; inflation, 405; land reform, 133; population, 305, 307, 310, 327, 328, 329–30, 332. *See also* Argentina; Brazil; Mexico; Peru
America, North: agricultural methods, 309; capital-income ratio, 202, 205; economic freedom, 78; foreign investment, 346; immigration, 357, 365; industrial welfare, 194; nutrition, 308; population, 330, 424; soil erosion, 125. *See also* Canada, U.S.A.
Anthropology, 14, 55, 144, 371
Apprenticeship, 161, 181, 186–7, 194–5, 359–60. *See also* Guilds; Trade unions